the
Analysis
of
Political
Structure

the Analysis of Political Structure

David Easton

New York •
London

Published in 1990 by

Routledge
An imprint of Routledge, Chapman and Hall, Inc.
29 West 35 Street
New York, NY 10001

Published in Great Britain by

Routledge
11 New Fetter Lane
London EC4P 4EE

Library of Congress Cataloging in Publication Data

Easton, David,
    The analysis of political structure / by David Easton.
      p.   cm.
    Includes bibliographical references.
    ISBN 0-415-90310-6
    1. Political Science.   2. Structuralism.   I. Title.
JA74.E19   1990
320—dc20   89-78476

British Library Cataloguing in Publication Data also available.

To Stephanie and Malcolm
for a more secure future

Contents

Preface

This book is about general theory. It continues an effort over the last several decades to take some initial steps toward developing an empirically oriented theory that will help guide research about the way in which any and all political systems operate.

In the past I have been concerned with identifying those kinds of activities that must be characteristic of all types of societies if they are to be able to sustain a political system. In this book I shall raise some questions about a theory of political structure.

Structure was once a very popular word, verging on faddism, as I shall later note. We used to hear much about structural anthropology, structural linguistics, structural Marxism, structural effects, structural constraints and the like, but strangely not about structural political science. Somehow the latter was virtually impervious to these broader trends.

This book will not offer a structural theory about politics. Rather, it will explore how the analysis of structure fits into a general theory of politics. A theory about the structure of the political system is very different from a structural theory about such systems. The latter kind of theory would, as we shall see, offer a special theory in which structure would play a central explanatory role, so much so that it would color the nature of the whole theory.

I have found it useful to interpret a political system as all those interactions through which values are allocated authoritatively for a society. In all societies capable of providing for these kinds of allocations, I have argued, we must find evidence of variations in inputs of demands and support, conversion mechanisms through which these are transformed into outputs, and feedback processes whereby the results of these activities make themselves felt on subsequent support and demands. This so-called black box model was, at the time it was first presented in 1957, a rather unusual way of representing pictorially those vast and complex forms of behavior that we call politics. Nevertheless, its very simplicity served to summarize a great deal of information. It presented in skeletal form the crude outlines of the processes with which political scientists were intimately familiar but which we had had difficulty conceptualizing in their totality.

It was clear to me then, as it is now, that I was only seeking to organize our thinking about what goes into a political system, what constitutes the raw materials with which it has to operate, and what comes out. Two critical additional factors were missing. One was the determinants of these inputs, outputs, and conversion processes. To the extent that we can make propositions about the conditions that influence variations in the demands and levels of support put into a political system and the forces that shape the conversion processes and their relationship to outputs or policies, the closer a conceptual framework moves towards a theory in the full sense of the word.

A second factor, however, was clearly missing. I had had little to say about the way in which inputs were transformed into outputs. It was clear, of course, that here I was referring to the complex of studies that political science already had at its disposal after some two thousand years of development. Within the black box occurred those multifarious activities that in modern industrialized societies go by the name of parties, interest groups, lobbies, the military, administration, legislation, judicial behavior, voting, and the like. But specifying what is already so well known to the merest novitiate in political science is not very helpful. My critics were appropriately impatient.

In my earlier publications I have dealt with the central activities in which members of a political system engage so that binding decisions for a society can be made and implemented. What I had not considered, at the same level of abstraction as other matters, was how these things get done and the constraints on them. At the time this distinction, between *what* gets done and *how* it gets done, seemed a reasonable way of distinguishing something called process from what was universally called structure. I have since learned better, as this book will illustrate.

At any rate, this book fulfills a commitment to deal with this transparent and acknowledged "gap" in my previous work. It was an omission, however, only because things have to take their own course and move at their own speed. I had promised to consider the theoretical problems relevant to what happens within the black box, but only at some future date.

This book is, then, a theoretical foray into that box. It will deal with some general problems pertaining to the nature of the structures which circumscribe or facilitate conversion processes, the way policy decisions are made. In that sense it will provide the beginning of a theory of political structure.

I have learned by this time to write a little defensively so as to anticipate what may appear to my critics as legitimate complaints. I can easily anticipate that they will not be satisfied with my present efforts at filling in some of the structural "details" of the black box. Their discontent may be revealed in disappointment at finding that as I deal with the structure of the political system I still do not come to grips with the same kind of reality so common in contemporary political science, a kind of reality that I might be accused of neglecting. Not that I ignore parties, groups, legislatures, voting, socialization, policy-making, social issues, nation building, governmental intervention, and the like. These are the stock-in-trade of all political scientists. But I do not seek to use them as the primary building blocks of a theoretical approach about the way in which operations inside the political system are organized and constrained.

This apparent neglect of these bread-and-butter subjects of political science is of course deliberate. I view most of them as kinds of structures, to be sure. They will, however, prove to be of secondary or derivative interest; they represent largely historically conditioned and, therefore, possibly transient phenomena. Many of them did not even exist in the last century, except perhaps in embryo. Many of them may not exist by the end of the next century, except perhaps in vestigial form. They constitute what I shall call observed structures, or "political relations," comparable to what Lévi-Strauss calls "social relations." New forms of political organization may well arise in the future to perform their functions better, even when tested against our present formal criteria of adequacy. Certainly structures so closely associated with the maintenance of poverty, environmental pollution, inequality in the distribution of wealth, and pervasive venality in public and business life may become subject to considerable questioning and modification.

If indeed the political structures that serve to reproduce or sustain these conditions prove to be happenstances of history rather than inescapable devices for political action, it would seem shortsighted to attempt to found a theory, applying to any and all political systems, on their presence or their functioning. In the short run they must be dealt with and local theories of their operation will be valuable. Such partial theories might be helpful in coping with day-to-day operations of such structures and, if successful, would point in the directions of the kinds of changes necessary to achieve any specific goals at a given time and place. If, however, we seek to go beyond an understanding of what may be historically only transient structures and to explore the part that structure in general plays in the operation of political systems, regardless of time and place, then we have to adopt a different strategy. We have to search for a fundamental understanding of the place of structures in political systems.

I remain committed to the search for such fundamental knowledge in political science. This is a luxury that both political science and society can afford, perhaps, if not too many of us engage in this kind of work—and today this does not represent a clear and present danger. The opposite may be the case. Too few are engaged in basic research. As someone has said, if there is any one law of research, it is that applied research tends to drive out pure research, and we have witnessed this in the 1980s.

Based upon the reception of my other books, I believe I can make a fairly good guess about the trajectory of the present one. I suspect it will receive very varied responses. Sociologists will be curious that political science has at last awakened to the importance of structure; postmodernists will become noisily alarmed that the human subject (intention, purpose, and desire) may once again be lost from sight (which it is not) in my work; empirical political research workers will find the work too abstract and will be unhappy with my criticisms of their research; traditional political theorists will worry that I have shorted philosophy in favor of empirical inquiry; critics of positivism will condemn me for holding fast to the idea of a science of politics; and unregenerate positivists will be displeased with me for what they will view as excessive concessions to interpretive analysis, despite my explicit plea for a modernized and revised conception of the philosophy of science.

In short, there may be little agreement with my diagnosis, analysis, or remedies.

But I do have confidence that once the initial dust has settled, the significance of the broader political structures about which I speak cannot help but become a major new item on the research agenda of political science.

The outline for this book began to take shape over a decade ago, before I took early retirement from the University of Chicago to accept my present position at the University of California, Irvine. During a long period such as that I have incurred many debts.

My initial research was supported by the Division of the Social Sciences at the University of Chicago. It was subsequently generously aided by the School of Social Sciences at UCI under the leadership of its perceptive and inventive dean, William Schonfeld.

I have also received the wise counsel and advice of colleagues, too numerous to list exhaustively. I would not want to let this occasion go by, however, without special mention of a number of them from a variety of disciplines: Istvan Anhalt, Henrik Bang, Frank Cancian, Stephen Easton, Lutz Erbring, Linton Freeman, David Greenstone, Russell Hardin, Mark Petracca, Adam Przeworski, Shawn Rosenberg, Marshall Sahlins, David Schneider, and Duncan Snidal.

I also profited enormously over the years from the intellectual exchanges, on problems of structure, in my graduate seminars at both the University of Chicago and UCI, as well as from the dedicated and creative research assistance of former graduate students, a number of whom are now well into careers of their own: William Coleman, Munroe Eagles, Robert Gamage, Robert Grafstein, Ernest V. Underhill, and James Whalen.

As with all my intellectual efforts, this book would have suffered measurably, in content and style, but for the patient yet unrelenting critical assessment of every thought and word by my wife and life-long colleague, Sylvia Easton, whose capacity to combine a lifetime of vigorous public advocacy with continuing scholarly acumen has added to the wisdom of her advice.

Prologue

When my publisher asked me to tell him, very briefly, what my manuscript was all about so that he could make a decision with regard to its publication, I sent him information of the following kind. I thought I might share this with the reader as a quick introduction to what follows in a rather long and not uncomplex manuscript.

For the last ten years I have been at work trying to understand the nature of political structure. At the end of my earlier book, *A Systems Analysis of Political Life*, I had committed myself to writing on this subject. I found the going more difficult than I had anticipated. Part of the reason for this was the fact that there is very little in the discipline on which I could build. I was unable to find a single article, let alone a book, dealing with the subject of structure in the study of politics. I had to build up the conceptual grounds for my study virtually from scratch. Accordingly, it became my belief that the appearance of my present book might well open up a new subfield of inquiry in political research, much the same as my essay on political anthropology, my publications on political socialization (1957 ff), and my *World Politics* article on political systems analysis did for those fields.

My manuscript deals with political structures of two kinds: those that are obvious to us on a day-to-day basis; and those that shape the former and that act like an unseen force operating on the political system. The latter kind of political structures can be found in the way in which political systems as wholes are organized; they stand as a basic limit or constraint, or at times even as a facilitating factor, influencing the nature and direction of public policy and the more readily observed forms (regime structures) taken by political activity.

The way in which a political system is organized for making decisions (its regime) both reflects and helps to determine how power is distributed and, therefore, how and what kinds of public policies are pursued. My book focuses initially on these regime forms or easily observed structural parts of political life.

Political science has been relatively unsuccessful in accounting for the great variety of regimes (so-called types of political systems) that have appeared historically and that exist today. For example, despite all our research in these areas we really know little about the conditions for the emergence, maintenance, or decline of democratic or authoritarian types of regime structures. The transformations currently (1989) taking place in Eastern European countries as well as the USSR have come as a complete surprise to those with scholarly as well as practical interests in the areas.

I attribute a major part of this incapacity to anticipate the nature of regime changes to the kind of decompositional research we typically undertake in political science. I argue that if we are to understand the shape taken by regimes, we shall be forced to see them in the context of the structure of political systems viewed as wholes, opting thereby for an unconventional "holistic" approach to analysis.

To get to this conclusion I find it necessary to point out that political science has never demonstrated an explicit interest in the structures within which political behavior is imbedded. But I also acknowledge that this may seem a poor time to try to resurrect an interest in structure. In recent years deconstruction and other forms of postmodernism have subjected structural analysis to vigorous attack, with the result that structuralists, for example, as a prominent school committed to the importance of structure, have been forced into a wholesale retreat.

However, despite this transparent modern turn away from structure, I prepare the groundwork for a revival of a concern for structure by relating it to the social and political experiences of the countercultural revolution of the sixties and seventies. As I discuss in the book, this was a period dominated by convictions about the power of sheer will. By the end of the seventies, however, the failure of such voluntarism to achieve basic social change was clearly recognized. It left us with the need to account for the failure of mere desire and social urgency to bring about the expected social changes.

I find an important source of this failure to lie in the continued neglect of the limits imposed, on desires for change, by the nature of the political structure as represented in the way in which political systems as wholes are put together and operate. And I point to the arrival and patent influence, in the United States, by the 1980s, of structuralist Marxism and neostatism as evidence of the search for a way to understand the nature of constraints on the will to political change.

Since political science has historically paid so little attention to structure, my argument continues by establishing what we ought to mean by the notion of political structure, concretely specifying various types of structures with which political scientists typically deal (natural or informal vs. formal structures), analyzing the deficiencies of current empirical research, especially in comparative politics, with regard to regime structures, and demonstrating the role of whole system constraints. In the process I analyze structuralism—Lévi-Strauss's variety—as a movement, and the deficiencies which have led to its rejection. However, I seek to salvage certain underlying truths in structuralism that reinforce my own arguments with regard to the importance of the whole political system—the overarching structure—as a major influence on structural parts.

To strengthen my case, I engage in a close and fairly lengthy critical analysis of the work of Nicos Poulantzas, a structural Marxist and follower of the eminent modern Marxist philosopher Althusser. I demonstrate that the work of Poulantzas is one of the influences that lies behind the present neostatist movement in the social sciences as a whole, especially in the United States, to "bring the state back in," as the popular phrase has it, but that those who share in this effort tend either not to be aware of their own structuralist roots in his work or not to give due acknowledgment to the latter. Poulantzas fails in his project to relate varying forms of political regimes, such as democracy or military dictatorships, to the social wholes (what he calls the modes of production) in which they are imbedded. But an understanding of the sources of this failure provides the necessary grist for my own mill. It enables me to conclude with a proposal for the way in which we may improve our capacity in political research to locate the major determinants of the enormous variety we find in political structures.

I conclude with a plea for the recognition of the way in which the organization of political systems as whole entities—their overarching structures—shape the form that regimes take and thereby influence the nature of public policies themselves. I acknowledge, however, that we have yet to devise methods, that conform to acceptable rigorous standards of inquiry, for discovering and validating the nature of this influence. Hence I can point to our theoretical needs without presuming to be able to specify the methods necessary for meeting them.

Part 1

Structure in
Political Research

1

Structure in Contemporary Political Analysis

Political structure is like an invisible force operating in the background of the political system. The time is long past due for bringing it into critical focus. No systematic explanation of political life could be complete without exploring in depth this long-obscured dimension. Such an exploration is the broad goal of this book.

Politics is about the making of decisions of a certain kind, those that are considered binding by most members of society most of the time.[1] Through them nations set their goals, design their institutions, and seek to cope with their present and future. The extent to which and the manner in which we survive the global challenges we have created for ourselves in this century—unparalleled threats to the environment, severe inequalities in the international distribution of income and wealth, pervasive violence at all levels of existence, and nuclear winter hovering menacingly in the background—will depend in no small measure on our capacity to understand how we got to where we are and the nature of the limits that stand in the way of extricating ourselves.

Recently a half-million-dollar prize was announced in a public competition for the best book that could work out a realistic scenario for the world to solve its major problems and that could at the same time project a rosy picture for the future. So gloomy have global prospects for the 1990s become that apparently we have had to be prepared to pay handsomely to entice people to cast off their longstanding pessimism and to begin to think about a possible bright and happy future based not on utopian dreams but on specific, plausible means for achieving it.

Institutional redesign does not come easily, however. Public decisions are not made in the abstract, isolated from the existing broad institutional context of which they are part. Rather, they are shaped by these conditions and in turn shape them. They reflect as well the intentions and goals of the political authorities as decision makers. To take fate by the forelock and twist it to our purposes, as Machiavelli encouraged us in *The Prince*, demands many strategies, not the least of which is a fundamental understanding of the conditions that circumscribe our capacity to act politically. Among these conditions, the overarching structure of the political system itself looms large. Yet it has all but been neglected. The objective of this book is to identify the nature of this structure, to distinguish it from other structures, and to explore a theoretical approach necessary for its understanding.

The Discovery of the Structural Context

Despite the fact that structural limits on public policy and on the organization of political life are presumed to be well known, in retrospect it is crystal clear that

3

during the 1950s and 1960s behavioralism in political research had managed to neglect the broad context in which political activity takes place. Nor has one of the most vigorous theoretical tendencies of the post-behavioral period of the 1980s, the rational actor model, done much better. It too has taken the context of the actor as a given, subject to acknowledgment but not to the analysis of its effects on the nature of the choices made by the rational actor and on the range of excluded options.[2]

Not that there has been a shortage of critics ready to draw this oversight to the attention of political science. The critics of power pluralism, for example, deplored its failure to take into account the various "faces of power," as it was put in those days, that helped to determine what kinds of demands got onto the decision-making agenda of the power elites.[3] In due course this contributed to what I have called the third coming of Marxism to American political science[4]—about which, more in the next chapter. This new arrival of Marxism, in the 1970s, took, in good part, a structuralist form that had been developed in France by Louis Althusser and Nicos Poulantzas—about whom much more will be said in still later chapters. It emphasized the impact of the mode of production—capitalism in the present case—on political phenomena and the need to take that broadest of contexts into account in any adequate explanation.

Whatever one may think of it as a social theory, structuralist Marxism was an important conceptual innovation for American political science, even though it has never been given its proper due for the impact it has had on political research. By the late 1970s it inspired a new generation of scholars to take seriously the need to explore the social context, in its broadest sense, within which political action takes place, or, as they put it, within which the state operates.[5] Most of these scholars are by no means Marxists; some may even see themselves as vigorous opponents. But unwittingly they have been influenced by the sharp focus that Marxism has consistently drawn on the so-called structural conditions which, in one way or another, shape social behavior and institutions.

This new-found sensitivity to structure has contributed significantly to the flowering, in the 1980s, of a new political economy, an area of research in which economic variables, in almost as broad a sense as Poulantzas's notion of mode of production, are seen as central to an understanding of politics. It has spawned a new and lively interest in the nature of the state, its historical origins, its various forms, and its contributions to social change.

Neostatism, as we may call this most recent theoretical tendency in political research, has represented one of the major manifestations of discontent with the structural limitations of behavioralism together with most of its post-behavioral successors.[6] It has revived attention to the structural setting in which political action, policy, and institutions are imbedded.

The Political System as a Comprehensive Structure

This book is about these structural conditions within which politics takes place. These conditions are usually thought of as social in character—class, cultural, economic and the like, and even psychological. This book concludes first, that, in the strict sense, *political*, not nonpolitical social conditions, represent the immediate environment of any political act or structure; and second, that unless we are prepared to leave room for the influence of the political structure itself, taken in the broadest meaning of the term, on any action in or on any part of the political system, an adequate explanation of such phenomena will inevitably elude us.

In pursuit of an understanding of the nature and influence of such structural conditions on the operation of the political system, this book poses a simple ancillary question: To what extent can we explain why even individual parts of the overall structure of a political system, such as may be found in its party, interest-group, or regime structures, take the form they do? This question stands at the center of the present analysis.

I shall propose that we cannot expect a full understanding of any major part of the structure of a political system without taking into account the relationship of such a part to what I shall call the overarching or higher-order political structure itself. In more general terms, the argument will be that we cannot hope for a complete explanation of a component part of a whole independently of the place of that part in the whole.

To illustrate this point, I could attempt to show the influence of the overall structure of the political system on its patterns of inputs, outputs, conversion processes, and various types of associated behavior. Instead, however, because of its critical significance for the operation of political systems, I shall pay special attention to regime structures, together with certain other structures closely associated with them, as major parts of the overall political system. The purpose is to give a sharper, more precise focus to the analysis than would otherwise be possible. My ultimate conclusions, however, should apply equally to any other significant part of the structure of a political system, such as its party, interest group, elite, or power structure—or, for that matter, to any pattern of actions within a political system such as those involved in the making of public policies.

Is it appropriate to view regimes as parts of a political system that merit special detailed attention? Are they important for political outcomes or are they mere epiphenomena, derivative from power struggles but not themselves of much intrinsic significance? The answers may seem self-evident but they have in fact been questioned. I shall return to such doubts in chapter 6 in order to justify the attention that we will be giving to regime structures.

For the moment, however, let us assume that if social conflicts are organized, for example, through democratic, authoritarian, or dictatorial regimes, the structural differences implied in these types will influence the kinds of policies pursued by political authorities, and their outcomes. This judgment is already implicit in the decades-old, and perhaps now outmoded, dispute among students of American politics about the relative merits of the presidential as against the British two-party responsible government as subtypes of democratic regimes. If the relationships between parties and legislatures had not been considered important, what would have been the point of the perpetual debates about the merits of one structural arrangement over the other?

If for the moment we may continue to assume that regime structures do count for something, it would be vital to inquire into how we can best explain the emergence and survival of and changes in different types of regimes and, within them, of historical subtypes. To what extent are the forces that influence their form all *external* to the political system? To what extent are there any factors *internal* to a political system that need to be invoked for any comprehensive explanation? And if they are internal, what political factors do we need to call on to explain these varying regime forms?

It will be a major conclusion of this book that our explanations have been deficient in the degree to which they have neglected the role played by the overarching structure of the whole political system in shaping all its major parts. To make the point I shall illustrate this, as I have indicated, by special attention to that part of a system called its regime. This conclusion will lead us to identify the study of political structure as a possible new and largely unexplored territory for the agenda of systematic theoretical inquiry and empirical research. It represents an area of explicit inquiry largely ignored, until recently, in mainstream political science.

The Age of the Subject?

It may seem strange, or, at the very least, countercyclical, to argue for increased attention to structure. If there is any single movement notable in social science of the 1980s, it is the discovery, or perhaps we should say, rediscovery that in politics individuals do have some control over their own fate. We no longer see ourselves as necessarily trapped by the way the system is organized. We are no longer prone to think that we are caught in a structural vise over which we have little if any power.

In recent years there has been a powerful movement in virtually all the human disciplines to focus on the actor, whether individual or collective, and to interpret outcomes as consequences, in whole or in significant part, of subjective intentions. In this so-called post-structuralist era of the 1980s, agents have come into their own; their behavior is no longer likely to be thought of as concealed behind objective structures or as epiphenomenal or even as mere responses to social stimuli or conditions. Except for Marxist and for the occasional non-Marxist analyst in political science, structure has receded into the background as a phenomenon and as a topic of interest. Even within Marxism, as we shall see, this pressure to recognize the role of the individual in shaping society has meant that the initiative of the subject has had to be taken into account in some systematic way.

The Enlightenment had posed the dilemma: how to bridge the gulf between the objective social order and the self.[7] Progress was defined as the application of human reason to an understanding of the way in which the world functions. The reasoning subject became the outside observer of objects, much as the ancient Greeks had defined the theorist—hence the origin of the term—as the dispassionate onlooker at the feast. In time this initial division of the Enlightenment developed into a separation of subjective and objective spheres and posed the question of the relationships between the two and of how they could be brought together again. In effect it was the social version of Descartes' mind-body problem without the pineal gland as a possible linkage.

In many ways, social inquiry since then has been a gloss on this question. In the nineteenth century Marx and Durkheim had swung the pendulum toward social structure and social facts, objective relationships over which the individual has little control. Society became a strictly social phenomenon, not a product of individual will. Individuals as such could hope to modify those relationships only marginally, if at all, but there was little way for individuals to escape their influence.

Such was the message from the nineteenth century's discovery of the constraints imposed by social structure. The French Revolution had seemed to reveal the capacity of human beings to alter the course of history. The nineteenth-century reaction was to explore the limits to human efforts in face of the laws of social change: hence either the Romantic conclusion that human beings had it in their capacity to undo what the revolution had wrought; or, as the mighty triumvirate— Comte, Marx, and Spencer—had proclaimed, the laws of progress were a part of nature. Human hands might slow down or accelerate the process of change; they could not deflect it. By the twentieth century, this concern for constraints reached its apex in *structuralism*, a specific school of thought elaborated, for the social sciences, by Lévi-Strauss. For him, genetic intellective structure, an objective and ever present reality, determined observable social relationships. There was no escape from its clutches.

By the 1980s it was clear that the age of objectivism (if the period of structuralist determinism can be so called, even if it had never had the field to itself) had begun to wane. Indeed, the very school of structuralism may have been its last major expression in the twentieth century. We seem to have entered a new stage of thought, that of the reassertion of the subject, in which the intent, meaning, and preferences of the actor have begun to come into their own once again.

In the 1980s many signs point toward this resurgence of a recognition of the individual's influence on social relationships. The revival of Weber's interpretive understanding—with stress on the viewpoint of the actor, on Piaget's analysis of the individual as a reasoning, thinking being who processes information in different ways that may affect social outcomes, on the implications of this perspective for the independent effects of cognition in social processes,[8] and on the spread of the rational actor model with its concentration on choice—all come to a sharp focus on the individual actor. Various kinds of action-oriented philosophical theories proclaim that we do have reasons for what we do, as minimally expressed in our intentions and purposes, and they are constitutive of behavior. All these tendencies to bring the individual into the foreground of social analysis indicate that we have indeed moved into the age of the subject.

Furthermore, in discovering that the individual is not only an acting being but a thinking one as well, the 1980s have also stumbled on the equally vital but hitherto obscured fact—however elementary—that thinking itself is a way the individual has of operating on and influencing the environment. The mind is the bridge between the agent and society. Individuals can be expected to behave differently depending on the way they perceive and reflect on their environment.

Hence their attitudes and behavior, although not totally independent of influences from their environment, will be mediated by the actors' cognitive processes.

Rational modelers, in borrowing their assumptions from economics, tend to see such cognition as a uniform, standardized faculty among all human actors. Others, however, see variations in individual attitudes, beliefs, and understandings as a function of variations in how persons see, reflect on, interpret, and reason about their experiences with their environment. In this way, following up on cues from phenomenology, subject-actors, as centers for processing information, may reason in significantly different ways. These different styles of reasoning threaten the utility of the economic model—with its reasoning processes standardized across all human beings—and become salient variables in behavior.[9]

In political science, these themes have been translated into the discovery—or is it really rediscovery?—that public policy is not just a reflection of class relationships, economic, regional, ethnic, or religious cleavages, pressure of interest groups, or the state of public opinion. The actor, whether as an individual or group, is also likely to be seen as having an independent effect on policy outputs.

This has been the underlying if unwitting message of rationality-based inquiry, perhaps the most assertive theoretical tendency in political science in the 1980s. As I have suggested, choices of the actor become the salient factor for understanding behavior, not the social conditions under which the individual acts, which are taken as givens. If the path so discovered, through logic, is the one we are in fact likely to select in the real world, as many of the new rationalists imply or declare, this clear evidence of the importance of reason must demonstrate the independent influence of the agent in political action.[10] The subject as a rational chooser among alternatives has gained a central and credible position in political analysis; it is the choice and action following on it, under the specified conditions, that yield political results. Understanding of behavior thus leans heavily upon a subject-centered explanation.

Reduction of explanation to the rational choices of the individual has not had the stage to itself, however. The will of collective actors has been included in one way or another. We have been exhorted by neostatists "to bring the state back in"[11] with the dire warning that unless we are prepared to do so, we will have lost sight of the independent influence of this group of actors and institutions, the state, in setting public policy. The "state," it is argued, can no longer be viewed as a mere instrument or reflection of other social forces, such as classes or interest groups. It re-enters the political arena with interests and goals of its own that may override pressure from others.

In practice it appears that, at times, the state is virtually a free agent, with a mind of its own, far less restricted in its choice of purposes and goals, or far more autonomous, as it is put, than society-centered analysis would have had us believe. In place of the voluntarism of the individual subject we come dangerously close to finding a state with its own collective will, harking back to a belief in a kind of group or corporate mind, a not unpopular view in the late nineteenth and early twentieth centuries.[12]

This is not to say that constraints have dropped out of sight. It would be unreasonable to believe that whatever the enthusiasm for the newly rediscovered role of the subject, research has blissfully ignored the obvious: political behavior does not take place in a vacuum. However rational an individual may be or however independently the state may at times appear to act, they are both seen as operating within a restrictive structure of some sort. Even the rational modelers themselves acknowledge this, since they see choices as being made within a set of givens, with the options changing as these conditions themselves change. Nonetheless, for rational modelers the emphasis has tended to lie in the logical basis for the decisions of actors, not on the influence of the givens in narrowing or broadening the range of choices. The givens tend to fall into the background.

Similarly, the neostatists readily acknowledge the structural limits within which states operate. But in the first flush of the rediscovery that the state (political authorities?) may indeed act to serve its own interests, neostatists, too, concentrate, to an extreme, on the so-called autonomy of the state, and in the process begin to shift the focus away from its determinants or contexts.

The resurgent concern for the voluntaristic basis of individual or collective (state) behavior may have already gone too far. The deconstructionist extreme among post-structuralists, for example, has already raised an urgent flag of warning.[13] As a powerful reaction to the rigors of structuralism, deconstruction may at the same time represent the last hurrah for individualism, at least of an unbridled sort. For deconstruction, the interpretation of the meaning of texts seems, in the end, to rest with the individual reader of the text, despite protests of its proponents to the contrary. Hence the frequent charge, levied against deconstruction, that it leads to interpretive anarchy, better at *de*constructing than at *con*structing. Since each reader becomes the ultimate arbiter of meaning, structure simply collapses and a Berkeleyan solipsistic chaos seems to fill the void. And since texts at times may be interpreted as passing beyond communications to include behavior as well, deconstruction may also reduce behavior itself to the realm of perpetually uncertain meaning. What is ignored or lost from sight are the larger constraints on political action, those factors in the environment of action that help to determine or limit the nature of public choices (political outputs). The cost of deconstruction, in the extreme, to be sure, is a descent into a political world of utter disorder.

If it is now the case that the subjectivist pendulum may indeed be swinging too far in a voluntarist direction, it seems imperative to pull ourselves up short. It is none too early to return, once again, to a consideration of the place of constraint on political actions and policies. This is the emphasis that serves as the point of departure for this book.

The Return to Constraints

Early on in the development of the behavioral movement in political science, there was clear evidence of discontent with the tendency in political research to marginalize the study of constraints. As I noted earlier in passing, in the 1960s objections had already been raised about the egregious failure of power pluralism to give a systematic place to broader power relationships, the various so-called faces of power, which severely limit the range of options open to plural elites and the agenda for public debate.[14] We have, however, also seen more recent evidence of this emerging fear of an excessive voluntarism, in the announcement of a *new institutionalism*—the discovery that political action takes place within an institutional framework—even if for more old-fashioned political scientists, the *old* institutionalists, if they will suffer that name—this was no news at all.[15] We see even further evidence in the preoccupation with contextual analysis, in voting behavior, on the grounds that of all the determinants of voting, the context or institutional elements in the environment of the voter has not been sufficiently or systematically taken into account.[16]

Furthermore, the rediscovery of history in the 1980s, in all areas of human knowledge, opened anew the question of the extent to which the past constrains the present. It echoes a dissatisfaction with immersion in facts and theorems of the here and now, undisciplined by an awareness of a past which casts its shadow over the present. Sensitivity has been reawakened to change over long spans of time and to its possible relevance for the present. History becomes the broadest contextual constraint of all. More than any other change in contemporary epistemology, the turn to historical inquiry in all areas of knowledge testifies to the continuing deep concern and search for the limits on human action despite (or perhaps because of) the rediscovered role for the human agent.[17]

The invocation of institutions, contexts, and historical conditions represents a response to what had happened in political analysis and in society from the 1960s through the 1980s. Social events seem to have contributed significantly to a general reawakening of the role of structure as a major type of constraint, one formed, as we shall see, from patterns of social relationships over which the individual actor, as such, may have little control. In the next chapter I shall have more to say about the influence of this period in reviving a social interest in constraints and thereby, in the end, an intellectual interest as well.

Forms of States versus Forms of Regimes

Before we can proceed further with these introductory remarks, however, we must pause to identify just what the object of our inquiry is, namely, the "forms of the regime," subject as they are, as I shall be arguing, to broad structural constraints. As the reader will quickly discern, I do not find it helpful or necessary to adopt a neostatist vocabulary and talk of forms of "states." As basically a concept that has recently been retrieved from the nineteenth century, the state leaves much to be desired. It has continued to carry with it all the ambiguities and opacities it had borne in earlier centuries of traditional use, characteristics which unfortunately will continue to plague those who value clarity of expression, precision of meaning and absence of unnecessary intellectual baggage. I have had much to say about this[18] and will have more to say in chapter 14.

At the moment, to make some progress I shall adopt the simple assumption here that at times the term state is used loosely to refer to the whole political system and at other times to what I call the political regime. If so, in talking about the form of the state it is not implausible to conclude that neo-statists may on occasion, again very loosely speaking, have in mind what I am calling the regime. To avoid the pitfalls inherent in the state concept, however, for theoretical reasons fully developed elsewhere some time ago,[19] I shall refer to the form or type of a political system as its regime.

Even though I shall avoid using neo-statist discourse, nonetheless it is instructive to realize that neostatists themselves confirm the importance of variations in the form of the regime or, as they would put it perhaps, in the forms of the state. As I observed earlier, recent exhortations by neo-statists "to bring the state back," into social analysis represented the conviction that we had in the past made too much about the extent to which the state as a major political actor was either epiphenomenal or simply a direct response to external societal forces. Even if we are now instructed to view the state as a relatively autonomous force in its own right, with interests, intentions, and goals of its own that it seeks to implement through its policies,[20] this does not relieve us of the obligation to explore the structure of the state (the regime) itself. However independent the state may be, its own internal structure could still be expected to influence its policies, even if we would no longer need to focus virtually exclusively on the societal (as against the strictly political) context within which the state operates, as we shall see later.

Of course, political science, as distinguished from sociology, had never really neglected the independent effects of the political authorities, presumably a major component of the state in anybody's lexicon.[21] But aside from the question of the validity of the sociological claim, the important point is that at the same time that the state was being interpreted as a subject capable of action with independent effects, our attention was being directed to the structure of the state itself as providing something of an internal constraint that has an important impact on the kinds of policies the state might pursue.[22] Thus, even though societal constraints are reduced in their determinative consequences, the state is, in this new political discourse, not free to make history out of whole cloth. Its own structure imposes its own limits.

I take the neostatists at their word (even though, for sake of clarity, we shall have to change the words they use): that the "structure of the state" is indeed a central phenomenon worthy of investigation if we are to understand political outputs and outcomes, or policies and their consequences.[23] And if the form or structure of the state is so important, it is appropriate to pose the further question: How does it happen that different "states" assume different structural forms?

As I have pointed out, this is the very question that sets the central problem of this book. If the structure of a "state" (in my terms, the political regime) has a significance bearing on the policies it is likely to pursue, how can we account for the variety of forms it assumes? This question is remarkable for the ease with which it can be posed and for the extraordinary difficulty it raises in finding an answer.

The structures of political regimes come in many different shapes and forms— as democracies, dictatorships, or monarchies, as absolutist, constitutional, republican, developing, traditional types, and the like. Within each category we have many subtypes, such as presidential as compared to parliamentary democracies, totalitarian as against authoritarian orders, military versus civilian dictatorships. Although we have many names for such types of political regimes, even after two thousand years of political discourse we have not as yet succeeded in devising a stable, widely accepted method for classifying political systems or their regimes. We still await our Linnaeus. But even as we wait, we can address the issue of how to account for the variety of structures we do observe.

It would be legitimate and important to inquire into the various forms taken by political structures such as these, as well as of many other kinds. Because of the special significance that forms of regime have played historically, however, it seems appropriate and theoretically useful to focus on regimes. In any event, as I have already indicated, whatever I shall have to say about them will apply, *pari passu*, to all other structures. Hence, even those who might wish to focus on other kinds of structures, such as various informal power arrangements in a political system, ought to feel comfortable with my attention to regimes.

Nature of the Regime

Specifically, to what might we refer when speaking of the regime of a political system? As implied in this question, I shall continue to identify the most comprehensive manifestations of political life, not as the state but as a political system. Within it we have political authorities, a political community, and a regime. In this context a regime refers to the goals or values of a political system, the norms or rules of the game, and the structure of authority.[24]

Each of these elements of the political regime has its own structure, as we shall see when we come to discuss just what we mean by structure. But typically, the structure of a regime draws our attention to the relationships among the political authorities and, in turn, their relationship, as political authorities, to the other members of the political system. In other words, it points to the distribution of that kind of power we call authority and the informal political power relationships associated with such authority.

As I have put the matter earlier,

The regime as sets of constraints on political interaction in all systems may be broken down into three components: values (goals and principles), norms, and structure of authority. The values serve as broad limits with regard to what can be taken for granted in the guidance of day-to-day policy without violating deep feelings of important segments of the community. The norms specify the kinds of procedures that are expected and acceptable in the processing and implementation of demands [as well as support and conversion processes]. The structure of authority designates the formal and informal patterns in which power is distributed and organized with regard to the authoritative making and implementing of decisions—the roles and their relationships through which authority is distributed and exercised. The goals, norms, and structure of authority both limit and validate political actions and in this way provide what tends to become a context for political interactions. This context changes more slowly than other kinds of political relationships.[25]

It is important to bear in mind that the structure of the regime is narrower than that of the political system as a whole or of the regime itself. The structure of the political system, for example, would include the structure of nonauthoritative power in a system (elite-mass relationships or class-based power, for example); the patterns of nonauthoritative relationships among interest groups and political parties; various roles such as those of opinion leaders, political bosses, and voters; electoral and other political cleavages; and all those other groups and roles that wield political power (except the the kind we call political authority, which is characteristic of the influence exercised through the regime). As I have described these other structures of the political system elsewhere,

> In the processing of demands and . . . in the generation of support, the roles of opinion leaders, interest groups, and influentials of all sorts together with a vast complex of interpersonal [and intergroup] relationships constitute the components of the general political structure through which power may be wielded. But they are not included in the regime. They are not part of the structure of authority even though at times some of these roles may be so incorporated; and usually they are all of some political significance to the extent that they are ultimately able to influence the authorities.[26]

This difference between the regime and other structures will become important at a later stage. I shall then be claiming that there is an important connection between the structure of a regime and its associated structures, on the one side, and something that I shall call the political system as a whole, on the other. But this is jumping ahead of ourselves.

It is enough here to note that for the more obscure notion about forms of "state" I shall be substituting what I hope is a clearer statement of the problem: How can we account for the variety of forms of regimes that we find in political systems? This is an important question if we accept the postulate, as I shall argue we must (chapter 5), that such forms do make a difference in political outcomes. Indeed, it underlies all neostatist inquiry in the 1980s. Democratic regimes, we can assume for the moment, are not likely to produce policies that are identical with those of authoritarian ones, even though, as I shall point out in chapter 5, this is a postulate that has not gone unchallenged. But the very fact that it is subject to some doubt makes even more important an understanding of the sources of variety in the forms of regimes.

Explanations of Variations in Regime Structures

Traditionally, in political science, as we shall see in chapter 6, we have sought to explain variations in political structures by relating them to specific societal variables. We have sought explanations, following Montesquieu, in geography (size of country, its climate and topology), as well as in ethnic homogeneity or diversity, linguistic variety, class and other kinds of cleavages, international setting and levels of industrial development, education, communication technology, energy, and the like. If differences in such factors fail to give us a convincing explanation for the existence of one or another type of regime, we have always felt free to call on history and tradition.

As we shall have occasion to note more closely in chapter 8, in the end, after centuries of effort, no single explanation accounts for very much of the variance in overall institutional arrangements. Worse yet, all the explanations together do not fare much better. If we were able to sum the variance in political structures accounted for by each variable, to get an overall measure of their explanatory power, we would still be able to account for only a small fraction of the differences we find in the structures or forms of regimes.

If we are intent on understanding why systems differ in their regime structure, we are left with several alternatives. First, we could continue to decompose structures into their elementary parts. Although I shall pursue this matter further at a later point, we can here assume that the regime includes at least such institutions as administrative organizations, chief executives, legislatures, central-local governmental arrangements, and so on. By decomposing political structure into such parts as these and their relationships, we could, for example, explore why regimes based on multiparty as against two-party structures occur, why collegial as against unitary executives arise, or why the way in which one set of authorities are organized leaves it more responsive than another set which is organized differently. There is little limit to the number of such parts of the structure of a system that we could examine through this *decompositional* approach.

Second, by use of what we might call an *incremental* method we could go on adding to the number of individual variables which seem to us to account for at least some of the differences among these parts of a political structure. We could explore the influence of industrialization, educational, ethnic, religious, regional, historical, and racial cleavages, and other such independent variables that might seem to be associated with the presence of one or another structural arrangement.

No one would want to interfere with this process of painstakingly adding to our store of effects of individually selected factors. This has been the bread-and-butter activity of all social research. However, if experience with most areas of research of this sort is any guide, after we are through exploring the influence of one variable after another on some central phenomenon in politics, such as the form of a political system, we are likely to feel a deep sense of disappointment. We will discover, as I have suggested, that very little of the variation under examination is usually explained. This would normally drive us into looking for other factors that might be able to account for more of the variance. At most we are likely then to uncover only another small part of the reason for the variance we are examining, and so on. There will usually be no end to the number of factors that might be involved in an explanation.

The piling of explanatory factor on explanatory factor does, of course, give us additional understanding. The increment of knowledge, however, for the effort expended may be so small for any one factor and, as I have already suggested, what is more depressing, for all factors taken together, that the light at the end of the explanatory tunnel all too frequently just seems to recede indefinitely.

If we are dissatisfied with the *decompositional* as well as the *incremental* approach, we still have a third alternative left, a *holistic* one, to which we will be driven. We can turn our attention to the connection between the observable structural or institutional forms of a political system—its regime structure—and the not so visible way in which the political system itself is put together and operates, its overall structure. We could raise the following question: Do the democratic, authoritarian, or totalitarian forms, or any of their variants, for example, depend only on such separate sets of *societal* facts as the level of industrialization, ethnic composition, degree of social conflict, external threats, geographic location, or roll of the historical dice (to use Weber's imagery)? Or may they also be closely related to structural properties of the *political* system that cannot be detected by confining ourselves to research on any of its parts. In other words, to what extent is any deficiency in our understanding of variations in regime structures a product of our neglect of the structure of political constraints represented by the character of the overall political system itself?

Parties, interest groups, chief executives, voters, local governments, power cleavages, electoral relationships, political opinion leaders, and so forth—components that I shall detail in a succeeding chapter—on this assumption constitute a complex, the properties of which ultimately are explainable only if we find an empirically rigorous way of addressing the political system as a whole entity. Such attributes of political systems as responsiveness of authorities (matching of outputs to inputs of demands), stability, representativeness of a structure, multiplicity of points of access in the structure, and feedback processes, for example, may all be a function of not only single sets of variables but of the whole complex of relationships which constitute the political system. Similarly, from this point of view, what is critical is that the reason for a political regime assuming the particular form it does may depend not only upon the character of the *social* system in which it is imbedded but also upon the nature of the complex of structures represented by the *political* system itself viewed as an interdependent set of relationships. The socioeconomic reductionism of traditional Marxism as well as of much of past social inquiry tells only part of the story about variations in forms of regimes (as well as of other political structures).

Stated directly, I am here posing the following issue: To what extent are the forms of the political system—its regime structure—appropriately explained as products of an unlimited and undefined set of particular societal or even political variables severally understood, the effects of which are then summed in one or another manner? Or to what extent does a satisfactory explanation require us also to conceptualize the political structure as a whole entity and, in turn, to explore the relationship of the regime, as well as other structures, to this whole? Are we not now at the stage in which, as I have suggested, we have pushed too far in the direction of tracing out independent effects of the subject, including collective actors such as the state? Is it not time to think of bringing political structure itself back in, once again, and this time at the highest level within the political system?

When the question is put in this direct, bald way, it immediately raises a further question: To what extent does it make sense to talk of structure, on the one hand, as the form of a political system (its regime structure) and, at the same time, to talk about the overarching structure of the political system which somehow influences its own regime (and other) structures? What meaning can we be giving to the term *structure* that permits us to refer to it in these two seemingly different senses? Does talking about the regime structure and the structure of a political system as a whole involve two different meanings for the term *structure* itself, as (we shall see), the structuralists would argue?[27]

Furthermore, how can we sensibly even think about isolating the effect of the whole structure of a political system on one of its parts, such as the regime, without decomposing the whole political structure into its various parts, and still hope to meet the demands of rigorous empirical research? On the other hand, can we reasonably hope to understand the structural differences we transparently observe among regimes without considering the overall way in which political systems are put together, that is, are structured? It is questions such as these that I shall address as I seek to formulate, not a structuralist theory of politics in the genre of Lévi-Strauss, for example, and not a theory in the strict sense about the structure of the political system as a whole, but rather just a theoretical first step to the understanding of political structures.

The Plan

Before we can expect to come within sight of a comprehensive theory about political structure, some conceptual underbrush needs to be cleared away and the essential groundwork must be prepared. This is a book, then, about some of the more important issues we must confront as we take the first major steps toward a theory about political structures. Although we might have focused on any structure for illustrative purposes, because of the central significance of the regime in all political systems I have chosen its structure, together with certain other structures closely associated with it, for special attention.

At one time it had seemed to me that such a start toward the formulation of a theory about political structure might take a different path. Upon completing *A Systems Analysis of Political Life* I had thought that my next book, one on structure, would address itself to the ways in which political structures constrain the inputs of demands and support, help to shape the nature of the outputs, and limit the ways in which conversion processes might operate. In fact, given the attention that I had devoted to such major processual elements of a political system, it would have been legitimate to expect that in turning to the regime and its associated structures I would have sought to trace out the effects of variations in such forms on these elements. Insofar as different structures impede, facilitate, distort, or shape such inputs, conversion processes, outputs, and feedback, it would certainly be helpful to have a theoretical approach that would clarify the ways in which this might occur. Indeed, this was my original intention.

As I proceeded to try to determine the effects of variations in structures on these major elements of a political system, however, it quickly became apparent that structure was not the simple, readily usable concept that it had seemed to me at the outset, or that it appeared to be from the insouciant way in which we political scientists have used it. Outside of political science there is an enormous literature about structure. But for one reason or another these ideas have had little obvious impact on our thinking. We do not have a clear idea about the multitudinous ways in which the term has been used in political science, or elsewhere for that matter. Nor do we have a tradition that directs us to view the idea of structure as problematic.

It is clear to me now that even though questions about the impact of structure on inputs, outputs, and the like continue to be important, such an approach to structure would lead only to a partial answer about the way in which structures might determine or limit these central political processes. It would not be complete. It would not help us understand what makes these very regimes and their related structures what they are. In short, a theory revealing the way structures limit inputs, conversion processes, and outputs might lead us to a better understanding of the effects of these structures. It would, however, offer us little understanding of the conditions within which these structures themselves operate, as parts of the larger structure of the political system, and that give them the form they take with the effects they have.

Hence, as I progressed in my understanding of structures, it became clear that explanation of the way in which they influence the major kinds of activities in political systems requires prior understanding of the factors that help to shape these structures themselves. It became equally clear that this prior knowledge must take center stage. Whatever effect visible political structures might have on the central political processes—inputs, conversion, and outputs—ultimately these effects would themselves be dependent on the very forces that facilitated, limited or determined these visible structures.[28]

The choice, then, was between a theoretical approach that stressed an understanding of immediate structural effects or one that focused on the broader factors that give birth or shape to the immediately observable structures that might bring about these effects themselves. It was evident that the first step in the direction of a theory of structure should address itself to the latter issues. From an explanatory perspective it is fundamental as well as logically prior.

As structure is a concept notorious for its ambiguities, my discussion will be directed, initially, toward its clarification. In the process I shall not be able to avoid taking into account, nor would I wish to even if I could, social structures other than political ones. In the end, however, I shall return to the relevance of our conclusions for an understanding of political structures.

After considering the conditions, that, during the late 1970s and 1980s, might explain a revival in political science of an interest in structure (chapter 2), I shall seek to specify an appropriate meaning for political structure. This will enable us to identify those components traditionally included as part of political structures (chapter 3) and inquire into the source of the importance that political science has traditionally attributed to structures because of their presumed consequences for the functioning of the political system (chapters 4–7). Unless we are able to demonstrate convincingly that regime structures are seen to have significant effects, there would be little reason to pursue further our concern for the determinants, if any, of such structures.

These preliminary chapters will clear the way for consideration of a major intellectual movement, structuralism, that focused on efforts to explain visible social structures. For some explainable reasons this movement all but passed political science by, although we will see that to the extent it did intrude, it sneaked in unobtrusively through a back door opened by structuralist Marxism. We will discover that whatever its shortcomings—and they are numerous and serious— stucturalism does at least have the merit of identifying and opening up the problem of the how we go about seeking an explanation of the factors that shape visible structures. In the justified rejection of structuralism, however, we will want to see whether, in that overused but still descriptive sentence, we can rescue the baby from being thrown out with the bathwater (chapter 8). This will put us in a position to explore the way in which political science in the past has sought to address the issue of variability in regime structure and to note and assess its shortcomings in this effort (chapter 10).

Unable to find an appropriate way of handling the matter in political science and enticed by the fact that structuralism has been the only intellectual approach that has sought to raise the issue of variability of visible structures to a serious theoretical level, I shall undertake a fairly extensive analysis of the work of Nicos Poulantzas. It turns out that he alone among structuralists has attempted to apply one form of this approach—a neo-Marxist one—to part of the very question I have been posing: how to account for regime structure variability (chapters 11–16).

From the ashes of Poulantzas's efforts and those of conventional political science I shall then be in a position to raise up a possible alternative path of inquiry that gives hope of a meaningful theoretical approach for coping with the issues about structural constraints raised in this book. It will lead us to a consideration of the explanatory relationship between political life conceived as a complex system of interactions and the decisive and inescapable effect of this whole on that important part we have identified as its regime structures (chapters 17–19).

2

Political Structure Revived

During the last quarter of the nineteenth century, political science seemed almost obsessively concerned with the legal structures of political systems. In the twentieth century, however, political science has shown remarkably little interest in the whole area of political structure, at least until relatively recent times, as I noted in the preceding chapter. How can we account for this indifference to structural constraints? More important, how can we account for the revival of political structure as an area of concern in the 1980s? This chapter addresses these questions.

Neglect of Structure

Is it true that in this century, until very recently, American political science, at least, has virtually neglected structure? In contrast, much of European social science, in the same period, has passed through a structuralist phase and into a period of post-structuralism, marked even by such extreme types as deconstruction. In one sense, to the question just posed we would have to give a negative answer. In one way or another the bulk of empirical political research cannot help but touch on political structures—on governmental structures of all kinds, party structures, interest group structures, and the like. Comparative politics could scarcely survive if it were to exclude all attention to what we normally call political institutions, a term that at least includes political structures even if it may go beyond them.[1]

In another sense, however, if we refer to theoretical interests in structure, we would need to respond affirmatively to the question as to whether political science has neglected structure. As we shall see, nowhere in the literature, with the notable exception of Marxism,[2] can we find even the statement of a need for an explicit theory about the place of structure in the functioning of political systems, let alone the presence of such a theory. The discipline has not set as a central task the formulation of ideas about how political structures come into being, change their shape, and are displaced by new ones. Even though, through its recent rediscovery of the individual actor, as we noted in the preceding chapter, political science is joining the post-structuralism of the 1980s, it does so without having gone through the experience of a genuinely structuralist phase, one in which it had rung the theoretical changes on the place of structure in the political system. As the critics of rationalistic individualism have intimated,[3] we are in danger of bypassing structural constraints without having previously explored their significance.

Fragmentary ideas on these and other structural subjects do, of course, abound.

We debate the merits of various constitutional arrangements, test for or assume the effects of such constitutions, formulate philosophies about different structural orders such as democracy or totalitarianism, classify systems by their structures,[4] propose reforms of formal structures, dispute the merits of two-party versus multiparty structures, prescribe the conditions for stability of democratic systems (which include more than structures, of course), explore the effects of varying governmental structures on modernization, and so on. We typically work with these and other phenomena that we call political structures, analyze them, take them into account at every turn. Yet even though we have produced weighty essays and monographs on almost every other intellectual issue, from personality, ideology, participation, and socialization to survey research, voting behavior, rationality, policy-making, and world political systems, we have still to devote sustained theoretical attention to the idea of structure for the special problems it raises.

What is even more surprising is that in the literature on structural-functionalism in political science, a debate over the nature, place, effects, and determinants of structure has never been joined. We might well have expected such a debate if only because of the fact that this approach to research in comparative politics, under the ultimate influence of theoretical guidelines formulated by Talcott Parsons (and Malinowski before him, together with the British structural anthropologists, led by Radcliffe-Brown) once dominated this particular field for more than a decade. It is not clear that in political science the functional approach really disappeared even in the 1980s. Yet we will search in vain for any fundamental analysis of structure as a concept or theory not only in comparative research but in the study of politics as a whole.[5]

Furthermore, nowhere is the expectation raised that one day we ought to or might wish to collect whatever knowledge we do have into a partial theory of political structure. Nowhere do we even find discussion about the possible significance or relevance of such a theory. In political science the idea of structure in general has been neither salient nor problematic.

If, for example, we turn to the *International Encyclopedia of the Social Sciences*[6] we will be unable to locate a topical heading "political structure." We will find one on *social* structure, but it reflects exclusively the special concerns of sociologists and anthropologists. We will find an article on political *process* which, astonishingly, is able to discuss this topic with scarcely even a casual reference to structure. But no special topic called political structure finds a place there.

Aside from political science, structure as an idea has long been prevalent in the social sciences,[7] as I have already mentioned. Its meaning, however, has remained uncertain over the ages. As a term, it has become increasingly popular in the other social sciences, especially since the Second World War. Even its usage in political science has increased noticeably since the 1970s, a point to which I shall return shortly. This increased dependence on the term has done little, however, to bring about its clarification. Indeed, such a variety of meanings for the idea has evolved in the social sciences as a whole that there are those who throw up their hands in despair at the thought of trying to distill a common meaning for it. For them the term has picked up more connotations than can sensibly be handled in scientific discourse.

> Quite apart from the multiplicity of definitions [Boudon has argued], the use of the actual word 'structure' at least in certain contexts, gives rise in itself to considerable dissatisfaction. The variety of connotations characterizing the term when employed by different authors raises doubts as to the existence of a single meaning which could be attributed to it.[8]

It is truly remarkable that today, especially in a period that is already widely described as post-structuralist, most mainstream political scientists, virtually alone among the social sciences, have paid so little attention to the meaning of structure, despite its increasing use. And this is equally true of neostatists, comparative political historians, new institutionalists, and contextualists, however much we might have expected their turn to structural constraints to offer a signal for more deliberate attention to the concept. It is as though we thought the term so readily knowable to common sense that it does not merit special consideration. Indeed, we seem to leave the impression—falsely, as it turns out—that political scientists have agreed on a unique meaning for it.

Other social scientists, however, are far less sanguine about their ability to comprehend even the referents of the term, let alone the effects of structure, its origin and sources of change. In sociology and anthropology, for example, the notion of structure constitutes one of the central unresolved issues of the disciplines. A vast literature on the subject blankets their fields. In political science, on the other hand, we have had no theoretical tradition for dealing with structure. Even though Marx, Durkheim, and Simmel, for example, were as available to us as to sociology, we have seldom sought to build on them, except for Marx, and even with him, not for these purposes.

With political science typically concerned about redesign problems involved in the change and improvement of political systems, we might have thought that in recommending new forms for old institutions, political scientists would have been alerted to the structural assumptions and implications of their proposals. If proposed changes in administrative organizations and federal arrangements, or in the distribution of powers among legislatures, courts, and executives, are intended to bring about improvements in the performance of political systems, we might have thought that this would at least have raised more general theoretical issues.

To what extent, for example, can we expect that transformations in such obvious structures or forms of systems will lead to the attainment of the anticipated goals? How do we know what kinds of structures to change and what changes to introduce unless we have some idea about the factors that lead existing structures to take the form they do? Yet even though reference is made to problems such as these from time to time and judgments are readily expressed—as in the perennial debates about the merits of a two-party responsible government, on the British model, as compared to a Presidential structure, after the American type—the determinants and consequences of structural change have seldom been raised as explicit issues meriting sustained theoretical attention.

Why the Neglect?

How can we account for this past neglect of the theoretical status of political structures, which, on the surface would seem to be a central concern for political science? In retrospect it is not too hard to understand. The intellectual history of the discipline tells us how our interest came to be deflected from structure as a central topic.

As we know, the idea of structure fell into disrepute in the latter part of the nineteenth century. It was then associated with the arid deductive legalism of German Staatslehre scholarship, once the major source of inspiration for American political inquiry. The Staatswissenschaft school had interpreted political institutions as formal juridical realizations derivative from a self-conscious theory of the state based, in turn, on a theory of justice.[9] When Woodrow Wilson, following Walter Bagehot's lead from England, attributed transcending importance to those political activities that occur within and around the formal structures of government, students of politics lost confidence in the ability of political structures to explain much of significance. Structure, in the sense of a legal constitution or the formal arrangements of government, receded in theoretical and practical importance, nor did an interest in structure of an informal sort take its place.

Subsequent research seemed bent on throwing the wheat out with the chaff. This later nineteenth-century challenge to structural formalism exhorted us to devote ourselves to the activities or processes through which legislation was produced. The very notion of the political process acquired precious symbolic value as the flag of the opponents to the old formalism. Much as their own successors in the 1950s were prone to see themselves as different because they studied *behavior*, so these opponents of formalism sought to demonstrate their own modernity by asserting their commitment to the study of *the* political process.[10] The presence of the definite article and the use of the singular form—the political process, not the study of political processes—puzzled outsiders but comforted the members of the political science guild.[11] These conventions signaled colleagues that the given research worker was not allowing static political form or arid legalism to conceal dynamic content.

It is clear today that in shifting the emphasis of political research away from those aspects of the political system which were considered to be formal structures, our predecessors in political science were certainly taking a major step toward resolving the problem of legalism. They did so, however, only at the cost of a legacy of a new and perhaps equally difficult sort, a not atypical kind of change in science, as we know from Kuhn.[12] In rejecting structures as an interesting influence in politics, the anti-formalist revolt left us with the new question of just what that phenomenon was that was being discounted. What is the nature of these presumably ineffectual political structures? Are they really only of minor significance? Can structures ever be of any importance? And are the rejected structures the only significant ones in politics?

To be sure, the discovery of and concentration on the political process, and later on political behavior, did not rule out concern for structures at the day-to-day level of research. Without any fuss about or acknowledgment of the matter, little political research could forgo some important references both to formal political structures and to the influence of other kinds of structures largely untouched by nineteenth-century formalists—elements of the social structure, for example, such as social class, region, religion, and ethnicity. Even though, as I noted in the preceding chapter, we have no stable vocabulary for classifying political systems, it would be universally acknowledged that the terms we do use—democracy, totalitarianism, authoritarianism, dictatorship, bureaucratic state, and the like—refer at least in part to differences in structures, whether formal or otherwise. Even the more detailed inquiries into political systems through the identification of ruling classes as against subjects or subordinate classes, elites versus masses, the plural bases of power, and the relationship between the authorities and their electorate seem to use what most research workers would feel comfortable in calling structural categories.

Thus, even though toward the end of the last century political science had shifted its attention away from formal structures, this did not mean that it had really given up all interest in formal and other kinds of structures. As I have already suggested, no study of politics could proceed in happy abandonment of the structured relationships we find in political organizations and institutions and at the same time maintain contact with the real world. It is just that the process advocates had converted the prior theoretical interest in juridical structure, however misguided it may have been, into a mere *ad hoc* and practical interest. This led, until recently, to the unwitting neglect of a concern for developing the theoretical aspect of structure. It is as though structure were not a real issue or as though its understanding is simple enough to resolve, in passing, through *obiter dicta*.

It is now clear, I shall propose, that in rejecting the formalism of the last century, we in political science failed to detect the grain of truth that might have been extracted from the experience of that preceding generation of political scholarship. Structure does have major importance, even if not in the way the legal formalists would have had us believe and even if the term itself goes beyond mere form.

Structure in American Political Science

The neglect of a theory of political structure cannot be explained solely in terms of the internal history of political science itself. The revolt against legal formalism, during the late nineteenth century in the United States, may well have fixed our disciplinary attitudes initially. But this does not explain why we have not changed, especially when faced with the clear example of European scholars.

The preoccupation with structure in Europe, and in France particularly, had been growing rapidly, since the 1950s at least. In fact, in the particular version called structuralism, a fascination with structure passed even beyond the walls of academia. By the 1960s Lévi-Strauss's kind of structuralism, for example, was widely discussed in the public press, even in letters to the editor, on national television in France and on the Third Programme of the BBC.[13] The Althusserian form of Marxism transformed structuralism into a salient issue in Marxist and other socialist intellectual circles in Western Europe and Latin America (but not until the 1970s in the United States, and then only in a modest way).[14] This special kind of inquiry into the significance of structure as a possible universal phenomenon moved beyond the social sciences into literature, history, psychiatry, philosophy, mathematics, and other major areas of thought.[15] With such widespread concern about structure in other intellectual communities, we may well ask how political science in the United States managed to wall itself off from this major current so successfully, and for so long.[16]

An exhaustive discussion of the reasons would take us too far afield. Piaget has speculated that there are cognitive developmental grounds for the delay everywhere, until the mid-twentieth century, in coming to terms with what he considers the underlying ideas of structuralism, a particular kind of interest in structure.

> That it should have taken so long before its possibility was discovered [Piaget proposed], is, of course, primarily due to the natural tendency of the human mind to proceed from the simple to the complex, hence, to neglect interdependencies and systematic wholes until such time as problems of analysis force them upon our attention. It is also due to the fact that structures are not observable as such, being located at levels which can be reached only by abstracting forms of forms or systems of the nth degree; that is, the detection of structure calls for a special effort of reflective abstraction.[17]

In the United States there may be an additional ground for having neglected the issue of structure, especially of the variety to which Piaget refers, a subject to which I shall return in a later chapter. Pragmatic suspicion of theory continues to this day, despite the extensive discussion of the place of theory in basic inquiry and the inclusion of lower-level theory in most empirical research. Theory at the higher levels, what I have always referred to as general empirically oriented theory, has not yet lost its suspect character. Despite the inroads that general theory made in the decades following the Second World War, the going continues to be rough. Despite the arguments about general empirical theory in recent decades, in the end the pragmatic tradition has managed to mold the idea of such theory to its own purposes. With notable exceptions, it has virtually reduced the search for theory to middle-range or lower-level generalizations or hypotheses that can be readily operationalized for testing, or to issues in the philosophy of science. And the pressure, during the 1980s, for the application of knowledge to urgent social issues has reinforced this tendency.

It is arguable that if American political science had been more open to theory in general and less suspicious of European philosophical tendencies, from the 1950s through the 1970s, we might not have been quite so blind to our own virtually unexplored conceptions of structure. We might have been led to give greater credence, for the purposes of empirical research, to the changing philosophical perspectives in social science flowing out of Europe—phenomenology, structuralism, and now various post-structuralist tendencies. This might have helped us to broaden our understanding of structure. It could have opened our minds to the possibility of including less easily measured factors in and surrounding political systems, factors that may influence the operations of political systems no less significantly than such specific, measurable elements of social structure as patterns of religion, ethnicity, region, and social class. The latter reflect the differentiated social positions which may shape social interactions and in this way certainly pertain to structure. As we shall see, however, structural elements such as these, which we typically include in our research, need not and do not exhaust the structures relevant to political systems, and especially to that part that I shall be calling the regime structure.

Whatever truth there may be to this surmise, I shall hope to show that it is the less easily operationalized factors about the broad context within which political systems operate, toward which one of those theories, called structuralism, was pointing. In American political science the much narrower view of structure as differentiated social positions, whether separately or collectively considered, has put important limits on the insights and findings of empirical research itself.

In later chapters I shall have much more to say about structuralism as an interpretation of structure, including its severe shortcomings. The important point at the moment is that the general suspicion of theory, broadly conceived, deriving in part from the traditions of pragmatism as a specific philosophy, has been hard to drive out of political inquiry. Whatever inroads the discussion of general empirically oriented theory may have made in the last few decades, they were apparently not deep enough to open the way to a more serious and comprehensive examination of structure such as was already so prominently under way in Europe.

The latent pragmatism in American political research, then, the conversion of theoretical interest into the more limited sphere of theorems, the degeneration of theorizing to the discussion of problems in the philosophy of science, especially epistemology, and the recent commitment to the immediate application of knowledge (the policy analysis movement) have all reinforced the tendency to divert attention and energy away from the task of formulating more general substantive theories, including those about structure.

Changing Awareness about Structural Constraints

Despite our continued failure, especially in American political science, to provide the depth of analysis of structure to which it might be entitled, by the 1980s there had developed a new awareness of the significance of structure for an understanding of the way political systems operate. Neo-Marxism, neostatism, comparative historical sociology (as practiced by political scientists as well), the so-called new institutionalism, and contextualism, tendencies to which I shall return much later, all signify this emerging interest, as I suggested in chapter 1. They indicate that in political science we have indeed begun to be more receptive to ideas about structure, especially when interpreted as overarching structural constraints. How can we account for this?

The answer lies perhaps in the sociology of knowledge of our discipline. After the rejection of the significance of structure, toward the end of the nineteenth century, the revival in the 1970s and 1980s of a concern for it, at a new level of understanding, turns, in part, on the events of those and the immediately preceding decade.

The events of the 1960s in the United States and throughout the world created great expectations among many, and great fears among others, of deep and rapid social changes. The student counterculture movement helped young people, especially those residentially concentrated, in larger numbers than ever before, in educational institutions, to flex their social and political muscles.[18] Their initial successes evoked in them exhilarating feelings fired by a growing sense of efficacy about their participation in politics. They witnessed signal successes in shifting attitudes toward civil rights, in moving the Vietnam war to its conclusion, and in fundamentally altering social priorities in such central areas as freedom of attire, social ecology, health, poverty, sexism, and racial prejudice. It was an age of "the greening of America"[19] with great hopes and confidence in the ability of social movements to bring about what were considered fundamental transformations in society.

By the mid-1970s, despite the end of the Vietnam War, these hopes had begun to fade. The sparkle in young people's eyes began to dull as the promise of change seemed either much slower in coming than had been expected or seemed to disappear entirely. In the face of efforts to change the world, reality seemed much less cooperative and far more recalcitrant that had ever been imagined in the first burst of enthusiasm of the 1960s.

It is commonplace to point to the sense of powerlessness and alienation that slowly emerged as the political realities began to sink in. The intense popular minorities of the 1960s seemed less able to move legislatures and political leaders than the smaller, less visible minorities acting through corporate structures with respect to which individual actors felt helpless.[20] Society turned against education. The economy began to falter. Humanitarianism and altruism came under attack. Hedonism emerged in new forms, confronted by new kinds of poverty. The claims of the United States to dominant moral and military leadership no longer seemed as tenable as they had been in earlier days. New problems associated with the ongoing need for the international redistribution of wealth from the resource rich industrialized nations to the Third World, symbolized in the mounting international debts of developing countries, became more urgent than ever.

The story of this dramatic turnaround and tapering off of the activism of the 1970s by the 1980s is too well known to need recounting here. Its effect on the intellectual community of the United States, however, is not so self-evident. Entrenched prejudices and presuppositions were loosened. In the aftermath of the mobilization of energies and heightened social awareness attendant on the massive efforts of the student days came the realization that the mere desire to bring about social change and the mobilization of large numbers in peaceful or confrontational demonstrations was not enough. Bright hopes had been dimmed by reality.

Why? What was there, in the nature of that reality, that stood so solidly in the way of massive voluntaristic efforts? What is the source of resistance to change even in face of intensely felt feeling in its favor? How can a society manage to blind itself to what, to many people in the 1960s and later, seemed like vast areas of oppression and exploitation, both at home and abroad, and of transparent abuse of their environment? How did it come about that with so overwhelming a desire for social change, with the painful mobilization of vast energies on its behalf, and with the knowledge and understanding that social science had accumulated about society, nothing more than a modest realization of the desired ends could be achieved?

The assessment of the 1960s and 1970s is, of course, not over yet.[21] Nor is it my intention to balance off the genuine changes that have been associated with the counterculture movement against the extent to which things have remained as they are or even grown worse. The point here is that the activism of those generations did lead the involved and succeeding generation to pose a major new intellectual question, if only implicitly: How can we account for our limited capacity to bring about change? To what extent are these barriers to change a product of objective constraints, concealed to ordinary observation, but powerful in their determining or limiting effects?

Although no single person or group has taken the initiative in posing these questions so directly, they do subsume the discussion in much of the leading literature of the period. It helps to account for the new and serious turn to phenomonology, to the reception of Marxism in the United States, to the revival of elitist interpretations of democracy, to the search for outer limits of change,[22] and even to a preoccupation with what might appear as more mundane methodological matters such as contextualism and compositional and ecological effects (which embody important theoretical implications as well, as we shall see in due course).

In its critical application, for example, phenomenology implies that political science, like the other social sciences, had failed society by neglecting to recognize its own primary weakness as a theoretical discipline. It had been unable to take account of the constraints limiting the questions it can pose and the answers it dares to give. From this perspective political science is a prisoner of its own ideological and value structures. These determine the way it looks at the world: the kinds of questions it asks, the kinds of data it looks for, the kinds of evidence it accepts as proof, and the kinds of solutions it considers reasonable and sensible. In other words, political science has unwittingly been constructing and operating within its own reality, to invoke a well-known book title of earlier years,[23] and it perpetuates this construction through the way it socializes its novitiates in graduate school. Hence political science can be critical only within limits defined by the ideological "structure" within which it operates.

Marxism not only joined in this criticism. It went further and this provided for its "third coming" into American political inquiry.[24] It offered alternative possible explanations for the failure of voluntarism. Gramsci could attribute our intellectual blinders to capitalist ideological (cultural) hegemony which conceals the constraints under which we act. Other Marxists could depict social relationships as an "objective structure" which shapes the ideological structure itself and creates a powerful and inescapable set of determining forces for the social fabric as a whole and in its many parts. The Marxist critics had been around for over a century. But from the 1960s on, in Europe at least, a new and influential reanalysis of Marx, under the theoretical guidance of Althusser, as I have already noted, sought to emphasize, more strongly than ever before, the "structural" determinants of manifest social arrangements. This interpretation later had a strong appeal, in the United States, for those who were searching for some way to account for the resistance to change in society despite the passionate commitments and active involvement of so many in the movements of the 1960s and 1970s.

Nor were traditional political scientists themselves silent in the aftermath of the counterculture movements. As I suggested in the preceding chapter, power pluralism was found fundamentally wanting in its utter failure to take sufficient account of the socalled other faces of power. Elite theories of the political system, originating with Mosca and Pareto and revived in American political science by Lasswell, once thought to be only a historical critique, now began to surface again as appealing contemporary interpretations.[25] Their renaissance reflected the same feeling about the need to reach for a more persuasive explanation of the recalcitrance of society to change than was available in current theories of power pluralism or Marxism. For the elitists, the political system was captive of a structure consisting primarily of two hierchically organized elements, the elite and the people or masses. These decisively determine the location and distribution of power.

What these and other intellectual perspectives have in common is an effort to build a theory around what has suddenly been discovered, or should we say, rediscovered: that despite the enthusiastic expressions of human will and intention in the 1960s and 1970s, actors are not entirely free to determine their own fate. There are certain inescapable or objective constraints on actions of the subject or person. This new turn in social inquiry has led to a revival of what we might call an objectivist (or structural) as against a subjectivist epistemology as the assumption for research.[26]

Whether, in the United States, the emergence of an objectivist epistemology as a theoretical commitment is adequate or even useful, is not the question at the moment. What it does reveal is the renewal of an underlying awareness that we cannot understand society, after all, unless we are prepared to attend to the basic conditions that may shape or limit action despite subjective will or desire. In the process, as we might expect, this has revived the ancient debates about the place of the actor or of subjective intentions in the scheme of things and about the effects of the whole (holism) on individual actors.

In short, I am suggesting that, unlike the Old Left of the 1930s, the New Left and other counterculture social movements of the 1960s and 1970s were dominated by no special ideology or any single, well-articulated social philosophy. Many did, however, share a single philosophical premise, even if unarticulated, that voluntarism would work. In their behavior it was clear that there was a powerful belief that the mere force of human will, desire, and collective effort could turn society around. The apparent limited successes, the more visible and felt areas of failure, and the slow shifting of social concerns to a more conservative if not reactionary (in the strict sense) social philosophy in the 1980s, led to the simple query: How free are human efforts? How determined or limited?

In searching for answers, one major route of inquiry has been to appropriate one or another of those social theories—phenomenology, neo-Marxism, and structuralism—that had built into them central ideas about the limits on human action. Some few did just that. Another route has been to generate interest and concern for the nature of constraints in general that determine social interaction, or, as I shall argue, perhaps more appropriately, impose major limits on it. In political science we have given too little attention to this alternative. It will become a focus for our interest in this book.

In political science of the 1980s, the revival of an interest in structure is, therefore, not a product of caprice or mere historical accident. It seems to be closely related to the times in which we live and the real problems they have posed. Historically it evokes once again a continuing and major intellectual puzzle: How much freedom do human beings really have to change or master their collective fate? It need not do so, however, by relying exclusively on the traditional, overworked philosophical debates on this matter. It can search, rather, for answers that take these debates into account but go beyond them, answers based on and consistent with, although not necessarily limited, by the intellectual imperatives of contemporary changing social science.

We will find, surprisingly, that what looks like a simple idea—that of constraining structures—passes well beyond its normal and expected meaning in conventional political science, at first in the hands of European scholars and then among some in the United States. The notion of structure acquires new connotations which seem to be vastly different from those normally associated with it.

As we shall see, for some the idea seems to lead to the adoption of a broad theoretical interpretation or model of society, along systems lines in some instances, usually going beyond the political aspect alone. We will come to identify this tendency as structuralism in contrast to the traditional, if unarticulated, ways of analyzing structure. I shall have occasion to distinguish between these two perspectives to structure through designating the one as *structuralism* and the other as *structural analysis*.[27]

This simple and unassuming classification will help us keep clear two major and contending tendencies, however unavowed they may often be, for understanding a major source of regime variability. But before we can turn to the relationship of these two perspectives on structure, we need to establish what we may mean when we talk of structures—the explanation of the variability of which is our primary concern—as elements of a political system.

3

Structure in Political Explanation

Political systems are composed of a variety of structures, as well as processes. I am interested in the variability of these structures. As I have indicated, for illustrative purposes I shall be paying special attention to that subset of structures embodied in the regime. And I shall be arguing first, that although there are many influences at work in giving shape to any particular regime, in political science we have not been very successful in explaining the particular forms they do take; and second, that there is one influence that is characteristically omitted, that of the overall structure of the political system, which, we will find, is distinct from the structure of the regime. In the end, as I have already stated, my point will be that by bringing in the total political structure we will have added a dimension to our explanation that gives promise of eliminating this gap in our understanding of the variability of regimes, and of other structures as well.

In the last chapter we spoke about the decline and revival, in this century, of an interest in political structure as a central problem in political science. In this chapter, to try to illuminate further our use of the idea of structure in political science and, as a means for introducing us to an acceptable way of approaching the meaning of this concept, I shall turn to the way we enter it into our explanations. This discussion will reveal an implicit usage that has tended to narrow our ordinary conception of structure to a single type, one that deals largely with political behavior.

I shall conclude that, in itself, this usage cannot be faulted. It has been accompanied, however, by what I shall call a predominantly *physicalist* interpretation of structures, as though they were largely membership groups, out there in space and time, as much a part of phenomenal reality as directly visible chairs or dogs. This has created certain ambiguities if not confusion about the theoretical and ontological status of political structures. These need to be clarified if we are to be able to appreciate the shortcomings in the ways we have been dealing with the structure of regimes and of other parts of political systems.

I shall conclude that, by their very nature, political structures cannot be viewed as physical things. To construe them in this way is to confuse them with concrete institutions such as membership groups. The latter may be structured but they are not themselves structures. Structure, I shall propose, are not phenomena; they ought to be considered only as *properties* of things, not as the things themselves. To do otherwise is to be guilty of what we might call a fallacy of misplaced concreteness—the substitution of the property of a thing for the thing itself. Such a stricter conception of the ontological nature of structures will prepare the ground for a broader, and, in my view, a more useful conception of political structure which will appear in later chapters.

Misplaced Concreteness

In chapter 5 we shall look at various kinds of structures commonly introduced into political explanations. These structures are formed by such elements as interest groups, formal governmental arrangements, various political roles, groupings such as elites versus masses, party systems, and the like. Normally we assume that in one way or another, such structures help to determine the way the system works by shaping inputs, outputs, conversion processes, and feedback to use a systems conception of political processes.

What are we in fact trying to do, however, when we see structures as such determinants? When we look at the attribution of this kind of influence to structures, although we may have a number of explanatory purposes in mind, one of them stands out. Normally we will be trying to prove that political structures, as such, have an independent and separable effect on such things as policies, attitudes, and behavior. By implication, since the effects of political structures are separated out for independent treatment, it suggests that they need to be differentiated from other kinds of effects such as those brought about by culture, personality, or actual behavior (political activities and processes). We wish to isolate political structures, whatever their form, to show their separable consequences.

The reader might well ask: Why should I take the trouble to draw attention to this view of structure? The matter appears to be only too obvious. Presumably our objective in identifying structures as a set of variables is precisely to show their specific influence on one or another aspect of the political system and the outcomes of its operation. There would be little point in being interested in structures if we did not suspect them of having some important independent effects.[1] If so, it is only natural for us to want to isolate those effects if we are to enrich our understanding of how structures may be involved in the way political systems operate.

Unfortunately, the matter is not quite so simple. If it were just a matter of trying to show the independent effects of structure there would be little to cavil about. The task of all research is to unveil important relationships. It is the way we typically do it, however, that raises serious questions about our apparent interpretations of the meaning of structure.

Thus, standard usage requires that we carefully try to discriminate the consequences of structures, such as those of regime, party, interest group, or political class, from the effects of other characteristic major categories of political phenomena, such as political culture, personality, or even political behavior. In other words, it appears that we frequently and automatically conceive of structure as being on the same theoretical level with other classes of presumed major determinants. We consider it a class of determinant which is separable from culture, personality, and behavior and which may need to be taken into account whenever these other sets of variables are entered into an explanation, if we wish to estimate the effects of all the major parameters in a given situation.

More than that may, however, be involved when we speak of political structures. We seem to look at them in this light because of the special ontological status we give them. We seem to consider that structures are real entities out there in the objective world. We can infer this from the fact that when we talk about political structure we seem to have in mind some concrete kind of entity in space and time. When we speak of the structure of government, for example, we normally seem to have in mind organized entities, made up of human beings, to which we can point, in perhaps the same way that we can point to the walls or girders of a building as its physical structure. The structure seems to be the whole membership group.

Closer analysis will reveal that this attribution of concreteness to political structure involves us in a special conception of political structure that reduces its scope unnecessarily and thereby its analytic power. I shall seek to show that, our apparent usage to the contrary, structure has not got the same theoretical status as certain other major determinants with which it is often contrasted (such as political culture or political personality), at least implicitly since we have seldom had occasion to consider this matter seriously in the discipline.

As I have indicated, I shall argue that to give structure any sensible meaning for the purposes to which we put it, we must construe it only as a *property* of these other aspects of a political system (political culture, personality, behavior, etc.), with which it appears to have a similar theoretical status. It is not physically separable from them as though it were an independent entity existing in space and time, a view that only too often seems to be implied in our ordinary usage. Rather, structure is entailed in each of these other elements of a political system. It can be separated from them only in the sense that we can abstract it out analytically. As an analytic concept it refers not to the concrete total activities of groups of persons, such as those constituting a government or party system, but only to an aspect of their total behavior.[2]

Typically we have failed to recognize this analytic nature of political structures, that they can have no independent spatiotemporal existence in a way that a membership group has. On the contrary, structures can only be a property of political phenomena some of which, such as membership groups, may exist in space and time, and others of which, such as culture (at least as defined here), may not have a spatial existence. In the case of those concrete objects that do have a spatiotemporal presence, we have fallen victim to the fallacy of misplaced concreteness by attributing to a property of an object (its structure) the concreteness of the object itself. It leads us to call the object by one of its properties; that is, we call the object a structure when all we can mean is that it has the attribute of being structured.

The idea of governmental structures is a classic illustration of this misplacement of concreteness. Government is composed of persons organized in certain ways and involved in certain kinds of interactions. We can point our finger, as it were, to the government so conceived. We know where it is or, at least, where its parts, such as organs and agencies, reside, we can locate its buildings, its visible symbols and its members, and we can identify the behavior that makes it work. In this sense, in speaking of the governmental structure we would seem to be referring to the complex of governmental agencies, institutions and practices located in space and time. The idea of the "structure" of government does not seem to be a way of identifying a particular property of a space-time entity called government. Rather, the two terms, governmental structure and government, seem to be interchangeable.

When we think of governmental and other political structures in such concrete terms, it is not difficult to think of structures as having impact. This imagery accords with the underlying billiard-ball notions of causality (asymmetrical or time-dependent relationships) that often prevail, however much in our stricter moments we may wish to consider "cause" to be represented by associative relationships only.

It is true we often also speak about the structure of attitudes or about personality structure, although not frequently about the structure of political culture, even though culture clearly does have structure. In doing so we are not likely to draw attention to the fact, or even become aware of it, that we might be using structure in different ways. Much less do we imagine that these different ways may have important implications for our general conceptualization of structure and for the neglect of certain vital aspects.

Classes of Explanatory Variables

If it were not for an emphasis over the years on what has seemed like the effects of political structure as a concrete separable object with space-time dimensions, there would have been little incentive in the twentieth century for paying so much attention to the effects of several other classes of variables. These, we have slowly come to believe, need to be taken into account, in addition to structures, for a full and adequate explanation of political phenomena. We call them personality, culture, the person as a biological organism (soma), and something called behavior or the processes that go on *within* those presumed concrete entities called political structures.

Undoubtedly we have been less self-conscious about the part these classes of explanatory variables play in our efforts to understand politics than a thoroughly rational approach to research might require. As we shall see, their theoretical status, as such sets of explanatory variables, has been far from clear. Their significance, however, is marked by the fact that they tend to become areas of subspecialization or of concentrated interest in the discipline.

Let us glance at these different categories of phenomena that we now typically introduce into political explanations. This will put us in a position to appreciate, by contrast, the misleading theoretical as well as ontological status we characteristically give to political structures if we think of them as concrete membership groups with an independent spatiotemporal existence.

One of these types of sets of variables that we consider to be different from political structure is political personality. Normally, structure and political personality seem to be distant from each other. We may describe personality as consisting of the predispositions, goals, and motives of individual actors and their learned patterns of behavior that come into play over a wide variety of behavioral domains.[3] The assumption is that each person learns to respond to political events and to political others in typical ways. Although personality is intro-epidermal,[4] it overlays the biological dispositions of the person. In any political system, characteristic personality types may be found, in the political elites or among the people, that may lead them to participate in politics, whether actively or otherwise, in different but predictable ways.

Political personality is typically separated from other kinds of political elements. As Parsons has pointed out, in this respect reflecting frequent social science practice, each person's "own behavioral system will be a *unique variant* of the culture and its particular patterns of action. It is therefore essential to consider the personality system as not reducible to either the organism or the cultural system. It comprises an analytically independent system."[5] Similarly, we may add, for the political system the literature on personality implies that we may extract the *political* personality as a separable element whose varied influence on politics needs to be assessed.[6]

Whether the differences indicated are analytical or concrete need not be settled here. It is clear that when psychological factors appear as elements in the understanding of political phenomena, they are intended to point to something very different from structural ones. The effects of a federal structure on political outputs, for example, are clearly seen as different from the effects of different personalities, as found among the political authorities, on the same outputs.

Just as in recent decades we have come to recognize the need to take personality more systematically into account in political explanations, we have also elevated culture to a separate and identifiable class of variables. Political culture is still an ambiguous term in political research, a residual catchall category.[7] Close examination might lead us to conclude that we intend it to refer at least to the system of meanings incorporated into language and symbols and transmitted from generation to generation in a political system. In this sense, culture would represent meanings that arise out of the collective experiences of a group rather than from the wishes of individuals considered severally. Such meanings thereby constrain or facilitate action in presumably specifiable ways. As has often been recognized, the inborn competence to create complex languages distinguishes human from nonhuman primate societies. Symbolic systems of meanings have their origin in this innate capacity. From this perspective, systems of *political* meanings help to define and limit the character of political behavior.

One characteristic aspect of culture that has commanded the attention of political science historically has been ideology. But ideology is too confining a concept for political culture, even though, as with Gramsci, on occasion it has been used as a surrogate for culture. Ideology represents only one component. All research into attitudes, the traditions of a political system as a guide and limit on current choices, the preferences and values implicit in political actions, the hopes, expectations, discontents, beliefs in legitimacy, and criteria for performance are facets of political culture. As such, the latter represents an analytically separable subsystem in politics. Only our failure to develop a more coherent theoretical approach to political culture, with its own transformation rules and interconnections, has reduced our readiness or capacity to recognize the extent to which political science, in practice, depends upon culture as a major explanatory element in the political system.

In using culture, broadly understood in this way, here too, as with personality, we see it as having an influence in politics which is distinctive from that of political structures. Pye puts this very clearly when he says:

> If the concept of political culture is to be effectively utilized, it needs to be supplemented with structural analysis, but the difficulty is that political structures can be seen on the one hand as products reflecting the political culture, while on the other hand they are also important 'givens' which shape the political culture.[8]

Political culture and political structure are in two different domains.

A further class of variables that enters into political explanation, one that emerged in the 1960s and 1970s—or perhaps it would be correct to say, re-emerged but in more vigorous and systematic form—is to be found in the organic aspect of the person, the aspect represented by the genetic constitution of the species. Political science, through political philosophy especially, has had much to say in the past about human nature as a basis for speculating about the ends and organization of political life. Yet, until recently, it has paid surprisingly little systematic attention to the newly revived interest in the somatic and genetic characteristics of the human being and their possible influence on political behavior.[9]

During the 1980s, however, momentum slowly gathered seeking to demonstrate that the state of the human organism itself may have a substantial effect on the way in which the individual participates in politics. Some have even maintained that the soma may provide us with measures of attitudes more reliable than the usual questionnaire surveys.[10] A few would also argue that we are all born with certain biologically endowed predispositions and capacities which may provide a direct genetic link to political action. These inescapable tendencies to act in certain ways have been concealed, it is said, by our failure to take seriously the possibility of genetic continuity between nonhuman and human primates. Standing as testimony to this is the large and growing literature on the presumed genetic origins of such politically germane traits as domination, territoriality, bonding, leadership, aggression, and even altruism.[11] Regardless of the validity of these claims—and much speculative interpretation with little concrete evidence has been advanced— once they are made they need to be assessed in any review of political determinants.

A final set of variables that appears to enter into political explanation, separately from political structure, can be identified under the residual category of behavior or actions or what, in political science, we often call, in the aggregate, *the* political process. What people do in politics would appear to be the fundamental explanandum. In the end it would seem that we are seeking to explain why people act in the way they do politically—vote, argue, revolt, negotiate, participate in political parties, make public choices, and so forth. We are looking for an explanation of the way in which structure, culture, personality, and the human organism influence political behavior and the functioning of political institutions. Behavior itself, of

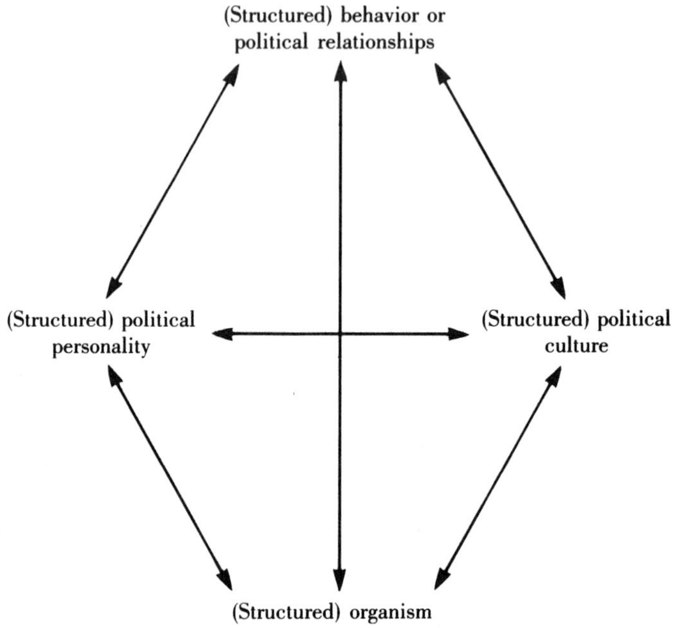

(Structured) behavior or
political relationships

(Structured) political
personality

(Structured) political
culture

(Structured) organism

Diagram 3.1   Types of Explanatory Variables and Their Relationships

course, is also seen, in turn, as having an impact on culture, personality, and even the organism, as well as on political structure. Its influence, therefore, has been separated from that of structure.

If we now collect all these elements we can see that the discipline seems to have been operating, since the 1950s at least, with a fivefold classification of the kinds of elements that we need to take into account in any adequate explanation: political structure, political culture, political personality, the human being as a biological organism, and a residual category, the central phenomenon to be understood, variously termed political action, activity, behavior, or process. These appear to be viewed as separable components of the political system.

If these elements do indeed exhaust all distinctive classes of explanatory variables, the state of any political system would constitute a particular product of the interaction among them, as represented on diagram 3.1. Presumably a fully developed political theory would systematically take into account the part that each of these elements plays in the operation of a political system.

Whether or not this classification is as comprehensive as it should be, is not critical for our purposes, however. Even if it is not, as long as these five elements do represent some of the major categories into which we segregate political phenomena, the essential point is that among them we are likely to view political structure as a concrete entity with an influence separable from those that I have mentioned.[12]

At the very least, this diagram, simplistic as it is, fairly accurately reflects the assumptions of most research about classes of variables, internal to the political system, that need to be brought into a comprehensive explanation.[13] But its simplicity is deceptive. In no uncertain terms it asserts an important point about structure: that structure is at the same theoretical level as the other elements and is sufficiently different so that it can therefore be separated out from them as an identifiable set of variables with a possible independent influence on all the other classes of explanatory variables. Furthermore, we leave the impression that it exists in space and time as such an independent or phenomenal object. Structure is therefore separable from other units of the same sort. Thus unless structure were to exhaust all reality, which it obviously does not, there must remain other phenomena that can be distinguished from it, and we have identified these in diagram 3.1.

The meaning of this implicit ontological claim with respect to political structure needs to be examined and questioned. Political structure is presumably different from the other elements and therefore can be isolated from them. In what ways is political structure different from these other explanatory elements? What do we mean when we say that it can be separated out as a set of variables for the analysis of its independent effects?

Analytic versus Concrete Structures

One element can be differentiated from another in either of two senses: analytically or concretely.[14] Whether the difference is of one or the other type is critical for our understanding of the nature of the element. If structure is separable from other elements only analytically, then it can be only a property of one or another of these other elements. In this sense it would constitute the form in which some of the elements appear.

The ontological status of chairs, for example, is clear. They are concrete entities; they are physically separate from each other and may be linked in different ways. Thus, for example, they may be set around in a circle. As such, they constitute a physical phenomenon. They exist, in that ordered way, in space and time. The structure (or form) of the collection of chairs, however, is their circularity, a property that is abstracted from the concrete entities constituting that particular physical collection of chairs. Unlike the chairs themselves, we cannot physically separate their circularity and transport it to some other location. As a property, circularity is inseparable physically from its object even though analytically we are able to do so. Otherwise we could not talk of the shape, called circularity, and compare it with other shapes and show their consequences, for example, on distortion of the communication process.[15] And the analytic character of shape, of course, does not leave it any less verifiable as an empirical phenomenon than the existence of the chairs themselves. A property can be as validly observed as any concrete entity.[16]

This difference between the collection of concrete entities, on the one hand (which are the entities or elements of which a structure is constituted), and their relationships (which form the structure), on the other, is so commonplace that it may seem unnecessary, if not tediously superfluous, to draw it to our attention, and in such detail. In practice, however, with regard to political phenomena, it is often neglected or its conceptual implications are not taken into account.

For example, this discussion has already implied an alternative conception of structure. The latter may be viewed not as a property of an object but as a concrete object itself which exists in space and time as does the organized collection of chairs. The circle of chairs *is* the structure. This seems to be the meaning that perhaps is intuitively and most frequently attributed to structure in political science. As one social scientist has expressed this position, "The *structure* of a system is the arrangement of its subsystems and components in three-dimensional space and time at a given moment of time. . . . The spatial organization of a system's parts is its structure."[17]

There is no reason, of course, why we could not use the term *structure* to refer to such parts in their relationships. In that event we would need to invent a term to refer to the structured relationship independently of the parts that enter into that relationship. Or we would need to use structure in two different senses: one, to identify the ordered constituent parts of an entity; the other, to refer to the abstracted nature of the order. Since we happen to lack such differentiated terms, for clarity of discussion it would seem useful to take an easier course and to reserve the term *structure* for the order and to speak of the parts, in their particular arrangement, simply as parts of an entity or as a subsystem. In much the same way we try to distinguish between the color of a box and the box itself even though no box-in-itself, devoid of color, is observable. Color is only a property of the box, not the box itself. To talk of a structured object as a structure is equivalent to talking of a blue box as a blue.

This ambiguity in our use of the term *structure* often appears when we talk about the governmental structure, as I noted earlier. In referring to government we seldom intend to point to the form of the government alone. Rather, we often have in mind the collection of political authorities as they exist in time and space, together with the concrete organizations of which they are part and their related behavior. In other words the government structure, in the American sense of the term, typically refers to a set of institutions and practices.[18] Indeed, in one large work on development, by Apter, government is explicitly defined as such concrete structures, and a whole theoretical approach is woven around this point of view.[19] In the same manner, we often speak of party and interest group structures and other nongovernmental structures as though the structures were the physical entities rather than the constituent parts in their organized or ordered behavior.

This usage of structure that we have just been discussing embodies what I shall now call a *physicalist* image of structure. It instructs us to view structures as physical things. We can step into and out of such structures, as it were, and in principle we could move them around from place to place. Even though structure is only a property of such objects as government, parties, interest groups, etc., the term is used to refer to all their aspects combined, as total membership groups. In doing so, we thus commit the fallacy of what I have called misplaced concreteness, identifying a concrete object by one of its properties and giving that property all of the attributes of the thing itself.

We can now see that the conception of structure as an entity, separate from the other elements in diagram 3.1, was not entirely fortuitous. It can be attributed in large part to one of the intuitive ways in which political science has come to think about structure. Seeing structure as a separable physical entity or membership group has led us to search for other explanatory elements of what we have conceived to be of a nonstructural sort. Plausibly, reality could not consist of physical structures alone; over the years political science sought out other explanatory variables such as personality, culture, biology, etc. Yet, as we shall shortly see, it is just these presumed nonstructural elements that give us the greatest conceptual trouble if we insist upon the physical nature of structure.

Origins of Physicalist Image

Let us examine this physicalist image further, since I am designating it as the likely source of confusion about the status of structure as a term in our explanation of political phenomena.[20] As I have noted, the conception of structure as a physical spatiotemporal entity is implicit in much of political research. The very term *structure* often carries with it, in common usage, a sense of solidity, a physical arrangement around and within which something occurs.

Thus, we speak about stepping into a given hierarchical or governmental structure as though they were buildings or other physical containers. We look for the structure not only because it provides such a physical frame but also because it is thought to give a degree of permanence to a social unit as it goes about its work. To some extent a legislature, as part of a governmental structure, is a legislature because it consists of certain parts that hang together: an assembly, committees, presiding officers, representatives, buildings, offices, even symbols. An organizational chart lays out the formal aspects of its internal structure, and it can be completed by describing the informal roles and groups through which the legislature actually conducts its business of debates, lobbying, mobilization of public sentiments, negotiations, compromises, and roll calls. It is as though the ordered parts provided an internal framework around which legislative activity is seen to occur, much as the skeletal structure does for the human body. The presence of structure as a frame within or around which actions take place seems so obvious to common sense that there seems to be little reason to think of even questioning its existence. It is just there, in space and time, much like an assembly of the physical parts of a machine or a building.

This imagery stands very much in the tradition out of which the word itself has arisen. *Struere,* the Latin verb in which structure has its etymological origins, means to build. Until the seventeenth century structure was largely associated with the idea of the physical framework around which a building takes shape.[21] It was later transported into biology and grammar. For most of us, as lay persons, our familiarity with the term probably derives from these architectural, biological, and linguistic sources.

All these early roots of the word conspire to reinforce its physicalist implications. In grammar, each language spatially locates parts of its sentences—its subject, verb, predicate, adjectives, adverbs, and the like—according to relatively stable ordering rules. In anatomy, the structure of the human organism is to be found in its skeleton on which flesh adheres and around which physiological processes occur. In architecture, the structure of a building is found in its physical members and spatial divisions through walls and the like. A structure in this sense has its own beauty; we are able to walk in and around it in admiration. Historically, biology and architecture gave substantive content to the very idea of structure, and it is this heritage that has left the term with a physicalist imagery. Since Herbert Spencer borrowed the term *structure* from biology and applied it to the social science, the contrast between its implications in these two areas of knowledge acquires some significance.[22]

Even though in biology the place of structure is handled, very simply and intuitively, in physicalist terms, a division comparable to anatomy (structure) and physiology (process) does not exist in the social science, Herbert Spencer notwithstanding. Yet despite this gap between the two areas of knowledge, biology and social science, much of the latent meaning of structure as used in biology is in fact carried over into social research. It is this spillover that has probably contributed to the ease with which we are ready to accept the existence of structure in itself as a concrete phenomenon or artifact.

Leighton has drawn our attention to a number of vital differences between what I am designating as the physicalist conception of structure in biology (as well as architecture and grammar) and the additional connotations of the term in the social sciences.[23] In our comprehension of structure we tend to gloss over these differences, and this permits an easy transposition of the physicalist imagery to social, and hence, to political phenomena.

For example, as we have noted, when biologists speak of the structure of an organism such as the human body, they refer to the anatomy. They contrast this with physiology, the processes for which the anatomy provides the necessary conditions. As Leighton remarks, "When one speaks of the structure of the heart he is talking about visible-palpable substance [upper and lower ventricles, muscles, arteries], not the rhythmical contractions. The latter are an aspect of functioning."[24] As he puts it more generally, in the natural sciences, "A structure is not something which keeps coming back in a regular flow of movement like a figure in a dance; it is something which just sits like a chair."[25]

Thus, for the physiologist the fact that there is a patterning in the flow of the blood through the vascular system or that there is a rhythm in the contractions of the heart or in the respiration of the lungs, does not lead the research worker to consider the stable relationships or patternings within this functioning of the organs to be part of their structure. "Yet," Leighton goes on to say, "it is precisely the analogue in behavior of these contractions, this regular functioning process, that is meant when one speaks of 'structure' in a society."[26]

Similarly, we might point out, the structure of representation, for example, consists of a set of stable interactions between represenatives and their constituents, a phenomenon that lacks the tangibility of structure in biology or for that matter, in other physical contexts, such as architecture. The structure here lies in the repetitive or stable patterns of relationships between representatives and constit-uents, not in the "palpable" behavior in which each engages. A relationship is composed of behavior. But the form—that is, the structure—of this behavior, its pattern of behavior, may vary.

For the political scientist, therefore, as for all social scientists, the matter is very different from that faced by the natural scientist. The repeatedly expressed preferences of a person for a political party or set of policies, the repetitive behavior (stable patterning) associated with political roles such as those of political leaders or representatives or party bosses, the patterns of conflict, and so on are the very aspects that can be said to give structure to the phenomena of which they are part. Structure and behavior are entwined. The matter is not the same for natural scientists, however, as we have seen. When *biological behavior*, such as physiological processes, ceases, the anatomical structure remains in place. When *social activities* cease, however, structure just disappears.[27]

Indecision Between Physicalist and Analytic Meanings

Whatever else we may make of structure in political science, we frequently see it as resembling what the physiologist rather than the anatomist deals with, namely, some patterning of what we would call function, activity, or process. Yet, confusingly, as social scientists we will typically contrast structure to behavior or process or speak of the activities within structure, as, for example, within government structures, as though the behavior was something separate and apart from structure. True to our biological heritage in this area perhaps, we often contrast process (physiology) with structure (anatomy) as though the former took place within the latter. We seem to be agreeing with the biological division into physical structure on the one side, and process on the other.

Yet at times we may seem to want to reserve the right to see structure in process. When we talk about fluctuations between stability and instability in the history of a political system, cycles of centralization as against decentralization in federal systems, or changing patterns of governmental intervention, we are thereby attributing structure to processes. But if processes themselves may have structure, it compounds our difficulty with the term to speak of the processes within, say, governmental structures. Needless to say, such oscillation in or indecision about meaning does introduce needless ambiguity, if not confusion, into our use of the idea of structure.

In our day-to-day research we can clearly see this ambivalence, if not contradiction, in our use of structure. Although I have not yet directly confronted the issue about alternative meanings for structure as a concept, in political science, despite our frequent physicalist implications, the fact is that at times we do talk about structure as though it were not a concrete membership group but some broad abstraction. We speak of democratic, authoritarian, centralized, federal, or other kinds of political structures. In using the term in this way we are clearly abstracting these patterns of political relationships out of the particular historical units in which they appear. A federal structure remains such regardless of whether we find it in a Canadian, Swiss, Australian, or American political system. Intuitively we often identify structure in this way. We extract the pattern of political interactions from among the relevant concrete components or institutions and characterize these relationships as federal. Thereby, at least implicitly, we are acknowledging the federal structure as just a *property* of the relationships among participating concrete political units, and not as the actual agencies and representative organs at the national and state or provincial levels in their ordered relationships.

However, despite our frequent intuitive recognition of structure as such a property abstracted from the concrete acting units in a relationship, our practice is far from consistent. We also frequently speak as though, in any individual instance, we considered the concrete institutions, existing in space and time, to be themselves the structures. We indifferently use the concepts of institutions and structures as synonyms. We look on them as physical constraints, like containers or buildings, on the behavior of which they are constituted, as I have already indicated. Thus, we may look upon federal structures as a combination of courts, legislatures, administrative organizations, and the like, at national and at lower regional levels, which shape or mold the behavior or processes that take place within them. Federalism, as a form of political relationships, quickly becomes transformed into a set of institutional physical presences, a framework or skeletal arrangement, as it were, that helps to shape and channel behavior. Typically we will contrast such structures with the informal behavior that occurs in and around them. Still true to our intellectual heritage from biology, we often say that the structure represents a frame, composed of various governmental organizations (often called "structures"), for example, to which culture, personality, and behavior add flesh and blood.

I am not suggesting that federalism, for example, is nothing but structure in an abstracted sense, that is, a pattern of political relationships which reflects the allocation of jurisdiction and power among a number of different political levels. Behavior is of course involved; this is what works the system conceptually. The entities—such as courts, legislatures, or administrative organizations—which engage in activities as part of this structure, are the "bearers" of the property, much as, for a blue box, the box is the bearer of its color. I am only pointing out that the structure refers not to any one or another of the entities or to the behavior of the entities themselves but to their relationships, the way in which they are patterned. A legislature is not a structure, any more than a blue box is a blue. The legislature is only an element which participates in a number of relationships. It is the latter that describe the external structure of which the legislature is one of the constituent elements. Alternatively, the legislature is composed of its own elements the relationships among which make up its internal structure.

As I have suggested, in political science we oscillate rather indifferently and often inconsistently between these two meanings of structure. One presents us with an image of structure in physicalist or concrete terms, as an entity or set of institutions out there in space and time, like a box or a building into which we pour content such as behavior, personalities, or cultural habits. The other image is that of an abstractable pattern of relationships, a form which may occur independently of the concrete units that are involved in the relationships but which manifests itself, of course, only through the concrete interactions among persons and institutions. This is what it means to say that structure is a property of behavior.

We thus seem to be using structure with two meanings. In the one it refers to membership units, concrete entities; in the other it refers to one aspect or property of the interactions among the entities, namely, the pattern of their relationships.

Structure Reclassified

The use of structure in these two ways is not only confusing; it leads to an unacceptable contradiction in analysis. We would not be able to discriminate behavior and process, on the one hand, from structure, on the other. And if structure referred to both the object and the relations, we would not be able to separate the object which engages in a relationship from the latter itself. Yet, if diagram 3.1 is accurate, it is precisely these conceptual contradictions with which we have traditionally and frequently operated.

Let us examine these contradictions more closely. In the first place, the classification in diagram 3.1 seems to restrict structures to objects only, to hard things out there in space and time, as we have observed. If structure were different in this way from behavior, then clearly it would be impossible to discover structure in behavior. Indeed this dichotomy between structure and behavior might even leave the impression that all behavior is random, that is, unstructured, which violates ordinary common sense. Even worse, if behavior has no structure it could not be taken systematically into account in any scientific explanation. If so, political science would not likely be interested in it except to recognize its presence in any explanation or to treat it as a unique account of what happens, narrative history.

In fact, as we have seen, processes (behavior over time) may be structured; it does not seem to make sense to adopt a classification that separates structure and behavior. Hence it behooves us to adopt a meaning for structure that permits us to recognize the presence of such processual structures and to take them into account in explaining at least historical phenomena.

In the second place, if structure is the element or object that engages in a relationship—a case of misplaced concreteness in which a property is considered equivalent to the object itself, as we have seen—we would need to invent a word to refer to the patterned relationships that manifestly exist among objects. We see patterns among party systems that we call multiparty as against two-party or single party; we see patterns among major organs of government that we call the separation of powers or federalism, as the case may be; we see relationships between interest groups that we call pluralism or corporatism; and so forth. If the concept structure is seized to describe the elements that engage in these relationships—parties, governmental organs, interest groups, etc.—we are left without a generic term to refer to the patterns of behavior in which such political elements engage. There does not seem to be any compelling reason to handicap ourselves conceptually in this way.

We must conclude that if structure is to be given any useful, stable, and consistent meaning, it cannot be interpreted as a separable spatiotemporal element, theoretically equivalent to behavior, personality, culture, and the soma, as part of a political explanation. As I have suggested, such a position has derived from our physicalist imagery of structure and is buried deep in the early etymological roots of the term. Where such an imagery seeps into our thinking it induces us to look for an aspect of social or political behavior which appears to give us something resembling the palpability of the structural members of a building or the skeleton of the human anatomy. It automatically inclines us to look for the activities surrounding and constrained by the structures which give them life or which flesh them out, what we have traditionally called the political processes within political structures. It has led us, at least implicitly and unavowedly, to try to distinguish conceptually between structure on the one side and behavior, culture, personality, etc., as in diagram 3.1, on the other.

In fact, as our analysis reveals, the relationship among these elements is conceptually better depicted in diagram 3.2. There we see that structure does not enter into the explanation directly as a separable element at the same level as the others. Structure becomes, rather, a property of each of the other dimensions. As such a property, possessed by many different elements, it may of course have many aspects in common; hence we can talk of structures in general terms just as we can write dissertations on other properties such as the color blue, its wave length, composition, hues, compatibility with other colors, and so forth. We could generate a theory about structure as a property of behavior, of culture, of personality, etc., cutting across all areas. And to some degree I shall be doing just that in this book. But as a specific explanation of political phenomena, it needs to be seen for what

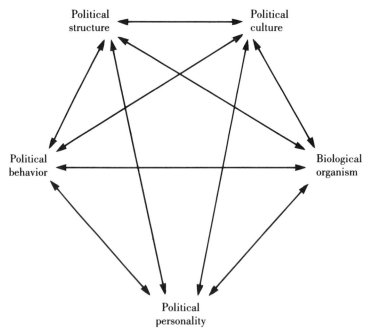

Diagram 3.2   Types of Explanatory Variables and Their Relationships

it is: just a property of behavior, culture, personality, and the like. Diagram 3.2, then, assumes that each of the components in a political explanation may have the property of being random or being structured. Structure cannot be considered by itself as a concrete set of elements or an entity separable in space and time from all the others and at the same conceptual level. It enters an explanation of political phenomena, rather, only as a property of one or another of the other elements.

Conventional discourse in political science, however, tends to constrain the way in which we may use structure as a term. Typically, when we speak of a structure as a component of a political system, such as federal or governmental structures, we are apt to have in mind only structure of behavior in these membership groups, unless the context clearly indicates otherwise. Presumably this is also what we mean when we speak of political relationships. The latter concept is a synonym for political structure which, in turn, implies just the structure of political behavior, giving the term a narrow construction. Certainly we do recognize that cultural attitudes, beliefs, and the like have structure, as do personalities. Nevertheless, if we intend to refer to such nonbehavioral structures, and thereby give the term a broader scope, we are likely to say so explicitly, unless the context clearly implies it.

Strictly speaking, however, if we wished to be consistent, the simple phrase *political structure* should be used in the broader sense to embrace the structures to be found in all the elements in diagram 3.2. It includes not only political relationships—that is, the structure of behavior—but the structure of all the other political elements. However, tradition has dictated the more limited narrower meaning for the concept.

There would be little purpose, or, for that matter, likelihood of success, in now trying to bring about a change in our linguistic practice by proposing a stricter construction, namely, that whenever we speak of political structure we ought to specify whether we mean the structure of behavior (political relationships), or of political personality, or of political culture and the like. Accordingly, I shall abide by convention and use the idea of political structure in the narrower sense—to refer to the structure of political behavior—unless the context clearly indicates otherwise.

In this chapter, then, I have addressed the question of the theoretical and ontological status of structure as we seek to introduce it into our explanations of political phenomena. I have concluded that political structure is best interpreted not as a physical entity in space and time and not as a discrete part of phenomenal reality but as a special kind of property of this reality. It may be an attribute of a political object that is a physical entity, such as a group of persons and, therefore, is empirically or verifiably present, in the same sense that blue is present in a box as a physical object. But, of course, structure may also be a property of analytic elements themselves such as political culture (attitudes, beliefs, ideas, etc.) or personalities. Finally, we noted that we shall be discussing such structures in two senses: as a generalized property of a political system as a whole; and as a property typically thought of in relation to the behavior of individuals and the operation of institutions.

4

Meaning of Political Structure

In the last chapter we addressed the question of the theoretical status of structure and concluded that structure is best interpreted not as a physical entity in space and time but as a special kind of property of such an entity. It is now time to abandon assumptions about the intuitive understanding of the term, on which we have proceeded to this point, and to turn to a closer examination of just what we might mean by it. Accordingly, in this chapter I shall raise the question of what meaning we might give to political structure as a concept.

Defining Political Structure

The Political Nature of Political Structure

As a concept, political structure has two aspects: the political and the structural. Let us begin with the first. What distinguishes a *political* structure from other kinds of social structures? This clearly depends upon our theoretical presuppositions about what we are going to accept as political phenomena. My conceptions on this score are well known; hence I need do little but mention them in this context.

Members of a society interact with each other in a variety of relationships. Through some of them the members are collectively able to make decisions for the society that most of them will come to accept as binding most of the time. Those who actually make the decisions or are effectively involved in doing so may, of course, range from very few to very many, in systems ranging from a dictatorship to a direct democracy. But regardless of the numbers actually involved, the fact that these kinds of relationships are more or less directly concerned with the making of these kinds of decisions will enable us to distinguish them as political.[1] We may describe structures as political rather than economic or broadly societal, for example, by virtue of this close involvement in the making of such decisions.

The Structural Nature of Political Structure

As I noted in the preceding chapter on physicalism, structure is nothing more than one kind of property of political phenomena. As Radcliffe-Brown, a distinguished British anthropologist had put it, in an often quoted passage:

> One may say that the characteristics of a society are determined by two things: first, by the simple fact that the society is composed of human beings; and second, by the

46

internal nature of those human beings. No amount of investigation can explain the characteristics of society by simple reference to the nature of human beings; but by an investigation of human beings *arranged in a certain order, yes. The social scientist is studying the structural arrangement of the units and takes the internal structure of the units for granted.*[2]

And the same remarks may be made about political arrangements. They represent one inescapable and fundamental aspect of political life. If so, it is appropriate now, after having identified what gives structures their political character, to inquire about how we might go about deciding on the precise nature of this property we are calling fundamental.

If our understanding of structure is to assist us in formulating theories about how political systems operate, what do we and what ought we to mean by structure as a property of political relationships? A complete answer will emerge in time as our discussion proceeds throughout this book, so I shall not pretend that the present chapter will do more than introduce the matter.

What is clear at the outset is the absence in political science of any theory or organized conceptualization to guide us in settling on a stable idea of structure. The supply of meanings in the social sciences as a whole is virtually unlimited. The same is true in political science, perhaps because of the very fact that in our case we have not elevated the notion for special attention.[3] In actual usage the meanings are so varied that it would be fruitless to attempt to collect all of them in the hope of ultimately distilling some common content. In part, as Kroeber, in a frequently quoted remark, has complained, use of the term some time ago became almost a fad, a way of showing that one was *au courant* with the language of social science. As he wrote:

'Structure' appears to be just a yielding to a word that has a perfectly good meaning but suddenly becomes fashionably attractive for a decade or so—like 'streamlining'—and during its vogue tends to be applied indiscriminately because of the pleasurable connotations of its sound.[4]

During the 1980s, unfortunately, political science revived the habit.

In part, however, we cannot escape concluding that this variable usage may just represent a genuine attempt to come to grips with an underlying consciousness that not everything is possible. Constraints are built into the human condition. They are of various sorts: internal in the sense of genetic or merely biological, internal in the sense of motives and predispositions (personality), geographical, cultural, and so forth. One of them has to do with the way human beings organize their social ties, that is, the structure of their relationships. The attempt to cope with this awareness has led to as many ways of conceiving structure as there are ideas about how social relationships limit or determine action. Structure has long been an everyman concept.

The French sociologist Boudon has concluded that the word *structure* has been caught up in such a complex web of polysemous, homonymic and synonymic meanings that it defies any effort to induce a single acceptable connotation. And there are good grounds for this indeterminacy, he suggests.

> When a concept has its support in objective reality, as for example, 'dog,' a concept dear to Kant, it is possible to attempt its definition by comparing and abstracting the elements common to those objects which it designates. In our example, the concept of dog would be defined by comparing and abstracting the elements common to all individual dogs. But what of the concept of 'structure'? Clearly, comparing and abstracting would take place on the level of secondary sources and could not use any other material than the definitions of the concept of structure propounded by different authors in different disciplines. While dogs exist and have a reality independent from the definitions which could be given to the concept of dog, this does not hold for 'structures,' which do not exist until they have been defined.[5]

We can set aside the dubious metaphysic expressed here about the objective reality of dogs as against a presumed subjectivism of structures. Of interest to us at the moment is Boudon's ultimate conclusion that it is necessary to attempt not an intrinsic but an extrinsic definition of the term. He sets out to do this by analyzing not the meanings common to all definitions but what he views as the function of the concept in ongoing scientific research.[6]

In apparent disagreement with Kroeber, Boudon finds that the popularity of structure stems not from faddism but from important changes taking place in social science. These, in his opinion, have led to the discovery of the interdependence of phenomena and the special properties of wholes that are not derivable from their parts. Although he does not put it in this way, in effect he is associating the popularity of the idea of structure with a transformation in our thinking in the mid-twentieth century that has led us to conceive of our subject matter in social science as systems. For Boudon it appears to be a product of what I would identify as the systems revolution in our thinking.[7]

Boudon finally instructs us that social scientists use the concept in such a way that it can be reduced to two major implications. These he designates as its *intentional* and its *operative* meanings. In the intentional sense, when a social scientist speaks about the structure of an object, such as a body of ideas, behavior, motivations, or culture, he or she may be referring to a variety of different properties. But in the end they all express an *intention* to view the object as composed of interdependent parts or wholes rather than as mere aggregates. Whether the term *system* is or is not used, Boudon claims, the intention is to treat the object as such.

Where the idea of structure goes beyond such mere intention, Boudon argues, it can be demonstrated to involve the formulation of a theory about the nature of the interdependence of the parts in the object-system. This gives structure an operative meaning. "In the case of an *operative* definition, what is involved is an attempt to determine the structure of a given object."[8] The idea of structure arises not simply to imply an intention to treat a subject as a system but also as a way of actually trying to understand the structure of the object-system, that is, to develop a theory about how the parts of a system hang together and operate.

For Boudon, the analysis of structure in this *operative* sense would, therefore, lead to the construction of a theory. For him, such a theory would consist of a set of stated or implicit axioms as well as propositions about the relationship of the parts. Together they would yield an understanding of what he calls the "apparent" characteristics of the system, that is, the observed way in which members of a system interact with each other, either individually or in groups.

Thus, where different conceptions of the structure of an object are not just an expression of an *intention* to interpret an object as a system, for him they represent efforts at formulating different kinds of theories about the relationships among the elements of such systems. Such structural theories will use different parts or elements of the the same object, such as society, out of which to build their theories and/or arrive at different conclusions about the relationships among the elements.

From his decision to find the meaning of structure as a concept in the function it performs in social research—its *operative* meaning—what Boudon in effect has done is to conclude that the analysis of structure is just another way of committing oneself to the construction of alternative social theories. In this interpretation, then, *structuralist* analysis is no different from ordinary theory building. "To sum up, a structure is always the theory of a system—and it is nothing else."[9] If so, there is no basis for the claim by scholars, such as Lévi-Strauss, that *structuralism* offers not a theory but a special method for understanding society.[10] If the analysis of structure is, in the end, nothing more than a commitment to formulating theories about social behavior, then it can scarcely lay claim to being a special method, despite Lévi-Strauss's insistence to the contrary. At most, it can represent only a theory different from others.

Aside from its implications for structuralism, a school of thought associated particularly with the name of Claude Lévi-Strauss,[11] if we were to accept Boudon's point of view it would certainly end the enormous conflict over the meaning of the idea of structure. Unfortunately, as tempting as the thought is, the reduction of structuralist or structural analysis to theory construction would leave too many questions unanswered about the use of structure in political science, and in all social research, for that matter. Certainly many who deal with structure are oriented to theory. But not all theories are structural in character, emphasize structures, or even take them systematically into account. This neglect of structure in theories of power pluralism, for example, had once been the source of the most trenchant criticisms of it.[12]

The critical issue is the very one that Boudon evades in his analysis: Even if social theories, by the very nature of their interest in social relationships, must in fact involve themselves in the identification of structures, just what gives some theories a special structural character? This brings us right back to our starting point. To distinguish structurally oriented theories from other kinds requires us to settle on a meaning for structure.

Regardless of the utility of Boudon's ultimate conclusion, however, what he has done is to demonstrate the difficulty, if not futility, of trying to discover a meaning for the concept by searching for some core common to all uses. I shall follow his example and refrain from pursuing this unprofitable course. I shall not seek to identify all the varying uses of the term *structure* in political research, much less try to distill a common meaning from the multitude of ways it has been used there. Instead, I shall try to establish a theoretically justifiable interpretation for it as we attempt to understand regime and associated political structures by looking at their relationship to the overall system structure.

Pursuit of this objective will lead us, in the next chapter, to identify various classes of political structures and their components which political science has typically considered important. Without challenging the wisdom of our discipline in designating these objects as structurally relevant, I shall then seek to demonstrate, in succeeding chapters, that if we were to consider only such objects as structures, one of the most significant problem raised by this decision would be left unanswered, namely, how to account for their varying forms and shapes.

Meaning of Structure in Ordinary Usage

I shall turn, then, to an alternative way of establishing an initial working conception of structure. Political relationships, whether among individuals or collectivities, have many properties. They may vary in salience for the participants, in frequency of occurrence, in valence (hostile or friendly, exploitive or cooperative, for example), in status (dominant or subordinate, equal or unequal), and so on. Of significance for us is the fact that political relationships may also vary in the property of being structured. Some may have very little structure as in the case of casual and fleeting political contacts. Others may display well-defined and durable kinds of structures, as in the connections among executives, legislatures, and courts in stable political systems.

What is the nature of this variable property called structure? If we begin with its use in ordinary language it usually refers, as Boudon confirmed, to patterns found in political relationships among elements of a system, that is, to relatively stable arrangements among members of the system or among other political units such as collectivities or aggregates. A party boss may relate to individual members of a party in a superordinate way; interest groups as collectivities may relate to each other so as to form a structure called peak organizations; an elite as an aggregate may stand in a relationship of domination to the masses, another aggregate, in a pyramidal structure.

This ordinary usage suggests several things about structure. First, it implies that an object can have a structure only if it has parts. If an object could not be decomposed into parts, we would be left with an irreducible whole with respect to which it would be unintelligible to speak of its internal structure.

Second, in all instances, whether the object is composed of individuals, groups or aggregates, it is the arrangement among the parts that constitutes its structure, not any part taken by itself. In a circle of marbles, a single marble can be said to be part of the structure of marbles; the structure is the circular arrangement. Similarly, the elite does not constitute the structure of a political system. An elite structure would consist of the power arrangement in the system between an elite and the mass, or among various components of the elite itself.

Third, just as the circularity of the marbles is a property separate from the other properties of the marbles—their color, texture, mass, hardness, etc.—so the arrangement of individuals, groups, or aggregates in a political system represents a property abstractable from the objects of which the arrangement is composed. As a property, structure in this sense can have no independent existence. The form of any relationship is only analytically separable from the parts that enter into it. We have already seen this to be so, in the preceding chapter.

Fourth and finally, as we also saw in that chapter, this property is observable (a concept to which I shall return again) or can be directly inferred, and, accordingly, will be confirmable. We can readily tell when we are looking at a circle rather than an oval or square of marbles.

In short, structure is an empirical, describable property referring to the relatively stable relationships among the parts of an object or among objects themselves. This concept clearly refers to the most general meaning of the term in its ordinary usage. Normally, it would appear, when we speak of the structure of a political object we intend to point to this kind of relationship, a meaning regularly confirmed in the other social sciences. Thus, the anthropologist Nadel defined structure as "an ordered arrangement of parts, which can be treated as transposable, being relatively invariant, while the parts themselves are variable."[13] In similar vein, sociologist Blau speaks of social structure as "the patterns discernible in social life, the regularities observed, the configurations detected."[14]

From this view of structure, federal relationships, for example, would constitute a political structure. They represent stable patterns of behavior, among individuals and collectivities, through which power is regionally dispersed. Identifying the structure of a political culture, on the other hand, would point to the stable patterns of attitudes in a political system, such as an ideological subsystem. An object has structure when its parts reveal some specific kind of relatively durable relationships. This is true whether we confine the term *political structure* to political relationships (behavior) or broaden it to all other explanatory elements of diagram 3.2, for example.

A central but easily overlooked point about this conception of structure, however, is precisely what it fails to say. It assumes that structure is just a description of the relationships among the parts of an object, not a theory about them. That is to say, it does not leave open the possibility that to speak of the structure is to present a theory that helps us to understand why the visible property we call structure, in ordinary language, takes the form it does.

For some social scientists, such as Lévi-Strauss and Poulantzas, as we shall see, social structure is precisely that, a theory about the factors that give shape to the reality. The theory can represent the structure, from this point of view, because it is the theoretically defined factors themselves that are presumed to give structure to the visible world. They are the structure underlying what ordinary usage had hitherto thought of as the structure. In Lévi-Stauss's oft-quoted sentence, "The term 'social structure' has nothing to do with empirical reality but with models which are built up after it."[15] This interpretation led Lévi-Strauss to speak of the visible structure of ordinary discourse as mere "social relations" as contrasted with "social structure," which can be specified only through a "model" of basic relationships underlying the observed social relations.[16]

On the face of it, this difference between structure viewed as a description of the world as against an underlying theory about it, would not necessarily seem to be contradictory or necessarily incompatible. In fact, however, the debate about the meaning to be given to structure—mere description as against a theoretical statement—and its many implications for the effects of structure represents one of the sharpest conflicts about the nature of structure that has divided scholarship for over a century, if we take Marx as the starting point. Without entering into the dispute at the moment, suffice it to say that I shall seek to bridge the chasm that has separated the two points of view—between what I shall designate as *structural* (descriptive) as against *structuralist* (theoretical) analysis.[17] I shall try to do this through the adoption of a deceptively simple conceptualization: the identification and discrimination between higher and lower-order structures, terms that have already begun to creep into my discussion and that will be explored extensively as we proceed.

Structure as Constraints

To return, however, to the issue under consideration here: Even if we content ourselves for the moment with the everyday usage of the term—structure as a describable empirical pattern or arrangement among the parts of an object—why should we be interested in structure as a property? Seldom do we put this elementary and elemental question to ourselves. Yet the kind of answer we give will in large part shape the conceptualization we develop for the study of structure.

As I suggested at the outset of this chapter, we must assume that the way parts of an object are related at the very least imposes some sort of important constraints on the behavior or performance of that object, in its parts or as a whole. Much further along in our analysis we shall find that structures do more than constrain; they may also facilitate activity.[18] For the moment, however, we may neglect this aspect and examine only the constraining consequences of structure, which in any event looms largest in most research.

The Nature of Constraints

What is a constraint? In its most general sense, a constraint is a limit on the variety of choices open to an individual or collectivity. It is a condition that reduces choices from infinity to some finite number. The smaller the number of choices the greater the constraint. As Ashby states it formally, "Constraint is a *relation* between two sets, and occurs when the variety that exists under one condition is less than the variety that exists under another. . . . Constraints may be slight [that is, they eliminate few options] or they may be severe [eliminating many]."[19] Where there are absolutely no limits on choices, there is complete freedom; where there are no choices, behavior would be fully determined. Neither extreme is often encountered in nature, whether physical, biological, or social. Constraints normally leave room for some variety. The question is what kind, how much, under what conditions, and with what consequences.

Constraints on human behavior are of course virtually infinite. At the beginning of *The Social Contract* Rousseau had cried out in anguish against political constraints: "Man is born free; everywhere he is in chains." The fact is that the physical environment, the state of one's soma and psyche, the mere presence of others—in short, everything in an actor's internal and external environment—may limit the expression of his or her preferences. If structure were to be used to refer to all such constraints, the concept would quickly lose its utility. What we are called upon to do is to distinguish structural from other kinds of constraints.

As we shall ourselves see in due course, the term *structure* itself has often been so broadened, through its popular association with constraints, that is seems to refer to almost any kind of restriction on choice not subject to individual control or modification. By the 1980s it had begun to appear as though it was acceptable to use *structure* to refer to any social conditions to which individual actors are necessarily and inescapably subjected. Such a usage would quickly destroy its potency for the understanding of any unique phenomenon, such as relationships, that we might wish to include in the term.

Some scholars have been rather more restrictive in their conception of structure. Among them, there are those who have argued that the most important structural constraints are to be found in social norms, others, in visible social interactions, and still others, in some theoretically defined underlying relationships such as in the economy (Marx), in the intellect (Lévi-Strauss), or in culture (Gramsci). What links these alternative conceptions is that they are all intuitively searching for an understanding of factors associated with social relationships that reduce the variety of choice for individuals, groups, or even whole systems.

If, for the moment, we set aside these broadened usages, however, not all persons would necessarily agree that structured relationships, even in the narrower sense in which we have been discussing them to this point, constitute constraints on behavior. For some ethnomethodologists, for example, this is a debatable proposition. I shall return to their point of view in later chapters. Many of them interpret structure as an effect, not a cause. Structures do not limit choice but are, rather, just the precipitates of choices already made, almost epiphenomenal in character. This view has never received wide acceptance, nor has political science ever devoted much attention to it, but it does raise some important issues that we shall need to consider.

However, from my point of view the argument for interpreting structure as a constraint of some sort can be put rather simply. A political system is seldom total chaos even under the most unstable conditions.[20] Independently of our wishes we are born into a political system in which our relationships with others are regulated by certain rules. These relationships define part of the constraints under which we may act. They may also give us the opportunity to modify or change the rules substantially or even completely and, thereby, the nature of the pattern of relationships to others in which we may engage. This represents the important facilitative or enabling functions of structure (to which I shall return in chapter 18). But despite

Rousseau's anarchistic longings, we seldom if ever find ourselves able to cast off all rule-governed relationships. By the very nature of society, some constraints on the choices of individuals or collectivities always remain. It is never a matter of being or not being part of a structure of political relationships. It is just a matter of what kind of structural constraints prevail, the conditions that shape them, the effects they may have, the way these effects are brought about, and how they may be changed so as to permit different results.

Structural Constraints as Patterns of Relationships

To understand political structure as a constraint, it is necessary to stress, by examining further, a point that I have already touched upon: political structure involves more than just a part or aggregate of parts of the political system. In and of themselves parts do not a structure make, despite the fact that through the fallacy of misplaced concreteness we often consider a part itself to be a structure, as we saw in the preceding chapter. Rather, the structure derives its force as a constraint from the *pattern* of relationships among the parts. If we are to understand how political structures restrict or facilitate behavior in any way, it must be to the variations in these patterns that we must look.[21]

For example, even if we were to recognize a set of social classes to be related to each other, to talk about the structural effects of this class structure it would not be enough to locate each person in a social class and to connect such location to some kind of activity or belief of such person. At most, this would yield only the effect of one of the parts of the class structure. Yet this is what is frequently meant by structural analysis, as one example, chosen virtually at random, illustrates so well:

> Certainly, there is no absence of interest in structural analysis in the literature. It is rare to find a student of Latin American politics who does not take for granted the link between stratification and politics. *The political attitudes, aspirations, interests, and ideology of different strata are constantly being imputed.*[22]

In other words, as frequently occurs, to account for the possible effect of structure, the authors are content to describe the various social classes (strata) and discover their presumed effects on those individuals who belong to them. I am arguing, on the contrary, that we ought not to accept this as an example of the effect of structure. Whatever the effect of membership in a class may be, such a class, in and of itself, does not constitute a social structure. It is, rather, only an *element* of a class structure. The latter is something very different. It is more useful and powerful, as a tool of analysis, to think of structure as consisting of the *pattern* created by the relationships between two or more classes, as, for example, one of dominance or of inequality among social classes in Latin America.[23]

The structure of social classes would seem to refer to the class pattern created by the interdependence of the classes in the set. To understand the effect of class structure on the behavior of groups or individuals requires us to explore the effects of variations in class patterns, and not only variations in specific class membership. It is the dominant-subordinate power relationships among classes, for example, that may have more to do with an individual's "life chances," in Weber's terms, than mere membership, as such, in a class. The reason why mere membership has often worked as a useful category for analysis is because such membership will normally expose an individual in a given class to the structural effects of the position of the class in the pattern among classes. To be a member of the working class in Latin America, for example, normally is to be part of a structure in which one is in a subordinate power status, with all the implications that has for one's life chances. Hence the notion of class membership at times may stand successfully as a surrogate expression, a metonym, for referring to participation in a particular pattern of class relationships.

As a further example of this metonymic practice—the substitution of a part for the whole—consider Canada during the nineteenth and early twentieth centuries. The lack of the development of a middle class in the western prairie provinces left the poor and the rich, in that region, confronting each other directly. This condition, in which no middle class stood as a buffer between the two, it is said, so sharpened class visibility and antagonisms that it provided fertile soil in which socialism could flourish. The western prairies became the birth place for the Cooperative Commonwealth Federation (CCF), the predecessor of the present labor-farmer New Democratic Party (NDP). In eastern Canada, on the other hand, the presence of a significant middle class is said to have buffered relations between the class extremes and reduced the appeal of the western-based Socialist party. In fact, the latter has had persistent difficulty in getting a secure foothold in the eastern part of the country. It was not the presence of the two polarized social classes or mere absence of a middle class that had these presumed effects; it was the pattern of class relationships, the way they stood in relation to each other, with no intermediary class, that is presumed to have provided the soil for the growth of a socialist party.

Visibility of Behavioral Structures as Constraints

Structure in the initial sense that has been arrived at here, then, is a pattern of relationships that constrains behavior of individuals or collectivities. As I have already suggested, structural constraints of this sort, as found in patterns of voting practices, various political roles, federal or centralized relationships, interest group formations, party organizations, and the like, are the stock-in-trade observations of political research. We have little difficulty in identifying or finding empirical referents for them. This enormously facilitates our search for their determinants and effects.

We are relatively familiar with such structures. For many of them one does not even have to be a professional political scientist to be able to observe and talk about them. Hence I shall begin by referring to them as visible or observable structures. Whether they are directly visible is of course very debatable. As I shall soon have occasion to point out, they are no less a product of abstraction than other kinds of less familiar structures to which we shall have occasion to turn our attention. For that reason, among others, I find it more useful and pertinent to characterize them as *lower-order* structures.

At the moment it is enough to say that we need have little difficulty in understanding the appropriateness of this concept, lower-order structures, for speaking about the kinds of political relationships denoted above. They are lower-order in the sense that traditionally they are at the most accessible level of observation in political research. The central reason for adopting this terminology will, however, become more apparent when, in chapter 5, we denote such lower-order structures extensively and contrast them with structures of what I shall call a higher-order kind.

Nonbehavioral Structures as Constraints

I have been speaking about structure as a constraint based on patterns of behavior. As we have seen in the preceding chapter, there may be many sources of structural constraints on human behavior other than those deriving from the patterns of behavior themselves. These other sources may not be so self-evident, however, since they are linked to less readily observed aspects of society: political personality, political culture and genetic predispositions, the elements other than behavior in diagram 3.2. As I noted at the time we spoke about that diagram, these other elements in a political system also have their structures, that is, internal patterns of relationships or organization among their constituent parts.

Like the structure of behavior itself, the structure of these elements also impose some constraints on the parts themselves and on any behavior related to them. For example, when we speak of political personality types we have in mind the relatively stable relationships among components of personality such as motives, attitudes, cognitive practices, and the like. These constitute parts of the structure of the political personality that help to account for the way in which a person apprehends and participates in political processes.

Similarly, when we speak of patterns of political attitudes, systems of beliefs or of ideologies, we have identified parts of the structure (stable patterns of relationships) of political culture.[24] For example, there is little question about the importance of such aspects of culture as beliefs in the legitimacy of political authorities influencing the operation of political systems. Weber's classification of such belief structures into traditional, legal-rational, and charismatic would be a case in point about the presumed relevance of that part of the structure of culture.[25]

In addition to beliefs, rules may represent a vital and characteristic part of political culture and insofar as they exhibit some degree of stability they may constitute part of the structure of such culture. For example, in most political systems described as democratic, we find interrelated sets of rules that state that the majority should prevail, minorities ought to have certain reserved rights, provision should be made for freedom of association and speech, each person should have one vote, public decisions should be made through representatives who are elected with a certain frequency and the like. Such rules do not of course represent behavior; they are norms to be followed.[26] They may influence behavior and, in this way, the structure of culture, as represented in a set of rules, may be reflected in the structure of behavior of a political system. Presumably, where there is a close fit between democratic rules and democratic practices we may have evidence of this influence. Nonetheless, the rules remain part of the structure of the culture.

The literature in the field of biopolitics is not as yet so well developed as in other areas of political inquiry. Nonetheless, we could easily imagine the day, if this aspect of biopolitics could claim some plausibility, when we might wish to call structural such components as the relationships among the various genetic predispositions and the presumed role of these patterns in determining kinds of political phenomena like sovereignty, political aggressiveness, bonding, dominance, altruism, or leadership.

We do not need to linger over the nature of structures as patterns of constraints in the area of personality, culture and genes, however. As I have already indicated, when we speak of political structures in the literature, we have normally intended to focus on behavior or processes. So, to state once again, unless future discussion requires specific attention to structures in these other areas, my remarks will be addressed specifically to structures in behavior and processes even though in fact structural analysis would have relevance for the other areas as well.

Related Terms

Micro versus Macro Dichotomy

In the sense of structure described here, the concept applies to both micro- and macrostructures as the terms are ordinarily used. The differences between these two approaches seem largely to involve the scale of the units constituting the structure and hence the different scope of analysis required. For example, our interest may lie in the political relationships among such small units as individuals, as between a legislative representative and his or her constituents. Does the representative stand in relationship to the constituent as a mere mouthpiece for the latter, or does the representative reserve varying degrees of independence?[27] In such an inquiry we would be focusing on aspects of microstructure. We might limit our scope in such a way so as to be able to detail the relationships, their possible effects and implications, and to explore in equal detail the processes through which the relationships are preserved or changed.[28]

Because of the narrow scope of the units entering into the relationships, the methods that can be used are those developed for the study of individual actors, as in survey research or rational choice deductions. They are techniques deemed appropriate for the examination of the behavior of individuals in a one-on-one relationship to each other.[29] They raise important questions about what is left out, that is, about the effects of what I shall be calling higher-order structures (which are only one kind of macrostructure)—but we shall return to this matter later on.

Alternatively, we might have an interest in understanding the patterns of relationships among much larger parts of a political system, as, for example, between various organs of government. In this event our concerns are typically described as being macrostructural in character. We cast our net more widely and consider group relationships or aggregate phenomena.

Because of the nature of the subject matter at the macrolevel, the concepts, methods, and conclusions are usually of a different character from those used in microstructural research. They may involve analysis of aggregate data, comparative historical research on evolving institutions, gross descriptions of relationships among such broad units as parties, interest groups, legislatures, and their electorates. And the conclusions will tend to be more sweeping in character than in the case of the study of individual relationships. Typically they may refer to transformations of such large-scale structures as democracies as a whole or dictatorships. What is more important perhaps than even the scale, though it is related because it is a product of the latter, is the significance of certain kinds of macrostructures, those that I call higher-order, for the effects and limits of microstructures. But as I have indicated, this will emerge as our discussion progresses.

These two approaches, however, the micro and the macro, are not necessarily mutually exclusive or competitive; they represent, rather, two different perspectives, with different objectives. The one permits us to fine tune the interactions among individual participants in a relationship; the other gives us insight into broader kinds of relationships the connection of which to microstructures may need to be taken into account for a full explanation of the latter.

There are those who would, of course, deny this distinction, arguing in effect that to be intelligible all structures must be reduced to the microlevel. Among them ethnomethodolgists loom largest. As I mentioned, we shall have occasion to return to them much later, in chapter 18. At the moment it will become clear that in arguing that there is a significant linkage between the regime structures of a political system, for example, and its overall structures, I shall be opting for a macrostructural route.

Organizations

To bear clearly in mind what we may mean by structure as a concept, we also need to distinguish it from other terms that are frequently used in its place. In political science we have perhaps not monitored our language about structure with the care exercised in other disciplines. We often use the terms *organizations* and *institutions* interchangeably with structures as though they might mean the same thing. In fact it is useful, if not, indeed, necessary, to discriminate among their meanings.

As a concept, organization usually draws attention to a particular kind of structure or pattern of relationships, one in which the parts are arranged according to known rules so as to meet some specifiable purposes.[30] We create organizations to mobilize an electorate, engage in direct political action, legislate or implement a policy. A system may be consciously organized or arranged in such a way that it solidifies the power in the hands of a ruling elite. There appears to be an element of consciousness or deliberation in the notion of organization, although there are undoubtedly instances in which the term may be used in a broad and loose way as a virtual synonym for structure.[31] I shall try to avoid this assimilation of meaning and reserve organization for the narrower meaning defined here.

Political Institutions

Similarly, we are prone to talk of political institutions as though they were identical with political structures. It can be argued, however, that institutions usually include structures but go beyond them. When we speak of institutions we will certainly have in mind the patterns of behavior of groups or other collectivities. But we would normally intend to include the rules governing such constituent parts, as well as concrete symbols such as the buildings they inhabit or the physical symbols they use. Thus Congress or the presidency, as institutions, refer to more than their occupants but to the rules by which they govern themselves, the buildings they occupy, and the symbols by which they are identified (the presidential seal as part of the institution of the presidency, for example).

Typically when we speak of institutions we also include institutionalized behavior, that is, a complex of actions that has achieved a certain stability and with respect to which an equally stable pattern of norms guiding that behavior has become established. This behavior refers both to processes and to structures; that is, to both what gets done as well as how it gets done. For example, we speak of the institution of marriage in this sense. It includes the physical correlates of marriage (nuclear families, physical residences, and local contiguity), the norms (expectations, rights, and obligations) governing marital and familial relationships, and the actual patterns of interaction typical of marriage in a society. The institution of marriage would also seem to embrace well-established (institutionalized) recipes for marriage, that is, how to find a mate, actually get married, raise a family, relate to in-laws and the like, as well as to the way the parts of marital institutions, such as the family, nuclear or extended, are and should be ordered. It is only this latter, the arranging of the parts, that constitutes structure of the family, at least in the initial way I am proposing to use the term here. If the parts we wish to refer to are the norms or rules and regulations, we have a normative structure. If, however, the parts are the behavior of the participants, we have structures of behavior. All other aspects—expectations, rights, obligations, prescriptive rules, physical elements, and so on—represent other parts of the broader, institutional basis of marriage.

Similarly, Congress as one of our political institutions raises up an image of the physical location of Congress in a special set of buildings, its own symbols of authority, the rules governing election to Congress and the internal operations of the latter, and the expected behavior, rights, and obligations (ethical and political norms) of its members. When we speak of congressional institutions we probably have in mind all these things. Among them it is only the stable patterns of behavior within Congress—its various internal parts such as committees, official positions such as speaker, majority, and minority leaders, whips, and so on—together with external relationships, as between Congress and other legislative and political bodies which, in the strict sense, I would call the structure of the institution. The other aspects of Congress, its rules, norms, expectations, and the like, certainly do have structure, that is, patterns of relationships among their constituent elements, as I have repeatedly indicated. But they are nonbehavioral or noninteractionist structures and, as such, are normally not included under the generic term *political structure*.

If we initially confine structure to an ordered arrangement of parts, the broadest and least restrictive meaning, or stable patterns of political interaction (behavior), it would not include either the physical objects or norms (rules) that typically seem to be included in references to political institutions. Both might indeed be very influential in the way in which patterns of behavior take shape. Norms (prescribed as contrasted to described rules to which participants may be socialized) especially may be powerful determinants of the way we behave, whether they are merely social norms or legal ones. As part of institutions, such norms will themselves undoubtedly be structured, as I noted earlier. But, as I have proposed, it would not be appropriate to confound the structure of norms with the structure of behavior. And in ordinary political discourse either we do in fact wish to draw attention to the patterns of behavior themselves when we talk about the structure of political relationships or, for purposes of clarity, I am proposing, we should wish to reserve a concept, such as structure, for that purpose.

Norms will certainly help to give structure to behavior and thus will be among the determinants of the latter, as noted earlier, and they may in turn themselves be shaped by behavior. But given our ingrained linguistic habits, it would now only add confusion to the term *structure* to use it to signal both kinds of structures—the structure of norms and the structure of behavior—simultaneously, unless the context makes this unmistakably clear. Accordingly, it would seem appropriate to distinguish structures from institutions and to use the latter term to continue to refer to the grab bag of constraints that includes structures other than and in addition to the structures of behavior.

Thus, more than structure, at least in the sense identified here, is clearly involved in the referents of institutions. In fact, in recent years, in the call for a new institutionalism,[32] there appears to be a return to a traditional use of the term *political institutions*.[33] It takes on the appearance of a broad and comprehensive, even if ill-defined, way for covering all those facets of political life often taken for granted when focusing excessively on individual actors and their choices, characteristic of rational choice perspectives. Its very ambiguity, however, represents its strength in this literature as it allows one to recognize the broad setting in which individual choice must be made. For our purposes, however, it represents a distinct weakness insofar as it confounds different kinds of structures as well as other, non-structural phenomena.

When we speak of political structures, then, initially, as a working conception, I shall use the term to refer to patterns of relationships among such elements as individuals, groups, classes, or aggregates, not to individual elements themselves. And to this point we have been speaking of those kinds of related elements that are visible or observable in the sense already described. Furthermore, at the moment, unless otherwise indicated, structures will be of the kinds created by individuals, groups, or aggregates interacting with each other rather than of the kinds we find in culture or personality, for example. Collectively I shall be designating them as lower-order structures. In that use, they need to be clearly distinguished from organizations and institutions, including, in the latter, prescriptive rules. It will become clear as we proceed that structure also implies broader kinds of political macro-relationships, higher-order ones, that play a central role in the operation of political systems.

In the next chapter I propose to look more narrowly and explicitly at the various classes of elements that make up these structures of behavior that have caught the attention of students of politics over the years. The reason for undertaking what may seem like the pedestrian task of detailing these structural components of a political system will emerge very quickly. They are presumed to have important effects in the functioning of political systems, and we shall want to look at this assumption in succeeding chapters.

5

Varieties of Political Structures

Now that we have had an opportunity to give some initial content to political structure as a concept, it is time to give content to the term by specifying objects in a political system that we may count as structures and their components. In illustrating the meaning for the term in this way, we will wish to confine our attention, of course, to those structures that we consider to be important for an understanding of how political systems operate to produce the kind of policy outputs that they do.

To begin with, one thing is certain. Political systems have many kinds of structures. Such structural variety within and among systems cannot be and has not been ignored or neglected by students of politics in their day-to-day research, however much the idea of structures as a theoretical concept may have been overlooked. Empirically, however, just what are these variable structures through which political actors, whether as individuals or collectivities, make and implement policies? How can we identify and describe them? I will direct our attention to these questions in this chapter.

Furthermore, what effects, if any, do these structures have? Presumably, if they had no consequences for the operation of political systems or if their effects were minimal, there would be little point in spending much time on them. I will deal with this matter in the next two chapters.

And finally, how can their variability be explained and understood? As we saw at the outset, this is the subject of this whole book. In later chapters, the explanation will lead us into the exploration of substantially different kinds of structures, those that are less accessible to direct empirical observation and that have therefore been more easily neglected. For that very reason they will prove less tractable to inquiry with the tools of empirical research invented and honed for application to other kinds of structures.

Higher- and Lower-Order Structures

As we develop a picture of the variety of things that we consider part of the structure of a political system, it will put us in the position of being able to differentiate between what, as I have noted, I shall call lower-order structures as against those that have typically been overlooked, the basic or higher-order structures. We shall find that the concept of lower-order or observed structures is an economical way of identifying those highly variable forms we are accustomed to seeing and examining in political systems across space and time. It is the variability of these kinds of empirical structures that requires explanation; the idea of a higher-order structure will prove useful in exploring an important part of a possible explanation. This distinction between lower- and higher-order structures will give us a major theoretical tool for this purpose.

In the end we shall find that, as an element in systematic analysis, political science has for the most part ignored higher-order structures, those that form the broadest pattern of relationships within the context of which political systems operate. In part the reason for this may be that, unlike the lower-order ones, which are observable, the former patterns of relationships are at a higher level of abstraction, an object of "reflective abstraction," as, we have noted, Piaget once put it.[1] Nonetheless, these higher-level structures are influentially related to the lower ones, so much so that we shall find that, despite research efforts to the contrary, regime and other lower-order structures will not be fully understandable except within the context of a higher-order structure, that of the political system as a whole. Hence the need to distinguish between the two types of structures and to explore their connections.

In the process of our discussion it will become apparent that in ordinary usage we do not have to penetrate very deeply into political relationships for the discovery of lower-order political structures. They seem to be given to understanding through immediate sensory experience even though in fact they are as much products of abstraction as are higher-order structures. But, as I suggested in the preceding chapter, they are so familiar to us in political research that no special effort of "reflective abstraction" is required. They seem to be directly visible and for that reason can be called observable. Others may prefer to refer to them as surface as against deep structures (structural linguists), base vs. superstructures (Marxists), or just political relationships (adapting Lévi-Strauss's terminology).[2] These other terms would be acceptable if it were not for the fact that they are imbedded in and hence evocative of theoretical approaches which my analysis does not necessarily presuppose.

What are these observable lower-order structures the adequacy of the conventional explanations of which I shall be questioning? If we had a tradition within our discipline of dealing with structural issues in an explicit and theoretical way, we would be spared much labor. The fact is, however, we have little literature to speak of on the subject. Accordingly, to clarify just what we in political science have been calling structure, I shall take the time to specify, at least broadly, various categories of lower-order structures that represent the bread-and-butter fare of our discipline. This will lay the groundwork for later discussion about the limits of our explanations of the variability of such structures. It will lead us to look at the way in which we have intuitively, and inadequately, sought to explain and understand these structures either by attributing their forms to specific types of factors or by embedding them in only vaguely identified higher-order ones.

Regime Structures

We can usefully classify lower-order political structures into two subtypes: regimes and what I shall call the differentiated structures closely associated with them. These two kinds of structures have typically attracted most attention in political research. Let us first look at regime structures.

Structure often assumes a somewhat restricted meaning in political analysis. Frequently such analysis focuses our attention on the presumed causal force of that aspect of the political system that I have called its regime structure. We see the kind of regime, whether it is democratic or authoritarian, for example, as critical for understanding the operations of a political system.

We should note, however, that at times, particularly in the 1980s, the idea of structure also often appears in association with the notion of "state." We hear talk of state structure, especially if the purpose is to draw attention to the oppressive or interventionist character of the state. If the state idea were just intended as another way of talking about the regime, then of course there would be no problem. It would always be included under the present discussion. But because of its inherent ambiguity as a concept, as I have already noted and as we will encounter in some detail in our discussion of Poulantzas later on, regime and state may at times suggest very different objects. Hence, regime and state structure may not always be interchangeable concepts, so that we need to be wary about automatically transferring what I shall have to say about the one to the other.

In any event, a regime, I have proposed,[3] may be understood to refer to a number of specific aspects of a political system: the formal structures of the authorities, often loosely called the government, together with the informal behavior and relationships that collect around it; formal (legal) and informal rules of behavior specifying rights and obligations for the authorities as well as for ordinary members of the system; and the values or goals associated with the given political system. Frequently, when we speak about the structure of a political system, we clearly have in mind just the structure of the regime, that is, the way power is organized and distributed among the political authorities and between them and the members of the political system as a whole. Structure here clearly refers to the stable patterns of power relationships among the major individual and collective actors in a political system.

This usage, although not always consistent, is nonetheless most obvious, for example, with respect to the way we classify political systems. Thus, we are prone to talk about democratic or authoritarian patterns of power structures, traditional or modernizing structures, presidential as against parliamentary structures, and the like. Such references usually seem to include large formal components of what I am calling the regime structure.

In this sense regime structure is something much less general than the overall or global political structure implied in the Aristotelean conception of regime, a meaning that still appears in lay and professional usage at times. In this conventional broader usage it embraces a wide range of relatively poorly defined elements which we may consider to have some central significance in determining how a political system operates. As such, regime often becomes confused with the political system as a whole.

Apter, for example, once directed his work in large measure to showing the effects on modernization of what we can conclude must be regime structures in my narrower meaning of the term. The arrangement of particular concern for him is governmental structures because of the peculiarly potent function he attributed to it in modernizing processes. But such governmental structures, in a strict sense, are difficult to distinguish from what I am calling regime structures.

Apter defined modernization as development and equity. Development refers to the expansion of the capacity to choose, and equity, to the criteria in terms of which choices about the distribution of goods and benefits are made.[4] Apter followed Parsons in viewing a *political system*, of which government is for him both a functional and structural component, as a mechanism of choice for a collectivity. As he put it, "A *political system* becomes a system of choice for a particular collectivity."[5] *Government*, on the other hand, one of the major structures within a political system, "is the mechanism for regulating choice."[6] One of the tasks of political inquiry is to discover the different effects that variations in omnibus governmental structures have upon the two criteria of modernization: expanded choice and equity.

In Apter's usage, the actual referents for government as a concept become cloaked in doubt if not obscurity. Whatever intentions to the contrary he may have had, the term assumes a relatively diffuse and elastic character even though, in its declared specific sense, it is equivalent to what I have been designating as the regime structure of a political system.

Thus, at the formal definitional level, he did well enough in containing its meaning. He described government "as a group of individuals sharing a defined responsibility for exercising power."[7] In practice, however, he was seldom able to confine himself to this limited meaning despite his explicit intentions. The term *government* quickly becomes sufficiently broad and vague to include most of what we might consider all visible structures in a political system. It does seem to include regime structures or patterns of relationships such as the formal division of labor among political authorities—members of the cabinet, chief executive, civil servants, legislators, etc.—elements normally part of the idea of government. But it frequently reaches beyond them to embrace associated elites such as managers, political entrepreneurs and brokers, professionals, and occupants of other designated roles thought to be important for the process of social modernization.[8] At times the scope even seems to widen to include most of the political and economic elites in a society, both in and out of what we would normally think of as government.

In this usage, government is a very broad and diffuse category indeed. It is one that would certainly make more intuitive sense, given the extraordinary influence that Apter chose to attribute to government in controlling the direction, rate, and quality of development and in managing the social and political tension occasioned by change. But it is, at the same time, a category that looks much more like all the structures in a political system than only like the narrower structures of government (or even of regime) which constitute just one part of any political system and with which Apter seemed to have begun his analysis.[9]

I have turned to Apter only for illustrative purposes. He does not stand alone. His is but part of a vast body of research that explores the extent to which modernization, variously defined, has been linked to the adoption of particular kinds of regime as well as associated political structures such as competitive party systems, centralized as against pluralized policy-making structures, efficiency-oriented administrative organizations, and the like. By and large, the performance of a political system, its capacity to set and implement modernizing goals, has been presumed to be related to the way in which the political authorities (that is, part of the regime structure, in my sense) as well as other parts of the political system are organized.

What is true for modernization applies equally to other areas of political research. In one way or another, the kinds of political structures included in what I have designated as the political regime are usually considered significant variables in shaping almost every aspect of the operations of political systems. In one sense, every classification of regimes—for example, into democratic, authoritarian, auto-cratic, totalitarian, oligarchic, elitist, or pluralist types—in effect represents an attempt to show that there is a relationship between such a structural type, on the one hand, and potential for change, representativeness, responsiveness, pacific or warlike proclivities, and so forth of the political system, on the other. As hard as our discipline has worked at the task from Plato and Aristotle on, we, of course, have not yet discovered a stable and generally accepted classificatory scheme for regimes. But the identification of regime structures in one way or another has remained a fixture in our attempts to understand the way political systems operate.

Formal Structures in Regimes

Regime structures characteristically appear in political research in both formal and informal guise. With regard to its formal aspects, we would have little capacity for understanding France, for example, if we did not recognize that since 1789 it has passed through five republican, one dictatorial, and one monarchical regime, or that since 1900 Germany has experienced a monarchical, a democratic, and a totalitarian regime. Despite the prominence of the formal aspect and despite the fact that the latter may linger in the background of virtually every political analysis, it has received little more than *pro forma* attention since the turn from legalism in political research, at the end of the nineteenth century, toward process analysis.

What might we or should we really have in mind when we speak of the formal political structure as part of the regime? The matter is not without some ambiguity, especially when we seek to distinguish formal from what we usually call informal structures.

Typically, formal structure refers to relationships among those organs that are established through some public procedure and through which the special kind of power we call political authority is allocated and organized. In literate societies, this procedure may require the specification of an arrangement of political relation-ships or organizations in a written document, such as a law, decree, or regulation. In nonliterate societies the arrangement may be prescribed through some special oracular or ceremonial statement. Rituals such as these that are associated with the initiation of the structure, whether they be in written documents or in ceremonial statements, prescribe the rules by which members are to define their roles and to conduct themselves.[10] As we know by this time, in my conceptualization these rules constitute not a part of the political structure but only the definition of the relationships or structure.

Since the formal structure as here described consists of a set of rules, we must consider them to be part of the cultural, not of the behavioral, structure."[11] They represent a pattern of norms or expectations that people hold in their head, as it were, about how members of a political systems ought to organize their relationships, not necessarily a description of how they in fact do behave.

What makes these rules of political culture formal is the ritual surrounding their introduction. This endows the structure with special recognition or legitimacy in the culture. In legal systems, for example, formal structures acquire the special recognition and sanctions associated with laws. In modern industrialized societies, organizations such as courts, legislatures, administrative services, and the like, together with their relationships to other organizations, are normally explicitly created through written rules (laws, decrees, regulations). By their very nature the rules are prescriptive; they describe the form that the relationships should take. This is why we typically refer to them as the basis of formal structures.

Political cultural rules such as these specify the character of a regime structure— its division of political labor as found in the organization of authority roles and offices. The legal rules indicate how people are expected or required to organize their political relationships, who is supposed to have the authority to do certain things, how they are to be done, how conflicts are to be resolved, how the rules themselves are to be changed, and so forth. As we know, a written constitution represents the clearest and most direct expression of a formal political structure. There is no limit to the kinds of prescriptions that have been included in such written specifications as witnessed by the well-known extensive written constitutions of various American states.

This nominal description of formal structure seems straightforward enough. When we examine it more closely, however, we find that it conceals certain ambiguities. In the first place, it is not that easy to distinguish formal structures from what have been called *crescive* ones,[12] that is, from kinds that seem to evolve naturally, without explicit or ritualistic establishment. For example, at the level of the political system as a whole, a pattern of interest groups may evolve independently of any specification in a constitution or in legislation. This structure of interest groups must therefore be considered part of the informal structure of the system. In some jurisdictions no systematic body of rules has been laid down to specify the location, relationships, or powers of the interest groups. They may have just gradually taken shape on their own and found a place in the system.

What we have just considered is true at the level of the political system as a whole.[13] If, however, we now drop down a level to the interest group subsystem itself, we find that these groups, in modern industrial societies at least, are likely to arise out of deliberate decisions by some or all of their membership to cooperate in the pursuit of shared objectives. In fact, close inspection may reveal that not only do the individual groups often originate through explicit rules written into a constitution, but federations or other umbrella organizations of interest groups—

peak structures—often take shape in the same way. They conform to our definition of a formal structure.

From the very way in which I have formulated the problem it is clear that to say that a lower-order structure may at the same time be formal and informal only gives the appearance of a contradiction. In fact, the formality of a structure depends on two criteria: its level and its origins. At a given level in the political system a structure of behavior will be formal or informal depending upon whether it originates through some special prescription or crescively. Thus, at a more general level a set of political relationships may typically arise without formal specification, as we have just seen, even though at a lower level in the system it may be a product of formal rules.

The first source of ambiguity about our use of the idea of formal structure derives, therefore, from our failure to recognize the significance of the structural level being analyzed. There is a second source, however, that we must take into account. When we describe a structure as formal, do we intend to refer only to the prescribed rules that define what the structure ought to be—that is, the culturally defined structure of the object—or do we also intend to include the actual behavior of those who participate in the relationships that form the political structure? For example, in the United States the two houses of Congress are clearly considered to be part of the formal structure. They are prescribed in the Constitution and have been further delineated in legislative rules. Yet we know that many informal patterns of behavior have arisen in both houses of Congress without which it would be impossible for the system to work, especially under changing conditions.

Now, however, let us shift our focus away from these informal practices to those patterns of interaction, say, in Congress, that conform faithfully to the rules laid down in the Constitution and ancillary legislation. When we speak of the formal structure of an entity such as Congress, do we mean to include within that notion of structure not only the prescriptive rules themselves (the cultural structure) but any concrete behavior that faithfully reflects the relationships defined by those very rules? Does formal structure refer to behavior as well as to prescriptions, to actual patterns of interactions as well as to tables of organization?

Again, the formal constitutional rules, in establishing a separation and balance of powers, structure the relationship between Congress and the presidency in such a way that the latter has the authority to veto legislation under certain circumstances. If the president acts in accordance with his power, when we refer to the formal structure of authority in the United States do we at the very least wish to include the actual relationship between Congress and the presidency with respect to the use of the veto power? In observing this relationship, since it does conform to the prescribing rules, would we be correct in saying that the patterns of actual behavior represent part of the formal structure of the American political system? Even if we exclude troublesome informal behavior, what we would seem to have in mind when speaking of the formal structure in this case would be not only the prescribing rules (cultural structure) but the actual behavior (empirical or behavioral structure) as well.

If this is so, it would appear that we would be in error to conclude that formal structure refers exclusively to rules that prescribe behavior. Presumably, it is intended to include actual patterns of interaction as well, at least to the extent that they conform to the prescribed rules.

Indeed, the disparity between formal rules and actual conforming or diverging patterns of behavior may become an important criterion for differentiating political systems and the way in which they perform. For example, Eckstein has told us that in Norway formal rules, laid down in great detail, regulate the relationships among members within national and local governing bodies. These rules are not only standards for behavior; they are actually incorporated into the behavior. In a system such as Norway's it is difficult to distinguish between formal rules and concrete behavior, they come so close to each other. Practice seems to match form. Yet even with such a close fit, it is never perfect.[14] There is always some discrepancy. Furthermore, systems such as these, where formal rules and behavior so closely approximate each other, are the exception rather than the rule.

In summary then, although the term *regime structure* embraces what has traditionally been called formal structure, the meaning of the latter concept has retained some irreducible ambiguity. In the first place, what is formal or informal will depend upon the level of analysis, as we have seen. In the second place, it is not always clear from our conceptual usages as to whether we intend to include, in the notion of formal structure, the prescribed rules as well as the actual patterns of interaction in which members of a political system engage—whether the formal structure is only a blueprint or whether it includes such behavior as well. The idea of formal structure, as part of the regime structure, seems to float uncertainly between exclusive reference to formal statements about ideals, expectations, or legal prescriptions on the one hand, and inclusion of a description of conforming practices on the other. In chapter 8, when we come to consider the possible influence of formal structure on behavior, I shall pursue the implications of this matter.

Differentiated Structures

Structural effects are explored in political science through a second category of structures. These are very different from those included in the regime but they are nonetheless closely associated with it. They are a type of structures that, in the past, has been much more frequently the object of empirical inquiry. This type I shall call *differentiated* structures.

These kinds of structures inform us of the different positions occupied by individual members of the political system as well as by political collectivities. The identification of these specialized or differentiated positions is a way of decomposing a political system into structural parts that are different from those of the regime but that have proved central to empirical research. Before identifying some of the major categories of these parts, however, it will be helpful, for understanding the usual approach to these types of structures, to look first at some of its theoretical presuppositions, even though they are seldom laid out explicitly or systematically.

We take it for granted that political structures have evolved through increases in specialization and differentiation of functions as revealed both in institutions and roles. For example, even though in small-scale tribal or peasant societies such differentiation may be low, it exists even there to some degree. No system is totally homogeneous with respect to the positions members occupy or the activities in which they engage. There has been and must always be a division of labor of some kind, even in the smallest unit, such as a familial band.[15]

The history of the increasing specialization and differentiation of royal authority in England stands as a classic model in Western society of what happens to a political system functionally and structurally as it increases in population, in geographic expanse and and in power, as it moves through feudalism to industrialized capitalism. Thus, in England the unified authority of the Crown gradually spun off an advisory privy council which, in turn, proliferated into courts, administrative organizations, a legislature, and later a cabinet. Around them grew up special groups for political involvement, such as parties. All these served to erode, circumscribe, and finally eliminate the effective powers of the monarch, except for residual authority in times of extreme crisis.[16] Structural inquiry in political science is based on this almost primal idea of increasing specialization and differentiation of functions and activities. It has provided the intuitive starting point for most research.

The notion of differentiation, however, in the examples just described, refers to both an activity or process and to a product or resultant. As an activity it represents the way in which a society or political system produces specialized or distinctive patterns of behavior for the performance of various characteristic tasks. In political science, however, this aspect of historical differentiation, once the reliable standby of constitutional political history, has been largely neglected, at least in the twentieth century. Instead we are likely to focus on the fact that this very process, when coupled with the specific conditions of industrialization, has yielded differentiated products, such as legislatures, courts, political roles, interest groups, political parties, etc. When we speak about differentiation and specialization with regard to structure, therefore, until interest in the 1980s turned once again to history, this time to the history of the state and the growth of its powers, we have usually been less concerned about studying the processes of differentiation than the various resultant specialized parts of a political system and their interrelationships. It states the obvious to point out that we do this because, with the rest of the social sciences, we have considered these structural products to have important effects on the behavior of persons or groups within the system and of the system taken as a unit. Hence, differentiated positions represent the structural outcomes of historical processes that we have tended to take for granted.

As we discovered in chapter 4, however, unless we join our discipline's practice of using the part as a metonym, it will be misleading to consider that we have addressed ourselves to a structural problem if we only seek to determine the effect of a part on the behavior of members of a political system or on the behavior of the system as a whole. We need to bear in mind that genuine structural analysis would require us to look at the patterned relationships among parts for their effect on behavior or system functioning, an issue to which I shall return, for much fuller discussion, in the next chapter.

With this caveat, then, I shall now denote briefly the parts into which we characteristically decompose the political system when we seek to understand the relationship of its structure to the way in which the system operates or its members behave. The immediate value of this list is that it will give us a concrete feeling for the kinds of elements we may typically have in mind when we refer to the structure of a system. This will put us in a favorable position to contrast this general idea of structure and its elements, the lower-order structure, with an alternative conception, the one that I have already labeled the higher-order structure.

Categorical Aggregates or Groupings.[17] On the basis of criteria that we as political scientists select, we may classify members of a political system into various categories or types. We are accustomed to doing this, of course, for elements of the *social* structure. For example, on grounds we consider analytically pertinent we may choose to locate the members of a system in social groupings which share such characteristics as ethnicity, religion, region, language, socio-economic status, and the like. These are not specifically organized groups such as trade unions; nor are they natural units such as families. Rather they are just statistical categories that, as political scientists, we create for analytic purposes and as guides for empirical research. We expect that persons with the properties of the categories will be associated with various kinds of predictable political actions or processes, such as voting, partisanship, socialization, and other forms of political involvement.

We follow the same practice in creating structural elements for the political system. We have found it useful to construct categories of members of the political system itself and to relate various kinds of political behavior to possession of the properties of one or another of these strictly political categories of structure. Thus we are accustomed to aggregate members of the political system, arbitrarily but for good reason, into such categories as participants of various sorts—party identifiers, issue-oriented partisans, apathetics, and the alienated. These are no less structural in character than the familiar status, ethnic, regional, religious, or linguistic groupings in the social system. What is common to both the political and social analytic parts of their respective structures is that the persons in them need not cohere in any organized fashion and need not even know or identify with each other.

These categories do not really give us parts of the political structures, however, in a way that corresponds to what we mean when we speak of concrete parts of the human skeletal structure, even though these social elements might at times be labeled as such. Rather, as Blau has pointed out,[18] they are only analytic elements of a system (political, for our purposes, social for his) which differentiate persons in that system along the specified dimensions, such as, in our political illustrations, apathy, issue orientation, or partisanship. We choose to consider members as belonging to a common type, such as a more or less participant subset, because we anticipate that the properties that induce us to consider them a common subset are also predictably associated with other phenomena of interest to us. Empirically, that is to say, in the phenomenal world, the strictly political position of a person will be defined by a number of dimensions based on his or her electoral grouping, party identification, activity score, and the like, as well, of course, as on the socioeconomic groupings in which such a person is placed. The task of research is to depict these combinations (patterns) of positions and to show their impact, singly or in combination, on some other characteristic of a person's political activity or relationships.

Theoretically, if we were to describe all the positions of all members of a political system along all possible political dimensions, we would have an exhaustive delineation of the political structure, at least when approached in these terms. There would be no reason for engaging in this exercise, however, unless we had some advance theoretical indication that the categories so created would contribute to our understanding of the behavior of the members of a system or the system itself taken as a unit.

Later, at a number of points (and especially in chapter 18), I shall return to the limitations of this piecemeal way of conceiving of political structure, as necessary as it is for much research. At the moment I wish to draw attention to one kind of position in this multidimensional political space that plays a very special part in political analysis. It is based not on a nominal classification of members by some criterion but on an ordering of members according to one special criterion: power.

The central significance of power in political systems has led us to differentiate, for example, the authorities from their subjects, an elite from the mass, or a ruling class from the ruled, in either Mosca's or Marx's sense. As social scientists we observe the political system and, according to our particular definition of power, we classify members as higher or lower by the influence we see them as exercising, by the method of either objective or reputational ranking. But regardless of the method used, the rank ordering by power groupings is constructed from criteria adopted by the observer. The members of such power strata or groupings need have no organized or purposively united existence. Power categories or strata, when seen as part of a pattern of power relationships, represent another way in which positions critical in the operation of a political system can be differentiated.

There are, of course, ways of looking at a power distribution such that members of a system can be interpreted as organizing themselves around this dimension, independently of the constructs used by the observer. We find this, for example, among those who interpret an elite as a self-conscious cohering unit in society[19] or who see shifting elites organizing for action as, occasionally, in power pluralist theory. We find a similar position among those who discern a ruling or a working class as a group whose identity and consciousness of self are ultimately established by their common position in relationship to ownership of the means of production. In that event we would have self-defined, self-conscious, organized power groups rather than mere power groupings. They would play a distinctive, purposive part, as organizations (organized structures), in the functioning of a political system.

Here I do not wish to refer to such organized power groups, important as they are. They belong to the next type of differentiated positions. Rather, at this point the power position being identified is only a classificatory grouping representing a way of organizing our understanding of certain aggregate phenomena and their consequences. Recognition of a person or collectivity as a member of the category "political elite," for example, alerts us to the characteristic influence such a person or collectivity may exercise in the formulation and administration of policy, independently, for the moment, of whether the elite is a purposively or self-consciously organized entity.

Regardless, then, of whether we are considering differentiated positions in the political system determined by degree of participation, partisanship, alienation, power, or the like, the point is that, as observers, we take the initiative in constructing this aspect of the political structure. It is not a given in nature, as it were, even though the persons and their positions will exist independently of us. We collect them together into our categories because thereby we hope to be able to use variations in such structural elements, and the way they combine, to explain variances in other parts of the political system.

In short, differentiated positions in political space are objective and independent of the investigator. They are real enough. But collecting them together conceptually is an artifact created by the research worker because it is thought useful, for explanatory purposes, to do so. As we shall now see, such structural elements in a political system are substantially different from those—namely, groups—that can be thought of as givens, just waiting to be identified.

Groups. As I have already indicated and as we well know, differentiated components of a political system may represent more than a reflection of the way in which political scientists find it helpful to sort out the members of a system for understanding their behavior. As political systems evolve, members may form into natural (crescive) membership groups. A group is natural or crescive if its members join together initially through no special or deliberate effort of their own or of others and yet they have a sense of belonging and acting together in the pursuit of political goals. Such natural groups appear in all political systems. Royal families, lineages in nonliterate societies, and spontaneous politically-oriented gangs (Chicago's Blackstone Rangers in their later years, for example) are clear instances of such natural groups that may participate in political life.

A group is formal if it has the same characteristics of natural groups except that its existence depends upon the someone's explicit initiative in bringing the group together and organizing it. We are very familiar with such groups since they occur in large numbers in most large-scale societies. They frequently cut across classificatory groupings of the kind mentioned in the previous section.

These specialized groups, whether crescive or formal in origin, are givens in nature from the point of view of students of politics. They do not depend for their identification on criteria of classification proposed by us. Their numbers are vast, especially in modern complex political systems. We know them as political parties, interest groups representing every aspect of life,[20] organized communal groups (often bound together by ties of religion, language, ethnicity, region, tradition), organized elites, organized representatives of social classes, the armed forces, and so on.

As we know, groups such as these constitute major means for political participation, even in nondemocratic societies.[21] Unlike mere classificatory groupings, but as organized units or corporate entities, in Weber's sense, they are capable of acting purposively to mobilize their membership and resources for the attainment of their goals. In this sense they are a type of differentiated part of a political system, that is, an element of its structure.

Political Roles. In combination with the preceding aspects of political structure, some political scientists have also chosen to focus on a further element, one in which the basic analytic unit is the actor-role. The approach parallels that of other social sciences which find it useful to consider social roles as a central element of social structure.[22] From this point of view, roles constitute a basic unit of the lower-order or observed political structure, and role specialization represents a further kind of differentiation. Despite the fact that the literature on role analysis is enormous in the other disciplines, it has received only limited explicit attention in political science as a possible unit of structural analysis. We need touch on it only briefly here.[23]

Roles may be defined in normative or behavioral terms. Normatively, they constitute the reciprocal expectations about rights and obligations that members of the system have of how persons ought to act when they occupy certain positions. These rights and obligations define the role and they are usually enforced by normative sanctions in the system. Thus, presidents expect to have certain powers, to relate to others in certain ways, whether the practices are constitutionally prescribed or just a matter of convention. Other members of the system will usually entertain similar sets of expectations about the rights and obligations of presidents and about their (the members') own rights and expectations. When these reciprocal expectations converge or diverge, there are foreseeable consequences for the system. For institutionalized rather than recently innovated roles, for example, breach of these reciprocal expectations may evoke behavior by relevant others to bring the deviating occupant into conformity, unless the role itself is undergoing change.

As described to this point, the role structure has been interpreted strictly as normative or cultural. The expectations constitute norms which operate to "structure" the behavior of the person occupying the role. Role behavior would here stand as the product or effect of the structure interpreted as an institutionalized set of norms.[24]

There is, however, an alternative conception of roles as structural units. They may be interpreted in behavioral rather than normative terms. We may see them as regularized patterns of interaction in which members of a political system visibly engage, and not just as expectations. What defines the role is not the rules that members of the system think ought to be followed but those that are practiced.[25] From this point of view, we would describe the role of president by observing how presidents typically behave in office toward their subordinates, other branches of government, the public, foreign governments, and so on. Norms and expectations about how presidents ought to act are not an intrinsic part of the defined role structure; they are only independent variables that help to explain the role behavior and they themselves may be shaped by the behavior.

There is an obvious way to handle this apparent dichotomy between the normative (cultural) and behavioral interpretations of role as a structural element. We may choose to combine the normative and behavioral conceptions and see role as composed of two complementary aspects, a normative and an observed one. In this way we might avoid the apparent conflict in conception. In this unified view, the rules would represent the ideal or expected (the culturally approved) role, behavior, the realized role. Conformity or variation between these two aspects of a role would help to account for role stability, strain, and change. Each would influence the other. In much the same way we have interpreted formal as compared to actual regime structures.

Regardless of the precise way in which we conceptualize roles, however, there are those who find it useful as a focal point for the analysis of political structures. In practice it appears that they define their task as one of identifying the major roles in a political system, describing their distribution, understanding the properties necessary for recruitment to the roles, exploring the effect of role variations on selected relevant aspects of political life, and finally, showing the relationship of roles to each other and to the functioning of the political system as a whole.

As the number of roles in any political system is more vast and complex than the variety of political systems themselves, the mere enumeration of roles would not prove helpful. In fact, those who do approach structure through role analysis lean on explicit or intuitive theoretical criteria to help them sort out what they consider the significant from the incidental roles. The structure of the system would then be definable, at least partly, if not wholly, in terms of the description, relationships, and consequences of these units.[26] Some of those who use role analysis as a way of handling the structure of a political system may do no more than describe and account for particular roles and attempt to show their consequences for some other aspect of the system, such as for the representative process or for modernization.[27] Others may go further and conceptualize the structure of political systems as configurations or patterns of roles.

As widespread as the commitment to role analysis as an important way to understand central parts of the social structure has been in sociology and anthropology, it has never found a commanding place in political research. Its advocates have been few. They have not carried their analyses very far. Yet it clearly reveals an important facet of lower-order political structures that would otherwise remain concealed.

These, then—the regime and various politically differentiated elements of the political system—are major types of components of political structures with which we typically deal in our research. Although I would make no claim that the classification presented here is exhaustive, it does give us a fairly comprehensive notion of what is concretely included in the class of structures I am calling lower-order ones. We associate certain behavior with members of the system who occupy a position in one or another or any combination of these parts (since they may cross-cut and influence each other). That is to say, we anticipate that the political actions of the members will vary with the kind of regime of which they are part, the formal structure in which they fit, the aggregates into which they fall, the organized groups to which they belong, the political roles they occupy.

Conventional research may also seek to show the effects of one or another part, or any combination of them, on one or another aspect or state of the political system, such as on its voting, system performance, policies, stability, integration, conflict, socialization processes, and the like, or on the actions of individual members or collectivities. Efforts are also made to account for their variability—why we have democratic as against totalitarian regimes, multiparty in contrast to two party structures, different patterns of relationships among interest groups (corporatism, for example), and so on.

We need to bear in mind, of course, and to stress once again, that we have addressed here only typical elements which political research has isolated as components of political structures. In and of themselves these elements do not constitute structures which, as we have seen, would consist of patterned relationships among elements such as these—a subject that I shall address again, more fully, in the next chapter.

Even though it is structural parts such as these that I shall include under the concept of lower-order or observed structures, no social phenomena such as these are, of course, directly observable, in any real sense, in the way that we can "see" Kant's dog.[28] To emphasize what we have already noted in chapter 4, they may be described as observed only in the sense that they represent kinds of political relationships that are accessible for relatively immediate and direct description and analysis. What these kinds of observable structures are relative to, will become apparent when we contrast them with the higher-order or overall system structures.

Unlike higher-order structures, lower-order ones seem to be directly available to sensory experience. But that is only because they are so familiar to us. The fact is, they are no less a product of abstraction than higher-order structures; the latter, as we shall see, are just at a higher level of abstraction. It is only because in political research we are so familiar with lower-order patterns of behavior and arrangements that no special reflective effort, in Piaget's sense of the term,[29] is required. For that reason they just appear to be directly observable.

It is nonetheless useful to continue to refer to these lower-order structures as observable, if only to remind ourselves that they do constitute the regular intellectual fare of political research into structure. We do need to bear in mind that this will only be a convenient convention. For ease and simplicity of reference, as indicated earlier,[30] I shall reserve the concept *structural* analysis—as contrasted in chapter 7, to *structuralist* analysis—to refer to the analysis of these lower-order or observed kinds of structures.[31]

Global (Higher-Order) Structures

Structures of the lower-order sort are so much a part of customary political research that we are apt to overlook an alternative conceptualization that has had little success in gaining acceptance in political science and yet that has refused to disappear. Indeed, use of the term in this alternative sense has gained in popularity since the reemergence, in the 1980s, of the kind of concern for constraints on behavior and institutions already discussed in chapter 2. It also presents us with the vaguest and, therefore, least controlled meaning of the notion of structure. Yet this looseness of content may be the very reason for its popularity.

We are apt to call on structure in this sense when we wish to point to the global constraints on the variations of any phenomenon in which we are interested. "In view of the assumption that health services are a subsystem of the larger society," one author writes, "it is well to set forth the main contours of the political and economic structure that shaped them."[32] Clearly the term here draws attention to the broadest context or constraints within which health services are provided.

Similarly, it has been the practice to call upon the structure of the social system, for example, to help us understand the sources of urban violence in the past in the United States. Within the context of such parameters as the juxtaposition of rich and poor in metropolitan regions, racial tensions, propensity to police lawlessness, thwarted expectations in a consumer-oriented society, and the like, some precipitating event, such as the assassination of Martin Luther King or an apparent random arrest of a citizen, has, in the past, led to violent flareups of discontent. The conditions within which the specific event occurs seem to exist independently of the will of the participants, and yet they also seem to help shape and direct the actions of the participants. Such conditions have often been characterized as the structural context of urban violence.

In this meaning, structure identifies no specific property of the social system. It just refers to a diffuse or undifferentiated global set of phenomena which, in one way or another, seems to provide the underlying conditions, determinants, or constraints for the events being described or explained.

We can, of course, accuse those who use the term *structure* in this global way of obscuring understanding. It is scarcely news to say that the broad context may influence action and institutions, including political structures themselves. Yet to some extent we are all probably guilty of this kind of usage. We speak of the historical conditions which shape or constrain events and their outcomes. Indeed, it has been a characteristic of the 1980s, in contrast to earlier decades, that we began to feel that we cannot understand political and social events in general without interpreting them as products of great historical movements originating in the medieval European period.[33] We often do this as a quick and shorthand way of drawing attention to a host of variables that it would otherwise be too tedious and distracting to attempt to describe.

At the moment I just wish to draw attention to the existence of this practice in our conceptual armamentorium. In effect, I shall later propose, especially in chapters 17 and 18, that it may be a way of pointing to the existence and significance of higher-order structures, however vaguely defined. We intuitively feel that we cannot hope to understand the here and now, including ordinary observed structures, without in some way seeing them interwoven in the total political (and social) fabric. In the end we shall see that there is a reality to this usage even though to be persuaded of it fully, we need a kind of justification and specification that I shall not be in a logical position to present until much later on.

In this chapter I have claimed that to set out on our exploration of political structures it is not only useful but also necessary to distinguish between those that seem to be given directly to us through observation (lower-order ones) and others that may need to be discovered through a more deliberate process of abstraction (higher-order structures). I have sought to give some flesh to this claim by reviewing regime and associated differentiated structures as examples of those that are already familiar to us.

To some extent, in political science, although concern began to change during the 1980s, we have tended to show a greater interest in the description and effects of these kinds of lower-order political structures, together with their specific determinants, than in their relation to the overall structure of the political system of which they are part. Effects are, of course, of central importance. But it has seemed to me that if we are convinced that lower-order structures do have effects— and, as we shall see, this is by no means a foregone conclusion in all instances— we might well begin our thinking about any theory of such structures by inquiring into why they take the form they do. Whatever consequences such structures do have, we may assume, may well be related to the form they take. And if we are searching for the determinants of their form, it will not be enough to look for specific determinants. We would need to take into consideration, I shall argue, the extent to which the form of observed structures, such as that of the regime, results from the overall structural context (the higher-order structure) of the political system itself.

The broad forces that make observed structures what they are would seem to invite inquiry that is at least coincident with if not prior to the study of their effects. Yet without establishing that structures may have important political effects, there would be little point in trying to uncover hitherto neglected factors that do shape such structures. Accordingly, in the next two chapters, for illustrative purposes I shall discuss a number of arguments about the possible consequences of observed structures.

As I have noted earlier, the idea that structures do have effects has not gone without serious challenge. Once we have satisfied ourselves that structure is not merely epiphenomenal, we can then move to the core of our argument and inquire into the way in which we may go about understanding the forces that influence the forms of observed structures, such as those found in regimes and their associated structures.

6

Effects of Nonformal
Political Structures

In the last chapters we have seen that structure is not a physical thing out there in space waiting to contain or constrain activity, as it were. Rather, structure is a property which imposes constraints on individuals and collectivities and may also facilitate their purposes. Regardless for the moment of any further meaning that we might attach to structure as a term, in this and the succeeding chapter I shall address a logically prior concern: To what extent are *observed* political structures of any significance in influencing political behavior or the operations of political systems? Unless we are convinced that such structures have more than marginal significance, there would be little value in pursuing our main purpose of trying to understand their possible determinants, especially of the kind I am calling higher-order structures.

One point is clear. Traditionally, in political science, we have accepted as a fact that structures—setting aside formal ones for the moment—do have determinable consequences. Indeed, by the 1980s a substantial literature had arisen around the criteria for the assessment of political institutions, especially in democratic political systems.[1] There would have been little point for political science to have decomposed political systems into the various structural parts described in the preceding chapter if the conviction did not prevail that structures composed of such parts had an important bearing on individual behavior or system performance.

It might appear that early on, what we now describe as orthodox Marxism, virtually alone launched a major challenge to this assumption; democratic forms were interpreted as a figleaf to conceal the true locus of power. However, although the point is not usually put in the following way, the fact that Marxism did see democratic structures as functioning successfully to conceal the true locus of power is itself incontrovertible evidence that even this theory saw such structures as having considerable consequences for the operation of political systems. By their very presence, democratic structures serve the critical ideological function of masking and thereby preserving the substance of rule by the capitalist class. Hence, even for early Marxism, despite apparent utterances to the contrary, observed kinds of structures might have a telling effect in politics, a point that, by the twentieth century, Gramsci had incorporated into a theory of ideology.

In its own orthodoxy, however, political science chose not to lock horns on this issue. Initially it simply acted as though we could take it for granted that at least nonformal structures do have an impact on the operation of political systems. Yet the mass of research that makes this assumption has not been compelling enough to suppress sharply contradictory points of view, even within conventional political science.[2] Some of the latter opinions have rested largely on philosophical grounds, but others have been documented by careful empirical research. The result is that this once unconventional strand in political science, one that denies the validity of assuming structural effects, is now also becoming incorporated into our research orthodoxy.

In this particular strand of the folklore in the discipline, as we shall see in this chapter, we often find the conviction that even if structure may be of some importance on occasion, its significance is very limited in face of the "real" sources of power in society. In this view, structure is relegated to a secondary or tertiary position. It can induce minor variations in the way in which power is used. It cannot alter the fundamental distribution and consequences of power. Structure follows power; power does not follow structure.

Strangely enough, at the very moment when conventional political science began to question its own assumptions and to wonder about the extent to which crescive structures were important, a recent modification in Marxist thinking in essence rejects the fig-leaf theory of such structural influence. In this new variant, the form and organization of the State—that is, the political "superstructure"—is now understood to have a profound importance for the way in which political systems formulate and administer policy. Although not always recognized or acknowledged, this new position received its inspiration from the work of Nicos Poulantzas, whose structuralist interpretation of Marxism I shall later examine in some detail from this very point of view. He argued that although the mode of production or infrastructure comes into play only "in the last instance," in the first instance, if I may use this phrase, what he, following Althusser, called the "relative autonomy of the State,"[3] in its varying forms will have a significant impact on the way a political system operates.

This introduction of the "State"[4] as a relatively autonomous actor of influence is just a more theoretical way of stating what most political scientists had taken for granted from time immemorial, namely, that the way the political regime or the "State" is organized may indeed matter with respect to the way in which decisions are processed and implemented. Contemporary structuralist Marxism, neo-Marxists, and others have only added to conventional political assumptions a more systematic or theoretical approach to the understanding of the possible influence of political structures such as the state.[5] This is a point, I have noted, which I shall have occasion to examine much later. Its significance for the moment is that when we now turn to the possible consequences of observed structures I shall be dealing directly with the issue raised by those neostatists who have recently discovered that we ought to "bring the state back in," as though even the most conventional political scientists, in sharp contrast to many sociologists, had ever had occasion to leave it out![6]

For the moment I will gloss over a certain ambiguity and even shift in meaning in the idea of structure as it appears in the preceding statements. In the hands of neostatists structure had begun to assume some broad contextual overtones that will become increasingly important as our discussion proceeds. For purposes of this chapter I will just continue to use the conventional meaning in political science, one that restricts the term to the more narrowly conceived formal and nonformal structures.

In the preceding chapter I have already indicated the way in which we might usefully interpret formal structures. They are structures that arise in some special manner—through written documents (laws, constitutions) or ritualistic procedures to signalize their important special status. Nonformal or crescive structures, on the other hand, are relationships that emerge naturally out of the day-to-day interactions in which members of a political system engage. And I continue to include both formal and crescive structures under the label of observed or lower-order structures.

I shall conclude this and the next chapter, which deal with crescive and formal structural effects, respectively, with the less-than-helpful judgment that under some circumstances observed political structures may have important consequences and under others they may not. One of the major outstanding tasks in political science is the invention of methods for isolating the kinds of differences, if any, political structures make under varying circumstances. This, however, is not our purpose. We need only conclude that if it appears that lower-order political structures may indeed have some substantially significant consequences, that finding in itself will sufficiently justify our efforts to ferret out any hitherto neglected forces that shape these structures.

Structure versus Reality

As I have already indicated, if we were to rely exclusively on traditional political research we would be left with little doubt that lower-order, formal structures have discernible consequences on various aspects of political life. Intuitively, political science has built many of its theories of democracy on this assumption. In the United States, for example, every time someone proposes to change the organization of some agency or to restructure relationships between the American Congress and the presidency, implicitly the claim is being made that this will lead to some significant changes in the functioning of the government.

As I have indicated, the sheer mass of research in this tradition has not gone unchallenged however. Remarkably contradictory opinions exist, some resting on largely quasi-philosophical grounds but others now documented by careful empirical research. I shall return later to the philosophical basis for arguing that observed structures may have less effect than we might think. At this moment I want to deal with the other strand of the discipline's folklore. In it we find the conviction that even if structures may be of some importance on occasion, their significance is very limited in face of the "real" sources of power in society. Observed structures recede into secondary or tertiary positions of influence. They can affect minor variations in the way in which power is used. They cannot alter the fundamental distribution and consequences of power.

In a sense this criticism returns us to the realist complaints of the late nineteenth century against the legalists who mistook the prescribed seats of power for the genuine product. Bagehot had exposed what he called the "paper description" or literary theory of England's unwritten constitution which construed the latter as providing for the distribution of power among King, Lords, and Commons.[7] In contrast, Bagehot discovered the "living reality" of power to reside rather in the Cabinet within the House of Commons, drawing its moral and material strength from the middle class. Building on Bagehot, Woodrow Wilson later located this reality, in the United States, in legislative committees, lobbies, and political parties.[8]

Virtually every radical critic, from Marx forward, has similarly warned against mistaking structure for reality. The structural arrangements provide political actors either with no power or with trivial amounts in comparison with the resources they obtain through other, less visible means, such as control over wealth, property, votes, or organizations.

Elitism, as well, as elaborated by Mosca, Pareto, and Michels, is a foremost representative of this opinion in the twentieth century. For it, no less than for Marxism, the structural trappings of democracy cannot reverse the distribution of political power, stemming as it does from the dominance of elites over the masses.

These views reflect deeper issues about the meaning of structure, to which I shall return. At the moment they serve to remind us that not everyone has shared the enthusiasm of traditional political science about the significance of observed political structures.

Negative Findings of Empirical Inquiry

The nineteenth-century critics, such as Bagehot, do not stand alone in questioning the efficacy of structures. In recent years they have received reinforcement, from unexpected sources, for their conviction that we have made too much of structural trappings, particularly in democratic systems. This time, however, their objections have been supported at a higher level of technological skills to prove the point. In fact, for proof they could now appeal to a small body of research that has been trying to discover, on the basis of rigorous empirical inquiry, the degree to which various lower-order political structures need to be taken into account in explaining variations in public policy.

This research moves in a direction different from that taken by those who have characteristically accepted structure to refer to the differentiated positions in or parts of the social or political structure, which I described in chapter 5. There we saw that associations between various kinds of political behavior—such as voting or recruitment to political office—and social class, region, ethnicity, or membership in various interest groups were interpreted as meeting the need to show a relationship to, and therefore a possible effect of, social and political structures. The literature on voting, socialization, violence, and the like has rung the changes on the influence of structures so conceived. The effect of structural location was interpreted to signify the impact of structure.

Here, however, I wish to turn to those who have interpreted structure more broadly to include not just individual parts of a structure but patterns of relationships within political systems, such as the structure of party systems or of whole regimes. Out of the unpredictable idiosyncrasies of ongoing research perhaps, these areas have been selected for particular attention, probably because they relate so transparently to the urgent social questions about the presumed consequences of one kind of lower-order political structure, democracy, for such goals as justice and human welfare.

At any rate, despite or perhaps because of the radical critics of democracy who saw it as a mere façade concealing the true location of power, it seemed to the proponents of democracy simply a matter of common sense that the form (regime) of a political system, whether democratic or otherwise, must have considerable influence on its policy outputs. Otherwise why would we have struggled historically to achieve, improve, and retain democratic forms? One of the major advantages of democracy, so the argument has gone, is that it has seemed to promise outputs more responsive to and more in harmony with popular needs and interests than any other type of political system. Among other factors, we have consistently attributed this outcome to the representative structures found in democracies, as reinforced by competitive party structures.

When, in recent years, this assumption was scrutinized more carefully, however, the matter was no longer so clear. It turned out that what little empirical research we have in this area seriously muddies the water in what we might have thought was a transparent case.

The original work of Dye and Cutright, among many others, has confounded our folklore. Despite a considerable body of subsequent research,[9] the doubts they have raised remain with us. The expected effects do not seem to occur universally even though in some instances, such as the separation and balance of powers among governmental organs, the existence of effects may appear to be too obvious to deny.

In a classic study Dye explored the effect on political outputs of four sets of variables: party structure (in the form of party competition), apportionment structure, party control of state government in the United States, and voter turnout. We might consider only the first two variables to be structures in anyone's usage of the term. The literature in American state politics has usually assumed that these factors have a discernible impact on political outputs. As Dye himself summarized the assumptions that he set out to question

> The belief that competition, participation and equality in representation had important consequences for public policy also squared with the value placed upon these variables in the prevailing pluralist ideology. States with higher voter participation, intense party competition, and fair apportionment—usually northern and midwestern states—suggested a normative model of pluralist democracy, which was expected to produce "good" public policies—liberal welfare benefits, generous educational spending, progressive taxation, advanced health and hospital care, and so on. In contrast, states with low voter participation, absence of party competition, and unfair apportionment—usually southern states—suggested a type of political system which was widely deplored among American political scientists. Moreover, such political systems were believed to produce meager welfare benefits . . . and so on.[10]

Dye's research revealed that

> these four commonly described characteristics [degree of interparty competition, extent of malapportionment, the level of voter turnout, and Democratic or Republican control

of state government] of pluralist political systems [had] *less* effect on public policy in the states *than* environmental variables reflecting the level of economic development . . . *[On] the whole* economic resources were more influential in shaping state policies than any of the political variables previously thought to be important in policy determination.[11]

From the point of view of our interest, the structures tested—namely, the competitive two-party structure and the structure of representation as provided by the apportionment rules—accounted for much less of the variance in outputs than would have been anticipated from traditional opinions among political scientists.[12]

The conclusions we can draw from this and related studies do not permit us, of course, to go beyond the consequences of the specific structures tested. They at least do suggest, however, that the presumption of the effectiveness of varying combinations or patterns of governmental structures underlying, for example, Apter's work on modernization,[13] may have less generality than anticipated and demand closer scrutiny.

A study by Cutright leads in the same direction but uses as its data base the cross-national arena.[14] Traditionally we have thought that the responsiveness of governments to popular needs is directly related to their democratic character and ideology. Cutright sought to determine whether the level of expenditures for social security (insurance against severe loss of income due to unemployment, old age, illness, and the like) in seventy-six different countries could be explained by their different ideologies and by their types of political systems as classified by degree of representativeness. He found, to the contrary, that social security coverage is more highly correlated with the level of economic development of the country than with its ideology or representativeness. Whatever effect observed structures might have was only marginal. Controlling for level of economic development only indicated that the more representative structures provided social security programs somewhat earlier than those that were less representative.[15]

Clearly this research at least raises the question as to whether, upon more careful empirical scrutiny, it might turn out that the crescive (as well as the formal) structures of political systems have considerably less influence on outputs than democratic theory would have led us to believe. Even so, of course, as I have observed in footnote 12, the research of Dye and Cutright still leaves moot the question as to whether political arrangements may not help to determine who benefits most from those outputs that in fact are produced. The research pays little attention to the question of distribution in a population. In addition, as we shall see in a moment, formal structure, or legal institutions as they are usually called, may have other kinds of consequences that the literature we are attending to here does not touch on. At the moment, however, it is interesting that in those instances where our methods of research about the consequences of observed structures seem to be moving in a more empirically reliable direction, as in the studies of the consequences of such structures for political outputs, the relationship between these phenomena does not show the kind of strength long held as axiomatic in the folklore of the discipline.

Negative Findings of Institutional Analysis

The negative results suggested so far in this area of research are reinforced by what has been a recurring theme in quasi-philosophical interpretations about the significance of political institutions in influencing social change. Some time ago, Reich, in *The Greening of America*, offered a restatement of this position.[16] It appeared at about the peak of student concerns in the United States during the 1960s and early 1970s.

In this book Reich argued against efforts to bring "the system" down. Systems, he held, are not transformed by destroying their structural or institutional arrangements as long as the people who run the system and occupy its chief offices continue to hold the same old values and attitudes. Only changes in the latter will ultimately bring about revolutions and transform the way social and political structures operate. Change of values and attitudes must precede change of structure if alterations in the latter are to be of value.

Reich interpreted student militancy as an expression of a new configuration of values about basic aspects of life: sex, dress, morality, international peace, and the like. The bearers of the new outlooks in these areas, the younger generation, will, he predicted, in time move through the system like locusts across the wheat-fields, not destroying, however, but constructively consuming and transforming everything before them. Gradually, as these new cohorts occupy the central positions of power, the structures themselves will change or the old ones will crumble to be displaced by ones that express the new consciousness.

Reich's confidence in the power of the human will echoes the thought of many distinguished contributors to social science in the past. Moral and cultural change must precede structural change. Where Reich seemed to differ is that he put special emphasis on the futility of altering onmibus structural arrangements; for him "the system" seemed to be represented by conventional political and economic institutions present in American society at the time. He directed his moral theory of social change against the notion that destruction of institutions, which, for him include structures, is a necessary act or one that would in itself have lasting effects. As he phrased it in another of his writings:

> Institutional change, without a new source of values, would thus be an empty exercise. The "reformed" structures would be worse than the old. Real change can take place only after new values are introduced, and the only possible source of such values is man, and a new awareness and culture created by him.[17]

We need not address the dubious validity of Reich's theory. History has already demonstrated that as the new cohorts of the sixties moved through the American system, it has been their values that have seemed more prone to change than the structures of the system. Nevertheless, the message carried by Reich's work was essentially the same as that of the empirical research into the effects of structure: We ought not to overestimate the influence of structures on behavior.

Despite the fact that empirical studies such as those by Dye and Cutright, as well as interpretive institutional analyses such as Reich's, move in the same direction, the important point for us is that neither need be accepted as decisive about the possible effects of political structures. Aside from the doubts just expressed about Reich, even the more rigorous empirical studies by no means account for all or even most structures in political systems. They examine only limited types, such as parties and those structures related to representativeness. Even where they are concerned the studies focus only on a narrow, albeit important, range of possible consequences, namely, on social welfare policies. There are numerous other kinds of structures and certainly limitless kinds of outputs with which such structures might conceivably be connected. As for the broader interpretive analyses, they usually rest on historical and logical reasoning that lend themselves to equally compelling counterarguments.

In short, whether structures can be shown to have effects may well depend on what we mean by structure, what effects we choose to look for and what specific structures we examine, some of which matters did not appear even as peripheral, let alone central, concerns of these studies. Regardless of their limitations, however, what these studies do impress on us is the fact that we cannot take for granted the relationship between structure, however conceived, and its presumed effects, positive or otherwise.

Empirical Methods for Discovering Effects

Structural versus Compositional Effects

What is perhaps strange about political science is that, until recently, and then in a limited way, largely in the policy area, we have paid so little attention to the development of carefully crafted methods for exposing the effects of political structures, however we define the latter. Not all the social sciences, however, have been so remiss in their responsibilities, at least in their own spheres of interest. Some, such as sociology, have struggled to find a method for demonstrating what political science has for the most part taken for granted. It is useful to glance at some of these efforts if only to identify difficulties blocking the way of uncovering the effects of social structures, difficulties which may similarly stand in the way of the examination of observed political structures.

There are two issues at stake here, aside, of course, from the continuing question of the possible varying meanings attached to the very term *structure* itself. One involves what it is we count as an effect of structure. This depends on just how we are interpreting the idea of structure. If we construe the latter to be a social fact in Durkheim's sense—an objective reality with an independent influence—we would find it necessary to demonstrate how such facts do shape human behavior. At the moment we are not ready to address this matter, but I shall return to it much later when discussing higher-order structures.

Another issue, however, involves technical ways of isolating structural effects whether or not we view them as broad social facts. In the 1980s, for example, sociology was as solidly founded on the study of social structure as it had been, in the early part of this century, on the idea of social process (such as group conflict and change). At the aggregate level, standard procedures for isolating the influence of selected parts of the social structure are well known. We have mentioned these in connection with structure interpreted as differentiated parts of a social system. Covariations between behavior—such as socialization, political recruitment, participation, voting, conflict, and the like on the one side, and so-called structural variables such as social class, ethnicity, power position, language group, or age on the other—have been routine. Such correlations are presumed to reveal the effects of the specified structural *parts* of the social system.

The word *parts* has been emphasized. It reflects the fact that there is some question about what ought to be called a structural analysis, as I have already stressed in the preceding chapter. As pointed out in chapter 4, Blau has challenged whether the relationship between a specified behavior or effect and some part of a social structure really tells us much about structural effects. All it informs us about is the way in which a *component* of a structure affects some particular outcome. It tells us nothing about the effects of the *whole* of a given structure, and this is what we are usually looking for, according to Blau, when we talk about structural effects.

As we have seen, structure for him refers to the *pattern* formed by the way the parts are organized. Thus, the influence of class structure would refer not to the impact of a social class on some designated behavior, for example, but to the way in which the pattern of class relationships affects the behavior. A social system in which the upper and lower classes were small in numbers and in proportion to the total population could be expected to influence the system differently from one in which the upper and lower classes were large both numerically and proportionately. The buffering effects of the middle class would be significantly less in the latter kind of class pattern or relationship. Similarly, a genuine structural analysis, in Blau's view, would lead us to an interest in the patterns of status and economic inequality, not in the poor alone, in religious patterns of a society, not in a person's location in any single religious group, in the patterns of power, not in the power of a given class or elite.[18]

Applying this to politics, presumably the influence of party structure would not be revealed by the way in which party membership or identification shaped voting or attitudes. Rather, to uncover the effects of party structure we would have to isolate the influence of the relationships among existing parties (the pattern of relationships formed by the parties) on such voting behavior or attitudes. For Blau, structure means more than the aggregation of effects of the parts of the social structure; structure refers to the pattern formed by these parts.[19]

Blau cites numerous examples of structural effects established in this way. Of these we may mention one. He calls attention to the research of Lipset, Trow, and Coleman,[20] who found that where most members of a printing shop agree on general political issues (a group attribute) they were more likely to be active in union affairs (the "structural effect")[21] than in cases where they have political differences. Their behavior was affected less by their political views than by the degree to which they agree or disagree with respect to them. Blau argues that "sufficient political consensus [provides] a basis for cordial discourse . . . encourages political talk at work, and this stimulates interest in political activities of the union."[22] In other words, Blau interprets the data to mean that consensus generates a new communication network or structure[23] in the group. This new structural pattern then acts as an intervening variable to encourage interest in union affairs by facilitating talk about and interest in union affairs.

In effect, Blau is saying that it is often possible to identify some property of a group (degree of consensus, in this instance) that takes the form of a frequency distribution and to use it to differentiate one group from another. This is a technique, of course, that has been associated with Durkheim. For the latter the group property, in his famous study of suicides, was the proportion of Protestants and Catholics and their relationship to suicide rates.[24] It has been a widely used technique, as we know. For Stouffer, the group property was the frequency of promotion in the army as associated with attitudes toward promotion,[25] and for Lipset *et al.* it was the degree of consensus with respect to political identification and its consequences for interest in union politics.

In short, where we find differences in the proportions of certain properties in the group—in its composition—we find corresponding differences in test effects. The initial group differences operate by generating internal structural changes to which variations in these effects are then traced. So Blau's argument runs.

However, even though this method is offered as a way of testing for structural influences, we may question whether this has been demonstrated. All Blau offers is an interpretation of data that makes an argument, for example, albeit a plausible one, for the influence of consensus on generating new social relationships. As Davis and his coauthors have suggested, the method used here really tells us little about such relationships. Instead, it only describes what they call "the composition of the group."[26] Davis *et al.* do not deny that structure may be involved but, since no evidence is presented, they prefer to avoid the dilemma this creates by referring to consequences of group variations as "compositional" effects. They allow others to debate the meaning of structure. They leave it as a moot point whether these effects are truly structural rather than merely attitudinal, or even group phenomena irreducible to individual behavior.

Here Davis and his colleagues would seem to be taking the more sensible course with regard to so-called structural effects. To be sure, it could be that compositional differences do reflect variations in the nature of internal relationships and thus would be structural in character by most people's definition of the term. However, the fact is that in the cases noted, accepting Blau's own data, we have evidence only of frequency distributions of certain individual—that is, subjective—characteristics, with no information about new social relationships (structural patterns) within the group. It would be equally plausible to assume that attitudes are disseminated by stable communication networks and that the group composition leads to the domination of certain kinds of attitudes which, upon communication, produce the effects noted for others in the group. In other words, communication structure could be constant across all instances.

We have insufficient evidence to decide on the correct interpretation. It appears that this method for isolating incontrovertible structural effects, viewed as patterns of relationships, does not in fact help us. It leaves us uncertain as to whether structure, as defined here, has been isolated as a specific factor. Yet despite the fact that in this instance there has been little success in isolating presumed structural effects, it does at least reveal the continuing explicit concern of sociology with the issue, something that has been lacking until recently in political science.

Small-Group and Network Analysis

Some time ago, research in the area of small groups, at the micro structural level, did devise a method, one based on experiment and rigorous observation, for separating the structure or patterns of relationships from other aspects of social behavior and for sorting out its consequences. For example, in a classic experiment, Bavelas tested for the results of variable patterns of communication (circle, chain, star, and Y-shape) on task performances of a small group.[27] Other research on small groups sought to isolate structures around such dimensions as power, authority, preferences, and sociometric choices (friendship).[28] To test for the effect of friendship structure, for example, what we might call a friendship parallelogram was constructed. As indicated in diagram 6.1, if A and B are friends, A and C are friends and B and D are friends, what are the probabilities D and A, on the one hand, and that D and C, on the other, will form friendship pairs? As we might expect, once the problem is posed in this way, D is more likely to become friendly with A than with C. As both A and D like B, this increases the probability that D and A will also like each other. On the other hand, with C a stranger to B, we have a less reliable basis for arriving at a judgment about D liking C.

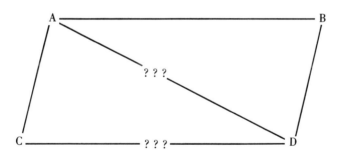

Diagram 6.1   Friendship Structure[29]

From efforts such as these to isolate patterns or structures of social relationships and to trace their effects empirically in small groups, some time ago there emerged a mathematical "theory" about structure. This formal analysis, known as directed graph or digraph theory, once sought to give precise meaning to "such ideas as the degree of connectedness of a structure, its diameter, its vulnerability, and its stratification levels."[30]

As the authors of this quotation recognize they were more successful in providing us with a body of definitions than with theory. However, from our point of view this is less important than the fact that their work applies largely to small groups. Its relevance for the central issues of political analysis is very limited. Small-group interaction is more easily described and tested than the larger amorphous relationships, at a macrostructural level, which make up a political system. The methods appropriate for isolating and detecting the effects of patterns of relationships among small groups are not readily transferred to larger and more complex social entities. And little advice is offered about how to combine the analysis of the structure of small groups into the vast network of relationships typical of large-scale political systems.

The innovative work on small groups just discussed has been continued during the 1970s and 1980s through elaborate, mathematically-infused network analysis.[31] Its underlying assumption is that network relationships do guide individual behavior. As one critic has expressed it,

> These purposively-constructed networks provide flexible and fluid conditions that help to shape future individual decisions and network relationships in at least two ways: (a) individual decisions and bonding processes will be based on and therefore affected by information and resources that flow through already-established network links, and (b) existing network links will be treated as exchangeable resources; that is, during their negotiations and transactions individuals . . . can and do make social contact available to one another at an agreed-upon price.[32]

However, as with earlier network analysis the transfer of knowledge from the networks of small entities to the macro level has continued to challenge the technical skills as yet available, at least for carrying us beyond formal models to an understanding of empirical phenomena.[33] Yet the conviction remains that if variations in structures have consequences for behavior at the lower levels of a social system, this must be equally true at the overarching levels.

Ethnoscience as a Theory about Structural Effects

Structure and its effects have also shaped the problematic of so-called ethnoscience (ethnomethodology), the movement toward a cognitive social science which sees the "knowing active subject as the source of human conduct."[34] Without at the moment entering into the debates about ethnomethodological approaches to an understanding of structure—a subject to which I shall return in chapter 17—we can assume fairly wide agreement with the proposition that ethnoscience, like network analysis, also remains largely at the micro level. There may be some question as to whether some of the advocates of this approach even deal with anything more than process. However, even if we limit ourselves to those among them who do seek to illuminate structure, with a few exceptions they confine themselves to the relationships among individual actors and the way in which such interactions and perceptions constrain behavior. Some ethnomethodologists hold out the hope, as do network analysts, that one day all this micro-derived knowledge will be assembled into a picture of the macrostructure of which we are all part.

This day is so far in the future, however, that no specifications are now offered about how this combining of knowledge at the individual level will occur, and if it does, how it will be able to depict the overarching qualities usually attributed to macrostructures.

Aside, however, from the often conflicting ideas about structure among ethnomethodologists themselves, some advocates of this approach accept the idea that structures do have some influence. It is just a matter of determining how we are to go about understanding that influence. For the proponents of this view structure does not have an objective existence over and above the behavior of individual subjects with an effect separable from the activities of these subjects. There are no forces acting "behind the backs"[35] of individuals forcing them to behave in certain ways. Rather, if there is structure and if it has an effect, it can be understood only, as one proponent has put it, by focusing on "what native speakers have to know (implicitly) about their culture in order to function adequately as competent members of their respective societies."[36] It is clear, therefore, that in this view particular structures may have effects; it is just a matter of how we go about conceptualizing structure and looking for these effects.

Impact of Structure of the State

In raising the issue about the possible effects of observed political structures, it may also appear that I am indirectly touching on questions about the relative autonomy of the state structure. This is true to some extent. The issue of the autonomy of the state necessarily points to the impact of the structure of the state on some political variables. As one proponent puts it,

> State power cannot be understood only as an instrument of class domination, nor can changes in state structures be explained primarily in terms of class conflicts. In France, Russia, and China, class conflicts—especially between peasants and landlords— were pivotal during the revolutionary interregnums. But both the occurrence of the revolutionary situations in the first place and the nature of the New Regimes that emerged from the revolutionary conflicts *depended fundamentally upon the structures of the state organizations and their partially autonomous and dynamic relationships to domestic class and political forces*, as well as their positions in relation to the other states abroad.[37]

The author states explicitly that the "structures of the state organizations"— presumably what I am calling observed structures—do have central importance for the presence of revolutionary conditions and for the nature of the succeeding new regimes. She goes further and points out that we can understand these observed structures, at least as they emerge from a revolutionary condition, only by reference to the preexisting state structures as well as to their relationship to social classes and foreign powers.

This question about the factors that shape a given regime does ultimately go to the heart of my concerns of course. At the moment, however, I am not addressing this problem. Rather, my focus here and in the next chapter is on demonstrating that political structure is worth exploring because it is not just ephiphenomenal. If neo-statists, in their new attempts at analyzing the state, had considered structures of the state, in the sense of its form and organization, to be a mere façade, their work would have offered little support to my purpose here.[38] To the extent that at least some of the literature on the autonomy of the state does consider structures, such as those of the state itself, to have a central effect on the creation of revolutionary conditions and on the shape of succeeding regimes, it gives added reasons for seeking to improve our understanding of the determinants of such structures.

Despite this newfound concern for the effects of state action, the weight of the discussion about state autonomy does not lie in the area of the effects of varying state forms or structures. It reawakens us to the importance of the "design of political institutions,"[39] which we may interpret as including not only the power of the state and of occupants of state positions but the effects of their varying structures as well. But the literature is more likely to dwell on the sources of the capacity of the state, as a so-called autonomous actor, to pursue policies that are independent of societal forces. As analysis usually puts the matter, it seeks to demonstrate that policies are state- rather than society-centered or -determined. Neostatist advocates of this view are asserting that under most conditions the political authorities or governmental rulers have the capacity to pursue goals independent of the social interests—whether of classes or of groups—they might be thought to represent. In the extreme, the state has the means to pursue courses of action that various social classes or groups in society, upon whom the state actors—the political authorities, in my terms—might otherwise depend, find objectionable and even damaging to what they conceive to be their long-term interests.

These kinds of state effects would be of moment to us if they could be attributed, in large part or in whole, to the structure of the state; they would then be structural effects. Customarily, however, those who speak about reviving the state as a focus of political analysis are not especially concerned about showing how structural variations in the state lead to varying degrees of autonomy or varying types of policies. Rather, they are more preoccupied first, with presenting evidence that the state—often viewed, for this purpose, as an undifferentiated actor—does indeed have some degree of autonomy in policy matters, and second, with accounting for this apparent capacity of the state. In doing so, there is little indication, except incidentally and in passing, about the extent to which they would attribute varying state effects over policies to differences in state (regime?) structures.

In other words, the main concern of neostatist analysis is with the fact and sources of the state's ability to define its own interests and courses of action—independent of such external social forces as classes or interest groups—rather than with any effort to account for this autonomy or particular policy preferences in terms of the way the state itself is structured.[40] Poulantzas is a notable exception, and I shall, therefore, later find it necessary and useful to analyze his work in some detail.

The few examples we have looked at, which could be multiplied by others, highlight the problems we have in sorting out empirically the possible consequences of nonformal lower-order structures. If nothing else emerges, it is clear that the attempt to uncover structural effects is bound up with the ambiguity surrounding the term *structure* itself. If we take it to mean only parts of structures—groups, classes, roles, agencies, organizations, and the like—we could of course ease the task of empirical research. Convincing correlations abound testifying to the degree of variance that can be attributed to the location of an actor in one or another of these parts. However, if we go beyond this narrow idea of structure to the broader one proposed by Blau and used by many others—as varying patterns of relationships among such component parts—the proof becomes much more difficult, at least if we look for empirically rigorous methods of demonstration through measurement or testable formal modeling.

Yet the intuitive belief in the existence of the effects of nonformal or crescive structures at both the macro and micro levels is hard to vanquish. Whatever else that can be said, it is clear, even from our cursory analysis of the relevant literature, not all lower-order structures need have consequences and that of those that do, not all need be of equal importance. Nor need they have significant consequences at all times or under all conditions.[41]

If the possibility of the influence of at least some observable crescive structures remains an unshakable conviction, we would find it difficult to deny the importance of seeking to understand the factors that give such structures whatever forms they assume. However, before entering into that discussion, there remains another class of lower-order structure to consider, namely, formal structures.

In the conventions of the political science there would appear to be little evidence that such structures need have anything but marginal effects on behavior or the operations of political systems as a whole. After all, it is well known that at the end of the nineteenth century the realists in political research turned away from legal formalism with the firm conviction that formal structure was of secondary significance. Would it now really be worth devoting serious attention to the determinants of such structures as part of our concern about the forces shaping political regimes? Can we say they have consequences of sufficient importance to merit our attention? I turn to these questions in the next chapter.

7

Effects of Formal Political
Structures

Although political science has put some effort into tracing the influence of various kinds of lower-order, nonformal structures, as we have just seen in the preceding chapter, it is really remarkable that in the one area that, we might have thought, would have attracted immediate attention, little rigorous analysis has as yet been undertaken. I refer here to the field of formal structures. As we saw in chapter 5, such structures are of special relevance for us, of course, as they are important constituent elements of political regimes in the way I defined the latter earlier. Since that is so, it seems appropriate in this chapter to examine the extent to which the belief prevails that formal structures may have some influence on the functioning of political systems. If they do, this would add further justification for undertaking to explore the determinants of lower-order structures in general, including the formal type.

In the preceding chapter I had noted that, traditionally, both the early radical critics of society, such as Marx with his fig-leaf theory of democracy as well as the nineteenth-century advocates of political realism, had rejected the existing legalistic tendency to consider formal structures equivalent to a description of actual institutional operations. Nevertheless, even after the presumed effects of formal structures came under suspicion, political science has not failed to continue to take them into account. In practice, few students of politics really believe that the legally prescribed organs of government or other political organizations have negligible effects on how people behave or institutions operate.

Evidence for this abounds. For example, every beginning text in comparative politics somewhere finds it necessary and desirable to describe the formal arrangements of the constitution, written or unwritten, on the assumption that understanding of the particular unfamiliar political system would otherwise be deficient if not impossible. Indeed, most current studies of politics at least take for granted the formal or legal framework within which behavior occurs and organizations operate, and account is taken of this structure as common sense dictates. On rare occasions direct arguments are even made on behalf of formal institutions, including political structures, in face of transparent tendencies to neglect them. As one scholar has put it,

In constitutional democracies, that is to say in states where the law is obeyed (Watergate notwithstanding), formal arrangements are an important, and in the immediate run an independent, factor in determining the way a political system operates. I do not say that they are the most important in all cases, just as I do not say that behavioural patterns will not reshape them indirectly in the long run through formal amendment. All I claim is that they deserve study in their own right.[1]

Despite this reluctance or inability to reject an interest in the formal (legal) arrangements of a political system, however, very little effort has been directed toward demonstrating their empirical effects, at least with the same careful tools of research devised for other areas in politics. Nonetheless, as I have just noted, in practice the claim seems to be made in the literature, if only implicitly, that structure, in the formal sense, may have a definable influence on political behavior and processes. The presence of this claim requires us to review and analyze, at least briefly, where we stand in the arguments on its behalf.

Do formal structures affect political life? If so, how? And why should we expect this to be the case?

Formal Rule Structure versus Formal Empirical Structure

In chapter 5 we have already noted that formal structures are part of that component of the political system that I am referring to as the regime. In that chapter I suggested that the term *formal structure* is typically used in two senses, and these are not always distinguished: first, to refer to the fact that a concrete set of political relationships—the empirical or behavioral structure—may have arisen out of a legal document, such as a written constitution, or from some ritualistic procedures, and that it may conform to them; second, to refer not to practices or behavior but to prescriptions or rules for the behavior of political actors in their relationships to each other, that is, to our desires or expectations about how given institutions ought to be organized and how actors ought to behave as participants in them.

To the extent that formal structure refers to a design for patterns of political interaction (rules, our second meaning) rather than to the actual political arrangements, the question of the influence of such a rule structure must ultimately reduce to the way in which rules make themselves felt in a political system. If so, their effect will depend in part on the special types of rules that they represent and the consequences that they have.

It is clear from our discussion in chapters 2 and 5 that insofar as formal structure refers to the rules prescribing behavior, what we are dealing with, in effect, is part of the structure of a political culture. In this sense, a constitution in and of itself does not represent a pattern of actual relationships among members of a system; it is not a political structure in the behavioral sense in which we have been using that term. Rather, it represents only a patterned set of rules which may or may not reflect the actual interactions of the members of the system. If this is so, to the extent that reference to the formal structure points to the rules by which members of the system are expected to organize their political relationships, the formal structure can be described only as part of the structure of the political culture, not of the structure of behavior. As I have already indicated in chapter 5, where it is necessary to distinguish these two meanings of formal structure, I shall refer to the one as formal rule structure and to the other as formal empirical structure.

If we accept this distinction, then whenever we talk about the influence of a formal structure we will be faced with two ancillary questions. Do we mean, what is the effect of a pattern of rules as laid out in some constitution or legislation? Or do we mean, what is the influence of the actual patterns of behavior to the extent to which they conform to those formal rules?

Usage in the literature does not often discriminate clearly between two such possible meanings. We cannot always be confident whether, when speaking of formal structure, the intention is to focus on the prescriptions (rules) as contained, say, in constitutions or statutes, the cultural aspect of structure, or on the actual behavior found in the structures so defined, that is, on the extent to which actors, in their interactions, conform to the political rules. Most of the time reference is to an indiscriminate mixture of both kinds of structures, thereby leaving much analytic as well as empirical ambiguity.

As I have already suggested, in chapter 5, what distinguishes those rules that are often ambiguously spoken of as formal structures is that they are explicitly stated in some written or other formal manner, whereas many other kinds of rules, informal ones, guiding political behavior, simply evolve through custom. For example, informal norms may regulate the organization and activity of interest groups, the way political leaders behave (the definition of their roles) as they seek to acquire and hold a following, or the multifarious activities in which members of a legislature engage on a day-to-day basis. Formal norms or prescriptions, on the other hand, are of a special kind partly because of their origins. They frequently represent those aspects of political life that for one reason or another the politically relevant members[2] of a system consider salient.

For example, constitutional rules specifying the ways in which a legislature is to be organized, its powers and its relationship to other organs of government often represent a historic compromise negotiated after severe social conflict. The reduction to writing serves as a public way of confirming the historical settlement and as a means of inducing dissidents to abide by it. Many written constitutions, such as those associated with the French and American revolutions, are of this sort. Yet since the parties to the agreement recognize that no settlement can be for ever, rules are usually introduced to permit change from time to time. However, participants are not likely to welcome easy changes of hard-won settlements; hence the customary presence of restrictive amending procedures in most written constitutions.

The question for us, however, is: Do such structures described by the rules or the empirical structures which arise in conformity with them, have any independent political influence? Do they give the occupants of the positions defined by the rules and the structures so created any power they would not otherwise have?

The answers are not so straightforward as we might expect. After all, the revolt against legal formalism in political science at the end of the nineteenth century would seem to suggest otherwise. The realists thought they saw formal structure as an empty shell with effective power being located elsewhere. Confidence in this wisdom of our predecessors has been reinforced by the now prevalent conviction that the formal description of a political system, as provided in constitutional prescriptions and the formal powers of positions defined therein, tells us little about how people behave and institutions do in fact operate.

In posing the issue in this way, we can immediately see the analytic difficulties in which we find ourselves. If we think of formal structure just in terms of *rules* of behavior, then to establish its influence we would need to demonstrate the way such rules do in fact shape the actual behavior of members of a system. That creates no special problems (unless we assume that political culture is only a reflection of activity and not a guide to it). However, if we conceive of formal structure as the actual patterns of interaction in which members of a system engage, then to speak of the influence of formal structure would lead us into studies such as those of Dye and Cutright. We would need to demonstrate first, that the structure we are looking at is formal in the sense that it conforms to the rules laid down for such classes of behavior and second, that it influences other aspects of the political system, such as policy outputs.

When put in this way, the problem is clear. In rejecting the influence of formal structure, the nineteenth-century realists were clearly thinking of structure in a cultural sense, as constitutional rules. If they had differentiated analytically between formal rule structure and formal empirical structure, it would have been impossible for them to have condemned both kinds as ineffectual, out of hand. They could feel confidence in their judgment about formal structure because, conceived implicitly as rule structure (expectations of how power was to be divided), eyeball observation, say, for Bagehot, Ostrogorski, or Woodrow Wilson revealed the disparity between what the rules said about where political power should lie and its actual location in the British Cabinet for Bagehot, in party "wirepullers" (bosses) for Ostrogorski, and in legislative committees and political parties for Wilson.[3] If, however, they had discriminated between rule and empirical structure and had conceived of the latter as faithfully reflecting the former, then they would have been called upon to explain why the formal empirical structure retained no influence. Indeed, it was left to Lord Balfour, who wrote the preface to one of the later editions of Bagehot's *English Constitution*,[4] to chide the author for having neglected to point out that despite the truth of what he had to say about the disappearing power of Parliament, the Crown (part of the formal structure) still retained some residual authority through its prerogatives as well as its popularity. And these powers were not to be ruled out as insignificant.

The Influence of Formal Rule Structures

Bearing in mind these differences in the two possible meanings of formal structure, let us now scrutinize more closely just what we might mean when we speak of the influence of these two kinds of structures and the relationship between them.

Despite the earlier realist disaffection from legal formalism (as found in constitutional arrangements) in favor of actual political processes, we can readily appreciate why, within any given political settlement, there may be purely instrumental grounds for a formal prescription of structures. Complex social systems, of the kind found in most large-scale societies at any rate, require such prescription if they are to extend the bounded rationality of individual members and to create an influence structure for the attainment of political goals.[5] That is to say, the specification of desired political relationships (formal rule structure) may be vital to facilitate the achievement of organizational goals.

Formal Rules in Organizations

In this respect a political system itself takes on some of the characteristics of a formal organization. Long ago such organizations were defined as "a planned system of cooperative effort in which each participant has a recognized role to play and duties or tasks to perform. These duties are assigned to achieve the organizational purposes."[6] Through rules that provide for specialization and a division of labor, a hierarchical arrangement of offices, and specification of operating regulations, an organized collectivity has the potential for achieving goals that would otherwise elude its members if they were to act as individuals, severally or in the aggregate. At the same time such a set of formal rules represents a way of seeking to create incentives for its membership to cooperate and to provide a means for socializing them to the purposes and ways of the organization. The rules formally define the desired organizational structure. Traditionally we refer to the table of organization and the prescriptions for the various offices so specified as the formal organization or structure.

Political systems are not formal organizations, however, even though they do share some important characteristics of the latter. It has been said that "formal organizations are characterized by explicit goals, an elaborate system of explicit rules and regulations, and a formal status structure with clearly marked lines of communication and authority."[7] Political systems are clearly different in some important respects. They are seldom organized *ab initio* rather than arising out of some preexisting system; they seldom state their purposes as explicitly as most organizations; they are often able to define and redefine their purposes continuously; they usually command a range of resources for mobilizing their membership unavailable to most organizations; unlike the restricted membership of most organizations, they embrace the whole of a society; and finally, political systems have a monopoly of coercive means at their disposal, usually denied to organization, as Weber has instructed us.

Aside from such differences as these between political systems and formal organizations, formal prescriptions, as special kinds of rules (usually called constitutional) in political systems, may have consequences not too different from those in formal organizations. The primary source of influence of formal rules in such organizations lies in the fact that they endow the occupants of defined positions with a power of legitimate action denied to others. The formal rules permit the organization to recruit and socialize members, shape their incentives and sanction their behavior. In this sense it seems plausible to argue that in political systems formal structure, as formal prescription of arrangements, may influence behavior.

Formal rules in political systems

Reasoning by analogy, then, it would seem plausible to expect formal rules to play a role in political systems similar to the one they play in organizations. In fact, in one of the few attempts to search out systematically the sources of influence of formal structures in political systems—interpreted here as formal rule structures—Duchacek arrives at similar conclusions about the latter. He argues that national constitutions, clear instances of what we normally consider to be formal rule structures, create what he calls "power maps" or organizational charts.[8] Where they are not solely a façade, they serve to encode power relationships at a given time and place. Different power groups will vie for an arrangement of the formal rules to assert and freeze their own privileges and status. The rules represent a resource on which to fall back in case of challenge. They also serve to recognize publicly, and thereby reinforce, the various statuses of power groups. In short, they represent the historic settlements I mentioned earlier.

This assessment by Duchacek presupposes that in those societies in which rules are explicitly enunciated for the organization of political power there already exists a predisposition among members to accept the legitimacy—and, in legal systems, the legality—of such rules. In the end, whatever influence the occupants of offices established by formal rules can exercise derives from the prior readiness of the members of the system to accept the rules as binding and, similarly, the actions these rules permit or encourage. This flows, of course, from the cultural nature of the rules.

In effect, it is an argument for the efficacy of the general political culture, first, in obtaining compliance with certain cultural rules, in this case, constitutional norms; and second, in strengthening the hand of those who obtain power through the behavioral structures so created and, thereby, in giving such political arrangements effects that they might not otherwise have had.

The kind of organizational power acquired by those who hold formal office plays so important a role in political systems that we give it a special name: political authority. In most societies persons are socialized to the acceptance of authority in the political sphere, at least so that when formal rules are laid down or changed, the expectation prevails that members will obey those who act within those rules.

If, for no other reasons, the empirical structures associated with formal rule structures thereby acquire high symbolic value through political socialization processes. Members are given an incentive to comply with the injunctions of those who hold positions of formal authority, although such compliance will vary with the degree of commitment to legalism or constitutionalism.[9] As Duchacek points out, constitutions may operate as important instruments of socialization to the extent that they encourage the acceptance of constitutionally defined structures and processes and the attitudes and practices embodied in the fundamental laws of the system. The very process of forming a constitution may be used to help generate mass interest and participation in the new regime, perpetuate an existing consensus, or forge a new one about goals and means for the system. Thereby, we may add, constitutions, and celebrations of their anniversaries and the like, may also serve as important mechanisms of control for a given class or leadership. They are system-maintaining structures by and large; constitutions do not provide for their own compulsory change even though they may allow for change through specified amending procedures.

If it were not for these and other presumed potential effects, constituent assemblies and their debates would be lacklustre affairs rather than, very frequently, dramatic power struggles searching for historic compromises among contending social forces. It is because of their potential significance that civil and international wars have been fought over control of the formal symbols of power, what Charles Merriam called the *credenda* and *miranda* of power.[10] However much we may consider constitutions to be window dressing, they are often thought worth fighting for as possible cloaks of authority, especially of a legitimate kind.[11]

Thus, in these various ways formal rules are presumed to influence the way in which members of systems interact with each other. The behavioral structures so created derive part of their efficacy from the special status that constitutional rules have in most societies. In this sense, then, behavioral structures which conform to those specified in that part of the structure of political culture that we call formal rules, affect the way the system actually operates. This does not account, of course, for those instances in which formal rules have little influence on the actual structure, as, say, in those systems where the constitution may be merely a sham.

Rational Modeling and Formal Rule Influence

In public choice theory we find an alternative way of accounting for the efficacy of formal rules in bringing about behavioral conformity with them.[12] In effect, this approach presents a way of accounting for the influence of rules, as part of the structure of culture, on the structure of behavior. Here the force of rules does not arise from their symbolic properties or from such processes as socialization, but from their appeal to self-interest.

The implications of public choice theory for the influence of formal rule structure rests on two assumptions. First, from a policy point of view, this theory informs us that it is useful to assume that persons will be more likely to follow their own self-interest than the interest of others. If so, then the second assumption is that to attain given policy goals we must be able to design institutions (which, by any definition, includes structures in our sense) which give individuals the necessary incentives to behave in a preferred way.[13] In this sense, institutions are not just outcomes of past rational choices and, therefore, exogenous constraints, such as boundaries that channel behavior. Rather, they are more likely to be creative forces, devices for motivating and channeling behavior, for appealing to the individual's sense of self-interest to follow one path rather than another. The task of institutional design or of informal changes in structures which occur as reactions to historical circumstances is to offer individuals some self-interested motives for conforming to new, prescribed structures. Institutional change, and that part of institutions which consists of formal rules, thereby become creative facilitative forces.

In applying a theory about the efficiency of the market place to institutional arrangements, where only those persons who are given an incentive to and do indeed follow their self-interest are likely to succeed, the argument here clearly follows the path of neoclassical economics.[14] This line of reasoning suggests, for example, that to prevent the dominance of any one organ of government—such as the legislature, executive, or courts—by the other, optimally prescriptions for structural arrangements (formal rule structures) would succeed only through provision of an appropriate set of incentives. Thus, if the founding fathers of the United States hoped to prevent the tyranny that comes from one branch of government dominating all others, they had to be clever enough to invent a set of structural arrangements such that legislators, executives, or judges would find it in their respective self-interests not to seek to control decision making by themselves alone. And it is argued that this is precisely what is remarkable about the institutional arrangements (structural devices) that were invented in the American Constitution.[15]

By implication at least, shortcomings in this strict rationality approach in explaining conformity to prescribed institutional arrangements have been noted. Hardin, for example, has pointed out that the influence of constitutional rules depends not so much on incentives or sanctions as on the interest of the participants to abide by a constitution once it is in place.[16] For him, the binding effect of a set of constitutional rules rests not on any specific incentives or sanctions built into the rules themselves but on the inclination, once a constitution is in place, to avoid the considerable effort and potential conflict that it would take to undo an existing hard-won settlement.

In other words, as has been frequently noted in the historical literature, once a major power struggle among contending social forces has been resolved through incorporation into a basic document or understanding—what we usually call fundamental law—the effort required to open up, once again, the very issues so painfully resolved is a major force militating against change. However, it is not only that the rules give individual members an incentive to conform, as rational modeling would have us believe. That may indeed be one important influence at work. But conformity may also be encouraged and reinforced by the resources in the hands of those who see themselves as profiting from the rules. Those who have the status, power, money, and skills, or the support of politically relevant members of the system, may use these resources to their own advantage and to block the actions of others.

Thus, political power, outside of and independent of any incentives shaped by constitutional rules, may dictate or compel conformity to the formal rule structure or may, in turn, give birth to efforts to change these structures or even to behavior to evade them through the creation of various kinds of informal structures. Indeed, the vast body of research in political science, beginning with the twentieth century, has been devoted to exploring these very informal (crescive) behavioral structures that seem to have arisen to serve these interest. Another way of putting this is that perhaps the incentives in the Constitution did not work as effectively as the founding fathers might have wished, otherwise there would have been little need for many of these informal patterns to arise!

However, whether self-interest is driven by an incentive to follow rules, for whatever reason, or whether it derives from other sources, such as the nature of the power structure (behavioral), is not an issue vital to our immediate concerns. The important point is that even a rational-modeling approach to formal structure, interpreted as rules, has argued for the latter's influence on behavior.

Evidence of Effects of Formal Rule Structures

As we have seen, folklore, plausible reasoning from general knowledge and even rational-choice theory converge in claiming that formal structure as rule structure probably does have important consequences. What, however, might count as evidence for the influence of formal structures, viewed as rules, on actual patterns of behavior, that is, on empirical structures? Here we are on less certain ground.

For example, the mere fact that certain empirical structures which exist in the political system seem to be associated with the presence of given kinds of formal rules need not be accepted as evidence that the former are the consequences of the latter. Even where the actual relationships in a system correspond to and articulate with the formal prescriptions, this fact in itself need not represent irrefutable evidence about the effects of the formal rule structures. We might well ask: Is it the set of formal rules that *produces* the conformity, or do the rules only *reflect* accepted convention or power relationships, just as the English common law did not create new laws but was presumed only to codify existing practices? It is the latter, what we might call a *reflective* relationship, that may be the case, say, in Norway, as we noted in chapter 5. There a legalistic culture encodes existing practices into law so that when we know the formal rules, as incorporated in law, we have a faithful description of actual relationships.[17] The legal prescriptions are less of an influence on behavior than they are a reflection of it. In our terms, formal structure, interpreted as prescribing rules, simply echoes the empirical structures as they come into existence. In itself, the mere fact of correspondence between formal structure and actual patterns of behavior need tell us little about the direction in which the effects flow.

Formal rule structure and formal empirical structure may combine in a number of ways, and these are seldom investigated systematically. For example, we may find a mutually *interactive* effect in which both prescribing rules and actual patterns of interaction depend on reinforcement from each other. In some systems the formal rules may be decisively *determinant*. We have numerous suggestions that in a compliant, legalistic, or traditional culture, obedience to formal injunctions will be more probable;[18] or that in a system in which members distrust and fear one another and instability threatens, there may be a tendency to stick with the letter of the law.[19] In such instances formal rule structure would seem to be influential for or causative of behavior. We also find the frequent observation, however, that many constitutions are not worth the paper on which they are written. Here formal rule structure would be merely *epiphenomenal*, although attempts by dissidents in the USSR, since the 1970s, to use their constitution on behalf of the legitimacy of their claims to individual rights should now give one cause to reconsider. In addition, during the 1980s, in the period of *perestroika*, it has been helpful, given the desire to transfer real power to the Supreme Soviet, to have had the legal authority already present in the constitution.

Only in extreme cases are the facts clear enough, even at a purely interpretive level of analysis, to decide whether the formal rule structure is reflective, interactive, determinant, or epiphenomenal with regard to formal empirical structure. Otherwise there is usually inadequate *prima facie* evidence to establish the nature of the relationship between formal structure, interpreted as a set of explicitly enunciated rules or prescriptions, and formal structure viewed as actual patterns of political interaction.

Relation of Rule Structure to Formal Structure

As we have noted, when speaking of formal structure we may have one or both of two things in mind: relationships simply defined or specified in formal rules— a part of the cultural structure—on the one hand, or formal behavioral structure on the other. In normal use, the term *formal structure* seems to apply—and for this reason, ambiguously—to both. At times we seem to use it to refer to a set of rules intended to design a set of relationships in the real world. At others we seem to mean it also to include the resulting empirical structure, that is, the behavior and arrangements flowing from the existence of those rules. In short, the idea of formal structure may refer simultaneously, hence ambiguously, both to an intention as well as to the extent to which that intention is fulfilled in political practice.

If we accept this interpretation, formal structure is at times reduced to an elliptical way of talking about the *structuring* of political interactions through the use of formal prescriptions or rules. In this usage the study of the effects of formal structure would be one way of encouraging the search for generalizations about how codified cultural rules influence actual behavior. In other words, we begin by identifying the rules as the formal structure. We question the nature of their effects. To the extent that they do influence actual political relationships, we are then comfortable in describing these as part of the formal structure; insofar as they fail to do so, we identify a cleavage between the formal structures and those that actually prevail.

It would appear that normally this is probably what we are about when we search for the effects of formal structure. It is a way of directing our attention to the relationship between formal political rules and their consequences for actual political practice, that is, between formal rule structure and formal empirical structure, in our terms.

Influence of Formal Empirical Structures

Constitutions as one kind of formal prescription of political relationships may have such influence as we have discussed. However, this still does not address the issue as to whether formal empirical structures themselves have a separate and independent effect on, say, political outputs or on the operation of other significant parts of the political system. For example, do structures, such as those formed by governmental offices, agencies, and the like, set up through constitutional authority, necessarily partake of this influence?

At one time, we scarcely need to be reminded once more, political science rebelled against the notion that such was the case. This was the basis of the realist rejection of legal formalism at the end of the nineteenth century. But reconsideration has revealed what was never intuitively forgotten, at least by what we may call the "old" or traditional institutionalists in political research.[20] Formal empirical structures, that is, those positions and collective units such as chief executives, legislatures, administrative organizations and courts, defined by and conforming to formal rules, need not be powerless simply because they conform, to one degree or another, to formal prescriptions. Indeed, the very opposite may be the case. At times prescription itself may serve as a power resource, a possibility that used to be neglected if not forgotten.[21] What we need is a way of discriminating between the varying degrees of autonomous power given by the possession of formal authority (an office or political position defined by formal rules) and the dependence of the formal office-holder on the influence of others.

In one of the earliest and now classic studies of community power structure, Hunter seemed to be skirting this very point.[22] He brushed aside the notion that city councilors of the community under investigation, occupants of the formal authority structure, could have any effective power. He saw them largely as pass-throughs or mouthpieces for other, more influential members of the political system whose informal power dominated the formal authority of those in office.

Recognition of some independent effects of the formal political structure bears important implications for an analysis like Hunter's. Even though municipal councilors may at times be puppets in the hands of invisible power brokers, it could be difficult to get them to perform acts that exceed the capacity of their offices or even that critically threaten their support base in the community. As occupants of offices in a formal structure of authority, councilors have a power of last resort, an ultimate barrier of resistance available to them, under certain circumstances, that Hunter neglected.[23]

By the very fact that council members are required to authenticate or legitimate decisions, they may thereby retain some residual power. In the end, they alone can make decisions that are accepted as binding by the community. Even if the effective power relationships are such that power brokers call the tune, they, the power brokers, cannot themselves make these *public* decisions. Given necessity or opportune moments, this authority may become a source of action, independent of outside power groups, and, therefore, a source of the councilors' own relative autonomy, to borrow a phrase more likely to be applied to national than to local political units, but nonetheless equally appropriate.

The formal empirical structures, then, need not be ciphers on the power scale. It is always a question of discovering the conditions under which any inherent influence of the political authorities may be able to assert itself, that is, the conditions for asserting the autonomy of formal officeholders. On a small scale, in a democratic system the fear of losing popular support may compel an elected official to use the power of an office even against the interests of influentials in the environment on whom the officeholder may traditionally depend. On a larger scale, Bonapartism is a well-known phenomenon in which social forces are balanced off against each other so that those who have nominal legal power may also exercise the actual power. Despite Lenin's fig-leaf theory of bourgeois democracy, presumably it is because of such inherent potentials that antagonists in political and social revolutions struggle so desperately to gain the cover of legitimacy offered by the possession of the formal trappings of authority.

In addition, on this basis, of what we may call legalism—a variable, learned propensity to abide by rules considered to have the force of law—formal behavioral structure has been thought to have several other characteristic effects. For example, it is thought to provide stability and predictability for the actions of individuals whose powers are assigned by the structure. Once we are able to identify a person's position in a pattern of relationships within an organization or political system, we automatically acquire significant information not only about the possible constraints that the rules impose on that person's behavior but also about his or her formal opportunities for action. This is the reason why we normally find it important to orient ourselves in unfamiliar political systems by finding out who has the nominal power to act in situations of interest to us.

That at least is a base line from which to start. To know that a person is a chief executive in a political system, for example, does not begin to tell us everything or most of what we would want to know about the role occupant's actual power and behavior. It does, however, give us a starting point. Knowledge of a person's position in the authority structure permits us to make some informed guesses about his or her possible power. We can better appreciate this point, perhaps, from the converse. If there were no formally defined positions related to each other, at least in larger scale political systems, or if such rule-defined relationships were constantly changing, we would be uncertain about how to locate ourselves in a new organizational setting.[24]

Formal empirical structures may not only have legitimating and stabilizing consequences. They may also facilitate the performance of tasks, a consequence of structures to which I earlier drew attention. They often open up opportunities for action to the occupants of relevant formal positions, kinds of opportunities that otherwise might not be available. Legal rules providing for the initiation of money bills in the more popular legislative branch of many governments are a case in point. The power acquired through location in the formal structure may also at times prove to be a critical source of actual control. The residual prerogative of the British Crown or its representative in the Commonwealth—for example, the discretionary power to request a political leader to form a government and thereby decide on the next prime minister—has been used in the past, and may still be used in the future, to intervene in party politics in Britain, Canada, and Australia. The veto authority of the American president and the legal right of Congress to investigate, however much limited by the realities of power relationships, are undeniable additional sources of influence, as long as the predisposition in the system to accept legal legitimacy prevails.

These comments do not exhaust the possible consequences of formal empirical structures. The latter, for example, often give certain persons access to and control over information generated in a system from which other members of the system may be excluded. They may give certain persons power over agenda setting and the establishment of priorities. And they may offer high visibility to persons occupying certain formal roles. Control over information and the establishment of priorities as well as high visibility are all powerful resources in any political system, but especially in a mass society.

Even though all such presumed effects of formal behavioral structures arising out of constitutional prescriptions seem plausible enough—their signaling of saliency and of an instrumental, socializing, stabilizing, facilitative, and controlling capacity—the fact is that most of our research has done little except to repeat and accept past folklore on the matter without subjecting it to more rigorous testing. Furthermore, by its sheer mass the research that automatically assumes the importance of formal empirical structures has seemed to suppress any sustained theoretical or empirical effort to explore the question.

There is perhaps one exception, and this is to be found in the analysis of the so-called autonomy of the state. Whether we consider this an exception will depend largely on our definition of the state. There are literally hundreds of such definitions,[25] so there would be little point or value in even trying to review them. There is one conception, however, that does fit in with our notion of formal empirical structure, that specified by Nordlinger.[26] He set out to try to test what he took to be a hypothesis that was gaining prevalence in neostatist political analysis: that the state could achieve varying degrees of autonomy. To do this he found himself forced to develop a conceptualization of the state and of the idea of autonomy that would permit any investigator to demonstrate this empirically.

He clearly sought to cut through the ambiguities and complexities of various abstract conceptions of the state, especially as found in the neo-Marxist literature, where, as we saw in chapter 6, the idea of the autonomy of the state originated. Indeed, he rejects these alternative views as well as past liberal interpretations, perhaps for the very fact that they do not lend themselves readily to empirical application through conventional methods of nonhistorical research. In any event, he chose to identify the state as a set of actors in the roles of public officials, a group that is clearly part of the general political elite.[27] As such, these are clearly a subset of the political authorities, in my use of the term. That is to say, they are occupants of roles formally specified in a political system. In other words, the state for Nordlinger is part of the formal empirical structure about which we have been talking.

In an effort to operationalize the term, he argues for a particular conception of autonomy that is somewhat different from the notion of *relative* autonomy that Poulantzas had in mind and presumably that much of the current neo-Marxist literature may intend. For Nordlinger, autonomy is couched in preference terms. Autonomy of the state is determined by the degree to which the preferences of the public officials coincide with or diverge from those of the general public. To the extent that divergence occurs and public policy reflects the preferences of the state actors, the latter can be said to display a degree of autonomy from the general public over whom they govern. [28]

We need not pause at the moment to discuss how this conception of the state, by neglecting the broad structural limits within which the state operates, succeeds in eviscerating the state problem as it is posed in the Marxist and neo-Marxist literature. Nor need we take into consideration whether Nordlinger, without taking such constraints into account, could ever successfully argue his point that the state, as arbitrarily defined, does achieve a measure of autonomy, as he interprets the latter. The important thing for us is that what he is trying to do—a point easily lost sight of in any assessment of his book—is to reveal the extent to which a significant part of the formal empirical structure of a political system may have independent effects on political outputs. To that degree he has the distinct merit of being one of the few who has squarely faced up to the task of trying to devise a method that would permit testing for the effects, on public policy, of formal empirical structures.

We may draw at least one unambiguous conclusion from this discussion: the effects of formal structures, interpreted as behavioral rather than cultural structures, are not likely to be nil all the time. Such effects are variable. They may range from total effectiveness, as it were, to the epiphenominality that some of the earlier realist critics seem to have implied. Just where any given formal empirical structure stands on this continuum is a subject that requires close scrutiny through research techniques that have yet to be explored fully in the discipline.

Whatever the evidence for such effects, however, the issue here is that the case has been made repeatedly for the influence, on political behavior, of formal structure, whether conceived as relationships prescribed by rules or as behavior in rule-defined relationships. There are enough plausible instances of rules influencing the real political world to justify considering that such observed or lower-order structures as formal ones, in the rule as well as the empirical sense, can be neglected at our peril if we hope to understand political behavior and institutions.

The Case for Structural Effects

From our discussion in this and in the preceding chapter it is clear that whether or not lower-order structures have any effects will depend on at least three factors: first, on what we mean by structure, that is, whether they are formal or nonformal; second, on which among such types of structures we select for inquiry; and third, on the conditions under which they operate—at times they may have no effects, at others, they may have effects in varying degrees. In short, it all depends on what we identify as a structure and the prevailing conditions.

Clearly, this does not say a great deal by way of permitting us to identify in advance those structures that are indeed important because of the consequences they do or are likely to produce. What this discussion does, however, is to make clear that observed or lower-order structures, in all their variety, may be of significance for the functioning of political systems and that, indeed, there are ample and plausible *a priori* grounds, buttressed by a small body of empirical research, for thinking this to be so.

Much attention has been paid during the 1980s to the possible effects of structures. We have already noted the beginning of this interest, in the early work of Robinson and Dye, and the considerable literature following upon it. We have also seen another upsurge in this concern during the 1980s as the United States prepared for the celebration of the two hundredth anniversary of its Constitution. This event revived interest in formal structures created by constitutions and the extent to which and the means through which the institutions they establish do succeed in bringing about their intended effects.

For the very reason that I have paid so much attention to the effects of structures, it is important to remind ourselves that this is **not** the matter that has stood or will stand at the heart of our concerns in this book. Without question it is an important issue, even if political science has yet to develop clear-cut answers about the exact nature of that influence and about empirical methods for its study. My pursuit of the matter may indeed have seemed something of a diversion from our main concern. It does, however, seem a necessary one if we are to be convinced of the value of looking at other issues about observed structures. If we had plunged directly into a discussion of our central concern, the possible factors shaping these structures, we would have lacked the minimal reassurance at the outset that we were engaged in a worthy and meaningful enterprise.

This means that for those who are primarily interested in the outcomes of structural variations—and they are legion in the discipline—I will be addressing a logically prior question, as I have repeatedly stressed: How can we explain or understand the emergence of varying kinds of observed lower-order structures, especially those that are embodied in regimes? No one would deny the importance of trying to trace out the effects on public policy or on other aspects of the political system of one or another kind of such observed structures. Yet, without understanding how we happen to have these structures in the first place, or what their limits are, we would be left severely handicaped in any effort to modify their effects. In short, the search for the determinants of these structures is inescapable if we are to be able to use our knowledge of their effects to attempt to alter or control these very effects themselves.

8

Structuralism as a
Theory of Determination

In the previous chapters I have argued that the interest of political science in structures is not accidental. Recent history has made us aware of the crucial significance of structures in shaping the course of events. I have concluded that structures are not physical things or separable empirical phenomena, out there in space and time. They appear in nature not as concrete, independent entities but only as empirical properties or aspects of such things. We have explored the kinds of components that we may consider to be included within political structures. And I have suggested that in political science there is ample evidence—even if it is not unchallenged—to point to the specific significance structures may have on the way authoritative decisions for society (public policies) are made and on the content of these decisions themselves.

Finally, although we have not yet found the need to settle on any single conception of structure, there is one at least that is acceptable for working purposes, if only because it is the most prevalent in the discipline: Structures are stable patterns of relationships among political actors and collectivities. For reasons already given and yet to be developed, I have proposed calling these kinds of structures lower-order (observable) in contrast to higher-order ones.

In this chapter I shall for the first time confront my central problem directly: To what extent and in what ways are we able to account for the enormous variations in lower-order political structures around the world as well as historically? We can hope to explain such variability only if we have some method for approaching the question with at least the beginning of a theory about political structures. As we have already seen, one of the major shortcomings of the way in which our discipline has dealt with political structure has simply been its failure to conceive of structure as a central issue. At the theoretical level, out of sight has also meant out of mind.

In this and the following chapter I shall examine briefly the special approach to structure called structuralism, one of the most influential attempts in this century to come to grips with lower-order structural variability. We shall wish to discover the extent to which structuralism presumes to help us understand how and why observed structures display the variability they do and some of the relevant limitations of structuralism as an approach.

Regardless of the extent of its influence, however, I shall try to show that whatever its many variants—and they have been legion, cutting across literary criticism, history, linguistics, psychology, mathematics, and philosophy, as well as the social sciences—structuralism did make at least one central contribution, one that has not as yet been sufficiently well recognized, let alone acknowledged or proclaimed in political science. It did have the effect of elevating the issue of structural determination—the effort to account for variability of observed structures—to high visibility as a central theoretical issue. It must be credited with more than that, however. Despite its many deficiencies, which have appropriately led to its decline as a mode of inquiry, it still has the merit of offering us a major clue about the direction in which answers to this central theoretical issue in political analysis may lie. In effect, it has steered inquiry toward higher-order structures, and toward one in particular: the structure of a system as a whole.

The fact that structuralism has succumbed to wholesale criticisms from a variety of directions—from deconstruction, actor-oriented philosophies, and postmodernism in general—can easily blind us to this insight. We shall find that despite the demise of structuralism due to its transparent theoretical, methodological and philosophical limitations, it did in fact manage to shed new light on how and why observed structures display their obvious variability. We shall find that one of the major and hitherto unrecognized contributions of structuralism is that it pointed us in the important and potentially rewarding direction of the role of whole systems. In doing so, I shall be maintaining, it put its finger, however unwittingly, on an inescapable conceptual device for exploring and possibly explaining this critical but neglected factor, one that can make a central contribution to the comprehensiveness of our understanding of the factors that account for the variable shapes of lower-order structures.

Indeed, it will help establish the initial plausibility of turning to whole systems for this purpose; it will also open up for us the possibility of finding in such whole systems the higher-order structure to which I have been referring. Let us now begin to look at how this comes about.

The Essential Contributions of Structuralism

During the 1970s, as discussed in chapter 2, a newfound interest in structure arose in the social sciences other than political science. Somewhat earlier, during the 1960s, there took shape a particular way of analyzing observed social relationships, now well known as structuralism. This school of thought, directed explicitly to understanding the nature of structures, had its origins in Europe, in France in particular, under the inspiration of Lévi-Strauss in anthropology. Yet, despite its widespread popularity there and its specific concentration on structural variability as its central problem, structuralism never did manage to send deep roots into American social science, aside from a modest penetration by the Marxist version. This is a point to which I shall return in the next chapter.

French structuralists were scarcely the first, or the last, for that matter, to raise structure as a major theoretical problem. From the very beginning of social inquiry, in classical antiquity, structure has commanded serious attention. In the present century it has led some sociologists to argue that structural phenomena lie at the heart of their discipline. In contrast to the commitment to process (especially group conflict) among social scientists in the late nineteenth and early twentieth centuries, many contemporary scholars would follow Parsons in virtually defining sociology as the study of social structure and would trace this focus through Plato and Aristotle to Comte, Marx, Spencer, Durkheim, Tönnies, and Simmel, and on to the present.[1] Bottomore and Nisbet, for example, interpret sociological inquiry very broadly as the discovery of "the fundamental, constitutive, *structures* into which the sensory data of human observation and experience fall."[2]

It would be stretching the notion of structure too far, however, and would strip it of its conceptual utility to suggest that even if we were correct in describing structure as the domain of contemporary sociology, this puts the discipline in the structuralist camp, as Bottomore and Nisbet seem to do. Not all preoccupation with structure need be structuralist in nature. Rather, at the very least, French structuralism represents a special theoretical point of view in the analysis of structure. As such, it has many well-known distinctive features, and only some of these are particularly relevant to our analysis of the sources of structural variability.

For example, structuralism is antisubjective. The human actor with his or her conscious intentions and purposes has little causative power in the structuralist scheme of things. Structural causation lies at the core of social explanation. A structure has an objective existence which seems of its own nature to be able to influence outcomes. Unlike Parsons, for example, structuralists do not find the need to show the processes mediating between the subject and the objective structures. The social system is energized and changed as the structures themselves, through their own internal processes, come into some kind of contradiction. It is for this reason that structuralism has been said to be antihumanist, a legitimate charge if we do not allow the terminology to imply that structuralists must thereby be deficient in their sense of compassion or humanity.

Structuralism at times has also appeared to be antihistorical. In the hands of some of its practitioners, such as Lévi-Strauss and some Marxists, society is interpreted in synchronic terms. Lévi-Strauss seeks to match society to the underlying structure of the human mind; and the structural Marxists such as Althusser and Poulantzas are most interested in discovering the effects of the "social formation" (their terminology for the basic structural components of society) on social appearances. Marxist structuralists are less likely to be insensitive to social change through time, but Lévi-Strauss never really came to terms with it when operating strictly within the limits of his structuralism.

As I have mentioned, the antisubjectivist and antihistorical character will not be matters of central concern for my analysis, however important they might be if we were assessing the full implications of this point of view. Rather, as we shall see in a moment, structuralism has another characteristic that points up its unique contribution to the understanding of structure. It instructs us to search for a possible underlying logic in society, a body of relationships concealed from ordinary observation and yet critical for ordering the social relationships we usually observe. For our purposes it is this aspect of structuralist thinking that distinguishes it from most prior thought about social structure.

Because of its unique theoretical position, as a specific way of approaching the study of structure, I shall hope to give it here the attention that it has richly deserved from political science but which has as yet been denied. In this and the next chapters I shall show first, that it has the special merit, from our point of view, of directing our attention to what are essentially higher-order structures, for explaining lower-order structure variability; second, that it suggests the need to call into question the premises of comparative (cross-country) research in all the social sciences, including, implicitly, political science; and third, that it encourages us to consider the link between structural theory and systems analysis, an insight that will prove critical as my own analysis proceeds.

Structural Analysis vs *Structuralism*

Geological Explanation: Surface versus Deep Structure

Let us now turn to the way in which structuralists handle the connection between those social relationships visible to ordinary observation, normally called structures but rejected as such by structuralism, and their explanation in structuralist terms. If major proponents of structuralism such as Lévi-Strauss, Althusser, Foucault (in an early phase), Chomsky, Leach, and Piaget have agreed on very little else, most of them have shared at least three premises in their search for social structure.

First, the main task of the social scientist lies in seeking to account for the observed reality among social relationships, or lower-order structures, to use my terms. These observed relationships, the major dependent variables of structuralist analysis, are designated from time to time as surface structures, empiricist relationships or superstructures (Poulantzas), social appearances, or abstracted forms of social relationships (Lévi-Strauss).

Second, we cannot understand these visible and apparent social relationships in society in their own terms. We cannot hope to explain such structures solely by reference to other similarly observed phenomena. Rather, an adequate explanation of them requires us to move to a different level of abstraction, to the way the whole social system works.

Finally, although the language that the advocates of structuralism use varies enormously, they all share a similar "geological" imagery[3] about structure: We must differentiate between "deep" and "surface" structures and show the critical influence of the former on the latter. This constitutes the central ontological point of all forms of structuralism: that there is an apparent or empiricist reality—the readily observable social relationships—and that it is ordered by what are called underlying relationships, also known as deep structures, theories, infrastructure, base, and models.[4] The appearances only represent the product of a succession of transformations that can be traced back to this underlying structure, however invisible the latter may be.[5] Some relationships are immediately given or accessible to our senses; these are the surface phenomena which, however, can only describe social ties. Other relationships, which "underlie" these surface phenomena, and which are invisible, need to be discovered through reflection and abstraction. They, and they alone, can explain why the observed relationships take the form they do. These underlying relationships represent the true "structure" of a society.[6]

The nature of this so-called underlying structural determinant differs significantly among alternative conceptions of structuralism. For some it takes the form of an explanatory theory; for other it is just a model; for still others, a method. All proponents of this view, however, agree that this infrastructure, regardless of how it is conceptualized, does impose its own inescapable imperatives on the observed reality. In effect, this geological metaphor, the layering of social phenomena into "deep" and "surface" structures, points to different theoretical models or methods, depending on the particular interpretation, in terms of which the variable structures of such surface phenomena as social relationships, culture, or attitudes can be understood.[7]

For Lévi-Strauss, for example, by all accounts one of the dominant figures in the structuralist movement in Europe in the past, this deeper structural stratum is an intellective quality, inherent in the human mind, something of the nature of a Kantian categorical imperative. It seems to compel individuals to order their social relationships in the form of complementary opposites. The apparent multiplicity of kinship ties within nonliterate societies throughout the world, for example, Lévi-Strauss would interpret as historically conditioned permutations and combinations of this tendency of the mind (an object different from the brain but otherwise not identified[8]) to view things as mutual and complementary opposites. He felt his theory weathered the acid test of reality when he claimed, through it, to be able to solve the hitherto intractable avunculate problem in anthropology.[9] It was indeed that presumed solution that helped to dramatize and popularize his form of structuralism.

For Althusser and his prime disciple in political science, Nicos Poulantzas, the structure which represents a level of reality behind empiricist social relationships is composed of the general mode of production in a society. For them, social practice, including observable political relationships, are results of the way the mode of production operates in given historical circumstances. Their "hidden" reality or "structure" is this mode of production, a set of causal forces which alone can adequately explain perceived political relationships.

For Freud, who is counted as an early and unwitting structuralist, the explanatory model consisted of the relationship among such constructs as the id, ego, superego, and libido. It is the structure of their relationships that Freud used to explain the observed or surface neuroses. No amount of describing and comparing neuroses (the analogue in psychiatry to the comparative method in political science, perhaps) or of explanations based on life experiences could by themselves give us an adequate understanding of them. In Freudian theory, we have to refer back to the way in which the underlying elements combine.

This final point, then, concerning a geological imagery, is about as far as different structuralists would go in their agreement. They share the idea that there are underlying, inferred relationships which are decisive for the character of observed structure. As Glucksmann points out, they would agree further that these layers are not of equivalent importance but "are linked by relations of determination."[10] As we shall later see in passing, however, even though all would share the view that structure, in the strict structuralist sense, does shape the observable reality, the epistemological status of the underlying structure receives different interpretations depending upon whom we read.

Structural versus Structuralist Explanation

For purposes of our analysis of alternative conceptions of structure, let us for the moment accept this ontological discrimination between surface and deep structures proposed by the structuralists. To simplify references to this view, as I have already pointed out, I shall follow Glucksmann in calling it the *structuralist* approach.[11] On the other hand, again accepting her lead, to signify the prevalent conventional efforts to understand observed structures in terms of other observable phenomena, at the surface or empirical level, as the structuralists would put it, I shall use the term *structural analysis*. This will differ from the *structuralist* analysis in that the former will look for explanation by comparing social relationships and other kinds of phenomena at a "surface" or "empiricist" level.

Thus, the structure of partisan attitudes might be correlated with social class, childhood socialization, regional location and the like. Both the *explanandum* and *explanans* tend to be at a similar level of observation. In political science we are accustomed to pursuing such explanation either within or across systems. Its basic premise is that explanation requires us to show the logical structure within so-called apparent or empirical relationships.

The shift in thinking as we move from structural analysis to structuralism is clear.[12] In declaiming against the utility of seeking to explain surface phenomena through the use of the normal comparative methods of research, that is, in their own terms, structuralists, such as Lévi-Strauss, took as their starting point the notion that experience with such phenomena make them immediately accessible to the senses. Lévi-Strauss was here reacting to the research of the British school of anthropology led by Radcliffe-Brown. The latter held that social structure had the same ontological status as the individual; both are concrete reals. Hence, social structure and its component social relationships are as directly observable as the human beings engaging in them. For Radcliffe-Brown social structure is a "concrete reality . . . of actually existing relations at a given moment of time, which link together certain human beings. It is on this that we can make direct observations."[13]

Lévi-Strauss accepted, as his own point of departure, this claim by Radcliffe-Brown about the observability of the social relationships. But for his part Lévi-Strauss declared such observed structures to be inadequate as a valid basis for explaining their form. They are only surface phenomena, immediately accessible to the senses, but of little explanatory value. To penetrate the sources of their variability, he argued, we need to go beneath these changing empirical phenomena, which he designated as social relationships, to the constant relationships underlying them and which give rise to them. For these alone would he allow the name social structure.

There is more to the difference between structuralism and structural analysis, however, than their ontological status. The idea that an understanding of structures requires us to distinguish between observable surface and invisible deep or underlying structures is only the beginning of the differences between the two approaches. Furthermore, from our point of view, it is not necessarily the most interesting one, especially since its epistemological validity is subject to serious challenge, as we shall see. Other differences are more helpful in enabling us to appreciate the real contribution that structuralism can make to our understanding of political structures.

Although structural and structuralist analysis share the view that any kind of structure must represent a stable set of relationships—hence their denotation as structure—beyond that they part company. In the first place, for structuralism if the parts of an entity are to constitute a genuine structure, they must not only have the stability associated with structures, but these parts must hang together or cohere in some way. They must constitute a set of interdependent elements. A defining characteristic of such sets is that they tend to persist as a group of elements with relatively stable relationships. This aspect of structuralism led to the explicit notion among many of its major proponents that society and its parts must be interpreted as a *system* of behavior or institutions. For Lévi-Strauss, for example, if a set of elements is to constitute a structure it must exhibit "the characteristics of a system."[14] For Piaget as well, "structure can live only in systems."[15]

In the second place, structuralism is holistic, that is, the underlying structure is a property of the whole system. It postulates that we cannot understand the behavior of any part except by seeing it as dependent on all other parts. We cannot understand a part in isolation. The whole entity or object being analyzed conditions the way in which any part operates. For Lévi-Strauss, for example, the true nature of (observed) kinship structures, especially the so-called avunculate problem, as we have already seen, must elude us, if we just continue to look at and compare the role of the uncle in different tribal societies.[16] The variable role of mother's brother is understandable only in the context of a complex set of relationships involving a much larger specifiable number of kin. This one part, the uncle, can be understood only in the context of a whole set of kinship ties. Put in another way, the specific "surface" structure—the role of mother's brother in relationship to mother's son—is derived from the way the whole system of kin relationships, the "deep" structure, functions.[17]

This holistic systems outlook of structuralism leads it along paths that are very different from those normally taken by purely structural analysis. In structuralist terms, if we are to grasp how the parts of a system cohere, that is, how the system operates, we are led to search for the rules, regularities, or laws that govern the interdependence of the parts. By understanding such operating rules of a system, we will have an explanation as to why a system reveals itself in the way it does, that is, why it takes the particular form (surface structure) it does at any given time and place. Such operating rules of the system will lead it to produce those variable visible or empirical results, in the form of social relationships, that typically draw the attention of *structural* analysts.

From this point of view, efforts of structural analysts to understand these variable empirical phenomena in their own terms alone must founder. To use a political example, it is as if they were saying that we may seek to explain the persistence of democratic structures, as we typically have done in the past, by reference to their association with such factors as levels of economic development, popular education, and energy, number of telephones *per capita*, ideology, and traditions.[18] The structuralists would hold that this kind of correlational analysis can give us only an incomplete if not superficial explanation. From their point of view, the very social relationships for which an explanation is being sought, through all kinds of comparative and correlational analyses, cannot be the results of one or another factor with which they may be empirically associated. They are rather the products of the nonvisible rules by which the system as a whole is ordered at a given time and place.

In the third place, once we have discovered these rules that underlie a given system—such as Lévi-Strauss's rules of complementary opposites, indigenous to the mind, or Althusser's laws of the mode of production, or Piaget's laws of transformation[19]—we have nothing less than a method (for Lévi-Strauss) or a special theory (for most other structuralists) of a particular system. Such rules inform us about the way a system transforms or rearranges one of its states or forms (observed structural patterns) into another. We end up with a theory of the transformational rules or "laws" of the system, even though Lévi-Strauss would demur at the notion of calling his analysis anything more than the description of a method. When we know the rules that order the parts of a system and lend it coherence, we have a theory about what it is that structures the system or, as Piaget puts it, we have a model of the system.[20] I shall later critically assess the extent to which, Poulantzas, as a structuralist Marxist, successfully implemented this aspect of the structuralist project.

In brief, then, the logic here is evident. In the strict sense of the term, *structure* for structuralists does not refer to the form or properties of social relationships descriptively abstracted from behavior but to "the principles of operation underlying observed data."[21] To use terms common among structuralists, it is an abstraction that lies at a "deeper" level, hence the geological contrast between surface and deep structure.

Structure: Product versus Process

It is clear that in giving the underlying structure a causative force, the structuralists introduced an interesting and unexpected change in the meaning of the word *structure*. In effect, they have transformed it from a noun into a verb. They are no longer looking for historical products called structures, as it were; they now want to know how a system gives rise to or, we may say, orders or *structures* patterns of behavior (so-called surface relationships) within it. The noun *structure* takes on the meaning of the verb *structuring*.[22] As in generative grammars in linguistics, the search for that elusive geological formation called the underlying structure becomes a search for the determinants of the visible surface structures, for that which, in my terms, structures the lower-order structures.

As normally pursued in political science structural analysis has been concerned with the properties of objects called their structures, that is, the abstractable forms or patterns that observable political relationships may take at a given time and place—party structure, governmental structure, interest group structure, role structure, and the like, the varieties of which we looked at in chapter 5. Without denying the existence or significance of such structural objects, in the hands of the structuralists these surface structures decline in explanatory significance. They are now to be considered only derivative from the transformational rules of the specified system under given spatiotemporal circumstances. They represent products of the way in which a system operates under such conditions.

That these surface structures themselves may have second order effects is not denied by the structuralists. What is being asserted, however, is that these surface structures are themselves effects. Hence, their own effects are just second-order ones, effects of effects, as it were, of the way the system operates. On this assumption, structuralism directs us to attend to the more important issue of the processes through which a system structures its parts and thereby produces the social relationships (empirical, surface, or observed structures) of the particular historical circumstances. Structuralism, in distancing itself from structural analysis, takes the form of a theory of structural causation or determination.

Clearly, structuralism succeeded in shifting the focus of the analysis of Radcliffe-Brown's observed structures to the structuring force of the system in which such structures are imbedded. As we shall see in the next chapter, at least in the hands of Lévi-Strauss, structuralism thereby fired the opening gun, in European social science, in the continuing battle between conventional statistical or correlational and asymmetric causal analysis, on the one hand, and a more holistic approach as found in a systems orientation, on the other. We need to pause, therefore, in the next chapter, to explore this connection between structuralism and systems analysis to see how this has, in the end, served to prepare the ground for a better understanding between lower- and higher-order structures in the political system.

9

Structuralism, Systems Analysis, and Higher-Order Structures

Implicit in the structuralist idea that the underlying structure of a system yields certain visible relationships is a conceptual orientation that is not always clearly understood even by structuralists themselves, or is simply overlooked by them. If all that structuralism is saying is that we need to view an object of reference as a system governed by rules, it would not have gone far beyond an idea that has appeared elsewhere in the history of Western thought. From time immemorial we can find the notion of system, at least in the social sphere. It was familiar to Aristotle and in recent years it has been a concept common in economics, sociology, and political science, if not all the social science disciplines. There, as elsewhere, it has always conveyed the idea of interdependence and in some fields, such as economics, of synchronic laws describing this interdependence. Insofar as these ideas were adopted by structuralism we cannot look upon them as a novel discovery.

Something more is implied in structuralism, however, even though it has seldom been recognized for the critical innovation that it represented. This added implication is closely linked to the systems revolution in thought that occurred after World War II. In this chapter I shall pursue this hidden connection between structuralism and systems analysis for the light that it will help shed on the nature of higher-order structures as a possible fundamental determinant of lower-order political structures.

Systems Analysis as Dynamic Theory

The clue to the concealed but vital message that lay hidden in structuralism is a conceptual orientation found explicitly in systems analysis. Let us turn to this mode of analysis to remind ourselves of one of its central and operative characteristics.

What distinguishes modern thinking about systems from past usage of the idea is a very simple yet profound discovery: that social systems do something. They just do not sit there with their elements interacting and changing their states through displacement from some presumed equilibrium with a tendency to return to the initial point of equilibrium, a time-honored idea borrowed from economics which in turn had long ago borrowed it from the natural sciences.[1] Nor is a system just a collection of elements that are interrelated or that covary in some determinable way, the normal assumption of social science in investigating any set of phenomena. Rather, a system represents a kind of dynamic coherence among the parts that generates special properties. One such property, feedback, for example, that is

118

central to most social systems, makes it possible for a system to learn and to regulate itself and thereby to provide for self-maintenance and goal-oriented change.[2]

The most significant overall result of a variety of specifically system properties is that they permit the system as a whole to get something done. In the case of political systems I have identified these products as binding outputs, special kinds of decisions that are usually accepted as authoritative for the given society. In this special sense a system is not just a congeries of parts; it is an interdependent set of activities which, because of its special dynamic properties, *produces or generates* something, including the reproduction or change of the relationships among its own parts.[3]

Simple as this idea of production or generation is, its discovery in recent years, **before** the emergence of structuralism,[4] brought about a fundamental transformation in the way we can look at social phenomena such as the political system. The question need no longer be: How do the elements of such a system interact, covary and influence each other? This of course remains a sensible procedure for certain purposes. But it is now central to ask: What does the the system characteristically produce through such interactions, and how does it continue or fail to do this? How does it transform something, the raw materials (in political systems, demands and support), into something else (in political systems, public policies, for example)? In formal terms, we may view systems as wholes that create something new out of the raw materials put into them, that have the capacity to regulate themselves, and in which the relationship among the elements are organized by dynamical or transformational rules.

It is this very property of political systems which the revival of the idea of the state in the 1980s sought to signalize. From this point of view, it is not a matter of bringing the "state" back in; as I have already indicated, the state has never really been left out, at least by political science. It is rather a matter of changing our focus so as to be able to understand what the "state" does and why it does this. This new focus derives, of course, from a growing interest in policy analysis from the 1970s on.

To get at this central performance characteristic of political systems, what the so-called systems revolution in thinking did in political science was to direct attention for the moment away from the obvious parts of the political system—from its interest groups, organizations, legislatures, parties, electorate, and the like, and their interrelationships—to a more abstract set of elements. I have suggested these elements are inputs (demands and support), outputs (public policies), conversion processes, and feedback.

The reason for this shift in focus in the case of political analysis is obvious. Not all political systems need have such immediately observable and variable parts as groups, parties, electorates, etc. These may be just a function of a given time and place. If, however, the elements central to the analysis of political systems are to be valid *general* theoretical concepts, they cannot be uniquely associated with a given set of historical circumstances. They must be found in all political systems, regardless of time and place. And if the relationships among these elements are to be of the same theoretical status, they too will have to be covered by universal laws in the sense that the relationships among inputs, outputs, and conversion processes will have to transcend any specific time and place. Of course, such laws have not yet been discovered; they are an aspiration, not a fact. But without them no general theory or model of the operations of political systems will exist either. All we can be left with is a historical description of the workings of a unique system or class of systems under given historical circumstances.[5]

Systems Ideas in Structuralist Analysis

What I have been saying about the nature of systems analysis may look like a digression from our main purpose. In fact it is not. As I point out later in this chapter, recalling the fact and nature of the systems revolution in our mode of thinking since World War II helps us to understand better the popularity of structuralism in Europe, however short-lived it has been. Unwittingly structuralism has been a response to and part and parcel of the systems transformation in the thought modes of our own day.

Evidence for Systems Orientation in Structuralism

Evidence for this affinity to systems analysis lies precisely in the fact that we find in structuralism the central ideas of system as well as of production. Although most structuralists have not adopted what might be called a full-fledged systems orientation, nonetheless, as I have already noted, the point of departure for most of them is the notion that society does constitute a coherent, interrelated whole and, what is for us critical, that this whole does give rise to or "produce" varying kinds of "surface" phenomena.

For example, Piaget, who was much more sensitive to the systems assumptions of structuralism than most other structuralists, pointed out that not all "forms" (so-called empiricist patterns of relationships) constitute structures in the special sense used by structuralists. Structures in this latter meaning are for Piaget "forms of forms."[6] By this, Piaget meant that the surface patterns of relationships (forms or structures) are themselves "formed" or ordered by an underlying pattern of relationships. Together with all other structuralists, he would reserve the word structure for that underlying form (form of forms) that produces or determines surface forms.

Thus, for Piaget, structure in this strict structuralist sense is a kind of form that is not just a pattern of behavior. Rather, it is a kind that constitutes a set of dynamic relationships among interdependent elements, and these permit the set to be self-regulating. As he himself explicitly formulates it,

> A structure is a system of transformations. Inasmuch as it is a system and not a mere collection of elements and their properties, these transformations involve laws: the structure is preserved or enriched by the interplay of its transformation laws. . . . In short, the notion of structure is comprised of three key ideas: the idea of wholeness, the idea of transformation, and the idea of self-regulation.[7]

Structure in this sense is equivalent to a self-regulating system characterized by transformational laws.

Few other structuralists would feel the need to go this far, perhaps. If they did there would be little difference between identifying a "deep" or underlying structure and describing the operation of the whole system of which the so-called surface structure or social relationships are part. They would simply be systems analysts, and this has not been their interest, desire, or intention. In going as far as he did, however, Piaget was able to draw the inference critical to an appreciation of the whole structuralist project. In his own words, structuralism postulates " 'deep' structures from which [empirical systems] are in some manner derivable."[8] That is to say, the particular form of the system or its surface structure can be derived from our knowledge of the transformational laws of the system. Although the specific term production does not figure significantly in his writing, the acceptance of the idea of transformation laws is just another way of saying that the underlying structure produces the surface structure.

As I have noted, Piaget was somewhat more cognizant of the systems roots of structuralist thinking. Others, however, such as Lévi-Strauss, in their more restricted use of a systems point of view are not so conscious of this implication (even though Lévi-Strauss does adopt the idea of system for rather limited purposes).[9] Nonetheless, even in Lévi-Strauss's thinking the mentalistic propensities of human beings, which constitute the deep structure, do give rise to (produce) surface phenomena. In turn, the latter will, of necessity, reflect the tendency to think in terms of mutual opposites.

Thus, as we noted in the preceding chapter, kinship ties are not just accidents of history or random arrangements. In the many nonliterate societies of the world, what appear to be enormously varied complex relationships among father, mother, brother, and sister are, for Lévi-Strauss, identical in their fundamentals. They are all informed or structured by the inescapable tendency of human beings to order their relationships in terms of complementary opposites. Mere comparison of kinship groups, as was the entrenched custom of British anthropologists under the leadership of Radcliffe-Brown,[10] had never been able to reveal this underlying order. As Piaget later expressed it, as I have already noted, what was required was a special effort of "reflective abstraction"[11] to detect that the apparent kinship ties, however varied they were spatiotemporally, had really been produced by the universal principles of the mind.

The specific notion of the production of surface phenomena by underlying ones appears only by implication in Lévi-Strauss. It is, however, explicit and self-conscious in the thinking of Althusser. The latter makes the idea of production central to his reinterpretation of Marx.[12] Each of the subsystems which Althusser identifies as part of the social formation (society)—the polity, ideology, economy, and scientific knowledge—as well as any given social formation as a whole are products of the underlying variable mode of production. And of course, as we shall see in our analysis of Poulantzas, contrary to the "economism" of vulgar Marxists, the mode of production includes much more than the economy. But regardless of the meaning of the concept mode of production, the fact that it is the determinative set of factors in shaping the historical character of a society indicates the importance for this version of Marxism—so-called structuralist Marxism—of the idea of production.

Structuralist as against *structural* analysis,[13] therefore, does not interpret structure as an object for description and explanation by reference to variables or forces at the same level of observation. Rather, as already indicated in the previous chapter, it leads directly to the search for theoretical statements about factors that may not appear to be closely associated with these apparent structures and that represent a higher or ordering type of structure. For structuralism, we have described the structure of a system when we understand those laws governing the interdependence of the parts of that higher-order system; those laws will explain how the system generates or produces the structures we see around us. The search for structure is transformed from a description of the stable patterns formed by the elements of a social system into a quest for the basic or higher-order elements of a system and the rules governing their relationships. As these relationships among the elements themselves change under different conditions, these rules determine the way the surface patterns of relationships are themselves reordered or restructured.

Limits of Structuralism as a Form of Systems Analysis

From this analysis, however—and this is the point here—we can also see that we ought not to confuse structuralist theories with systems analysis in the strict sense. Although a structuralist approach toward structure was a genuine innovation insofar as it used, as its foundation, the idea of system, it did not need to nor did it wish to go the full way. It is not and does not pretend to be a comprehensive analysis of any social system, modern or primitive. Rather, it tends to use systems thinking for a single purpose: to enable it to explain and understand better the nature of observed social structures. This is all that Piaget could mean when he said, as we have already noted, that "structure can live only in systems" or that surface structures can be "derived from" the transformational laws.[14] Structuralism is a theory (or, for Lévi-Strauss, only a method) that adopts a systems perspective only to the extent necessary to help account for the variability of social relationships, what I have been calling the lower-order forms or structures taken by a social system.

In the end, this is all that can be meant by structuralism. At most, it is a theory about structure that in most cases leans on or subsumes a systems perspective. Systems analysis, on the other hand, represents a way of understanding the functioning of systems in all respects and not only with regard to the determinants of their observed structures. For structuralists, the objective of theoretical inquiry is to be able to explain variability in what I have been calling observed or lower-order structures. This special purpose skews their theoretical thinking in a direction somewhat more limiting than the kind of thinking that might go into the development of a general theory of any system. In doing so, however, structuralists were responding, in this limited way, to the new systems mode of thinking that, by the 1960s, had already begun to make deep inroads into the intellectual life of the Western world.[15]

Structuralist Analysis as Explanatory Theory

In retrospect, then, structuralism is not so unique as it may have appeared when it first arose. Rather, in a real sense it may have been no more than a way of coming to grips with the systems revolution in thinking that was beginning to infuse the twentieth century.

The Theoretical Basis of Structuralism

Let us look at this suggestion a little more closely. It will help us understand why structuralism, as an intellectual tendency, should have had so profound an impact in Europe in the 1960s and 1970s, or at least in France, whereas it barely scratched the surface of American social inquiry. In the end I shall argue that the reason for this is that structuralism represents one of Europe's widespread ways of coping with the new concern for theory in social research that arose following World War II. Another such way was Marxism, but even it was caught up in the structuralist and systems waves. In the United States, however, we had already set out on a different path for expressing our renewed concern for theory in political science as well as in the social sciences as a whole. Hence, it is understandable that we should find structuralism a less than inviting mode of analysis.

If we set aside the claim that, in retrospect, Marx or Freud may perhaps be hailed as the first intuitive structuralists, Lévi-Strauss, as the founder of structuralism in the social sciences, was very much aware of the shift that his work represented toward theory, despite his puzzling insistence on interpreting structuralism merely as a new method. In fact he was so insistent on its *theoretical* nature that he misconstrued the character of the anthropology he was hoping to displace. For example, in declaiming against the utility of inquiry located at the level of surface phenomena alone—characteristic of British anthropology at the time as represented by Radcliffe-Brown, as I have already noted—Lévi-Strauss considered that such phenomena were immediately accessible to the senses and, accordingly, not theoretically determined. As I observed earlier, he would probably not object to Piaget's view that even though such phenomena are directly observable, apprehension of the true social structure requires some special effort of "reflective abstraction."

Clearly, the source of an interpretation such as this lies in the pristine positivist notion that the external world is directly apprehended by the senses, unmediated by our preconceptions. Although in the 1960s, when structuralism first became prominent, this interpretation of scientific epistemology may have had some plausibility, today we have learned differently. We are no longer hospitable to the illusions of early positivist ideas about immaculate perception, as Nietzsche put it. It has become clear that every effort at cognition involves some degree of prior recognition, organization, and abstraction from the total blooming buzzing confusion of the Jamesian world.

In that event, there can be no genuine cognitive difference between structural analysis and structuralism. Superficially, it may appear that the one is purely descriptive and the other theoretical. As I have suggested, however, the difference between surface and deep structure cannot lie in the fact that the one involves direct perception, unmediated by the mind, whereas the other, some kind of theoretically determined abstraction, as Piaget would appear to have it. The apprehension of both observed and "deep" structures requires abstraction. It is true that, *structural* analysts may believe they are describing and explaining specific structures (such as party or interest group structures) free from any theoretical presuppositions. In fact, it seems just a matter of common sense today to say that any selection of variables assumes at least some inarticulate broader theoretical premises. The fact that the analyst is unaware of them or even denies them cannot drive them away.

What can and does distinguish identification of the two types of structures is the degree of articulation or self-awareness. The one is often more intuitive and, in that sense, less theoretically informed and requires fewer conscious logical operations than the other. It is at a lower level of abstraction. That is why we may call some things directly observable. We have an immediately available organizing context into which to put them. The degree of abstracting effort is less. A chair is directly accessible to cognition not because it imprints itself in some pristine manner on our senses but because the theoretical context that organizes our external physical world for us comes so early in our intellectual development and is so familiar, we no longer need to make some special cognitive effort or to be explicit about it.

When, however, we look for less familiar and less concrete objects such as the structuralist's underlying structure, as the adjective underlying implies we need to be somewhat more self-conscious and deliberate about developing a theory to explain our constructs. This is especially true since we do not directly observe such underlying relationships. They can only be inferred, and we need rules to guide us in these inferences. This is the function of theory.

In short, when we move to the so-called deep or underlying structure, we consciously engage in developing a theory or model about the way in which the social entity in which we are interested generates or orders variations in those relationships which, because they are more familiar to us, are more accessible to our senses. We signalize this process by calling these more familiar objects, direct observations, the better to distinguish them from the products of our special cognitive efforts that result in less tangible constructs. Such a theory, in effect, serves to correct our observation and understanding of these more familiar relationships which will have been identified and interpreted according to the intuitive contexts in normal use. We have moved to a higher level of abstraction, and with it, to a higher order of structure.

Both structural analysis and structuralism are, then, in the end, theoretically based, but just at different levels of abstraction. The self-conscious character of structuralism reflects the shift in the direction of greater awareness of theory building that, after World War II, took place in European social sciences. Despite the efforts of Lévi-Strauss, Piaget, and others to see it as a new theoretical or methodological departure, in fact it turns out to be at the very least, and perhaps at the very most, a natural extension of normal science in the direction of theory formulation. It simply presents the argument for a theory to explain observed structures, proposing that they are not intelligible in and of themselves. Ultimately, they can be understood only in the context of a theory about the way in which the system of which they are part operates and produces these manifest results.

Varieties of Structuralist Theories

By this chain of reasoning we are brought to the conclusion that the search for a so-called deep structure, characteristic of the structuralists, reflects a newfound awareness of the role that theory plays in social research. It represents an effort to penetrate more deeply into an understanding of our direct observations (in this case, variable structures) by constructing a model or theory about their determinants.

Interpretation of the nature of the models or theories constructed for this purpose varies with the structuralist. Lévi-Strauss, for one, went so far as to reject the notion that the intellective structure of complementary oppositions, which constitutes the basis of his structuralism, is a theory or even just a theoretic construct or heuristic device. For him it is descriptive of facts representing the way the hidden reality— in this case, the mind—is organized. This is why at times he insisted on calling his structuralism not a theory but only a *method* based on the way the mind is organized. Yet at other times he did introduce more than a little ambiguity by also referring to his ideas as theoretical and, as we have seen, even calling his structuralism a model.[16]

If we are to interpret Lévi-Strauss to give his thinking maximal consistency, we would have to assume that he meant by this characterization something like a physical (rather than a theoretical) model or a template which determines the shape of social relationships, the surface structure, and thereby orders experience for us. In other words, for him the mind really *does* force us to interpret the empirical world as mutual or complementary dichotomies, much as a template creates the shape of a finished product.[17]

In the "mind," a highly ambiguous concept in his writings,[18] there *exists*, therefore, this unconscious and hidden structure which expresses itself in and projects itself on the behavior of human beings. The identification of this intellective structure is not just a heuristic device. The dichotomies that Lévi-Strauss finds in kinship relations, gustatory interests, and taboos and myths accurately reflect the propensity of persons to organize their world in this way. Hence, he does not present his ideas about the nature of the mind as a theory or theoretical model but as a description of reality. Yet, by any understanding of the notion of theory itself, since the organization of the "mind" is not directly visible, his conception of the way the mind operates as it deals with the external world must be considered theoretical, an abstraction. It represents a statement about the structure of the mind which can be tested only indirectly by seeing the extent to which it fits the world of behavior. And that is precisely what he did in the areas of kinship, food habits, myths, and the like. His thinking represented a shift toward a pronounced theoretical approach in anthropology, whatever questions we may have about its substantive merits.

Although Lévi-Strauss went to considerable lengths to try to prevent his view of structuralism from being considered a theory, other structuralists have not been so eager to distance themselves from the idea of creating a theory. Althusser, for example, explicitly presents his structuralism—even though he shuns the term itself—as a substantive theory about the organization of reality. For him it is confirmed through the fact that the "deep" structure—a term he also avoids—in the form of the mode of production, composed of such elements as labor, means of production, relations of production etc., has a verifiable existence and influence. The theory of the mode of production is more than even just a model to be used for heuristic purposes without any necessary existential claims. [19]

Piaget, on the other hand, seemed to be willing to embrace structuralism as either a heuristic model or a substantive, testable theory. In either form it serves to illuminate the relationship between observed phenomena and the way a system is organized. And most other structuralists are also prepared to accept the idea that they are engaged in model or theory building.

Structuralism as Limited or Specialized Theory

If, then, structuralism as practiced must be considered some kind of social theory, what kind of theory does it represent substantively? As one reads the work of structuralists it might appear that they are offering an alternative general theory of society. They appear able to apply their way of looking at the world to all its aspects—kinship, food habits, ideology, psychiatry, history, mathematics, etc. [20] As I have already indicated, however, we would be misinterpreting the nature of structuralism if we gave it so wide a range. There is a marked difference between structuralist theory and general theories or models in the social sciences. And this difference is apart from whether a theory is expressed in quantitative or formal as against the purely qualitative interpretive terms of most structuralist analysis. [21] The difference lies rather in the fact that for most structuralists the special purpose of the theory lies in the subject matter with which it deals.

As I have suggested, structuralism aims directly at an explanation of the variability in observed structures, what Lévi-Strauss calls social relationships. It represents not a search for a general theory dealing with the way society operates; rather, it begins and ends with a commitment to an understanding of observed (or surface) structures or patterns of relationships. For our purposes, this very limitation will become a source of strength.

It is for this reason that we must consider that even so astute an analyst as Boudon, for example, goes too far when he rejects the claim of the structuralists that they represent a new method and theory in social science. He interprets structuralism as little more than a form of normal theory construction in the social sciences. [22] He does not, of course, misconstrue structuralism when he insists upon its theoretical nature, despite Lévi-Strauss's protests to the contrary. But Boudon does it less than justice when he fails to recognize the difference between structuralist theorizing about the determinants of observed structures and other kinds of theories which deal either with the whole social system, such as that of Parsons, or with some other special aspect, as in economics.

Similarly, Piaget would appear to be in error when he interpreted structuralism as just an alternative theory for organizing our understanding of the world, one that is different from others only because it is cast in systems terms. Piaget's own model of society as a self-regulating, self-equilibrating, and transformational system, which he considers the essential message of the structuralist approach, goes far beyond what is implied by Lévi-Strauss and most other structuralists.[23]

As I have noted, the peculiar characteristic of structuralism, to the extent that it is true to its main ambitions as Lévi-Strauss initially formulated them, is that the idea of system is just a vehicle to permit the theorist to carry forward the search for an explanation of observed social relationships. It does not and was not intended to serve as a first step on the way to a full-fledged systems theory. But the fact that in seeking to cope with the rules that order the relationships in observed behavior, noted structuralists felt impelled to cast their ideas in systems terms, reveals that structuralist theorizing does represent a receptive response to the systems revolution in thinking that was already under way in other parts of the world.

The enduring value of structuralism, to be salvaged from its decline, lies in its insistence on highlighting the importance of an alternative way of explaining lower-order structures. It was not successful in presenting us with a useful theory of social systems. But it did at least try to offer us an alternative way of going about the search for an explanation of what we ordinarily identify as structures. Whatever fundamental weaknesses structuralism may have had, which have appropriately led to its decline, if not disappearance, it at least had the merit of raising the issues, first, of how we are to explain observed or lower-order structures, and second, of the kind of broader structures, which I have been calling higher-order ones, that we may need to look at to be able to discover an adequate explanation for the variety of visible structures.

Structuralism in the United States

Given these circumstances within which structuralism took shape, we may well ask: How does it come about that this intellectual movement took root in Europe during the 1950s and 1960s and flourished there but spread so little in the United States? We might have thought that, particularly because of the scant attention given to structure in American political science, the appearance of a word such as *structuralism* might have caught its eye if not its fancy. Faddism may not have been without some modest influence, it has been said, even in the very limited acceptance of structuralism itself in American anthropology.[24]

Part of the explanation appears to lie in the function that structuralism played in European thought. There, as I have suggested, one of its consequences was to bring into prominence the importance of theorizing for an understanding of society. In the United States, however, the social sciences were already sensitized to theory through the way they were evolving under their own initiative. Until the 1970s there was little inclination or need to look elsewhere for additional inspiration along the same lines. Hence, the theoretical message of structuralism held no special attraction. In other words, American social science may have seen the theoretical message in structuralism, which it did not need, and neglected the strictly structural message, which it did not see itself as needing, deceptively so from my point of view. Let us pursue this thought for a moment.

Today the history of structuralism is common knowledge. Originating in linguistics with de Saussure in the nineteenth century, it spread, after World War II, into anthropology and from there to history, psychiatry, philosophy, literature, and other areas of knowledge, especially in France. There, of course, Lévi-Strauss became its major and most visible architect and exponent, through anthropology. In Europe itself, however, even in France, it did not touch political science more than lightly except through the structuralist Marxism of Althusser and his disciple, Poulantzas.[25]

Despite its long tenure and diffusion in Europe it collected few adherents in the United States in any fields other than linguistics. Even in Lévi-Strauss's own specialty, anthropology, his influence reached across the Atlantic in only a small way. And prolific as Poulantzas was in his short life, his kind of structuralism managed to migrate into only a few areas of social science, particularly into those that have been influenced by class conflict analysis, and even there largely indirectly and diffusely.[26]

In one sense, structuralism in Europe was a reaction to the excessive empiricism in the first half of this century, especially among the social sciences with their enchantment with readily observed historical and other facts.[27] In another sense it also represented a movement away from large-scale philosophical speculation, such as existentialism and phenomenology, toward a more empirically oriented way of coping with the world of behavior. In addition, it seemed to offer an alternative Weltanschauung to that of the orthodox Marxism prevalent immediately after World War II. Like its alternatives, structuralism sought a way of transcending the facts of time and place by reaching for some enduring level of analysis of a theoretical character. It sought to present social science with a theoretical way of interpreting the world but one that, unlike existentialism or phenomenology, also claimed empirical verifiability and predictability as essential parts of its approach. Thereby it could demonstrate its accord with prevailing ideas about the empirical responsibility of those committed to the scientific method modeled after the natural sciences. In Lévi-Strauss's own words, his mode of analysis "demonstrate[d] that henceforth in the social sciences, theory and [empirical] research are indissolubly linked."[28]

The very strength of structuralism in Europe, however, as a bridge between theory and empirical knowledge enables us to grasp why it might fail to find a solid footing in the United States. By the mid-twentieth century, independently of the structuralist formulations but nonetheless in response to the same dissatisfaction with hyperfactualism and grand speculation, the pendulum of social research in the United States had swung far into the region of empirically oriented theoretical explanation.[29] This concern for empirical theory expressed itself partly in the development of a number of alternative general theoretical approaches such as decision making, functionalism, systems analysis, and rational modeling. However, of equal significance, it also encouraged a reexamination and reconstruction of our under-standing of the fundamental nature of scientific method.

One of the critical outcomes of this reassessment of scientific method was the realization that, contrary to earlier ideas, the heart of the scientific enterprise lay not in the accumulation of new facts but in the development of theory or models which would lead to facts for disconfirmation or otherwise. For some, indeed, a fact became not a datum given in nature but a theoretically informed way of ordering nature. For them theory is constitutive of reality.[30] Although most social theorist would not go that far, it is now taken for granted that, in research, theoretical presuppositions are unavoidable and that they help to shape our conceptions of reality. Equally important, it is commonplace to point out that today we generally accept the premise that adequate explanation must be go beyond facts to the theories that give them relevance.

Clearly, there already was substantial theoretical activity in progress in the United States and scientific epistemology was already undergoing important trans-formations by the time structuralism made its appearance in strength during the late 1960s and 1970s in Europe. This activity left American social science with little incentive to look elsewhere, especially abroad, for further theoretical inspira-tion that it did not need. In fact, we need only recall that, in the immediate post-World War II period, American social science was already providing innovative leadership both in theory and methods of research, a condition about which Euro-pean intellectuals were very much aware, however considerable the objections from some of them to the substance and direction of this leadership.

Accordingly, precisely what structuralism was doing for its European audience by awakening it to the role of theory, in the United States our revised understanding of scientific method and of the central place of theory in it had already accomplished for American social science. The latter found no urgent need to lean on or to borrow from structuralism as a way of strengthening its existing strong convictions about the value of theory.

Furthermore, a secondary message conveyed by structuralism added to the expectable disinterest in it among social scientists in the United States. As it was developed in the founding work of Lévi-Strauss, a systems conceptualization served as a fundamental premise, as we have seen. The salience of this notion, at least in this version of structuralism, was confirmed in the importance that Piaget attached to it in his own formulation. As we have also noted, structuralism for him was nothing more than a systems theory about an object such as society. We could even obtain further confirmation through detailing the way in which the system idea intruded imperceptibly into structuralist Marxism itself, at least as practised by Poulantzas.[31]

To be sure, systems analysis as a type of theory construction is designed to be more comprehensive than most forms of structuralism. But the point here is that as far as it goes, many variants of structuralism do adopt as a major premise the idea that society and its major components can be usefully interpreted as an interdependent system of behavior and institutions, as we have just seen. In short, structuralism became the historic vehicle, as it were, for reflecting what I have suggested was one of the most important epistemological transformations in knowledge in the twentieth century—the discovery of the utility of viewing all kinds of entities as systems, usually complex one, rather than as mechanical assemblies or aggregates or as simple sets of interacting elements.

In retrospect we can see that this absorption of a systems orientation occurred simultaneously in many different disciplines during the twentieth century. In the physical sciences, it highlighted the limitations of the decompositional method, inherited from Galilean and Newtonian science and articulated by Descartes, which glossed over those properties of wholes that cannot be directly inferred from a knowledge of the parts alone. In biology, it helped to transform the discipline from a description of organisms into a search for a theory about the way in which they function as homeostatic entities.[32] In communications it offered, through cybernetics, a way of explaining goal-oriented behavior or purposes that could rest on efficient rather than the final causes implied in biological functionalism and vitalism, and that gave the *coup de grâce* to any remnants of nineteenth-century vitalism. In linguistics, which Lévi-Strauss used as his guiding light, it redirected attention from spoken grammar and syntax to underlying linguistic rules at various levels of abstraction which produce the meaning of sentences. The surface structure of sounds may not be intrinsic to the communication of meaning. This structure is far more variable than the underlying structure of linguistic rules that give rise to variable forms of communication. And in political science, systems thinking has offered us an opportunity to interpret political life not just as a combination or collection of parts that interact with each other, but as a complex of relationships that does something, that is, produces outputs or policies.

Clearly, then, structuralism was not a unique and unaccountable occurrence of recent years. It has to be seen in the context of the new theoretical orientation toward social phenomena that was already underway in systems thinking. It seems to represent an early way in which European, or at least French, thought came to grips with this new and powerful intellectual invention of the twentieth century.

This very function of structuralism, however, as I have suggested, also helps to account for the relative disinterest that the social sciences in the United States showed in it as a specific theoretical approach linking up with a systems conception. Systems thinking itself had been under development for some time by the time structuralism came into full bloom, and systems theorizing had proceeded far beyond the elementary usage to which structuralism was able to put it. Hence here, even as a specific application of systems thinking there was still little incentive for theorists to turn to structuralism as a way of informing themselves further.

In the social sciences, therefore, structuralism had failed to make the voyage across the Atlantic successfully. There was little need for it either as an inducement to become more theoretical or, in doing so, to draw on its version of a systems approach. The resulting absence of structuralism from the American scene, however, could not help but contribute to delaying the time when American social science, including political science, would be forced to face up to the major substantive issue posed by structuralism: how to explain the nature and variability of observed structures. Although we need not engage in the debate about the otherwise dubious merits of structuralism as an intellectual movement, at least it had this one beneficial result: we can now use it to alert us to the value of directing our attention to that unresolved problem in social research. In turning a deaf ear, appropriately, to the theoretical and systems tunes that structuralism was playing, we failed to hear its more compelling *leitmotif* about the possible forces that shape observed structures.

Residual Value of Structuralism

We might wonder why, after the 1980s, American political science, and sociology in particular, should now be prepared, as I have suggested, to listen more attentively to what structuralism had to say, especially when they had virtually ignored it at the height of its popularity in Europe during the 1960s and 1970s. The reasons are not hard to find.

As I suggested in chapter 2, after the Vietnam War and the high hopes of the counter-culture movement it is understandable that social scientists should begin to pose questions about what there is in their environment that has made society, if not indifferent, at least resistant to fundamental change. If structure has any universally accepted meaning, it conveys at the very least the notion of constraint, as we noted long ago. Since their various moments of introduction into political science, the lower-order kinds of political structures we examined in earlier chapters—role patterns, differentiated social positions such as classes, organized interest groups and the like, and formal organizations—were always understood to limit or to influence alternatives for action. However, insofar as historical events of recent decades have encouraged students of politics to turn elsewhere, especially to fundamental constraints on behavior and policies (as well as to the effects of the "state" structure), where better could they look for an understanding of them than to those theories, such as structuralism and its Marxist versions in particular, that have made such constraints their central concerns? It is for this reason that I shall shortly turn to a detailed examination of the structuralist work of Poulantzas to explore what we can salvage from his analysis of the sources and consequences of such constraints.

The grammatical step that structuralism took between the two kinds of uses of the word *structure*—from a noun to a verb—is a simple and a short one. Yet it is this very step that has seemed to have profound implications for the alternatives in research strategies about structures, and perhaps in some instances even for the theories in the strict sense. As I have proposed, it can lead us to separate out patterns of behavior or relationships at two levels: the observed or lower-order ones and those higher-order ones on which they may be based. It leads us to ask whether there are higher-order structures, related to the way a system as a whole is organized, that can help us to explain and understand the variegated forms assumed by the manifest political structures, with their equally varied policy and other effects. It is this question that enables us to distinguish the essence of structuralism from structural analysis and to recognize the potential assistance of the former's residual and ultimate message for political research.

As we shall see, this salvageable help comes at a very appropriate moment in the evolution of the social sciences as a whole. By the 1980s a widespread reaction had set in against the deterministic character of structuralism and, indeed, of behavioralism in the social sciences in general, and in political science in particular.

Post-structural critics of the iron cage of structuralism are now commonplace: actor-oriented philosophy with its insistence on the centrality of intention in the rediscovered role of the subject; deconstruction with its virtual elimination of all causality; the revolt against all formal method itself;[33] and the rediscovery of the role of the subject in social action. In the social sciences, this reaction has revealed itself particularly in the rediscovery of the active role of the state.[34]

In a virtual torrent of publications, exhilaration with this new perspective has driven neostatists to elaborate their own discourse centering in the notion of the power and autonomy of the state, the degrees of freedom it has from societal constraints. As though confirming Abraham Kaplan's law of the hammer,[35] neostatists have discovered all sorts of effects that can now be brought to light through the application of this notion.

Peculiarly enough, this claim that the state, as one kind of variable political structure, may indeed have a substantial degree of policy independence from the rest of society, makes even more salient the position I am developing here. However free a "state" (regime, perhaps, in my terms) may be to create policy after its own preferences, the point of my argument is that this very emphasis on the relative freedom of the state with its capacity to implement its own intentions, carries a new danger. In hot pursuit of state effects, what may be lost from sight are the real structural constraints on the state itself.

Such constraints may be of two sorts. First, it seems strange, so many years after Marx, Durkheim, and Weber, to need to make the case, once again, that even the state cannot "make history out of whole cloth." Yet that is precisely what has become incumbent on us in face of this headlong rush to find, in the state, such extraordinary powers for bringing about political reforms and for managing the course of its own history and that of the world. There are limits; there are determinants; there are barriers. And among them, I have been claiming, is one that has yet to attract our attention, the higher-order structure, a constraint related to the political system as a whole.

Second, neostatists recognize, of course, that not all states are the same. There are those that are weak or strong, authoritarian or democratic, ideological or pragmatic, and so forth. Each type may produce its own characteristic domestic and foreign policies. If so, it is not only appropriate but essential to put the question as to how and why such "states" take the form they do. What factors shape their own structures and make them different?

There is no *a priori* reason to believe that even with its newly discovered autonomy, the varied structural forms of the "state" should have little or no effect on the way that it tries to use that freedom of action. To whatever extent the "state" may seek to pursue its own policy preferences, it is not conceivably able to liberate itself totally from society or from that part of society with which it is peculiarly enmeshed, the political system. In other words, structurally there is still likely to be a constraining relationship between the forms of "states" and the political system as a whole (the higher-order structure), and this can be neglected at our peril. This is a message that can and needs to be salvaged from the collapse of structuralism.

It is time now to turn to examples of the way in which actual political research has gone about seeking to account for the variability of political structures, especially those very "state" structures to which such freedom is being attributed. How have we typically accounted for the different kinds of "states" we find in the world? As we know by this time, *regime* probably represents the closest approximation to that notoriously elastic term, the state. Hence, my question is in fact directed to regimes. Accordingly, it is to sources of regime variability, as depicted in political research, that I shall now turn.

10

Comparative Research and Whole-System Constraint

Our discussion in the early chapters permitted us to return, in the preceding chapter, to the issue central to our analysis. How can we account for the enormous variability of visible structures in political systems? Structuralism, we saw, offered one answer: search for the relationship of these structures to some "underlying" structure of the whole system. It sought to establish the underlying organizing principle of operation of the whole social system. For Lévi-Strauss this principle took the form of complementary opposites, reflecting Kantian-like categories through which the mind manifests itself in social relationships. For Poulantzas, we shall shortly find, the principle involves a more complex theory of the structure of the whole social system. The important point is that for both the emphasis is on the need to turn to *the whole system* in order to be able to make statements about observed structures.

I shall return to this solution somewhat later in this chapter. First, however, I shall devote some attention to the way political science itself has conventionally sought to explain observed structures, when it has sought to do so at all. And since most interest in this matter has been shown in comparative research, it is to that area that I shall turn.

I shall conclude, first, that the normal routines of comparative research have led the discipline to identify patterns of political relationships and correlate them with other factors; and second, that this conventional approach of comparative research suffers from a severe and long-recognized handicap: it overlooks the broad context within which observed relationships prevail. This neglect is part of the larger handicap of political science in finding it difficult to cope satisfactorily, according to accepted scientific criteria, with such properties as the structure of whole systems, the largest of the macrostructures. Efforts to do so have had to be content with a degree of imprecision and ambiguity that affronts those political scientist who are accustomed to more precisely measurable variables—if only because they normally deal with theoretical matters on a smaller and, quantitatively, more manageable scale.[1]

Configurative analysis in comparative politics, a category covering the so-called case-study approach, which persisted tenaciously throughout the behavioral phase of political research, has always tried to make the same point.[2] Its message has been rather ineffectual, however, if only because it has had difficulty in escaping from a purely interpretive mode of analysis and from a single system focus, findings from which cannot logically be generalized to other systems. This has left its inquiries overly descriptive and particularistic.

As I have had occasion to point out more than once, the modest renaissance of Marxist theory in political science, in the 1970s and 1980s, can in large part be understood if we see it precisely as an effort to compensate for the failure of conventional political research to deal persuasively with what are viewed as the broader constraints—the mode of production, in the case of Marxism—under which all political processes and institutions operate. And the recent revival of comparative historical sociology,[3] particularly the quasi-Marxist and the Weberian interpretive types (neostatism), can be partly accounted for on the same grounds.

Each of these appeals for some alternative conceptualization of political processes—the configurative, Marxist, comparative historical—represents, in its own way, a response to the disquieting practice, in conventional political science, of neglecting the overarching structural constraints or macroscopic context within which political life functions. Formal Marxist approaches aside, however, they lack a sufficiently broad theoretical base to be able to cope with the character of these constraints. And as I shall later seek to show, through an analysis of the work of Poulantzas—the only comprehensive Marxist attempt to relate higher-order to observed political structures—even there the effort falls far short of what is promised, and required.

In the end, as I have already indicated, I shall propose that observed or empirical structures, noted by structuralists in particular, may be better understood as a lower-order kind of structure. As such they would be objects that are determined, shaped or limited by the political system, conceived now as a higher-order structure.[4] Furthermore, we need to put the empirical or lower-order structures into the context, not of bits and pieces of the political system, but of the system conceived as a complexly organized whole entity.

From this perspective, if we ever hope to be able to explain structural variability adequately we would need a theory about how the political system, viewed as a higher-order set of arrangements, influences various lower-order structures which we observe in such systems. Normal comparative research, which compares different observed structures, is an *ad hoc* method, and in and of itself it has not been able to provide a satisfactory explanation. As I shall now proceed to demonstrate, at best the so-called comparative method, with its correlational analyses, on the one hand, holds out the hope of explaining only a small part of the variance in observed structures; and with its familiar system-level approach, on the other, takes into account only isolated system attributes rather than whole systems. Nor do the self-conscious comparative historical versions of whole systems analysis fare much better.

Limits of Comparative Method

Comparative Research versus Comparative Method

For a number of decades comparative politics has, in effect, sought to generate methods that would help distinguish so-called cross-system generalizations from those that are clearly system-specific, that is, statements about relationships that are not affected by the overall character of the system of which they are part from those that are so influenced. I shall now turn briefly to that literature to see to what extent it can shed some light on the relationships between the overall structure of political systems and the forms of observed structures within them.

Some terminological underbrush needs to be cleared away first, however. Students of comparative politics customarily speak of their use of the comparative method. Insofar as they search for the effects of a system on political relationships, it would be through the use of this method. This leaves the impression that when we are engaged in comparative research we are using a special method of some sort.

It is arguable, however, whether comparison is indeed a special method or, whether, in its broadest sense, it is simply a description of conventionally conceived scientific method itself, as John Stuart Mill so convincingly argued.[5] If, however, we were to interpret comparative research as just an instance of the application of the normal comparative method inherent in all science, and if we were to reserve the phrase to refer exclusively to this normal method, we would still be left with the need for some term to alert us to the fact that we wished to conduct research across two or more political systems. This goes to the heart of the enterprise we call the study of comparative politics (even though the study of single countries foreign to the country of residence of the research worker also passes as comparative research, a well-known anomaly upon which I do not need to comment further).

We could, as some have proposed, restrict the terms *comparative method* and *comparative research* to that research in which differences between the properties of systems, as such, account for the differences we see within systems. Alternatively, we could agree to label this kind of inquiry as "cross-system" research and abandon the terms *comparative research* and *comparative method*. Traditionally, however, these twin terms have been applied to all research across systems even if the differences so noted refer only to the attributes of individuals with little or no attention being paid to the effects of the system as such. Hence, even if we did arbitrarily decide to renounce these terms, we would still be faced with the fact that the term *comparative method* is already so widely used in the sense described here[6] and is so deeply entrenched that there would seem to be little reason to abandon it as a concept with its current meaning and to try to use it exclusively to refer to all research that looks for system-specific effects. Nor, for that matter, even if we tried, would we be likely to have much success in getting others to do so.

Prudence, therefore, would seem to dictate that we ought not to try to discard the terms *comparative research* and *comparative method*—so long as we bear in mind that they should not be confused with "comparative method," in the broader sense, as a description of the nature of all scientific research. We need have little trouble distinguishing the narrower disciplinary from the broader scientific meaning of these terms; the context should readily make that clear.

Neglect of the Effects of the System as a Whole

One of the ultimate goals in the development of cross-system generalizations, presumably, is to help us formulate theories, or at least hypotheses, about why we find similarities or differences among various political systems. It would appear, therefore, on the surface at least, that the literature in this area should be of some help to us in our search for a way of understanding variations in observed structures (such as regimes, including roles, patterns of behavior, formal governmental structures, party and interest group structures, and the like) among political systems. In fact, however, comparative research tends to skirt if not obscure this issue. The reason for this is simple. Comparative research normally neglects a central problem: the extent to which differences in structural and other variables among political systems are due, not to individual system characteristics but to the specific character of the system itself, that is, to the impact of the system as a totality. As Sartre might have put it, comparative research fails to totalize the system.

It is not easy to explain why comparative research should shy away from systematic consideration of the character of the system as a whole. But that it has devoted relatively few of its resources to sharpening our tools for whole-system comparison cannot be denied.[7] Perhaps the important and necessary commitment to precision through measurement of phenomena has driven attention away from the kind of qualitative assessments that may still be the only means available for dealing with such macro-level objects as whole political systems.

Whatever the source of whole-system neglect, however, one methodological matter has loomed large in comparative research: that of the "many variables, small N,"[8] a legitimate source of concern in the search for universals across systems. For obvious reasons, where the variables to be related are many and the universe is small in numbers, statistical analysis is seriously handicaped. This has left the comparativists with the task of justifying comparisons among whole systems even if they do lack the capacity to draw generalizations based on valid statistical inferences. Many plausible arguments have been advanced for the continuance of comparative research despite its clear quantitative limitations. As Lipjhard succinctly concludes while working toward a restrictive definition of comparative method (differentiating it from experimental, statistical and case-study methods), the advantage of this method lies in "selecting comparable cases for analysis and achieving a large measure of control as a result of their comparability."[9]

Regardless, however, of how we characterize the nature of the method itself, the focus of comparative research in general has normally been on ways of discovering and confirming generalizations about specific phenomena—such as political participation, electoral systems, or party structure—that apply to two or more political systems. Discussion is narrowly limited to the search for universals of this sort, a kind that seeks to relate two or more variables within a system, to account for one in terms of the other and to show the similarity or differences of the relationships across systems. What is normally set aside is the extent to which political relationships may be influenced by the kind of system, *in the sense of the overall or total organization of the system*, in which they occur and the nature of that influence.

In short, we will search in vain, in the extensive literature on comparative analysis, for extended discussions of the specific effect, if any, of the whole system on any part of its internal relationships or for sustained inquiry about methods appropriate for attaining rigor in such analyses. Research remains largely at a single level or, as we shall shortly see, confines itself to isolated attributes of the whole system. And insofar as structures are the object of attention, the research remains at the level of the lower-order observed structures, accounting for them in terms of other structures or other factors at the same level. Only occasionally does it turn to the higher-order level that we might call the whole system—where the structuralists find their deep structure—as in the case of configurative analysis, to the limitations of which I shall return shortly.

Cross-System Individual-Level Explanation

It may seem strange indeed to argue that this limitation is an essential outcome of contemporary comparative research. We might perhaps have expected otherwise, especially since this research has been concerned precisely with comparing relationships in different political systems, at times for the very purpose of isolating the effects of such systems. This has been the driving force behind its very existence. How can we sensibly argue, then, that it has neglected the very concern that we might have expected to lie at the center of its efforts?

The apparent dominant interests of comparative research are somewhat misleading, however. To be sure, in its pursuit for differences occasioned by the nature of the political systems in which given relationships may occur, it has turned to two kinds of explanations: cross-system (same-level) individual-based as against system-specific (system-level) explanations. We might have thought that at least the latter kind of explanation would have directed attention to whole-system matters. As we shall see in a moment, however, this turns out not to be the case. The appeal to the system level can easily be deceiving. Neither mode of explanation offers a genuine incorporation of the whole system as an explanatory factor.

Let us look first at the cross-system individual-level explanation. It refers to those instances in which we seek to understand certain characteristics of individual behavior, usually aggregated for a population, by reference to other characteristics of the individual. The dependent and independent variables are both at the same level, that of the individual.

Typically, we find this single-level approach in voting research where, for example, we may relate the degree of political participation by individuals to variations in their education, social class, religion, or ethnicity. In instances such as these, a common dependent variable across systems—political participation by individuals—is explained by common independent variables across systems—the education, social class, etc., of such individuals. Similarly, individual feelings of anomie may be related to the breakdown of a sense of identification with the political community, attachment to political authorities and regime may be traced to early cathexis by children of personalized political figures,[10] violence may be seen to vary inversely with freedom to participate in and discuss political issues, education may be isolated as the most powerful determinant of political attitudes in various democracies, economic development (average wealth, degree of industrialization and urbanization, level of education, etc.) may be related to level of democratic development ("the more well-to-do a nation, the greater the chance it will sustain democracy"),[11] and so on.

In other words, what we are doing is seeking to uncover generalizations on a single variable across two or more systems, at the same level (of individuals). The implicit assumption is that the kind of systems in which the individuals are located will make no significant difference with regard to the subject matter under investigation or that system effects, if any, can be held constant. In each instance a common dependent variable found in a number of different systems—political participation, voting, feelings toward political authorities, the use of violence, and the like—is explained by common independent variables, in these same systems, which describe properties of the same individuals, such as their education, class, etc.

If all the variance of the dependent variable were really explained by such individual properties, an ideal in social science never attained, we could conclude that the differences in systems in which we find the individuals have little effect. The systems as such could be ignored. Thus, regardless of type of system, variations in political participation or violent behavior or individual civic attitudes could be fully accounted for by variations in the values of other individual properties—education, religion, ethnicity, and the like. In that event, we would not have to change levels; we could remain at the level of the individual across systems.

A great deal of comparative research of a quantitative sort utilizes this kind of explanation. It represents the search for cross-system generalizations on one level. These are to be distinguished from generalizations across levels within a single system or covering many systems, as, for example, where behavior at the individual level is explained by reference to independent variables at the system level, such as the stability of systems or their performance. Here the variables being associated are at different levels within each system. The analysis is across levels (the individual level and the presumed system level) within each system in which the system-level properties become a focus of attention.[12] Methodologically, generalizations across systems at a single level have seemed to be easier to handle.

Even though in political research we have been able to identify many cross-system single-level generalizations, it is not at all clear that the results so obtained give us an understanding that is any different from the same generalizations generated and favorably tested exclusively within a single system. Cross-national comparisons of this sort, encompassing varying cultures and types of political systems, do, of course, add to the conditions under which the relationships occur. Thereby they may improve the reliability of the generalizations. This is no mean achievement in itself, of course, since it might at least unearth some universals genuinely independent of spatial, cultural, and structural parameters.

On the other hand, even though the idea is not always well articulated, it has usually been clear in political research that characteristics at the individual level alone could scarcely be expected to explain all the differences we find among systems, even at the individual level itself. In fact, single-level analysis is notable for the small degree of variance it usually explains. Perhaps for this reason, despite the lack of quantitative tools for the purpose, we retain the impression that overall characteristics of the system would have to be brought in to help us understand at least some neglected grounds for the behavior within the system.

Cross-System System-Level Explanation

Traditionally, especially in the more interpretive literature, often based on configurative analysis, we have turned from characteristics of individuals to a second kind of explanation, one resting on what has variously been called a structural or macrostructural premise, one that somehow involves reference to the whole system itself. Thus, differences, say, in voting behavior, might also be attributable in part to differences in the properties of the systems within which the voting occurs. The explanation of cross-system differences would require us to cut across levels in each of the political systems in order to explore the extent to which the differences are due, perhaps, not only to the differences in individual characteristics across systems, but to the differences in system properties among the systems being compared.

For example, we may wish to look for the way in which economic status, an individual property, is associated with voting preference, another property of an individual. But in addition we might wish to explore whether voting preferences may not also be influenced by some system property, which differs between systems, such as a dominant labor-socialist tradition in one system as against a dominant capitalist free-market tradition in another. These traditions would represent system-level properties which might also account for some of the variance in the voting behavior of individuals. For this reason this method is usually referred to as a system-level explanation.[13] This shift in perspective is, in effect, a response to questions about the relatively low amount of variance that can usually be explained by research at a single level only.

Now, it might easily appear that this selection of system-level properties represents a turn to explanation in terms of the basic structure, that is, of the higher-order structure represented by the whole system considered as a dominating influence. The notion of system property or system level, with the emphasis on attributes of the system as part of the explanation, would surely seem to imply that we intend to relate differences found in the behavior of individuals, in different political systems, to differences in the way such systems are put together and work. Reference to system property as an explanatory variable seems to suggest that we are seeking to discover the impact of the specific political system, as a whole, on some institutions or patterns of behavior within it.

To draw this inference, however, would be to trap ourselves into a major misconstruction of the nature of this kind of research. Perhaps we have here one major reason why comparative research has not taken off in hot pursuit of a rigorous way for uncovering whole system effects. The identification of system-specific properties as sources of within-system variations has give the appearance of addressing the whole-system issue.

This second kind of explanation, however, at the presumed system level, merits somewhat closer inspection. It is not always what it seems to be. In the end, I shall argue, it has little relevance for helping us understand the possible relationship between the overall structure of a political system and the prevailing kinds of observed structures.

System Property as a Concept

The concept of system-level property is a spin-off of the discovery of the significance of the idea of systems for an understanding of political phenomena. Conceiving of political life as a system of behavior, it would seem transparent that the system itself, the way it is organized, might have some decisive influence on its various parts. If this influence varied with system types, then observed differences, say, in the performance of individuals or of systems themselves, or in the structure of organizations or institutions within them, could be attributed to the overall properties of the systems. Are there system-level or system-specific properties which influence the behavior or structure of the system or any of its parts?

Reasonable enough as this shift in direction may be, the fact is that the meaning of the terms *system level* or *system property* is not without serious ambiguity. It usually fails to select out the one system attribute that I have been suggesting may be very significant for understanding the way in which systems do shape, influence, and limit their internal forms—the overall structure of the system itself.

We might have avoided this neglect if we had subjected the term *system property* to the exacting scrutiny it merits, even though it has now been around for many years. We would have found that the idea of system property contains at least three undifferentiated kinds of referents: aggregate characteristics, states of the system, and institutional patterns. It typically identifies these three different aspects or properties of systems without, however, including the one property that may prove to be the most significant, namely, that of the system taken as a totality or what we might call the structure of the whole.

Thus, at times the term *system property* calls attention to certain *aggregate characteristics* of a system. These refer to the frequencies of properties which, in describing the aggregate behavior of individuals, also serve to distinguish the kind of system, in which they occur, from other systems. We speak of systems with such aggregate properties as high or low voter turnout rates, high or low levels of political crimes, or varying turnover rates of elites.

At other times, however, the notion of system property describes overall *states* of the political system. Here we may have in mind the stability of a system, its sense of legality, degree of internal conflict, militarism, effectiveness in performance, condition of war or depression. These represent pervasive rather than aggregated properties.

At still other times, the notion of system-level or system-specific property points to *institutional patterns* as embraced in the idea of a parliamentary as compared to a congressional or presidential regime, degree of party competition or of democratization, a merely constitutional in comparison with a broader democratic order, varying patterns of political authority as described in Weber's well-known classification, or degrees of centralization and decentralization.

Whether we choose to identify the use of one or another of these three kinds of properties, as a system-level explanation, is a matter of labeling preference. However, to say that we have explained some political phenomenon by reference to the type of system in which it occurs would seem to suggest something more than merely invoking one or another of these specific properties of a system. To be sure, where system-level properties are involved, the explanation will differ radically from one based solely on characteristics of individuals which are associated with each other, that is, from cross-system comparisons at the same within-system level. In the latter instances, individual-level properties are selected *for* explanation and *as* explanation. Neither the explanandum nor the explanans is a system-level property falling into any of the three types just identified. In this sense the cross-system, single-level explanations are clearly different from those that turn to system-specific or system-level variables. It is significantly different, for example, to say, on the one hand, that the education of individuals is related to the likelihood of their voting and, on the other, that a system that has a higher educational level has a higher voter turnout. The first statement relates to characteristics of individuals, the latter to properties of a system.

Despite this difference in one respect, however, both approaches in effect adopt the same methodological assumption. Essentially, for both, the explanation of cross-system differences depends upon selecting parts or properties of a system and relating them to other parts or properties. In the one case the individual is the part, in the other, a property of the system. This comparative approach represents a method that reaches as far back as Herodotus in the nine books of his *History*, we are told,[14] even though J. S. Mill, in his description of the methods of agreement and differences in whole-system comparisons, was the first to work on its logic seriously, a logic that has been widely reexamined in the last couple of decades.[15] It is a method, however, that fails to differentiate the particular characteristics of systems from differences in the way they are organized as whole entities, and usually complex ones at that.

In each case, whether we deal with individual- or system-level properties we are able to explain only a limited amount of the variance. This approach sets in motion a search for other variables, at one or the other level, to account for more of the variance, and since in the social sciences no single factor usually accounts for much of the variance, the search appears unending. Indeed, it provides an unrestricted hunting license for each generation of scholars to see whether they can discover yet another individual- or system-level property that explains a little more of the variance.[16]

Underlying this approach to research is a Cartesian or decompositional assumption about the way theory is built and comprehension occurs. A rational analysis, we were informed by seventeenth century encounters with the natural world, suggests that one must decompose an entity into its parts, explore them and their relationships in detail, decompose their parts in turn, and so on, until we come to some irreducible elements. Only then will we be able to reconstitute and thereby understand the whole. Today we find the archetype of this approach in the physical sciences which have decomposed physical matter down to the apparently irreducible quark. From this perspective the notion exists, in the social sciences, that somehow, through the gradual accretion of knowledge about each of the parts or properties of the political system, some day a theory about the way the whole system operates will emerge. The totality lies at the end of the road; it is unmanageable and recalcitrant to research at the beginning. The whole becomes little more than the sum of the parts.[17]

What comparative research has, for the most part, questioned is not that this decompositional-reconstitutive assumption about the road to understanding may be a misleading bit of epistemological folklore. Rather, it has been calling our attention to the possibility that we have not been identifying either the correct or all the relevant parts of political systems if we want to understand the differences among them. The parts to explore, it has been saying, in effect, ought not to be only individual behavior, whether discretely considered or in aggregates, but also properties of whole systems, at the system level.

To be sure, this point is well taken. It is not incorrect to direct our attention to the importance of system-level properties. My central point bears repeating, however. The appeal to these kinds of properties seems to be acknowledging the importance of systems as totalities. It seems to be saying that we ought not to lose sight of the differences among systems, as such, if we are to understand various differences within such systems. In fact, however, most of the rhetoric around this topic of system-level analysis does little to bring the higher-order whole system itself into sharp focus as a possible determinant or limit. The system in this sense lurks in the background and cannot be brought forward explicitly because of the failure of students of comparative research to recognize the implications and limitations of their original epistemological stance. Most still assume that understanding of the whole, how and why it is organized in a particular way, and what its possible effects are, will some day emerge from the summation of knowledge about the parts, except that now we have discovered that some of the parts are also to be found at the level of the system rather than at that of the individual alone.

One of the important consequences of systems thinking for research in the twentieth century has been the realization that a system as a whole incorporates an overall structure which we can ignore at the peril of omitting one of the decisive influences on major parts of the system itself. And yet this is precisely what is neglected even in that comparative research in politics which seeks to deal with the effects of the system, that is, with system-level determinants. This being so, no amount of inquiry into the variance accounted for by specific, discrete variables or combinations of them, even if we shift from the individual to the system level, will be able to provide an adequate explanation of the influence of one or another class of political system on the observed structures within them. It is not simply a matter of one or another component of a higher-order structure shaping or limiting a lower-order one. It is a matter of the whole providing a combination of factors which together, in their organized complexity, shape or limit lower-order structures.

Overall System Effects

The operating assumption that within-system or between-system differences in political relationships cannot be satisfactorily explained without taking into account the complex structure of political systems as whole entities might, for example, shed some light on a problem faced by Teune and Ostrowski. Some years ago they attempted to compare the relationship between conflict and activeness (collective action) in Poland and the United States.[18] In their analysis they were confronted by the situation where a common dependent variable or the relationship between common dependent and independent variables have different effects in different systems. They found that

> in Poland, [perceived or reported] conflict within a local political unit accompanies a low level of collective performance in mobilizing the resources of the population and in involving individuals in structures of participation. In the United States, the opposite is generally true: conflict is a characteristic of collective level resource mobilization and popular involvement.[19]

Appropriately, the authors in this study sought to avoid attributing the difference to membership either in the Polish or the U.S. political system. To do so, they point out, would have "the effect of introducing proper names in 'theories' of conflict and collective behavior."[20] Appropriately, again, the central assumption of their analysis was that "theories ought to contain no proper names and that proper names are the logical equivalents of error terms. In other words, theory should be general in the sense of containing only property concepts."[21]

However, the authors were unable to find any specific system-level properties, separately or collectively, that could account for a significant part of the different effects of political conflict on collective behavior in the two systems. In the end they acknowledged that they had to fall back on the methodologically undesirable conclusion that membership in the named systems—Poland, the United States—was the best predictor of the varying relationships of conflict to collective behavior in the two systems.

The authors might not have gone quite far enough in their speculation however. They did ring the changes on the kinds of system characteristics that might be used to account for within-system differences. They referred to "characteristics of the 'whole' political system,"[22] by which they meant system-wide structures or practices such as competitive as against noncompetitive parties, nonstructural characteristics such as aggregated attributes of individuals, general "cultural-historical patterns"[23] and underlying social processes such as stage of social development. Nowhere, however, did the authors come to grips with the whole system, not in the sense of specific properties which are system wide in their scope, such as those just mentioned, but in the sense of the system as an entity, that is, as a set of interdependent parts organized in a particular way.

It is conceivable that no specific system-level properties, even in the aggregate, could account for the differences in the effects of the two systems. Yet there is this different kind of system "property," if we wish to call it that, that might be able to explain the matter more persuasively. It is summed up in the notion that systems may be put together differently and operate by different rules. As a result, they have different effects on relationships within the systems. They create a total context in which two or more connected variables, present in all systems, may themselves function differently in different systems.

Thus, if we interpret the United States as a member of a class of political systems different from that of Poland, we would be saying that each of these two classes of political systems could be expected to be organized differently and to operate by different rules, an obvious observation. What apparently has not been so obvious is the fact that in the one, an effect of the organization and rules of operation could be that they encourage conflict to stimulate collective participation by the members, whereas in the other, the opposite appears to occur.

From this point of view, the differences between these two systems with respect to the effects of conflict on participation need not lie in one or another system-level property such as age distribution, income levels, educational patterns, degree of political stability, population growth, and the like—variables the authors use. No such single specific set of variables in isolation or in various combinations need be relevant to the relationship between conflict and collective activity.

Neither would we have to fall back on the idiographic kind of conclusion the authors had set out to avoid. The attribute of Polishness or United States-ness would seem to refer to little other than the historical resultant of two vastly different sequences of experiences. The particular observed differences could, of course, be just that, an idiosyncratic, nonreplicable outcome of history. These political systems are what they have become over time and that could be the most that could be said about them in trying to account for the different relationship between conflict and collective action. But, as I am suggesting, it also could be that concealed in these apparently ineffable system differences are two desiderata: the systems are put together differently; they have generically different ways of operating, that is, there are different rules by which common elements in both systems function. In short, it is, in part, to the higher-order structure of each system to which we must turn if we wish to account for variations in their observed (lower-order) structures and behavior.

A commonplace if oversimplified illustration will make my point about the effect of overall structure on component parts and outcomes. Imagine a car stuck in the mud with ten people to help push it out. Let us assume that the collectivity—the system, for our purposes—is competitively structured into two units of five persons and that each group acts independently of the other and is so positioned that when one group pushes it exerts a force opposite to that of the other group. Let us assume, further, that we have no knowledge of the competitive antagonistic structure of the system, that indeed we believe it to be composed simply of an aggregate of individuals.

Clearly, the outcome would be very difficult to predict. No amount of research on the independent variables thought to influence the force applied by each individual, such as motivations, sex, nutritional intake, inherent strength, skills, etc., would be likely to reveal the ultimate outcome, except by chance. With some changes, the car might be pushed out of the mud; under others, it would not budge. It would depend on whether changes in the critical variables added to or diminished the strength of one or the other group or whether it left them with an equal collective force that would result in a stalemate. Clearly, what would be required to complete our understanding would be some knowledge of the structure of the totality—of how the system is put together (its competitive structure) and of its rules of operation.

Let us, however, now alter the structure of this system of ten people into a new form in which there are no subgroups but in which all individuals cooperate in given tasks. Clearly, not only does the outcome change but the influence of the independent variables will be different. Appropriate changes in motivations, nutritional intake, skills, sex composition, and so on, to increase the force being exerted by each individual, need no longer leave the outcome indeterminate. From knowledge of them we would be in a position to predict whether the car is likely to be pushed out of the mud and the speed at which it might occur. In the antagonistic structure such changes might, of course, also succeed in altering the force being exerted by each group and therefore the specific outcome at any moment. But whereas in the antagonistic situation, under the assumptions described, the changes would be inexplicably unpredictable, the same would not be true for our understanding of the cooperators. If we were not aware of the differences in the overall structures involved, we would be deeply puzzled by why it should take so much more individual effort to shove the car out of the mud in the one circumstance than in the other.

In simplistic settings such as the one described, of course, we intuitively take structure into account in our thinking about them. Yet, fundamentally, the same reasoning applies to the infinitely more complex situation of political systems. There, however, the very complexity may lull us into a certain neglect of the possible influence of the overall structure. If we have two political systems, each structured differently and operating by different rules, there is little reason for believing that changes in independent variables such as level of education, degree of conflict, voter turnout rates, and the like, whether they are at the individual or at the system level, need necessarily have the same consequences. Their effects will in all probability be shaped, at least in part, by the overall system structure within which they operate.

Contextualism

We might have thought that various approaches to comparative or even single-system analysis might have sought to take the overall structure of political systems into account. Contextual analysis, configurative research, functionalism, and comparative historical sociology[24] would all seem to suggest an interest in this very issue. Yet even the most cursory scrutiny reveals how inattentive they have been.

A critical assessment of each of these varied approaches would delay our progress unnecessarily. But for illustrative purposes, let us look at two of them from which we might have had the highest expectations, contextualism and configurative analysis.

Contextualism, which I discuss further in chapter 17, shows us how easy it is to overlook the impact of the overall structure. It seeks to describe an element in a system by reference to properties of the system or of its parts. Nominally, we might expect that this focus would lead to precisely the kind of analysis that I am suggesting is missing with regard to the effect of the overall structure on components of a system and its operation. It would seem particularly appropriate to hold such an expectation since contextualism refers to conditions, either at the system or intrasystem level, which cannot be ascribed to or directly derived from the characteristics of individual members of a system themselves. At the system level, the broadest context, such properties might include political rules of the game, ideological predispositions of a population, historical experiences, institutions such as electoral arrangements, degree of party competition or separation, and balance of powers. At the intrasystem level, a narrower context, where the bulk of formal contextual analysis has occurred, the properties deal with the possible influence of local political networks, neighborhoods, class composition of a geographical region, aggregate behavior, and the like.

We might have thought that at some point contextual analysis, by its very orientation, would address the issue of the most broadly relevant context—the overall system—within which behavior occurs. Take, for example, a commonplace situation used at times in philosophical discussions of the issue of context, that of the relationship between a bank teller and a customer. If any person, A, were to present a signed piece of paper to any person, B, asking for a sum of money, it is unlikely that the request would be honored. But if A goes through this procedure in the context of a banking system, A would be recognized as a customer by B, the teller, and the piece of paper as a check or withdrawal form, and the transaction could be completed. The higher-order context, the banking system, provides the conditions under which lower-order relationships, such as those between teller and customer, can be entered into with known and expected consequences.

Similarly, the activities constituting a roll call on a bill in a legislature make sense only within the context of a complex set of relationships we call the legislative system. The institutional context of the legislature sets up the necessary expectations and legitimacy for the activity to take place and have certain consequences. The dispensing and receipt of money and the roll calls involve visible patterns of behavior or structures which are influenced and shaped by the higher-order structures or relationships identified as banking and legislative institutions.

It is strange to find, however, that despite the occasional reference to such broad events as wars, depressions, and the like, contextual analysis does not usually concern itself with such overall relationships, that is, with the connection between higher- and lower-order structures. Rather, most of its efforts go into exploring the relationship between the individual and a social environment that is far more narrowly defined.

Robinson set the direction for contextual analysis in what has become its classic form: From aggregated data, he demonstrated, valid inferences cannot be made about the properties of individuals, the so-called ecological fallacy.[25] That is to say, normally we cannot successfully move from the properties of the collectivity to that of the individual. Conversely, inferences about the properties of a whole entity—group-level properties—cannot be drawn from knowledge about its constituent individuals, the so-called individualistic fallacy. The fact that most members of a society are authoritarian in personality need not lead to an authoritarian political regime. The organizational characteristics of the political system derive from more than a "summation" of the properties of its constituent members. As yet contextualism has scarcely done more than ring the changes on the initial statement by Lazarsfeld that decisive jurors do not necessarily a decisive jury make. A hung jury may be and often is composed of very decisive jurors.

The issues of contextualism are by now well known in social research, especially in research on voting and political attitudes. How do neighborhood, geographic area, group membership, local party activities and the like influence votes and political attitudes, independently of leadership, partisanship, and issues? And if the context does have some influence, what are the mechanisms through which it operates?[26]

However, even if the problems with which contextual analysis currently struggles were successfully resolved, this achievement would have little bearing on our own concerns, namely, of the influence of the whole on its parts. To be sure, if we wished, we could describe such system effects as one among many types of contextual effects. That is, the effect of the highest-order structure in a political system, its overall organization, could be specified as a context, one that is broadest in scope. However, contextual effects are usually cast in much narrower terms, what we could call subsystems of the political system— neighborhoods, group membership, regional class characteristics, and the like. As long as we remained within this narrower conception of context, even the identification of all contextual effects would still leave the overall system effect quite elusive.[27] The issue is not one of discovering the effects of one or another context, singly or in combination, but of addressing the influence of that factor operating at the system level, what I have been designating as the overall or highest-order structure of the system.

In other words, the system itself, being the broadest context, represents a special case. Whereas other contexts are themselves subsystems within a political system, the whole system effect on political relationships transcends and conditions all subsidiary contexts. And as the concept "system effects" is being interpreted here, it relates to the total organization of the system, the pattern created by its overall structure. Alternatively put, the question remains: How does the higher-order system control or limit, as the case may be, the shape of lower-order subsystems such as the observed structures? I shall return to this issue again in chapter 17, from a slightly different perspective but with the same conclusion.

Configurative Analysis

Political systems differ in their internal structures or forms. Some have democratic, others dictatorial, still others authoritarian regimes, to mention only a few broad categories. And even within these, such as democracies, no two are identical in their internal structures, nor even in their overall general structure. In seeking to account for differences among political regimes, comparative politics very reasonably wishes to account for them through the fact that there seem to be differences among the systems themselves. If electoral participation in Britain is at a higher rate than in the United States, the way to account for that is to find the relevant differences in the two systems.

However, all the technology developed in comparative research seems to have avoided what might have seemed a natural source for this variability. To what extent could it be attributed to the way the overall systems are put together and operate?

There may be good reason for an aversion to this course. To the extent that there has been any move to search for this variability in the overall character of the political system it has led to configurative analysis. The latter, however, has seemed to end in pure description or historical interpretation, kinds of outcomes toward which formal science has been inhospitable.

Despite its uneasy ties to formal science, or perhaps for that very reason, the ultimate objective of configurative analysis has still to receive the attention it merits in political science. It assumes that through detailed familiarity with the institutions of a political system in a given space and time, we are more likely to obtain a better understanding of how the system functions and why it takes the form it does. This form of analysis operates on the premise that the patterns of relationships in a system constitute a coherent and interdependent whole and that any parsing of the system must destroy our understanding of it. Only if we can grasp all major and essential aspects of a system simultaneously are we likely to be able to appreciate the significance and determinants of any single component—hence a dependence on detailed descriptions of interrelationships and on an effort to comprehend, if only intuitively, how all the parts taken together as an entity shape and limit each other.[28]

Although configurative analysis appears to share the approach advocated by those who see merit in the study of each political system as a special case—the case-study method—in fact it represents a very special instance of the latter. Most students who turn to case studies operate within the terms of the nomothetic method. They see each case as a legitimate means for discovering insights into possible generalizations valid across political systems and for taking into account the whole context represented in a single system. But configurative analysis lies closer to what Gordon Allport long ago sought to formulate as the idiographic as contrasted to nomothetic science.[29] Even though he hoped to be able to demonstrate that his method did not wander far from the normal canons of positivist science, he never did plead his case successfully enough to persuade his colleagues in psychology, let alone other social scientists.

In any event, configurative analysis in political research has still to find a systematic advocate like Allport. Without having one to point to, however, we can nonetheless attribute to configurative analysis the expectation that the formal understanding acquired through normal science needs to be enriched through the intuitive and empathic understanding, in a somewhat Weberian fashion, that comes from detailed description of institutions and their relationships. It is now rather fashionable to describe this as "thick description," in Geertz's suggestive phrase.[30] In making its case, configurative analysis at least has the merit of recognizing the deficiencies of research that either ignores the overall context or only nods to it in passing. In effect, configurative analysis has served to keep this issue alive.

Appropriately, however, the inability of configurative analysis to go beyond impressionistic even if well-grounded description encourages the conclusion that our research technology is still deficient for handling so complex an enterprise. We have no easy or summary methods for describing the differences in the ways that complex political systems are organized. And we have invented even fewer conceptual and technical tools for isolating the possible effects of such differences. Not even comparative historical political sociology has been able to overcome this handicap.

This situation is regrettable, to be sure. One thing is certain, however, at this stage in the development of our understanding about how understanding occurs: The lack of adequate technology cannot be allowed to stand in the way of a theoretic identification of the issues. If it did, we would never acquire the incentive to invent the conceptualization that would inspire us to search for the necessary tools to do the empirical job.

Whatever the validity of the above conclusion, I would clearly be overstating the case if I were to leave the impression that at present we have at hand the specialized technical means to launch a formal and rigorous exploration of this relationship between the part (observed structures) and the whole (the political system as a higher-order entity) or for even defining the relationship fully, a subject to which I shall return in chapter 18. To be sure, it would be enormously helpful for displacing our dependence on the correlational analysis of conventional comparative research (with its limited concern for whole-system effects) or on such alternatives as historical interpretive or contextual analysis if we could offer measurable statements or formal equations describing and expressing the nature of the relationship between observable lower-order patterns and the way a complex political system is organized. Nonetheless, at the present time the absence of the means for obtaining such formal or quantified conclusions about the relationship does not reduce the importance of discovering and demonstrating its existence with the best evidence available, of exploring an initial theoretical posture relevant to this, and of adopting as formal an analysis as the subject and our technology permit at this stage of their development. As I have noted, it is now routine to observe that the absence of adequate technical means of analysis ought not to be allowed to stand in the way of the development of the very insights for which such tools may need to be invented or refined.

We can go even further. The salutary effect of recent criticisms of positivist ingredients in science has been to bring about a reconsideration of what is involved in the use of scientific method.[31] It is now clearer than ever before that, since the level of precision, clarity, and formality of an analysis cannot exceed the capacity of a discipline at its given stage of development, one ought not to construe the methods of science narrowly. If we consider science to be not the arbitrary set of canons that the Vienna Circle derived from Hertz's *Theory of Mechanics* but criteria to be inferred from the way in which scientists have worked historically, the way they actually practice their positive science, then we find that scientific method does not preclude qualitative analysis where necessary or inescapable. And this is valid even if the results cannot avoid some degree of imprecision and ambiguity which normal, older-style, and excessively demanding positivism in the past has mistakenly put beyond the pale of scientific inquiry. In short, even though my conclusions will of necessity be cast in broad qualitative terms, as long as they can stand up to the rigorous rules of logic and have promise of ultimate empirical reference, our changing post-positivist understanding of scientific method dictates that we consider them as much a part of this method as any highly quantified research product.

Part 2

The Structuralism of
Nicos Poulantzas

11

Poulantzas: Marxism Redefined

As we have just seen in the preceding chapter, comparative research in political science has failed to instruct us on how to bridge the gap between the structure of the whole political system—the higher-order structure—and the particular observed structures or political relationships of which a system may be composed. I shall now turn to structuralism in one of its numerous versions, namely, a Marxist one—as formulated initially by Louis Althusser and as subsequently adapted by Nicos Poulantzas—to explore the extent to which it can do better.

What makes Poulantzas stand out from numerous other Marxists of his own generation is not that he used Althusser as a point of departure—many others, in Europe at least, did the same—but that he sought to remold Althusser's structuralism into an explicit theory of politics. It is as though he wanted to beat bourgeois political scientists at their own game by showing them what a real theory of politics should look like. Despite the enormity of his effort, however, in the end Poulantzas will not be able to give us an unambiguous answer about how to decipher the relationship between higher- and lower-order structures. Nonetheless, a close analysis of his structuralist reinterpretation of Marxism and the very identification of the sources of his lack of success will at least help to highlight for us those issues that may be central for an understanding of how regime structures take the form they do.

As we have seen in chapters 8 and 9, structuralism no longer has the compelling force that it had during the 1960s and 1970s, especially in Europe. Nonetheless, its decline today, due in part to its neglect of human intentions and action and in part to its imagery of an overly ordered and determined world, paralleled by its displacement by deconstruction and postmodernism, ought not to be allowed to mask the problem, critical for social analysis, that it was seeking to address: how to account for the transparent variations in observed structures? Its inability to offer a satisfactory answer to this central issue cannot be allowed to pass unnoticed.

As I observed at the outset of this book, part of our own failure in political science to understand the relationship between higher- and lower-order structures lies in our neglect of the issue heretofore. Not having seen it as a problem, except perhaps in the simplistic formulation of structural-functional analysis or in the intuitive strivings of interpretive case-study approaches, we have lacked the incentive to explore its elements and ramifications. At this stage we shall have to be satisfied if we can at least begin to recognize the relationship between higher-order and observed structures as a major problem for research and identify some of the salient dimensions.

As we have already seen, whatever we may think of structuralism in general at least it does represent an effort to translate what it saw as the underlying relationships of a system, as interpreted by different brands of structuralism, into universally acknowledged surface structures, and thereby to substitute theoretical for mere statistical significance in comparing systems. Perhaps it was this promise that helped draw Poulantzas to Althusser's structuralist reformulation of Marxism.

Lévi-Strauss and Structuralism

As I have already noted, the founder of modern structuralism, Lévi-Strauss, clearly brought out the salience of this part-whole relationship. He explicitly sought to formulate a theory of the observed structures in social anthropology. "It is to [the] theory of superstructures, scarcely touched on by Marx, that I hope to make a contribution," he clearly states.[1] His "theory," we have seen, is not presented as a theory at all, if we were to accept his repeated insistence that structuralism is only a method. For Lévi-Strauss it is presumably just a way of discovering an underlying set of autonomous, objective relationships, what he labels *the social structure*, that is constant for all societies, past and present. Only *social relations*, the observed or lower-order structures in my sense, are variable. Whether method or theory, the ultimate objective of Lévi-Strauss's structuralism is to explain, in some sense, the superstructures.

Much like political science, social anthropology has, from its beginning, been comparative in outlook and has, accordingly, been sensitive to the variety in cultural forms manifested across the face of the globe. Through cross-societal comparisons, anthropologists have typically sought to bring some order to this variety in the content of social behavior, looking for similarities and differences of social forms. The network of social relations expressed in kinship groups, social strata, and the like constituted the social structure. As noted earlier, Lévi-Strauss sought to break through the tedious comparisons of one set of such institutions after another by siding with structural linguistics and with Freud and Marx, among others, arguing that there may be some theoretical or organizing principles underlying empiricist reality (that part of the world obvious to the senses).[2]

Linguistics, from Saussure on, had sought a fundamental grammar behind the apparent syntax and grammar of languages in ordinary use—a deep structure to explain the empirical or surface structure. Lévi-Strauss adopted and adapted the perspectives of structural linguistics[3] by searching for a similar deeper order in society, which, as we have seen, he called social structure, underlying what he designated as the empiricist social relations of conventional anthropology. This objective order, the real social structure, would serve to "make intelligible"[4] the vast variety of concrete social relations, the facts of social life, that for him, must be the starting point in the search for this underlying structure.[5]

As I have already mentioned, the forms of kinship ties, for example, normally described in ethnography as the central component of the social structure of nonliterate societies, were for Lévi-Strauss only the visible surface phenomena. No amount of description of their content or search for their correlates through statistical manipulations[6] could enable us to understand why they assume the varied forms they do. For this we need to probe beneath the surface for the autonomous processes and relationships out of which they arise. This deeper level contains a universal social structure of which variable concrete ties or relations are just a particular manifestation in the given spatiotemporal context.

Lévi-Strauss goes even further. For him there is one and only one universal social structure even though there are many forms of social relations. The basic structure remains constant while the forms are variable.[7] The former gives coherence to what would otherwise look like a mere aggregate of social relations resulting from the accidents of history.

It is this common and universal underlying order or infrastructure that commands the attention of Lévi-Strauss. He speaks of it as though it consisted of two parts, although he asserts this dichotomy in an almost casual way: first, social arrangements, such as the economy; second, the mind. It is the latter, we have already observed, which he finds particularly relevant to social theory.[8] Just as structural linguists had come to believe that human beings possess an innate language capacity that expresses itself in a limited number of empirical forms called spoken language, Lévi-Strauss argues that in society the mind presents a similar structuring tendency that lends unsuspected coherence to the variety we find in concrete social organization and thought. The mental or intellectual operations of the mind—processes independent of human will or desire—seem to impose an order on behavior, and this order consists of discoverable forms, a system of complementary binary opposites.[9] This tendency to structure in terms of such opposites is, for Lévi-Strauss, a powerful, universal, and inescapable intellective force.

During the 1950s and 1960s, accordingly, through his theory of structuralism, Lévi-Strauss began to tussle with the issue of the theoretical connection between so-called superstructure and base. Until then, this way of looking at structures had largely been the preserve of Marxist theory and was certainly seen by others to be so. Although Lévi-Strauss did not provide any good specific leads toward a theory about the way in which such structures might influence each other—his once very popular approach has receded into virtual obscurity—he did at least affirm the utility of distinguishing between kinds of structures such as these and of postulating the existence of an important relationship between them. Perhaps most important of all, he did reestablish the significance of the problem by directing attention to an issue that, as he pointed out, even Marx had left unresolved, namely, a theory of the superstructure (however ambiguous the latter term may be): How can we account for the empirically observed structures?

Regardless of whether we consider Lévi-Strauss to have been successful in resolving the issue, he had at least addressed it in a way that made it germane to possible similar kinds of concerns in all the social sciences, including political science. Indeed, the fact that his particular kind of answer, structuralism, at one time spread rapidly throughout most areas of knowledge, in Europe at least, as I have noted, is testimony to the perceived relevance of his problem, if not of his structuralist solution.

As I have mentioned, concern for the relationship between so-called super- and infrastructures was not, of course, original to modern structuralism—as Lévi-Strauss was quick to acknowledge—but had first been expressed, long ago, by Marx himself. However, as formulated in the bulk of earlier orthodox Marxist literature (although, arguably, not by Marx himself), the problem had received virtually a uniform answer: The one determines the other; base determines superstructure. Furthermore, the superstructure itself remained virtually epiphenomenal. It seemed to have little effect on social outcomes. Although over the years there had been some objection to this formulation, inside as well as outside the Marxist movement, those who challenged the validity of the relationship (with an occasional exception perhaps, such as Gramsci) did little to attempt to formulate a systematic or theoretical alternative.

If we now turn to the Marxist framework, however, we do find at least one person, Nicos Poulantzas, who has argued, in effect, that Marxism does offer a theory along these lines. The trouble, from his point of view, is that this theory has always remained buried, inappropriately concealed, as it were, by a heavy layer of economic determinism (so-called economism). Following the guidance of the Marxist philosopher Althusser, Poulantzas felt that it was time to resurrect the issue for reanalysis, at least in the study of politics.

This plea for a revival of the matter obtained some encouragement not only from Lévi-Strauss's structuralism but from an independent strand of thinking in linguistics, as I indicated earlier. By the turn of this century, under the inspiration of de Saussure the difference between *langue* (language as an institutionalized set of practices) and *parole* (the particular words used by a speaker) had begun to play a role similar to that between base and superstructure. In linguistics, of course, the distinction was later described as that between deep and surface or empirical structure, a terminology that Lévi-Strauss borrowed, as we have already seen, at the same time as he acknowledged his indebtedness to Marx as another source for the idea. But whatever the concepts used, these streams of thought were converging on the notion that somehow structures immediately available to observation, "superstructures," needed to be seen as influenced in some important way by relationships that are not readily or directly accessible to the senses. As we have already discovered, the argument seemed to move in the direction of asserting that the fundamental way in which a system hangs together and operates has independent, separable and identifiable effects on the parts of the system such as the observed superstructures.

The Significance of Poulantzas

As I have proposed, we will now find it theoretically and methodologically rewarding to turn to Nicos Poulantzas as one further step on the road to enhancing our understanding of the possible relationships between higher- and lower-order structures in political systems. He virtually alone addresses directly the theoretical issue of the way in which the changes in the overarching structures of a social system translate themselves into the particular forms of structures through which political activity occurs. Analysis of the way in which he reanalyzes Marx, following a path cleared by Althusser, will help to point up the fact that to explore observed structures we need to see them not only as possible products of the way they correlate with other factors—such as electoral influence, interest groups, or recruitment to political roles, to take examples at random—but as objects which may be determined, or limited, as we shall later discover, by the nature of the organization of the broader social system of which they are part.

Despite his occasional protests to the contrary, Poulantzas was a disciple of Althusser.[10] The latter, in turn, had reconstructed Marxism as a philosophy and as a social theory,[11] building into it self-conscious elements of structuralism and, as we shall indirectly see through our examination of Poulantzas's thinking, even of systems analysis, two major intellectual currents of the twentieth century to which both he and Poulantzas were inevitably exposed. Poulantzas's thinking was far more limited than that of Althusser. He was not engaged in a fundamental reinterpretation of Marxism as a body of thought. Rather, he sought largely to trace out the implications of the new Althusserian formulations for the strictly political sphere, or "instance," as both of them would call it. Poulantzas was therefore seeking to clear a narrower path of understanding: to apply Marx's thinking, as it had been reformulated by Althusser and as he, Poulantzas, himself interpreted it, in the development of a specific theory of politics, the theory of the state under capitalism, as he put it. In the process he extended and even modified Althusser's thoughts as he applied them to certain traditional issues in political research.

If we were engaged in a critical analysis of Poulantzas as a political theorist, we might, of course, wish to trace his linkages to Althusser. Our purposes, however, are more limited. We are interested in Poulantzas only insofar as his analyses can help us to understand the nature of political structures and to illuminate the relationships between higher- and lower-order structures. Hence, we need not be concerned with the paternity of Poulantzas's ideas except where a full understanding of their implications requires an excursion into their origins in Althusser. We shall find that for the most part the validity or utility of Poulantzas's conceptualization and theories can be assessed independently of their ties even to similar theoretical formulations by Althusser.

While allowing Althusser to lurk in the background, to emerge only as clarity requires, we must at the outset be careful to note the kind of argument Poulantzas will be making. He is not proposing that variations in the overall structure of the *political* system account for changes in any one of its parts. Rather, for him the broader structure is the *social* system as a whole, what I would call the social environment with which the political system is enmeshed.[12] Thus he does not address the issue of the relationship between the *political system* as a complex overarching order and its observed structures. Nonetheless, his efforts to demonstrate a significant connection between the overall *social* structure and political structures will prove instructive if they highlight the need to find a method for dealing with a relationship of this kind.

The selection of the work of Poulantzas for special attention, rather than that of a number of other Marxists, needs little justification. Despite all that has been written by Marxists in recent years, and despite the waning of interest in the work of Poulantzas even in Europe—where during the sixties and seventies it commanded widespread attention—he nonetheless still must be considered an influential Marxist political sociologist of the twentieth century. Central ideas from his work continue to cast their shadow over political science, if not over the social sciences at large, even among those who do not claim to be Marxists or who cannot be counted among them. Scholars either explicitly use his structuralist approach or derivatives from it, or they deal with problems set by him whether or not they acknowledge it[13] or, perhaps, are even aware of it. Furthermore, the mere fact that Marxism itself has lost its popularity of the 1970s, both in Europe and in the United States, ought not to lead us to underestimate the significance of the issues which it left with the social sciences and the influence they continue to exert in setting certain parts of the agenda of research.

Laclau, a once prominent Marxist and sympathetic critic of Poulantzas. has perhaps best located the latter's position, in relation to the development of Marxism at least.

> The work of Nicos Poulantzas is of considerable theoretical importance . . . because Marxist thought did not begin to develop, until the last decade, a systematic theory about the nature and the role of the State in various socio-economic formations. Sketchy observations attempting to establish the *ultimate* coherence between socio-economic changes and the transformation of the political system, or not so sketchy observations attempting to establish mechanical relations of causality between the two, have dominated the area of analysis to such a point that we can only welcome a work which tries to establish on the theoretical level the specificity of the political and which systematically avoids purely impressionistic correlations.[14]

Poulantzas was familiar with contemporary political science, especially as it had progressed in the United States. It left him sensitive to the need for Marxism to formulate a competitive theory of its own about politics, or about the state, as he characteristically puts it. Indeed, Poulantzas was very much aware of and in tune with the applied or policy interests of contemporary political science. He begins his first major work by posing a simple question: How are state policies formed?[15] To answer this he sets about developing a theory of the state (identical with a theory of politics, for capitalist society at least, in his view),[16] one particular part of the superstructure of society in general Marxist terminology.

This objective led him directly to an effort to account for the different type of states and the forms they take. He assumed that, in the end, policy is explicable only in light of the types and forms of states that make such policy and that these types and forms take their character from the modes of production in which they are embedded. His quest for a theory of public policy thus led him to the relationship between state forms (a part) and the modes of production (the social whole). As we shall see, whether a state assumes a democratic, fascist, or dictatorial structure and the like can be explained, for Poulantzas, by what happens to the way the social system as a whole is organized, and for him the whole is identified by the concept mode of production.

At the theoretical level no one has carried these matters in Marxism further than Poulantzas. Nor has any other Marxist been as self-conscious, comprehensive, or ambitious about the formulation of a general theory of politics. Hence, from his experience we might expect to learn something about the relationships between higher- and lower-order structures. And if we fail at that, perhaps we can at least find revealed something about the nature of the problems encountered.

12

Structuralist Marxism and
Systems Analysis

How does it happen that Poulantzas turns to the problems of the effects of a whole system of relationships on the parts? In one sense it is intrinsic to Marxism as any reading of Marx makes evident. The state, as part of the social system, can be explained only in the context of the way the whole mode of production operates and changes. What remains to be explained, however, is why the matter should have emerged in recent decades as a special focus of concern and why it should have been recast in the form taken by structuralist Marxism as formulated by Poulantzas, following Althusser.[1]

Structuralism as a Variant of Systems Analysis

In general the part-whole question is, of course, not new. It has been debated over the ages and has reemerged in its most recent guise under the rubric of holism as against methodological individualism. The literature in this area is extensive and continuing, even if its analysis at the hands of philosophy has not always been of greatest assistance to social science. Furthermore, the relationship of the whole to the structure and functioning of the parts has also been treated as critical for the interpretation of Marx by Marxists who lay no claim to being structuralists.[2] Nevertheless, we can get some sense of the origins of a renewed interest in the part-whole controversy and the particular form that this interest takes if we turn to the role that structuralism in general, independent of Marxism, has itself played as an intellectual tendency in Europe.

In a very important sense, to remind ourselves of what we have already discussed in chapter 8, it is not misleading to interpret structuralism as a way through which European social science has come to terms with the need to develop general social science theory. In the United States the behavioral revolution, so-called,[3] had taken place during the 1950s and 1960s, but it was essentially resisted by European scholars in most branches of social science. Hence, the intellectual climate in Europe was less than hospitable to the development of social science theory, at least of the sort that could be cast in the behavioral language of social science. As I concluded in chapter 8, we may interpret structuralism, in its varied ideological predispositions, as a disguised way of making a strong case for the development of theory despite a climate in European social science that was hostile to it.

There is, however, a central point about this aspect of structuralism that we may easily overlook. The kind of theory the structuralists were seeking differed in two respects from that aspired to or found in traditional social science, to which it

162

seemed to stand in some opposition. In the first place, until World War II, social science, particularly in the United States, had looked for explanation in terms of the relationships among a limited number of specific variables, what has been called middle-range theory at its broadest. By the 1950s, however, a change had set in. The social sciences had begun to show an interest, however hesitantly, in a different course. They opened up a search for general theory, that is, the kind of theory that seeks to put the whole of a discipline in its broadest theoretical context.[4]

It is here that a strange thing happened. European social science, in its continued commitment to a more humanistic form of inquiry, for the most part rejected this pursuit of general theory as well as other aspects of the so-called behavioral transformations occurring in the United States. At the same time, however, primarily through the efforts of Lévi-Strauss, structuralism began to take shape in Europe. In the process, even if his purposes were not clearly defined or understood at the time, in effect he was making the case for a higher level of theory, as Boudon was later to point out about all structuralism.

Boudon was certainly correct as far as he went in exposing the unacknowledged theoretical bent of a traditional sort within structuralism, a point I have made earlier.[5] A somewhat broader message did seem to elude him, however. Hidden within the often esoteric language of structuralism was not a plea for the construction of a theory from the narrowest to the broadest, but rather a special argument on behalf of the most inclusive or general type of theory. This pursuit of general theory is what really made structuralism distinctive and set it apart from common garden variety lower-level theorizing as regularly found in conventional social science. In retrospect this new language of structuralism seemed almost unavoidable if those social scientists in Europe, sensitive to the newer trends in theory development, were to be able to sneak it unsuspectingly into the existing hostile humanistic environment. In this way the traditional humanist resistance to behavioral theory, as it was called in the United States, was outflanked if not disarmed.

In the second place, however, structuralism went further. It represented more than a plea for just any kind of general theory. Its inclination turned out to be more specific than that. In arguing the case, however indirectly, for general theory, structuralism, at least as it was presented by Lévi-Strauss, was in effect proposing a type that could be formulated in systems terms, as we have already seen.[6] The epistemological pressure to interpret many aspects of life in systems terms, unique to the latter half of the twentieth century, reveals itself clearly in structuralism. It is here that Piaget's slender volume *Structuralism* is right on target. He explicitly saw in structuralism an effort to formulate not just general theory but general theory of a systems type.[7] He intuitively recognized what many structuralists themselves failed to see or acknowledge—that structuralism in Europe was the local medium through which not just theory but a systems-type theory was being introduced and, we might add, without giving the appearance of either being done.

For this reason we would have difficulty appreciating the theoretical premises on which Poulantzas, as a structuralist as well as a Marxist, rests his thinking (following Althusser closely but not slavishly) unless we were prepared to recognize at the outset its specific affinity to a systems points of view. In some ultimate historical sense, structuralist Marxism, as an intellectual tendency invented by Althusser and adapted for political inquiry by Poulantzas, can be interpreted as a disguised way of incorporating systems thinking into traditional Marxist theory. From this perspective structuralism played the historical role of updating Marxism by seeking to bring it, however indirectly, into some kind of accommodation with the systems revolution in modern thought.[8]

We may go even further. However much Poulantzas would have protested this characterization of his work, fundamentally, as both Althusser and he interpret Marxism, they convert it into little more than a subset of systems analysis in general. Some Marxists would formulate this thought differently. They would argue that Marx was really the first systems theorist, well in advance of his time.[9] Whatever the truth may be, for our purposes at the moment it makes little difference how we interpret the relationship. As long as we accept Marxist structuralism, like most structuralism, as a possible concealed variant of systems thinking, we can see that it is not at all strange that a central problem of structuralist Marxism should turn out to be no different from that of systems analysis itself. Both seek to understand how, if at all, the whole structure or higher-order network of relationships we call a system, shapes its parts or subsystems.

Indeed, I shall demonstrate, somewhat later, that as Poulantzas develops his own formulations even in his early works—*Political Power and Social Classes* (1968) and *Fascism and Dictatorship* (1970)—increasingly he comes to adopt the concept of the political system, as do many other Marxists. In time the difference, in Poulantzas's work, between the idea of the state and that of the political system becomes hazy. We might wonder whether the retention of the state as a central concept remains more a matter of loyalty to nineteenth century Marxist terminology for partisan political purposes rather than a matter of conceptual or theoretical necessity.[10]

If I am now to demonstrate the plausibility of this interpretation of Poulantzas's Marxism, I shall have to produce some convincing evidence that Poulantzas is indeed caught up in systems thinking. Let us, then, turn to the way Poulantzas analyzes politics to see whether we can detect this tilt toward systems analysis and through it a reaffirmation of the saliency of the parts-whole relationship. This will lead us into an explanation of his major theoretical premises, an apparent digression that will, in due course, enable us to return to the central issues posed in this book.

Mode of Production as Structuralist Whole

Nature of the Mode of Production

As I have already suggested, Poulantzas starts out with a central problem that is at once simple in its formulation and familiar to conventional political science: Who has power in society over policy making through their capacity to dominate the "state"?[11] How can we account for the different forms through which state power manifests itself? The response is clear. In every mode of production hitherto known in history, power is concentrated in the hands of a ruling class. Such a class arises and obtains power not through its independent and calculated efforts but through the way a mode of production (social system) organizes its social relationships. A ruling class is functionally necessary. As he writes, "Power is not located in the levels of structures, but is an effect of the ensemble of these levels."[12] Furthermore, the forms of the state through which this power is manifested are equally products of this ensemble or whole. His theory of politics is designed to demonstrate the plausibility of these conclusions.

Poulantzas distinguishes the state from its "practices" (behavior). Although, as I shall have reason to note, all too frequently, he is far from consistent in his general use of his concepts, normally the state refers to a structure or level, political practice to the class struggle or conflict among the various classes. However, at times he also uses the concept of state or that of politics to refer to state and practices combined, adding not a little confusion to his meaning of these terms. In any event, together state and practices constitute the whole of politics. As I have indicated, following Althusser, Poulantzas considers that the state, in its various forms as well as in its varied kinds of class struggles or practices, takes its character from the given mode of production.[13]

What is this mode of production, however, that is so decisive for the existence, nature, and forms of the state, and what is the theoretical status of this concept? In the first place, the mode of production is a construct and, as such, a technical term for Poulantzas. It is a theoretical way of identifying whole societies in general.[14] It represents what he might have called the social system if he had been willing to accept what, for him, is a concept of bourgeois social science. It is to be distinguished from the social formation, a term that he reserves to refer to a specific society.[15]

In the second place, as I have noted, Poulantzas hypothesizes that the mode of production determines both the forms of the state and of the class struggles. However, he does not mean by that to equate the mode of production with the economy. Rather, the mode of production identifies abstracted relationships among the components of any concrete social formation or society. "By mode of production we shall designate not what is generally marked out as the economic (i.e., relations of production in the strict sense), but a specific combination of various structures and practices which, in combination appear as so many instances or levels, i.e., as so many regional structures of this mode."[16] As I have noted, the mode of production itself is, for Poulantzas, a theoretical idea, an abstraction referring to the social system as a whole.

In the third place, any given social formation (society) is normally characterized by more than one mode of production. In every society we find remnants of historical modes of production, even if the society may be organized under the dominance of a single mode.[17] Hence, any individual mode of production, such as capitalism, since it is only a construct can never be found empirically in a pure or unadulterated form. Remnants of earlier modes of production, such as the feudal, may be woven into it. Modes of production are, in effect, similar to Weberian ideal types.

In the fourth place, a mode of production is not an undifferentiated whole. Poulantzas quotes Engels to the effect that a mode of production "is composed of different levels or instances, the economic, political, ideological and theoretical" and practices associated with them.[18] The theoretical level, the only one that may not appear self-evident, refers to that element in society through which valid knowledge is created. Althusser, from whom this whole formulation is adapted, at times also calls it science.[19] However, as it turns out in Poulantzas's own "theoretical practices," to all intents and purposes he drops the theoretical instance from his discussion of the mode of production and speaks of the latter as though it were composed only of the remaining three elements. No reason is ever offered.[20]

This decomposition of society into three (or four) instances gives us its abstracted invariant elements. All these combined constitute the mode of production (also called the global structure or totality), and it is the particular nature of their combination that has specific and inescapable effects on the parts (which he variously calls instances, levels, or structures). Whatever else this combination does it compels all the parts to serve a single overarching function: the maintenance of the cohesion or unity of the whole.

We might question why the mode of production—the forces that give a society its shape and character and lead it to operate in the way it does—consists of only three elements (or four at most). The answer is hard to come by. As a sympathetic critic, Laclau, has put it,

> Why only three [instances]? What has been the method of their deduction? Does there exist any logical link between them? The response is silence to the first two questions and in the negative to the third—the only relation is their articulation, which depends on the mode of production in question. That is to say, we find ourselves with three instances established in a purely descriptive way.[21]

Place of the Economy in the Mode of Production: Relative Autonomy

Accepting this arbitrary decomposition of any and all societies into three instances, how do the latter "combine," as Poulantzas puts it, to produce a given mode of production? "The type of unity which characterizes a mode of production," he proposes, "is that of a *complex whole* dominated, in the last instance, by the economic."[22] This whole (the global structure) is of a kind that we might describe as a hierarchically ordered set, hierarchical because "in the last instance" the economy "dominates" the other two elements in all the modes of production. Poulantzas himself does not explicitly conceptualize the relationship as hierarchical; it is only implied in his formulations.

The meaning of this "domination in the last instance" which is supposed to order the basic relationships among the elements is, however, cloaked in a virtually impenetrable mist of words. Its obscurity has been compounded by the warning from Poulantzas that "the term *determination* will be reserved for this dominance in the last instance."[23] On the surface it would appear that Poulantzas might have intended this term to mean that the economy does *determine* the way the whole mode of production operates and, thereby, at least indirectly, determines the position and operation of each of the other elements in the mode of production, including the state. But this is clearly what he cannot and what he explicitly does not intend.

The reason for this is that Poulantzas's major antagonist within Marxism itself was economism or vulgar economic determinism. He rejected a traditional and widely adopted Marxist position in which the whole superstructure—politics, culture, and the like—is determined by the base (the economy) and is virtually epiphenomenal. Instead, he considered that the purely economic contradictions brought about by capital accumulation would not by themselves be enough to plunge a society into crisis and lead to a socialist transformation. With Althusser, Poulantzas viewed a purely economic interpretation as highly mechanistic without any validity in fact, in theory, or in the writings of Marx. He went further and argued that the superstructure, including the state, is not determined by any single element in the social system, and especially not by the economy as represented in the forces of production (composed of the means of production, labor and nonlabor) or by the relations of production (economic relationships). Rather, a regime "is fixed in its limits by the global structure of the mode of production and social formation."[24] It is the whole which is determinant. The crisis in capitalism and its collapse will occur as a result of crises in all aspects of the capitalist social system, each interlaced with the other.

Such a conclusion is, however, still too simple an explanation about the relationship of the parts of the mode of production to the whole or "global structure." Even though the state may be "fixed in its limits" by the whole—a weak statement about the relationship—and even though it may be "dominated in the last instance by the economic" as an earlier quotation declared—depicting a much stronger relationship, one of determination—in fact each of the elements of a mode of production remains "relatively autonomous" with respect to the other and even to the "global structure" itself. Just what the phrase "relatively autonomous" means is another central notion that remains a frustrating mystery in Poulantzas's analysis and that manages to confound the meaning even further.[25]

Even though the economy "dominates" (meaning determines) the mode of production "in the last instance," each structural level or element nonetheless remains "relatively autonomous" in the extent to which it contributes to the overall contradiction that brings about fundamental social change. In this way, the structural elements of society, such as the state, are freed from the economic base of traditional Marxist interpretation and may have independent effects of their own. Indeed, it is this very autonomy of the instances (subsystems) such as the state that gives credibility to the idea of the development of a special theory of the state, one that is separate from other general theories such as those about the mode of production or about ideology or about the economy. Whatever Poulantzas may mean by the idea of relative autonomy, it at least serves as his primary justification for undertaking the kind of separate inquiry into empirical political theory that he does.

If "determination in the last instance" by the economy does not mean that the economy directly shapes the other elements of the society and leads to crises in them, what can this phrase mean? Poulantzas is perhaps better at telling us what he does *not* intend. He does this as he tries to tell us what he means by the prominence of the whole mode of production in shaping its own parts or instances. Thus, in speaking of the more general proposition that a state, as an element or part, is "fixed in its limits by the global structure of the mode of production and social formation," Poulantzas declares that the relationship among all the elements, including the state and economy, is not one of "linear" causality. By this he seems to exclude asymmetric causality, where A must precede B in time if it is to be seen as causing B. Nor are the total effects of all elements combined to be construed as a result of mutual causality or interaction—of the way they interact with one another, presumably in some simple Parsonian, functionalist fashion. Nor is the "ensemble" of relations even a Hegelian kind of totality in which the effects of the whole are a product of "a type of simple and circular totality, composed of equivalent elements."[26]

Rather, the global structure has two distinctive features. The first is that its constituent elements are not *pre*formed. They take their character during the very process in which the totality itself is organized, a kind of simultaneous occurrence. The mode of production represents for Poulantzas a special kind of combination of the instances (subsystems?) in which each instance arises and takes its form from the simultaneous presence of the other instances (and, as we shall see, from the special function of the economy in this process).[27] The net effect is that the nature of the relationships among the elements is a product of the constant shaping and reshaping of the instances (such as the forms and types of states, one of the instances) as they develop with respect to each other.

The second feature of the mode of production—global structure, totality, whole, all meaning roughly the same thing—is that it represents not an interacting set of elements with equal status but an ordered set in which the "unity" of the whole is, as we might wish to phrase it, a product of the hierarchical relationship among the elements. The economy, as one of the structures, dominates, in the sense of determines, the whole, because it is "determinant in the last instance," as I have indicated. But it need not always play the dominant role. Here Poulantzas differentiates between determination and dominant role. As he puts it in another of his enigmatic formulations, "The fact that the structure of the whole is determined in the last instance by the economic does not mean that the economic always holds the *dominant role* in the structure."[28]

Poulantzas rests this obscure conclusion on one major premise—the special place of the economy. For Poulantzas the economic instance (subsystem) is the source of the major contradictions in society. For this reason it can determine the fundamental relationships among all the instances "in the last resort." Thus, the contradictions in the economy may operate in such a way as to allow the political or ideological levels to play the dominant (but not the determinant) role. For example, under feudalism the contradiction in the economy between social relations and forces of production dictated that ideology in the form of religion assumed the dominant role. Hence, the struggle among the classes revealed itself in the form of a religious struggle. In classical antiquity the slave mode of production required the dominance of the political as a means of maintaining the subordination of the slaves. Under capitalism, on the other hand, the economy is both determinant in the last instance as well as dominant:[29] that is, the economy gives to itself the special dominant role assigned to the other instances in other modes of production. As a result, under capitalism the economic class struggles constitute the stage on which the contradictions of this mode of production are worked out.

In effect, for Poulantzas, the economy operates like a master switching device. It alone can determine which of the other two instances comes into operation with that kind of special influence called the "dominant role." To change the metaphor, there is a control hierarchy among the three instances in which the economy is always supreme. But it may count itself out, as it were, on a day-to-day basis and yield operational control to other instances depending upon the nature of the contradictions created in the economy itself. It is this special kind of control relationship of the economy to the mode of production as a whole that leads Poulantzas to describe the theoretical notion of a mode of production, not as interacting Parsonian subsystems or Hegelian totalities, but as a global "structure in dominance."

The ambiguities and circumlocutions here are not accidental. Following Althusser, this is a carefully designed attempt to provide a theoretical justification for retaining some of the meaning of the traditional Marxist idea that the economy is not just *primus inter pares* among all structural elements (or subsystems). The objective clearly is to provide theoretical grounds for permitting the economy to continue to fulfill a special function in society without, however, conceding that there is a mechanical one-to-one or directly deterministic relationship between the economy and other aspects of a society. In this way the latter relationship, pure economic determinism or economism as it is called, can be rejected without, however, relegating the economy to a functional status equivalent to the remaining two elements, the political and ideological, in its contribution to the operation of the whole mode of production. A kind of economic determinism is saved but only at the price of a virtually impenetrable confusion about the position of the economy (determination in the last instance) and the relationship of the instances to each other (relative autonomy).[30]

Sources of the Economy's Central Functions

How does it happen that the economy fulfills this special function of controlling the nature of what Poulantzas calls the "articulation" among the three invariant elements? We need only summarize his own brief and formal treatment of the matter. The reason for the special consequences of the economy is that it also consists of certain invariant elements: the laborer, the means of production and the nonlaborer. This is true for all modes of production whether slave, feudal, or capitalist. What is critical for the way the instances (the economic, political, and ideological) of a mode of production articulate or combine is the way these elements of the economy themselves are related. This is what ultimately accounts for differences in modes of production.

Variations in two kinds of relationships among the three elements of the economy will influence the nature of the mode of production. The first relationship is that of *real appropriation*—the way in which the *laborer* stands to the means of production and its products.[31] Does he own either or both? Is he separated from them? The second relationship is that of *property*. It refers to the way in which the *nonlaborer* stands to the means of production and to labor power and their products. The nonlaborer may own either one or all.

When these two central relationships—real appropriation and property—combine in different ways, their effects spread through all levels (subsystems) of the mode of production and determine the way they "articulate." Under the capitalist mode of production, the relation of property is such that the laborer is separated from the means of labor, and the owners of property appropriate to themselves the surplus labor, part of the product of labor.[32] The laborer is also separated from the products of his labor. These kinds of relationships ultimately create major contradictions between the socialization of the productive processes and private ownership of the means of production and their products. This central contradiction in the economy creates contradictions within the other two levels and in the way the whole combination of the levels occurs. Varying forms of class struggles evolve at each level to express these contradictions; ultimately they make a new mode of production, socialism, possible. In this sense, for Poulantzas, the economy is determinant in the last instance.

If Poulantzas had just argued that for these reasons the economy determines the nature of the mode of production and if he had stopped there we would have little to cavil about the clarity of his formulations. To have done so, however, as we now know, would have led him into the very "economism" or vulgar economic determinism that he had set out to avoid at all costs. Its limits as an interpretation of society had become only too obvious by the middle of the twentieth century, when the importance of the "state" as a social actor had begun to seem incontrovertible. The task was to find some intermediate function for the economy that would give it a special status and yet keep its effects within reasonable bounds so that it could not be said to determine all structures and behavior with a heavy hand.

To put limits of this sort on the economy Poulantzas had adopted Althusser's formulation: The economy is determinant not in general but only in the last instance. This succeeded in keeping the economy in the game and in its place, as it were. Yet by putting it into competition with the overall mode of production (ensemble of all instances) as the alternative determinant of society, the exact determining forces, if any, become ambiguous and obscure. To constrain the economy even further, as we have seen, Poulantzas also freed the other instances from the economic base, following Althusser in designating them as "relatively autonomous" of each other and of the whole mode of production.

The net result is clear. The economy has lost its position of outright primacy. But it does retain a privileged status. Each instance is relatively autonomous. Yet each is at the same time in some way determined by the whole mode of production and the latter by the economy itself "in the last instance." In the end we cannot help but wonder whether an important if unavowed consequence of these enigmatic notions is not only to free the instances from the economy but to free the observer and analyst, in the person of Poulantzas himself, from most theoretical constraints about how to interpret the position of each of the instances.

To be sure, as we shall later see, the analyst is not entirely free. There is one major theoretical limitation. As an unavowed functionalist, Poulantzas ascribes certain inescapable "functions" to each of the instances, including the state. Yet, within the limits of these specified functions, the question will remain as to whether Poulantzas's theory really allows anything to be determined uniquely. Such an inference will be particularly pertinent to an understanding of the limits of his theory in accounting for variations in the state.

In summary, then, the ambiguities in Poulantzas's theoretical propositions about determination in the last instance by the economy and the relative autonomy of each instance create a profound indeterminacy in the application of and the inferences from his theories. With Althusser as his point of departure, Poulantzas seems to wish to turn, at least nominally, to the mode of production, a very abstract theoretical concept, and not to the economy, as the basic determinant of society. Within the capitalist mode of production, however, the economy does have a special function, and this is why, in Poulantzas's view, it has often been misinterpreted vulgarly as the single determinant of society. For him the economy is determinant, however, only "in the last instance." At the very least it has seemed to mean that the peculiar feature of the mode of production is that it reserves to the economy the decisive control over the degrees of freedom offered to other aspects of the "superstructure," such as ideology or politics.[33]

The state, therefore, is not simply a mirror of the economy, of other instances or of the mode of production as a whole. It has its own capacity to intervene in and shape society. At the same time it is not free to roam at will either. There is apparently a complex relationship of freedom, determination and, as we shall later see, even of a loose constraint (implied, at least, if not explicit).

In effect it is this kind of involved relationship between the state and economy, as structural elements of society, that Poulantzas sets out to describe. Thereby he hopes to demonstrate that the state is not merely an ephiphenomenal superstructure and that its structural forms and policies can be adequately accounted for in terms other than by the simplistic abstractions of the economism of vulgar Marxists. But from the qualifications he imposes on the conditions influencing the state we shall later find that Poulantzas virtually frees himself from almost all constraints as he seeks to explain variations in the forms and types of states.

This is the way, then, that Poulantzas conceptualizes the whole social order as he lays the groundwork for his subsequent analysis of one of its parts, the state, and for his efforts to explain the latter's different types and forms. As the overarching order, the mode of production, in his technical sense, represents what we can call the structuralist base that "accounts for," as he will put it, the form and outcomes of every part of society including the state.

Since Poulantzas is developing a theory of politics, his focus is on the state, the conceptual centerpiece of his theory. Since the state must take its forms and practices from the specific character of the mode of production, the task for

Poulantzas is to unravel the way the instances, in each transformation of the mode of production, are typically shaped and articulated with each other and the whole system. And, as he is especially concerned with the contemporary state, this means tracing the changes in the state as the mode of production shifts from what he call the early competitive to the most recent monopoly capitalism. Such transformations as these in the capitalist mode of production will "reflect" themselves, again in Poulantzas's language, in changes in each of the complexly interwoven instances, including the state. In short, the way in which Poulantzas poses his questions about the state inevitably leads him to the primary issue of how the whole, that is, the mode of production, is related to transformations in that part in which, as a self-declared student of politics, he is especially interested, namely, the state.

Poulantzas's Structuralism and Systems Analysis

Now that we have set out the skeletal structure of Poulantzas's thinking we are ready to return to the central concern of this chapter: How does his structuralism relate to system thinking with its emphasis on the part-whole relationship? By this point in our analysis no heroic effort is needed to read into Poulantzas's conceptualization an attempt to address himself to the same kind of questions that are to be found in a systems way of thinking about politics.[34] Even though the concepts he uses reflect a commitment to Marxist nineteenth-century terminology and its twentieth-century derivatives, in fact, at the hands of Poulantzas, as adapted from Althusser, they do betray an effort, however unwittingly, to introduce Marxism to a twentieth-century systems point of view, or to achieve some kind of loose accommodation between the two. In the end, this systems orientation leads Poulantzas to retrieve from traditional Marxism and to pose precisely the kind of question which had brought Teune and Ostrowski to a halt: To what extent are particular aspects of a political system a product, not of one or another isolable factor within or outside the system, but of the way in which the system as a whole, as a higher-order structure, is put together and operates?

Poulantzas formulates the issue, as I have noted, through the use of a vocabulary and mode of discourse inherited in part from the nineteenth century. Essentially, in following Althusser he adopts a systems formulation, however, almost transparently so, even though he covers his tracks with traditional Marxist language. At the simplest level, that of terminology, this systems inclination is ill concealed. Thus his concept *social formation* is little more than the concept *society* in disguise, with all the built-in imprecision of the latter term. His decomposition of the social formation into its invariant *instances* (elements, levels, regional structures) simply represents an alternative formulation for the specifications of the *subsystems* in a society. The *mode of production* (ensemble of instances, global structure) as a construct, referring collectively to these abstracted subsystems, substitutes for the idea of *social system*. Social formation, instances, mode of production or global structure stand, therefore, for society, subsystems and social system.

Even the names of the instances or subsystems differ little from those found in conventional systems terminology. Economy, ideology, and state are also well known as economic, cultural,[35] and political subsystems. Finally, in concluding that the state can be understood only as part of the overall mode of production and as an integral part of it, being constituted simultaneously with the transformation of the whole, he is operating on the premise that the political system is a product of and in turn helps to shape the social system itself.

Of course, his specific theory about how all this takes place—through conflict or contradictions within and among the instances—differs from that of most non-Marxist systems analyses, although if it were germane to our purposes it could be demonstrated that the abyss is not so great as Poulantzas himself would like to have imagined and as outsiders would like to believe. Indeed the schematic presentation in diagram 12.1 looks as though it might be a variant of one of the many similar systems diagrams by Parsons—and indeed Poulantzas has often been characterized as an essential Parsonian. He has on occasion even been called the Talcott Parsons of Marxism, and in this there is some justice.[36] Presumably, despite the enormous substantive differences between Poulantzas and Parsons, the comparison has been meant to emphasize, correctly, the functionalist formalism of both.

There is an even deeper similarity, however, in that Parsons is often represented as a systems analyst. Certainly in the second half of his career Parsons had decomposed society into four major subsystems, however differently they may be defined as compared to Poulantzas's subsystems. Poulantzas and Parsons are also alike, however, in that both adopted only a truncated systems point of view. Neither recognized feedback mechanisms as central to their analyses; at best, Parsons introduced it only in his later writings, and then only in a nominal sense. Their similarity goes even further. Each orders the relationship among their subsystems hierarchically, even though Parsons offers a dual hierarchy in which material conditions (the economy) and culture control in different ways, whereas Poulantzas remains with a single controlling subsystem, the economy (material conditions). Thus, in this formalistic functionalism, subdivision into similar subsystems, neglect of feedback, and hierarchic ordering of subsystems Poulantzas echoes Parsons, however much they may differ in the substantive theories at which they arrive through the use of these formal similarities.

Unlike Lévi-Strauss, who claimed to adopt a systems approach but in practice permitted it to have little influence on his work, Poulantzas made no pretensions to systems thinking, yet in practice the changing epistemological pressures of the mid-twentieth century toward system thinking did seem to mold his perspectives. Perhaps this is most clearly if only superficially revealed in his inability to escape an informal and unwitting adoption of the concept of system itself. It seems as though the systems orientation intruded on his thinking, whatever his intentions.

For example, even though the idea of system is already implicit in his earliest work, *Political Power and Social Classes*, he uses it there only infrequently.[37] By the time he writes *Fascism and Dictatorship* a mere two years later, however, his resistance to the term *political system* has begun to crumble. In the latter book he casually and regularly speaks of the state system, the juridical system, ideological subsystems, and the like. Indeed, in this book the idea of system almost seems to be on the way to displacing the concept of instance or level.[38] This shift was already

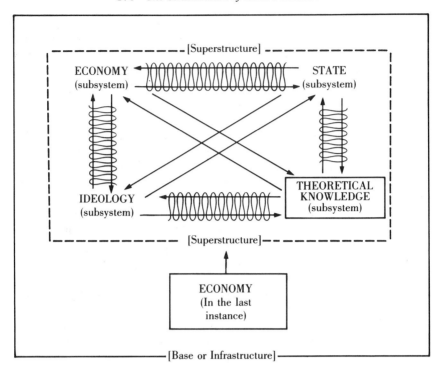

Diagram 12.1   Mode of Production

NOTES:

1. The diagram shows the hierarchical order in each mode of production.
2. Theoretical knowledge as a subsystem is boxed off as even though it is identified as an instance, it is not retained as an active component.
3. The economy appears twice, once as a subsystem and again as the economy "in the last instance" to represent the double function it serves.
4. The wiggles on the arrows alert us to Poulantzas's rejection of interaction as a description of the relation among the component subsystems. Rather, Poulantzas interprets the subsystems as "interpenetrating," "articulating with," or "inscribed in" each other. For a fuller discussion of these terms, see chapter 13. Thus the whole box, marked "mode of production," should be read to mean that the state of the whole system is produced by the "ensemble" of all subsystems "in their unity" (see *Political Power and Social Classes*, p. 95).
5. The wiggles on the arrows also alert us to the fact that the subsystems include the structures and practices (class struggles and conflicts). Within each and among them all, contradictions arise, the resolution of which is undertaken through the practices. The chief contradiction occurs in the economy. It leads to fundamental transformations in the whole system. Hence, it is "determinant in the last instance" and we may call the whole social system a hierarchical structure of contradictions.

foreshadowed in his essay on "The Problem of the Capitalist State,"[39] where the term is used extensively. Perhaps there he was influenced by the fact that Miliband, with whom he was debating, consciously adopts the idea of system to refer to the total political sphere within which the state itself functions. For Miliband, the state explicitly takes its place as a subsystem within the political system.[40] Nonetheless, it would be misleading to suggest that despite such forays into systems territory, the systems idea remains anything other than an uneasy and casual transient within Poulantzas's conceptualization.[41]

In effect, Poulantzas was trying to help Marxism catch up with bourgeois political science. He does this by accepting the possibility of constructing a special theory about politics, under capitalism at least, and by conceptualizing politics as a subsystem embedded in, influenced by, and, in turn, influencing the social system as a whole. In my own terms, he sees politics as a subsystem analytically separable from other social systems but empirically interwoven with them.[42] Not that Poulantzas would have admitted to this formulation of his enterprise, as I have already acknowledged. But I am trying to look at the reality rather than the rhetoric.

Unless we bear this systems perspective in mind, it is difficult to understand why Poulantzas grappled with such obscure and slippery ideas as "determination in the last instance" and "relative autonomy of the instances." He was not willing to give up entirely the traditional Marxist significance attaching to the asymmetric influence of the economy, nor was he prepared to ignore the modern view of multiple and simultaneous symmetric influences acting on such broad and complex variables as are represented in the political system, including factors internal to the political system itself. He adopted and sought to give sociological content to Althusser's obscure notions as a way of reconciling the old with the new.

Furthermore, "relative autonomy" was a vital innovative idea from Althusser that made feasible the introduction of a systems point of view into Marxism. As long as such superstructures as the state were derived from an economic base, there was no dynamism in or even real decomposability to the social system. All aspects of society were reduced to the economy. The idea of the possible relative autonomy of major subsystems freed the superstructures, as it were, including the state, from the so-called base or infrastructure and thereby freed the investigator to look for dynamic changing relationships among the various major elements of society, each being capable of influencing the other in greater or lesser degree. This new analytic flexibility brought Marxist methods of inquiry closer to conventional social science, especially as found in those adopting a point of view that saw society as analytically decomposable into interrelated subsystems.[43]

Peering into the conceptual world of systems analysis, through the side window, as it were, Poulantzas is, however, never able to make full use of the conceptual armamentorium of systems analysis. He thereby loses the opportunity to put certain powerful ideas to work, such as those of feedback or inputs. The unmistakable intrusion of a systems point of view into his own thinking, however, and the clear affinity of Marxism to systems thinking does help explain how it happens that Poulantzas should at this historical period pull out the particular problem of the part-whole relationship for special attention. The state, as a part of the whole social system, is no longer just a product of societal forces; it stands in a more complex relationship—one of relative autonomy—to the other instances or subsystems of society. And, as we have seen, Poulantzas places the state at the center of his contribution to the development of a Marxist political science. Specifically, he sees as his task the discovery of how the way the whole *social* system operates relates to the particular forms taken by the political system, that is, in his terms, the state.[44]

As I have suggested earlier, it is a difficult question, one that political science as a whole has failed to pose directly for itself and one to which political science has not even indirectly been able to offer any moderately adequate answers. It was to Poulantzas's credit that he does not dodge this central if neglected issue in political science but, rather, elevates it to a major, conscious purpose in his theory of the state.

Conclusion

As we shall see, Poulantzas is less than successful in demonstrating a linkage between states of the overall social system and the various forms of the political system. He has many hypotheses about this relationship but, as with conventional political science, the mechanisms elude him. His very failure, however, will at least illuminate the dimensions of the problem for us further. Not surprisingly, his unwitting escape hatch may be the only one currently available to social research in general.

In the end I shall conclude that, for a number of reasons, Poulantzas fails to make a convincing case for the kind of relationships he claims to find between variations in structural forms of the state and changes in the capitalist mode of production (social system). In the first place, his theoretical analysis is at such a high level of formality that he never makes the necessary linkages, even theoretically, let alone empirically, between the overarching structure of the social system and the identified variations in the state structures (such as normal and exceptional forms). For one pair of authors, Poulantzas's work represents "a political construction of the *Staatstheorie* kind, where the [empirical] connections between the state apparatus and the rest of the society appear flimsy and hard to grasp."[45]

The confirmation of such empirical connections would, however, be too much to ask of a theoretical work. We must grant that since Poulantzas is operating at the theoretical level he is really not called upon to demonstrate empirically the relationships he claims to discover. The deficiency is, rather, that he does not describe these possible empirical connections satisfactorily even at the *theoretical* level. Therein lies his fundamental weakness and his formalism.[46]

In the second place, his formalism flows from the epistemology associated with objective functionalism. He consistently refuses to allow, in theory at least, that actors, individually or collectively, may produce their own political and social effects, not just as pawns in the hands of history—*Träger*, as he calls actors, following Marx, or supports—but as actors whose rational calculations, intentions, motivations, and independently generated behavior may make a historical difference. In practice, however, he cannot help but assume some independence, in this sense, for the actor, or at least for class actors. We shall find unresolved tensions in his work between this structural objectivism and practical subjectivism.

Finally, I shall seek to show that he is ultimately forced by his own logic to concede, reluctantly even if unwittingly, that structures (types and forms of the state) are less likely to be determined, shaped, or molded than to be limited or constrained. There is a significant difference between these two possible positions. Poulantzas finds himself torn between the alternatives, and irresolute in face of them. What begins as a theory of determination ends at most as a theory of limits or possibilities, a conclusion vastly different from what he seemed to wish. From such a position it is impossible for him to deliver on his initial promise to account for variations in observed forms as direct effects of changes in the mode of production.

In the end his project fails. Our task will be to see what we can salvage from this failure for our understanding of the relationship between lower- and higher-order structures.

13

A Structuralist Explanation
of the State

Our objective is to understand how Poulantzas explains the different forms that the political system, or, in his terms, the state, assumes and to see what we can learn from his efforts. For Poulantzas the forms of the state are a product of two kinds of factors: the structure of the system as a whole and of the economy as a separable element. He would probably not admit to this characterization, at least to the extent it implies that he considers that the economy has a direct and independent influence on the form of the state. He is clearly hoping to explain the state by appealing to the so-called underlying structure of the social system as a whole (the mode of production) in which the economy occupies a special place. I shall conclude that he fails to make an effective case for this structuralist explanation.

In this chapter I shall begin the process leading to this conclusion by showing that part of the reason for his failure lies in the very nature of the type of explanation he attempts. His conclusion founders on his explanatory assumptions. Yet, as I shall point out, the nature of his explanation, whatever its shortcomings, does serve to highlight the issues faced by any attempt to understand the sources of variation in lower-order structures.

State Forms and Public Policy

Why does Poulantzas become extensively involved in differences among types and forms of states? This seems like a preoccupation with minutiae hitherto atypical of Marxist inquiry. Furthermore, given the general Marxist focus on the dynamics of class conflict in social systems, it comes as something of a surprise to discover, in this first intensive effort to develop a Marxist theory of politics, an unusual preoccupation with taxonomy.

The answer is that the emphasis on classification is deceptive. Even though it does occupy an inordinate amount of space in Poulantzas's writings, it is only derivative, not primary. His initial interest lies, rather, in variations of state policies. He sees them as at times contradictory, hesitating, subject to frequent voltes-face, as he put it. More important, they often appear to favor the workers, the very class against which the task of the state is to protect the dominant classes. If, as will appear, the primary function of the state is to preserve the capitalist mode of production and its dominant classes, how can policies which obviously favor the dominated classes, be explained? This is the question that drives his analysis.

The answer for Poulantzas is that policies are a function of the various changes which the types and forms of the state undergo. He therefore sees it as his task, in building a theory of politics, to explore the variations in the relationships among those structural elements that make up the types and forms of states, such as parties, police, courts, legislatures, and chief executives. The different relations among such components will explain, for Poulantzas, why major policies differ and at the same time will permit him to demonstrate how, appearances notwithstanding, they do in fact contribute to the protection of the dominant classes and to the preservation of capitalism as a mode of production.[1]

It is clear that Poulantzas is responding in part to the pressures of bourgeois political science to deal with public policies, reflecting the shift in conventional political research during the 1970s. But true to his Marxist origins, he does so from a different perspective. Unlike conventional political science, Poulantzas is less interested in understanding all the determinants and consequences of public policy than in demonstrating that, despite their bias in favor of the dominated classes at times, such policies are really a means whereby the state preserves the capitalist mode of production.

Herein lies the origin of Poulantzas's interest in types and forms of the state. He considers them to be the major determinants of policies. If he can show that they arise from changes in the modes of production (for him, the fundamental structure of the social system) and that the latter must always operate to perpetuate itself, then the policies of the state as an integral element in the mode of production, must serve the same end. This preoccupation with a designated underlying social structure also serves to put him into that category of analysis we have already considered under the name of structuralism.

Functionalist Explanation

For Poulantzas, as we shall see, states change their forms from liberal to interventionist and from democratic to fascist or authoritarian, for example. What is the character of such transformations? How are they to be explained? Are they due to the fallibilities of human behavior, to the interests of specific classes, leaders, or groups in society?

Poulantzas rejects any explanations such as these that see the state as a reflection of the interests and pressures of individuals or groups, or even of factions of the capitalist class. For him this approach invokes a humanist or "anthropological" account of the state. In it the human subject, with its interest, intentions, and desires, would shape structural forms and policies. This tendency, even for some Marxists, to consider the state as a Thing[2]—what Poulantzas calls an instrumental explanation—or of liberals to see it as a Subject able to act freely in terms of its independently established ends, he rejects. As we shall see, for Poulantzas, in structuralist vein, policies can be understood only as a reflection of "objective" contradictions, inherent in the capitalist mode of production, among the classes and "fractions" (parts of classes). The state (and its policies) "condenses" or refracts these contradictions, visible in class struggles at various levels, and expresses them in its varying policies.[3] In short, for Poulantzas the state takes its character from the objective infrastructure that he calls the mode of production.

His explanation of variations in state forms or structures turns on an attempt, at least in the first instance, to insist upon the exclusive influence of a presumed underlying objective structure—the mode of production—independent of the subjective intentions and desires of human actors. This objective structure becomes a "cause" in itself. Within this kind of structural context, various parts, such as the state, cannot escape serving certain functions. Paramount among these is the preservation and reproduction of the mode of production itself.

His structuralism is, therefore, closely tied to a functionalist point of view.[4] The existence of a particular structure leads him to explore the functions served by its parts. The parts of a structure are, in a favorite phrase of his, "accounted for" or understood only in terms of their functions in the whole structure, that is, in terms of the presumed purposes they serve for the whole. His critics have not been wrong in accusing him of being a structural-functionalist and to that extent he has not inappropriately been characterized, as we have noted, as the Talcott Parsons of Marxism.

Poulantzas is not, of course, a self-conscious or a self-avowed functionalist; he just operates as an intuitive one in most of his analyses.[5] We would, however, be misled by this conception of his work if we looked for consistency in his theoretical practice. Despite his claims to the contrary, he is reluctant to give up some critical dependence on ordinary causal (which he calls mechanical) determination in contrast to functional explanation. Causal and functionalist explanations need not necessarily be opposites, depending on how they are defined. But since Poulantzas explicitly rejects asymmetric causality, we are left with the impression that the only acceptable way of accounting for the forms and policies of the state is through the purposes they serve for the whole social system (mode of production). Nonetheless, we shall find that, in the end, he does in fact continue to depend to some degree on causal explanations, combining it with functionalism. In failing to face up to the different demands of these two commitments, however, he succeeds in entangling himself in an intricate web of explanation. Understandably, it has led to well-known complaints about his complexity and his formalism[6] and to comparisons, at least in his functionalism, with Talcott Parsons, as I have observed.

The difficulties that Poulantzas encounters in explaining the various forms of the state and their associated policies cannot be separated, therefore, from his assumptions about the character of an adequate explanation. As we shall discover in the end, his functionalism leads to virtually pure description, and he will be unable to fulfill the explanatory promise of even the residual causality reserved for the economy. He will be reduced to a kind of explanation that consists of a description of limits that differs little from what we find, from time to time, in conventional political science. And more important, his functionalist premises lead to presumptions about built-in purposes for such structures as the state that, by their very nature, are not likely to be demonstrable.

Method of "Interpenetration" as Functionalism Concealed

Poulantzas's methodological assumptions are easier to understand in what they deny than in what they affirm. In the first place, he rejects what he calls a "mechanistic"[7] explanation of the relationship of the base to the superstructure. He explicitly eschews any suggestion of social causation, that is, as we may put it, of time asymmetric relationships of the sort that say: if A, then B; if B, then A must first have occurred. This logic he associates with vulgar determinism or economism, an explanation in which the economic base is "mechanistically" seen as determining the political structure.[8]

Poulantzas's whole work is in some sense an attack on this interpretation, one that he finds prevalent in Marxism. Yet his unwillingness to deny a certain primacy to the economy, as we have seen in the preceding chapter, leads to an ambiguity in his explanation of the political system which compounds the difficulties already created by his functionalism. Despite his efforts, he is never able to find a cure for the resulting obscurity in his explanations.

Let us look further at the kinds of explanations he finds wanting. Not only does he reject mechanistic—that is, causal—determination, as he puts it, but he separates his analysis in summary fashion from the idea, first, that any level of society is simply a particular resultant of the impact of or the interaction with all other levels taken individually or collectively;[9] or second, that the condition of a social system as a whole is simply the outcome of the varying interactions among the subsystems along the lines of a Parsonian model. For Poulantzas a set of simultaneous equations showing the covariations among the subsystems (instances) would not be satisfactory for uncovering the linkages through which any one subsystem, such as the political, much less the totality, could be explained.

Poulantzas renounces these types of explanation because for him they lead us, wrongly, to conceive of each of the three instances—the economic, political, and ideological—as separable, pre-existing and invariant elements[10] of a mode of production that combine and recombine with each other to form the given social system. To take this view would lead to the assumptions that somehow each instance is preformed, that is, comes into being and maintains itself as an independent entity in society, that each subsystem is "external" to the other,[11] that each subsystem could then help to reproduce or maintain the others, and that the total effect of the particular way these elements interact and combine would be to give a social system (the mode of production) its special character. For Poulantzas such a position would justify the independent study of the way the economy or the political system took shape and evolved over time and of their reciprocal effects.

Poulantzas opposes this approach as assuming an independence among the elements that they do not and cannot possess.[12] Instead Poulantzas argues for what we might call a theory of "interpenetration." Each subsystem, from its very inception, is part and parcel of the whole mode of production, takes its character from its presence in the totality, and contributes to the nature of the whole social system. As he puts it, each subsystem or instance is "inscribed" in every other instance from the very outset, each part reflects the whole, and the whole derives it character from the "interpenetration" of the parts.[13] It is not a matter of each subsystem being separate and apart from the others and acting on each other from the outside. The task is to recognize that each is present in the other, all coming into being simultaneously. In Poulantzas's own words,

> a mode of production does not arise out of the combination of various instances, all of which possess an inalterable structure before they come into relation with one another. It is rather the mode of production itself—that totality of economic, political and ideological determinations—which fixes the boundaries of these spaces, sketching out their fields and defining their respective elements. They are from the very *beginning* constituted by their mutual relation and articulation—a process that is effected in each mode of production through the determining role of the relations of production. But that determination law always takes place within the unity of the mode of production.[14]

Time seems to disappear from this conception of relationships. Everything changes at once with the suddenness of creation. Nothing "causes" anything. Rather, in some formative or constitutive way, each element of the social system is involved in the other and in all elements together.

From the point of view of explanation, it is not a matter, therefore, of either structures (or, for that matter, even practices) "causing" or being associated (covarying) with certain effects. "External causation" is rejected,[15] as is covariation. Explanation, rather, requires us to identify the way the "interpenetration" of the instances or their "articulation" occur or to discover the degree to which one does or does not "correspond to or reflect" the other. Explanation must be sought through a description of the internal organization of a system, of how things fit together according to some uncertain criterion of coherence. "It is precisely because politico-ideological relations are already present in the actual constitution of the relations of production that they play such an essential role in their reproduction; that is also why the process of production and exploitation involves reproduction of the relations of politico-ideological domination and subordination."[16]

In thus shying away from notions of linear causation, simultaneous causal effects or mere covariation Poulantzas was of course moving in an important direction. He grasped a critical point, namely, that the parts of a social system, such as its political aspects, could not be fully understood either in their own terms or as products of one or another limited combination of social factors. Somehow the way the whole—for Poulantzas, the mode of production (social system)—is organized has a bearing on the form of the part itself, such as the political system. In this way he was preserving the issue raised by the structuralists, namely, of the relationship between the parts and the whole.

In this intuitive pursuit of the issue central to structuralism Poulantzas is driven to create a vocabulary to express his complex conception of how the state, as one of the instances, changes its form as the larger whole, the overall mode of production itself, changes over time. In the process, as I have noted, he reveals an unwitting acceptance of a functionalist mode of analysis. A part can be understood only if we can locate the way it serves some postulated end, such as the preservation of the whole, that is, the overall mode of production. Presumed teleological premises permeate his analysis.

The function or purposes of the political, for example, is not to reproduce the relations of production, that is, the economic relations in any simplistic sense.[17] The political and ideological levels are already present in the constitution of the relations of production, Poulantzas argues. As the relations of production take shape, they can do so only if the state is already there to preserve and guarantee them. And as the relations of production come into being they give rise to the necessity of the state. Each level or instance (subsystem) simultaneously and continuously involves the other; one is not analyzed as an "external" determinant of the other, as we might propose in conventional social analysis.[18]

Since nothing causes anything in his explanation (except, ambiguously, the economy, "in the last instance") or even covaries or even participates in producing simultaneous and reciprocal effects, Poulantzas is forced to search for a language to express the coherence he finds among the elements of a social system. Finding no single term that can satisfactorily express his obscure intentions, he seizes on a variety of terms that only reveals the inherent ambiguity in his thought. He speaks of "articulation" of the instances,[19] of the way the mode of production "governs" the instances,[20] or of how an instance "reflects,"[21] "corresponds to,"[22] "is present in,"[23] "is due to,"[24] the whole mode of production.[25]

These terms all seek to convey the notion that each instance can be understood only by interpreting it as participating in the formation and maintenance (reproduction) of the other two instances, with all instances combining to create a particular mode of production. Through these multiple terms describing this kind of relationship, Poulantzas is clearly groping for an imagery to express an ill-formed conception of the holistic nature of the relationships among the instances. Having excluded just about all major conceivable forms of that relationship, we need not wonder at the difficulty he encounters in finding a concept for describing the alternative.

The imagery here is difficult to grasp. Part of the reason is because it does reduce to the level of imagery or metaphor. Articulation, interpenetration, reflection, governance, and the like evoke images; they are more difficult to pin down logically and operationally. In fact, it is not clear how articulation and interpenetration differ from ordinary social interaction except that instead of A leaving a definitive and time-defined asymmetric impact on B, A and B simultaneously and continuously seem to affect each other in an undecomposable relationship.[26] This simultaneous interaction leads to changes in the state of the whole social system (mode of production). Formally, this might be expressed as a set of simultaneous equations. This route was clearly available to Poulantzas as a way of sorting out the nature of the interaction among the elements. He ignores it, however, and perhaps part of the reason lies in his unwitting dependence on a functionalist perspective.

The examination of the "articulation" of the instances is made more complex by the fact that not only may the *structures* (subsystems or instances) "correspond" to each other; they may also be in a condition of "dislocation" or disharmony. To compound the analytic difficulties further, each level or instance not only has a structure. There are processes within these structures which Poulantzas designates as class conflict and struggles. These practices may be in or out of synchronization with the structures. Thus, not only the instances but the practices (class struggles) as well may be out of phase and in conflict. They also contribute to systems maintenance ("reproduction") or change ("dislocation"). As he remarks, "*So what is important is to see that there are in fact two systems of relations here* . . . [and] the relations between these two series [systems] of relations [may] themselves [be] relations of dislocations characterized by an unambiguous non-correspondence between the terms of the respective levels of these systems."[27]

Poulantzas illustrates this system of relations between the instances (structures) and the practices with Marx's own analysis of Britain after 1680.[28] At that time there was a dislocation between the economic, the political, and the ideological in the sense that these subsystems were out of phase. At the very time when the capitalist economy was becoming dominant, two structures, the state and ideology, were still feudal.[29] At the level of practice or class struggle, it was the landed nobility as a class that was "in charge,"[30] as Marx put it, of the apparatus of the feudal state. Yet this class did not hold state power (in Poulantzas's technical sense, as we shall later see). State power had already moved into the hands of the bourgeoisie whose representative the feudal class in effect became. In short, "the juridico-political superstructure of the state is dislocated not simply in relation to other structures, but also in relation to the level of the political struggle of the bourgeoisie in the field of the class struggle."[31] That is to say, the state, being in the hands of the nobility, was "dislocated" both with respect to the economic structure which was capitalist-dominated and to the class struggle in which the capitalists already held power over the state but were not "in charge"[32] of the "state apparatus" (machinery of government). In this way Poulantzas tries to demonstrate that there is not necessarily a one-to-one correspondence between the economic level or structure and the economic class struggle, on the one side, and their political manifestations at the structural and class struggle levels, on the other.

A description such as this of the way in which the various elements (instances and practices) of the social system combine represents the closest thing to an explanation of the condition or state of any subsystem and of the whole social system. In other words, if Poulantzas is to explain the various forms taken by the political system (the state), he can do so only by showing how it is constituted by the remaining two structural elements in the mode of production, the economic and the ideological, and how the political system in turn helps to shape the latter.

To clarify what Poulantzas is trying to say almost forces us to give him a clarity not really possessed by his analysis. What he would seem to like to say is that there are moments when those who are economically dominant may not also be politically dominant. Such a situation can be expected to lead to political policies not necessarily hospitable to the demands of the economically powerful. But, as the preceding few paragraphs indicate, this is putting the matter too simply and mechanistically for Poulantzas. The economic and political instances (subsystems) are far more complexly related, each being, in some almost ineffable way, part of the other.

Poulantzas's method looks something like the Hegelian-derived "philosophy of internal relations" that Ollman has detected in Marx. As Ollman describes this method, "To state what is known about any one thing is to describe the system in which it exists; it is to present, as Hegel invariably did, each part as a facet of the whole."[33] As Ollman phrases it again, a little differently,

> Our common sense conceptions of 'whole' and 'part' are derived from a view of the world in which the whole (any whole) is the sum of its parts, themselves separate and distinct units which have simply been added together (an external relation). . . . [But] what is referred to as 'part' is a relational construct, a unit abstracted from reality for some particular end whose interdependence with other similarly constituted units is kept clearly in view; and 'whole' is just this interdependence which, again for special purposes, may be conceptualized within any of its parts.[34]

As we have seen, Poulantzas explicitly denies the validity of ascribing effects of one instance, such as the state, on the whole combination of instances (the "system" about which Ollman talks in the above quotation). This, for Poulantzas, represents the attribution of external causation. For Poulantzas, factors "interpenetrate" each other; they do not cause or covary with each other. If Ollman describes Marx's method as a "philosophy of internal relations" we are correct in calling Poulantzas's "the method interpenetration," as I have suggested.

It is this very method of interpenetration that represents the source of Poulantzas's functionalist analysis. In accounting for the existence of and variations in the state, Poulantzas moves effortlessly from mere description of its interpenetrating relations with other subsystems, and with the whole, into a discussion about and description of the presumed functions or purposes that the state serves in the whole social system. It would appear that his complex analysis of interpenetration is just a preface for an indirect and unavowed justification of a teleologically based explanation.

In effect Poulantzas wants us to believe that because of the interpenetrating character of all subsystems and the whole social system, we can say we understand the state when we have identified and described its functions in the whole. The mode of production as a whole is presumed to have certain requirements. The various levels or subsystems in the whole fulfill these requirements; this is their function or what they are required to do as a result of the way the overall mode of production is put together.

Thus, for example, the major functions of the state, in this view, are its contribution to the necessary cohesion of a social system and to the necessary reproduction (maintenance) of the mode of production (the whole social system). In his own words, "The State is precisely the factor of cohesion of a social formation and the factor of reproduction of the conditions of production of a system."[35] In short, for Poulantzas we understand the "interpenetration" of the subsystems and their "articulation" when we have described the presumed function of each in constituting and reproducing the other. To state the matter in its baldest form, this is why the instances, levels or subsystems exist; this is their function or purposes.

The argument here is, of course, dubious. In biology, from which the term *function* was ultimately derived, we do not feel we have adequately explained the long tongue of the anteater when we say it is there for the presumed function of enabling the animal to survive. Rather, the presence of the long tongue, as perhaps a mutation, enabled the animal to compete effectively in the pursuit of food and thereby helped it to survive. Suvival was not the purpose of the tongue; it was a consequence under the evolutionary conditions, a substantially different kind of explanation. Similarly, as I shall suggest in a moment, an understanding of the state does not come from declaring the functions it must serve but rather in pointing to its consequences under given conditions.

Explanatory Dualism: Functionalism and Causality

Understanding Poulantzas would be enormously simplified but for one major irritant in his style. He finds it virtually impossible to commit himself fully or consistently to a single methodological position. He fractures what might otherwise have been a pure functionalist approach by making a major concession to what he calls linear (asymmetric) causation even after having argued vigorously against it. This rupture originates in his effort to follow Althusser in salvaging something of the special place taken by the economy in Marx's own formulation.

As we will recall, Poulantzas maintains that "the type of unity which characterizes a mode of production is that of a *complex whole* dominated, in the last instance, by the economic. The term *determination* will be reserved for this dominance in the last instance."[36] This oft-repeated sentence, taken from Engels, remains shrouded in ambiguity. But whatever it may mean, at the very least it would seem to imply prior occurrence, a time asymmetry essential to the idea of causation. Functionalism seems, at least at this ultimate point, to yield to causal explanation.

Even here, however, as an earlier quotation[37] shows, Poulantzas does not easily give up his functionalism. The economy does not really "determine" in and of itself. If there is any causal effect it operates to compel the elements of the social system to "articulate," that is, to function so as to reproduce or change the system and its parts. If the phrase "determination in the last instance" has any meaning that is consistent with the rest of Poulantzas's analysis, it is that the economy brings about an inescapable (determining) condition in the social system through which each of the subsystems performs its "appropriate" function in maintaining or changing the mode of production. The ends of the subsystems are structurally defined and assigned, as it were; they are there to serve the postulated needs of the overall social structure. The state, for example, as one such subsystem "*has* to represent the long-term political interest of the whole bourgeoisie."[38] The task of inquiry is to clarify that position, that is, how the subsystem serves the postulated functions of a (capitalist) social system.

This is the only sensible way in which we can interpret the meaning of the quotation above in which Poulantzas states that the relationship of "articulation" is itself apparently "effected in each mode of production through the determining role of the relations of production (the economy)."[39] It would appear that to be "determinant in the last instance" does not really mean what it seems to say. Poulantzas would want it to mean only that the economy provides the *conditions* for the articulation or interpenetration of the instances. Yet in doing so the idea of *determination* suggests that the interpenetration is inescapable ("determining") because of the influence of the economy. Hence, much as Poulantzas may wish to escape any accusation of defending "mechanistic causation," his conception of "determination by the economy in the last instance"[40] would seem to make this impossible.

True to his functionalist approach, Poulantzas interprets the function of the economy in the mode of production as that of *compelling* all instances to "articulate" in a particular way. Functions make determination necessary as an energizing force, as it were. Thus, under capitalism economic relations leave no option but for each of the elements of the social system—the political and ideological as well as the economic itself—to serve the needs of the capitalist kind of mode of production. And as capitalism passes through its various "phases and stages"—from competitive through to monopoly capitalism—each subsystem will change to meet the new, postulated needs for the survival of the changing capitalist mode of production.[41]

It would appear, therefore, that functionalism itself presupposes an initial act of determination or causation as it were. Once the economy itself performs its primal act, as it were, by establishing or causing (determining) the nature of the mode of production, it sets in motion a kind of social system in which all the parts as well as the whole *must* function in one way or another to reproduce or change that system. The economy resembles the Puritan god who, through an act of creation, sets in motion not the mechanistic world of the seventeenth century but the functionally interdependent world of today in which each major part, the instances, are there for a purpose, namely, to preserve the whole system.

The task of a political theory (a theory of the state) becomes, then, to demonstrate the way the state fulfills its necessary ends under a given mode of production. In this way Poulantzas can have his cake and eat it. While surreptitiously adopting functionalism he can reject other conventional modes of analysis in social science such as the search for causes, covariations, interaction or deductive relationship, and yet accept his major *bête noire*, causality, as an external force that sets the whole process in motion and controls its change.

Unless we recognize this explanatory dualism in Poulantzas's methods, we are unable to account satisfactorily for his structuralism. Peculiarly enough, in his very preservation of causality (necessity) lies the "structuralist" base of his method. Without this turn to causality he would have found it impossible to argue that the mode of production, in which the economy has a privileged position, provides the context within which the whole and the parts can be understood. It enables him to see all parts of a system as "interpenetrating" with one another. But this functionalism in itself is insufficient; it only provides a method, teleological in premises, it turns out, for relating parts to the whole. Although some structuralists may be functionalist, not all functionalists are necessarily structuralists.

Poulantzas's structuralism derives from a primal act of causal necessity attributable to the economy. The latter determines, in the sense of compels, all parts of the social system to serve the maintenance (reproduction) needs of the whole.[42] Thus, for example, as we have seen, the fact that various forms of the state "serve" this function does not result from the wishes or intentions of social actors such as a ruling class. Rather, one or another fraction of the capitalist class must dominate in a society because of the kind of economic relations "in the last instance." Even though Poulantzas can explain how each element of the social system interpenetrates or articulates with all the other elements and contributes to maintaining this domination—a functionalist explanation—the inescapable, determinate, or necessary basis for this arises from the way the whole system is structured. "In the last analysis" this is determined by economic relations.

This primal cause penetrates the whole social system. It gives the economy the last voice (determination in the last instance), establishes which subsystem will play an especially dominant function (the structure in dominance, in Poulantzas's terminology), and provides for the "relative autonomy" of each instance.[43] The whole mode of production so formed *structures* the context within which all subsystems must serve their function.

Specifically, despite its relative autonomy and despite the motives, preferences or rational calculations of political actors, the state and its agents have little choice. The system as a whole takes over. Actors must always "reflect" or "correspond" to[44] or serve the interests and needs of the ruling class in a society. Otherwise the unity of the society, the way it is organized, under the dominance of a given ruling class, could not be maintained.

In short, the functions of the state are fixed by the way the social system is organized, its mode of production, not by the wishes or connivance of its members. The individual becomes a mere "support" or "bearer," virtually an automaton fulfilling the biddings of the mode of production, not the initiator or transformer or actor whose intentions and choices count in any significant way. Men are " 'bearers' of objective instances."[45] The human subject is explicitly excluded except as an agent of structural necessity. The objective structure is thereby designated as the major autonomous social force.

Poulantzas might have argued otherwise while retaining many of the major elements of his social theory. For example, he might have interpreted the economy only as a subsystem that establishes the *limits* within which other subsystems and the whole mode of production operates. He would have had here a theory of limits or possibilities rather than a theory of necessity. Gravity determines behavior not in the sense that it forces us to jump or throw objects but only in that if we do these things there are limits to what can happen. It determines behavior only in the sense of narrowing the options; it does not compel us to jump or to throw objects. For Poulantzas, however, the mode of production, determined as it is by the economy in the last instance, imposes necessary functions or ends on each of the subsystems, including the state. As we shall see, whatever the policies of the state, they must fulfill these necessary or predetermined functions, at least according to the theory. Alternatively, every state policy can be understood only if it is seen as a means of serving these functions, however indirectly.

As we shall also see, much later, however, Poulantzas finds it impossible to carry his theory of the objective necessity of the mode of production (the social structure) through to the end; the logic of his own analysis will drive him back to a theory of limits or possibilities. In *Fascism and Dictatorship* (1970) he shifts from the deterministic necessity of *Political Power and Social Classes* (1968) to possibilities. He withdraws from the sense of automaticity and inevitability and begins to take into account the possibilities created by class struggles or practices and sees a more innovative and unconstrained function for the state.[46] But that will come later.

At the moment, Poulantzas's efforts to escape the accusation of vulgar economic determination or economism led him to transfer the same necessity to the mode of production, the so-called global structure. Overall structuralist determinism displaces economic determinism. It is this that has lent a universally recognized obscurantist air to his whole enterprise. It led him to such arguments—opaque in themselves but revealing about the limits of his method—that "the structure is *not the simple principle which is exterior to* the institution; the structure is present in an allusive and inverted form in the institution itself, and it is in the reiteration of these successive hidden presences that we can discover the principle of elucidation of the institution."[47] The inner contradiction in his thought that led him to want to exclude "external" necessity and yet forced him to include it in the notion of mode of production created such a gap between his theory and his explanation that it exposed him to the charges, from Marxists and others, of "structural superdeterminism,"[48] "structuralist abstractionism,"[49] and "dogmatism."[50]

Conclusion

Why has it been important to look at Poulantzas's method of social explanation? Because it underlies or follows from his structuralism. It is difficult to sort out cause and effect here. But whatever the direction, his functionalism represents his way of handling the whole-part dilemma, as it does with all functionalists. Their merit lies in their identification of a major issue of our time: How can we recover knowledge and understanding of the properties of the whole after centuries of pursuing our traditional practice of decomposing the whole into its parts in the hope of ultimately reconstituting these parts into a whole? Functionalism sought to place the parts in context by describing their function for the maintenance (reproduction) or change of the whole.[51]

As I have noted, functionalism attributes ends to sets of relationships which somehow are supposed to explain the latter's presence. In one sense this might give a kind of explanation. This would be true, however, only if we could presume that human beings, by some explicit act, had created a state and sought to inform it with certain purposes. Then we could at least assert that its creators had agreed on certain goals for the state which its organization or structure was intended to fulfill. But Poulantzas was no contractarian, implicit or otherwise. For him the state emerges simultaneously with the mode of production and acquires its ends in the very process of formation, an assumption which, at best, is only heuristic even though it is used as though it were existential. The impersonal social forces of the mode of production seem to give the state—and other structural elements (levels, instances) of the social system—purposes which they must fulfill.

The attribution of functions in the sense of tasks to be performed by a social element is an assumption which is never demonstrated and which by its very nature is undemonstrable. Purposes are attributes of human subjects, not of abstract social processes and structures. The latter have consequences, of course, as I noted a little earlier. It could be that the processes and structures which are, for example, part of the state do indeed have the consequence, in all modes of production, of preserving and reproducing these modes. Such a statement would of course need to be demonstrated, but at least it is in principle empirically confirmable.

To speak, however, of the probable consequences of an instance (subsystem) is very different from asserting its necessary purposes or functions. A consequential analysis would leave room for the possibility, for example, that at times the state might act differently so as to support the dominated rather than the dominant classes. The task would then be to try to understand the conditions under which this outcome might occur. But once we assert, as does Poulantzas, that the end of the state is to preserve the mode of production, state policies that run counter to this purpose demand explanations of a convoluted sort in order to make them consistent with the original teleological premises.[52]

We will recall that Poulantzas had two objectives in his theory of the state: to understand social policies of the capitalist state; to explain their variations in terms of changing state types and forms. Whatever else that may be said about the way in which he attacks these goals, he was aware, as were few other Marxists, of the necessity to show something more than some formal coherence between the capitalist mode of production (the whole social system), in its various conditions, and the state. As we shall see shortly, he at least searched hard and seriously for some of the mechanisms linking the two. Yet even though it is to his credit that he recognized the need to find linkages, few could argue that he succeeded.

At the very most, as we shall see in due course, his functionalist analysis, underpinned by a quasi-economic determinism, gives us a theory of the forces that may limit the power of the authorities in a political system, not a theory that can explain the different structural forms which the "state" (or political system as a whole) takes. No better than conventional social science will he be able to account for variations in state structures, at least in terms of the conditions necessary and sufficient for them. His method of interpenetration, if such it can be called, is little more than an explanation of presumed functional coherence, not of cause or covariance. As such, the coherence or articulation of elements reveals, at best, vulnerable assumptions about purposes assigned to subordinate social processes and structures, such as the state, by the overall social processes and structures, the mode of production. As we shall see, for this reason Poulantzas is unable to reach his goal of explaining types and forms of states and their associated policies. All he is able to do is present a theory—whether valid or not—about how such forms and policies cannot go beyond certain limits, implicit in the purposes or functions of the state and imposed by the overarching whole interpreted as the mode of production. Even within those broad limits, empirically based explanations for variations in the specific types and forms of states, the primary aim of his analysis, will elude him.

14

The State as Structural Object*

If Poulantzas is to establish any kind of relationship between what he calls the state structure and the rest of society (the social structure), it is imperative to be able to grasp clearly what he has in mind when he speaks about such state structure. In this chapter I shall conclude that at the very point where we should be able to expect exceptional clarity we find instead extraordinary ambiguity if not outright confusion. In the theory of the state, which is the goal of his intellectual journey, the idea of the state itself continuously eludes not only us but Poulantzas himself. Hence, when he argues that states and their structures will vary with changes in the mode of production, representing our central interest in his work, we are left in a condition of permanent conceptual uncertainty about just what it is that varies.

The Concept of State

As we know, Poulantzas's ultimate objective is to formulate a theory of politics, a theory of the state in the broad sense of the term that we encountered earlier, in chapter 11. "The theory of the State and of political power," he reminds us "has, with rare exceptions such as Gramsci, been neglected by Marxist thought."[1]

Theories are never constructed in the abstract, however abstract a theory such as Poulantzas's may appear. They always take shape around some core problem. In Poulantzas's case, we will recall, this problem centers on the state and its policies and on the location of power over the state as a means of accounting for the policies of the state. As I noted in chapter 11, Poulantzas finds that the policies of the state are embodied in the different types and forms assumed by the state: liberal as against interventionist; normal versus exceptional; and in the latter, fascist, military dictatorship, and Bonapartist. As we shall find, these labels accent the ascendancy of different parts ("fractions") of the ruling class to positions of power over the state, a condition that makes possible policies likely to conform to the interests of these fractions. In this way Poulantzas's classification of states reflects the kinds of differences in broad policy commitments that he finds need to be "accounted for" in advanced capitalist society.

Poulantzas explicitly argues that these types and forms of states are determined not by economic relations alone. As we have seen, this would be economism of the

*The substance of this chapter was published as "The Political System Besieged by the State," in 9 *Political Theory* (1981) 303–25.

worst sort. Rather, they are a product of the social system viewed as a whole, what we know he calls the mode of production (or ensemble of instances). He explicitly maintains that his theory of the state will permit him to "account for" variations in state structures, in the sense of superstructures, a term he eschews, however, because of its association with economism.[2]

As I have indicated, for Poulantzas different state types and forms arise not from the subjective preferences or rational choices of actors, whether they be individuals, groups, or classes. Variations in state structures are a product, rather, of the objective conditions created by the transformations in the mode of production as well as by the "conjunctures"[3] in the class struggles. Even though the forms of the state structure themselves may change, however, the functions the state serves remain constant. As I have already discussed and will shortly look at again somewhat more closely, the state has no choice in its basic functions. Whatever its policies and actions and regardless of the structural forms it may assume, the objective structure of which it is part (the mode of production) leads it to act in such a way as to maintain the unity and cohesion of the social fabric. All we can do is try to account for the way the state modifies or transforms its own structures as part of the whole social system (mode of production) itself.

Even though Poulantzas studiously avoids the concept explanation and prefers instead to talk in such weaker terms as "accounting for" variations in the state, he does put forward the theory that such variable state structures can be directly related to changes in the underlying structure, the mode of production. Whatever else he may choose to call this relationship, it clearly is an effort to explain state variations in some sense.

However, before we can examine the way Poulantzas applies his theory to try to learn how the structural part of a social system, called the state, takes its character from the larger social whole, we must pose a prior and, to say the least, very pertinent question: What is this partial structure, the state, variations in which are to be accounted for in this way? As we shall later see, we are told that it appears in different types, these types assume different forms, and these in turn fall into several subcategories. But what is the "it" that manifests itself in these diverse ways?

We might have expected that in a work so explicitly devoted to the development of a theory of the state we would have found a definitive statement about the nature or general properties of the state. The astonishing discovery is that, even as the central political structure in his analysis, the state remains an "undecipherable mystery," to use one of Poulantzas's pet expressions. We learn about many of "its" characteristics, to be sure: how it originates, the forms it takes, the nature of its constituent parts, the functions it is supposed to serve, and the consequences (policies and outcomes) to which it may give rise. Yet even though Poulantzas's central purpose is avowedly to formulate what he considers to be a badly needed Marxist theory of the state (as superstructure),[4] we are never let into the secret of what this object is that the theory is supposed to explain. The state is the eternally elusive Pimpernel of Poulantzas's theory.

What the State Is Not

If we were to ask, however, what the state structure is not, we would not want for answers. In the first place, for Poulantzas it is not equivalent to the governmental apparatuses through which it manifests itself. This was the very point of his celebrated debate with Miliband.[5] The concrete apparatuses of the state, in both their repressive and ideological forms, are not the state itself but merely the means through which it acts.[6] To conceive of the state in such concrete terms would lend credence to the notion that it is a "Thing,"[7] object, or piece of machinery over which the social classes can fight for control, an unacceptable "instrumentalist" conception of the state held by Miliband and by too many other Marxists, in Poulantzas's view.[8] The dominant classes do not possess the state. Alternatively, the state does not act on their behalf just because they subjectively seek to and, in fact, may at times exercise direct control over it.

To see the state in such subjective and concrete terms would also be to mistake it for a "Subject" or collective actor "endowed with a rationalistic will" which can control various social classes or society as a whole.[9] This attributes to it a degree of independence from civil society which would enable it to serve as an arbiter or conciliator among the social classes.[10] This view of the state as the great conciliator and accommodator standing above the fray represents for Poulantzas the ideological position of liberal democracy. For him it is based on a false separation of state from civil society. In its classic extreme it assumes that the state acts as the great harmonizer of differences by playing one class off against another and, thereby, in Bonapartist fashion, exercising power independent of all social classes.[11]

For Poulantzas, the state is a product of and integrally involved in society. It cannot be set in opposition to civil society. As we have seen, it takes its character from the way the whole society is organized (the mode of production in a noneconomic sense). As part of a class-divided society under capitalism, for example, the state is a functionally determined partisan of one set of class interests, something more than a liberal interpretation would allow.

This much is clear then. The state is not its concrete structure, nor is it an instrument in the hands of any class. Neither is it a "Subject" or actor which can control the various classes independent of all of them. Nor is it an entity above and apart from the rest of society, somehow hovering over it and regulating it.

The Functions of the State

What, then, is the state? For Poulantzas, consistent with his explanatory assumptions already examined in chapter 13, the best first approximation to understanding its nature lies in clarifying the postulated functions it serves. In place of an instrumentalist (state as Thing), or liberal (state as Subject) theory of the state, I have already observed that Poulantzas offers us an unavowed functionalist one.[12]

To restate my analysis in the preceding chapter, this time in somewhat different form, the functions of the state can be derived from its relationship not to a class, even the dominant ones, but to the whole of society. As Poulantzas puts it, the state is "the State [not of a particular class but] of a society divided into classes."[13] It originates in objective necessity, out of the very logic of a mode of production (a social system), that is, by the way in which a mode of production organizes society into social classes and class struggles. For Poulantzas the state arises not as a mechanism of control deliberately sought by the dominant classes, as other Marxists would argue, nor as an historical instrument that has evolved to meet the needs of a people for welfare, security, justice, and the like, as traditional liberal theories would have it. The conscious behavior of individual or group actors plays no part in Poulantzas's functional determinism. Rather the state originates out of the way a mode of production is constituted, out of objective relations. *"The political field of the State . . . has always in different forms, been present in the constitution and reproduction of the relations of production."*[14] It is a condensation, résumé, or fusion of the contradictions in this kind of society.[15]

As such, we already know from the preceding chapter, the primary function of the state is to provide for the maintenance (reproduction) and integrity or cohesion of the social formation, to prevent it from "bursting apart."[16] Given the way a mode of production in class-divided societies works, the beneficiaries can only be the dominant classes. The state may often mask its political class character and parade as a popular-national state "incarnating" the will of the people and serving their welfare. But in a class-divided society, the state has no choice other than to serve the long-run interests of the dominant classes, however much it may appear to behave otherwise in the face of the class struggles. This is the inescapable function (postulated only, however) of the state. This is why, aligning himself with Marx, Poulantzas argues that the transformation of capitalism requires that the state be "smashed."[17] In this interpretation, the activities of the state are necessarily eufunctional[18] for the reproduction of the mode of production and the interests of the dominant classes. There seems to be little room for ignorance, error, or historical accident, at least in the long run, and subjective interest or will play no role in the ultimate outcome. The functions of the State are determined by the location of this structure in the overall structure formed by the mode of production.

The State as Institutionalized Power

We know, then, what the state structure is not and how it is to be "understood" in terms of its primary functions in society. But we are still not informed about what this object, called the state, is that is involved in doing or not doing the things associated with it.

Here the answer is less than clear. At different times Poulantzas offers us only two positive sets of statements about the nature of the state: it is institutionalized power; it is a material condensation of the relationship of forces among classes. I shall examine each of these in turn.

In the first definition of the state, Poulantzas describes it explicitly as "institutionalized political power."[19] Or as he puts it in context, "The specific objective of political practice [political class struggle] is the State, i.e., institutionalized political power, which is the cohesive factor in a determinate social formation and the nodal points of its transformations."[20]

On the surface, this definitional phrase, institutionalized political power, would seem to be straightforward enough. Power he defines somewhat narrowly as "the capacity of a social class to realize its specific objective interests."[21] We can gloss over the difficulties of conceptualizing power as a potential rather than as a relationship. Politics consists of "political practice," and this is a kind of activity that "has as its object the present moment and which either transforms (or else maintains) the unity of a formation. But this is the case only to the extent that political practice has the *political* structures of the state as its point of impact and specific strategic 'objective'."[22] If Poulantzas had restricted politics to action directed to maintaining or changing a society (social formation), he would have left us with a genuine, even if amorphous, definition of the term. But to escape the looseness of this part of his definition, it would appear, he then proceeds to undermine his own effort by limiting politics to the kind of activity that involves a struggle over control of the means (the *political* structure) for maintaining the integrity of a society or transforming it.

Here we immediately run into difficulty. Poulantzas is in the process of defining just what he means by the state. It is a particular kind of power called political. But the *political* in this context is itself defined as a conflict over "the *political* structures of the state." The political, a central term of the explicandum, is used within the explicans itself.

Clearly he fails to give us a conception of the political that is independent of and not already included in the very object he wishes to define, namely, the state. He leaves us as uninformed as ever about the *political* nature of power, and yet this is central to his conception of the state. The latter is just not institutionalized power; it is institutionalized *political* power. Nowhere does he resolve this issue. Just what he means by politics remains a nagging uncertainty throughout his writings.

Worse is yet to come. Not only is the state just a potential for achieving class goals (power) and a kind of potential labeled by this undefined term, political. The state, as I shall now show, for a while becomes a set of rules constraining behavior, and these seem to be what the struggle for power is all about. The state loses all "materiality," as Poulantzas himself might have put it.

In a way Poulantzas accidentally trapped himself, in his early writings, into characterizing the state as a set of rules. In a later work he tries to extricate himself by redefining what he means by the term *institutions*. In the process he confounds even further his idea of the state.

The setting for his difficulties has to do with the term *structure*. Even though it is central to Poulantzas's whole analysis—and, perhaps, for that very reason—he manages to confuse the reader by using it in several senses. In the first one, the term may refer to organized patterns of behavior as found say, in parties, legislatures, courts, administrative agencies, and the like—called superstructures in frequent Marxist usage.[23] Here he does not differ from regular Marxist social science. As we saw in chapter 5, neither is structure, as stable patterns of behavior, an unusual meaning in conventional social science. In a second sense, Poulantzas uses the term to identify one of the major elements or instances of a formation, what we might normally call a subsystem of society—the economic, political and ideological subsystems or structures. In this usage, "*political* structure" is synonymous with the state. The third meaning is perhaps most important for Poulantzas if only because this reflects the structuralism in his analysis. In this usage he speaks of the mode of production as a structure. Structure, therefore, is the combination of all the instances, the whole network of relations among the basic subsystems which constitute a society.

Nowhere does Poulantzas seriously explore the existence of and connections among his multiple usages. The most that we can say about his handling of the potential confusion is that where, occasionally, it becomes only too apparent and it interferes with the development of an idea, he will pause to specify the meaning for his immediate purposes. That is what he is forced to do in trying to define the state as "institutionalized political power." Institutions and structures are clearly related terms that need to be distinguished in some way.

Poulantzas initially goes to some length to demonstrate that we ought not to mistake institutions for structures. These terms have different meanings in his lexicon. The reason for this is that he carefully wants to steer clear of equating the state with the concrete superstructures with which many Marxists have recurringly identified it. If for no other reason, the state cannot be described as the "juridico-political institutions"[24] since institutions used in this sense represent only the so-called repressive apparatuses or structures in the sense of superstructures such as courts, police, administration, legislatures. With Gramsci, Poulantzas includes within the state, in addition, "ideological" (read: cultural) apparatuses or institutions, not necessarily provided for by law, such as churches, unions, and interest groups. But even taken together, these repressive and ideological apparatuses (structures, institutions) do not constitute the state. These political superstructures are at most only "centers" or settings in which the drama of the power struggle among social classes is played out. These superstructures do not even hold "state power;" such power resides only in the hands of one or another social class or parts thereof.[25] Institutions here, then, refer to structures in the first of the three meanings already noted.

To make this position unmistakable, Poulantzas at the same time introduces structure in the third sense. He does this by seeking this time to distinguish structure from institutions with the former becoming the broader term. In this sense of the word, structure describes "the *organizing* matrix of institutions and such structures [are] *not the simple principle or organization which is exterior to* the institutions: the structure is present in an allusive and inverted form in the institution itself."[26] Clearly following Parsons, Poulantzas then goes on to reserve the term *institutions* for "a system of norms or rules which is socially sanctioned."[27] They include legal as well as other social norms such as those found in ideology (or culture). The latter (accepting Gramsci in effect) Poulantzas saw as just as repressive as the juridical norms that are usually considered part of the state.[28]

From this perspective, even though Poulantzas did not put it in these words, in defining the state as institutionalized power he was in fact considering it to represent political power effected through a system of socially sanctioned (class repressive) rules, at least if we take seriously his conception of institutions just discussed. As we know from the preceding chapter, the state, now as a set of norms or rules, "interpenetrates" with the rest of the mode of production (or structure, in the global sense of the terms as used here) and gets its character from this "constitutive" relationship.

If this interpretation of Poulantzas is acceptable, we have at least clarified the power aspect of his conception of the state. We now know that it involves power made possible through the class enforced rules (institutionalized power) of a mode of production shot through with class conflict. However loose this conception of power may be, it would have served as a tolerable first approximation to an adequate description of the state. We could easily accept the notion that he who controls the rules of the game controls the game. If the system biases the rules in favor of one class, that class could certainly be said to dominate, as Poulantzas holds.

One fatal flaw remains, however, even if we ignore entirely the fact that Poulantzas nowhere stipulates the rules. He gives us no idea about how we are to identify the political nature of any rules, how we are to discriminate the political from other kinds of norms. As we have already seen, the political is itself still defined in its own terms, that is, as the struggle for control of the *political* structure, however we construe structure. The result is that even though we have some idea about what power means for Poulantzas (control of the rules of the game), since the political itself remains undefined we are still left on our own to decide just what this object, the state, might really be.

Still worse is yet to come, however. After wavering in his terminology, Poulantzas finally decided, two years after his extensive use of the term in this sense in *Political Power and Social Class*, to abandon institutions as a concept referring to normative rules. Instead, he now argued that he had always really meant the idea of state apparatus to be equivalent to the notion of state institutions, and since there is no point in using two terms, he proposed to adopt apparatus as the preferred one. "I think that the term 'institution,'" he writes, "can therefore be abandoned, since at least for the moment, I do not see what it can add to the concept of apparatus."[29] He had apparently forgotten about his earlier definition of institutions in rule terms or had chosen to ignore the inconsistency.

If Poulantzas had been willing to accept the consequences of this decision, we might possibly still have been able to make some sense of his notion of the state. We might take one of two tacks. In the first we could accept his new point of view as an indication that he really means apparatus (or structures in the sense of superstructures) to be identical with institutions. In that event, apparatus would just refer to socially sanctioned norms, and we would be back to the conceptual uncertainty from which we started.

A second tack might be more useful, however, and perhaps more faithful to Poulantzas's intention. Here we could assume that, despite his assertion that apparatus refers to institutions, he now intends us to accept the meaning he normally gives to the term *state apparatuses*. That is to say, he intends to assimilate the meaning of institutions into that of apparatus. From all his writings, it is unambiguous that apparatus refers not to institutions as socially sanctioned norms but to what he has joined Gramsci in calling repressive and ideological apparatuses or super-structures. These evoke the imagery of courts, legislatures, armies, police, execu-tives, and bureaucracies on the one side, and churches, trade unions, corporations, and the like (indoctrinating "private" organizations) on the other.[30] The state would be found in its structural "materiality and specificity," as Poulantzas himself might have put it.

Here we come straight up against a theoretical impasse. To identify the state as its apparatuses or superstructures would force Poulantzas to accept that very conceptualization of the state that he had been struggling to avoid. The apparatuses of the state are only the means through which the state acts and over which the social classes or their "fractions" (parts) compete for power. They are only the arena in which the power conflict for control of the state occurs; they are not the state itself.[31] This was the very point of acrimonious debate with Miliband in which Poulantzas repeatedly accused the latter of the cardinal sin of reducing the state to the state apparatus itself.[32] In short, after decisively rejecting the concretization of the state in its apparatuses or structures and continuing to protest against those who do, Poulantzas unwittingly and inadvertently, it would seem, boxed himself into the same interpretation. And yet even though the logic of his own analysis would thus lead him to associate the state with its apparatus, he is nowhere prepared to acknowledge or accept this outcome.

In the end, then, after having thought that, after all, we might have caught hold of some meaning for the state, it has turned to dust in our hands. Poulantzas refuses to accept the consequences of his own position. Both the idea of the political, as we saw, and of the state, remain essentially undefined and unconcretized. Poulant-zas feels free to speak of the state in terms of its existence in some way but has given us no firm idea about what the "it" is that, as he will go on to try to prove, manifests itself differently as the mode of production changes.

The State as Condensation of Class Conflict

As I indicated earlier, Poulantzas makes two positive statements about the nature of the state. We have examined the first, "institutionalized political power." We can now turn to the second, and it can be dispatched more quickly.

Perhaps because of his own discomfort, following his debate with Miliband, about the adequacy of his definition of the state in *Political Power and Social Classes* and the criticism from all sides of his excessive generality and formalism in that work, Poulantzas tried to pin down his meaning somewhat more firmly. In doing so he returns to Marx's view of one of the central functions of the state. In this new emphasis, the state serves as the locus or "condensation" for conflictual and unitary forces in society. It is where the struggle over the nature of the whole society takes place. This new stab at clarifying his meaning of the state does little better, however, than his previous attempt.

In *State, Power, Socialism*, his last book, Poulantzas rejects alternative conceptions of the state either as "a 'narrow' conception for which the State is in its essence an *apparatus*, [or] a 'broad' conception for which the State is simply the expression of a class *relationship*," that is, of the class struggle.[33] Instead, he says he wishes to take the opportunity to make some of his "earlier formulations . . . more precise."[34] Therefore, apparently in response to the ambiguity of his first conception, he now offers a new definition, or at least one with a different emphasis. "The (capitalist) State should not be regarded as an intrinsic entity: like 'capital,' *it is rather a relationship of forces, or more precisely that material condensation of such a relationship among classes and class fractions, such as this is expressed within the State in a necessarily specific form.*"[35]

This new view of the state diverges more sharply from his earlier one than he is willing to allow. Now he sees the state at least as a relationship of forces, a thought that appeared on occasion in his past writings but which did not then seem to be central to his understanding of the state as institutionalized political power. In fact, his very position opposed the notion that the state arose out of the class struggles (relationship of forces); it was rather a function of the way a mode of production as a whole operates, just as were the class struggles themselves.

However, even if we grant him this attempt to show continuity in his idea of the state, in this conception, Poulantzas, with his characteristic disconcerting verbal facility, returns to us with one hand what he had already taken away with the other. In the first place, the state may be a "relationship of forces;" but apparently this is only if we do not speak precisely. Assuming we wish "precision" for so central a concept, we must take Poulantzas at his word, in the above quotation, and accept that he really means the state to be "that material condensation of such a relationship among classes and class fractions."

What can he mean by this qualification in his pursuit of precision? It appears that Poulantzas returns us after all to the very conception of the state as an apparatus, one that he has all along been desperately trying to avoid. For after rejecting as "narrow" the idea that "the state is in its essence an *apparatus*," as we have just noted, he tells us in effect that it is "a material condensation" and by this phrase we can only understand him to mean material apparatuses. Time and again he speaks of the state in this way, "as a material condensation of a contradictory relationship."[36] The only reservation is that we need to recognize that this material manifestation takes its character from the continuing play of class forces working through it. That is, the nature of the apparatus will change with the vagaries of the class struggles.

This explicitness does not settle the matter, however, as we might by now have come to realize from the characteristic lack of rigor in Poulantzas's method of analysis. With customary indifference or oblivion, Poulantzas promptly denies us the conclusion to which we would seem to have been entitled from the logic of his argument. First, he characterizes the state as a relationship of forces. Then, for the sake of precision, he requires that we see the state as identifiable with its material condensation. But even this is not to be, after all. Poulantzas returns the state to some kind of essence over and beyond both class contradictions and their material expression.

> The State is not reducible to the relationship of forces; it exhibits an opacity and resistance of its own. To be sure, change in the class relationship of forces always affects the State; but it does not find expression in the State in a direct and immediate fashion. It adapts itself exactly to the materiality of the various state apparatuses, only becoming crystallized in the State in a refracted form that varies according to the apparatus.[37]

If we can probe this imagery—and the evocation of images is a characteristic method used by Poulantzas to cope with a certain obscurity in his own thought— it would appear that not only is the state not reducible to class struggles, it is not after all even equivalent to the "materiality of the various state apparatuses," as the preceding quotation clearly indicates. Yet, in an earlier quotation above, his insistence on a *precise* formulation had led him to describe the state as a "material condensation" of the class struggles. But earlier he had clearly ruled this out. We are thrown back, once again, to the idea that behind these apparatuses there looms something called the state which is affected by changes in class conflicts. But the state itself, being different from its material representation as we are now told, becomes invisible. It is like some essence (a Platonic idea?), the presence of which we infer only from its material expression in the apparatuses and from the effects of the class struggles. If we thought we at last had a handle on the state, we are once again doomed to find it slipping from our grasp.

What Can the State Be?

What then can the state be? It is not just political power, that is, class practices. It is not the class relationship of forces or class struggles. It is not an "intrinsic entity." It is not a Thing. It is not a Subject. It is not just a set of functions. It is not the governmental or ideological apparatuses, even if it manifests itself only through them.

Struggle as we may with Poulantzas's conception of the state, we must conclude that in the end, despite his continuing protests to the contrary, either the state is a vacuous term referring to some emergent, ineffable phenomenon which reveals itself only in the garb of its apparatuses, or it refers to nothing less than the apparatuses themselves, that is, to the governmental and nongovernmental institutions through which Poulantzas sees power being exercised, for example, in a capitalist society. In this event, the state is no more than a substitute term for the political authorities, or, if one wishes, for government together with associated nongovernmental political institutions.

This analysis may seem like a long road to travel to arrive at so banal a conclusion. But the verbal sleight of hand with which Poulantzas typically deals with problems of the state leaves such confusion or doubt that he gives every appearance of offering us some alternative conception of the state which upon close scrutiny just does not seem to be there. Indeed, when Poulantzas finally turns his energies (in *Political Power and Social Classes* and later works) to explaining variations in types and forms of the capitalist states, he is compelled by the nature both of his topic and of the ambiguity of his concept of the state to talk almost exclusively of the state in terms of its "materiality," that is, of its organizational apparatuses.

The state quickly becomes, in *Poulantzas's* practice, its observable structures. By that time, all refinements of language seem to have come to naught. State and apparatus are for all practical purposes fused into one, as will become apparent as my analysis proceeds, even though theoretically Poulantzas retains the notion of class forces and that these forces are "inscribed in its [the state's] very structure."[38] In fact, however, either the state is the very instrumental "substance" or "site"[39] which Poulantzas persistently rejects, or it is some kind of undefined and undefinable essence, a "ghost in the machine,"[40] knowable only through its variable manifestation.

It is clear that there is no resolution to the problem with which Poulantzas leaves us about the meaning of the state as a central political structure, except in a way that without question would be unacceptable to Poulantzas: to recognize that despite his protests to the contrary, when it comes down to specifics, he speaks of the state as though it did indeed consist of those very repressive and ideological apparatuses or structures for the use of which he had roundly condemned Miliband. In its most generous interpretation, politics for Poulantzas can be said to represent the struggle for class power over the state defined as a set of political structures (apparatuses) constrained by socially sanctioned (and, under capitalism, repressive) rules. It is not a conception that Poulantzas himself explicitly and forthrightly articulated; nor is it one on which he would have put his stamp of approval.

With fundamental confusion such as this about his meaning, however, it is perhaps best simply to proceed with our main task and accept the idea of state structure as a primitive and largely undefined term. Wherever this lacuna in his conceptualization threatens our understanding of the way in which he seeks to derive observable forms of the state structure from the basic social structure (the mode of production), we shall have to cope with the matter as best we can.

15

The Structural Forms of the Political System

As I noted at the outset, what makes Poulantzas, as a Marxist, interesting from my point of view is that he hypothesizes that the forms taken by a political system (state) are not determined by isolated characteristics of the social system of which they are part. The political system takes the form it does because of the effects on it of the whole context in which it operates. As part of this system of relationships, its form is different from what it would have been if it had been immersed in some other set. In short, Poulantzas is arguing for the importance of whole-system effects.

The question has been: Can Poulantzas instruct us about the nature of whole-system effects, the mechanisms at work and how we ought to go about discovering and documenting them? Can we learn from him how specifiable variations in the system of relationships, as an entity in itself, influence the structural forms of the political system?

Questions such as these would seem to be central to his whole theoretical enterprise. Now that we have clarified many of the assumptions of Poulantzas's theoretical approach, we have reached the point where we can hope to test the extent to which Poulantzas is able, through his various theoretical efforts, to "account for," in his words, the particular types and forms of observable (lower-order) state structures in capitalist society.

We have come some distance in his thinking. In general, he argued that that part of the whole social system (mode of production, in his terms) called the state could be accounted for only by the way it "articulates," interpenetrates or fits in with the rest of society, that is, through the functions it serves in the whole. For linear or causal analysis, we have seen, he tries to substitute what can only be described as functional analysis, already so well known and found wanting in conventional social science.

When, however, it came to describing the object of his theoretical pursuits, the state, we were defeated in our effort to discover any theoretical or empirically unique meaning for it. We were unable to put our finger on any clear-cut definition that would permit us to say what this object was that possesses the characteristics Poulantzas attributes to it or that undergoes various kinds of transformations. We could only proceed with our analysis of Poulantzas's theory by making the unwarranted assumption that we clearly understood what he was referring to when he spoke about the state. For better or for worse we have had to ignore the fact that our point of reference remains an object clouded in conceptual ambiguity.

On these premises and guidelines, we can now begin to appreciate the assumptions underlying Poulantzas's efforts to come to grips with the primary objective of what he calls his "science of politics." This objective is also the ultimate focus of our interest, namely, as he puts it in varied and uncertain terms: What "determines," "governs," "mirrors," "corresponds to," "is due to," or "characterizes" the types and forms of states in capitalist society?

In the end we shall discover first, that Poulantzas retains his implicit but all-pervasive commitment to a functionalist type of analysis; second, that the mechanism at work in shaping the structure of the state is not the overall structure of the social systems (mode of production) but the nature of the class struggle itself; and third, that a major source of confusion in Poulantzas's analysis of observed structures continues to flow from his indecision between determinants and limits. He cannot quite make up his mind whether he intends to account for these state structures by arguing that they are *determined* by the mode of production and its associated class struggles or whether the observed structures are only *limited* by these underlying structural factors.

Thus, from time to time he writes as though he means to inform us of the determinants of the different state forms and their subtypes. For example, he points out that

> a *significant* shift in the predominant branch in the State apparatus, or of the relation between these branches, cannot be *directly* established by the immediate exterior role of this branch, but is determined by *the modification of the whole system of the State apparatus and its form of international unity as such*: a modification which is itself due to changes in the relations of production and to developments in the class struggle.[1]

I shall later contrast this explicit use of the notion of determination ("determine," "is due to") with his tendency to see so many possibilities, at times, without being able to account for a unique outcome, that he is more often forced back to consider his parameters only as constraints or limits. The significance of the difference between determinants and limits is, of course, vast from the point of view of understanding and prediction.

Relationship between Modes of Production and the State

Let us look now at the way he moves from his broadest structuralist determinants to the historical manifestations of the state. How does Poulantzas, by descending from what he calls the most abstract-formal to the concrete-real level of thought,[2] account for state variations? In Poulantzas's epistemology he does this, not through a process of rigorous logical deduction from some theoretical model of the state. Rather, he starts with the general theory of society and through "theoretical elaboration" generates theoretical propositions to assist in the transition to experience, although his anti-empiricism makes that actual connection with experience, in his philosophy of science, somewhat dubious. These propositions, or theoretical principles, "will allow us," he says, "to give an account of what may be provisionally called its [the state's] *transformations*."[3]

To simplify this task of identifying and accounting for the transformations through which states pass, I shall now explore Poulantzas's method by identifying certain theoretical propositions or principles. I shall call them *transformation rules*, a term that Poulantzas does not use but which clearly expresses his intent to account for the way state types and structural forms are indeed transformed under varying conditions. I shall attempt to formalize these rules to the extent that their generality and all too frequent vagueness permit. Hopefully this procedure will enable us to understand the logic and methods involved in Poulantzas's effort to understand how and why the capitalist state assumes the various forms that it does.

Table 15.1 presents schematically the connections among the various forms, or what in the end turns out to be an elaborate typology of capitalist states.[4] The transformations are of several kinds. As my table reveals, Poulantzas engages in a "fury of classification," to use the characterization of a friendly Marxist critic.[5] In their pure form, at least, each different mode of production—slave, feudal, capitalist, and socialist—yields a different *type* of state of the same name. Since Poulantzas is especially concerned with the capitalist state only, the table describes the classification related to its transformations.

Each capitalist state may itself fall into one of two subtypes: pure or transitional.[6] The pure type subdivides into a competitive (nineteenth-century liberal) as against interventionist (twentieth-century regulatory) category. The latter assumes two major forms of regimes; normal (parliamentary democracy) or exceptional (crisis types). Normal regimes may be dominated by legislatures or by their executives but

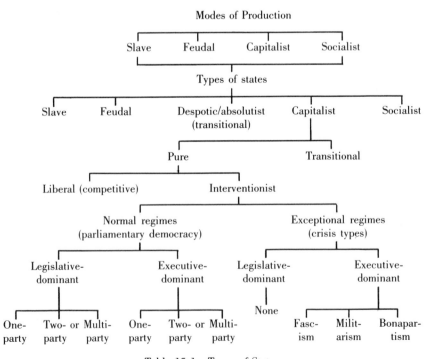

Table 15.1   Types of States

exceptional regimes are always executive dominant. Each normal regime is further classified by its party structure, that is, by the number of parties it contains, ranging from single to multiparty kinds. Exceptional regimes, crisis types, are fascist, military dictatorships, or Bonapartist.

Poulantzas sets himself the task of defining each of these various classes of states and of specifying the rules and conditions governing the transformation from one into the other. Not that Poulantzas expresses clearly what he is about. He offers no table of types, such as I have presented here, to clarify his schema; he volunteers no explicit formulation of the transformation rules. The predictable result is that he leaves plenty of room for doubt about how he does categorize different forms of the state and the conditions that bring them about. Within these limits, however, I shall indicate some of the major transformation rules to which he does seem to hold.

As I have suggested, the major problem that he poses for us, within the general deficiencies of functionalist analysis, is whether these rules *determine* the nature of the transformations from one type of state to another or whether they just *constrain or limit* the range of the alternatives, without dictating a unique outcome or even class of outcomes. This problem is, of course, independent of any legitimate concerns we may have about the validity of the transformational rules themselves or about whether they are even in principle confirmable. But whether they are valid or whether they are even testable, as presented, is not the central issue at the moment. Rather, I am concerned about whether Poulantzas offers us a plausible method or a theory that shows promise of permitting us to establish the effects of the whole set of relationships in a system on each of its parts, especially on the observed state (regime?) structures.

To simplify the exposition I shall divide the transformation rules or discussion of the conditions under which the state assumes one or another form, into several major categories: the transformation rules for *all* states regardless of types of states involved; those for all *capitalist* states regardless of subtypes; those specific to a given type of capitalist state, the *normal interventionist*; those specific to a second given type of capitalist state, the *exceptional interventionist* (which I shall examine in the next chapter). These are the kinds of states in which Poulantzas is particularly interested as they represent for him a formal description of states in the real world. In short, his whole classificatory scheme is designed to help us account for (explain would be too strong a term) the maintenance of parliamentary democracies (normal interventionist states) and their possible change into varying kinds of authoritarian systems (exceptional interventionist states), or the reverse, given the experiences of Portugal and Spain in the 1970s.

A. *Tranformation Rules for All States*

Rule 1. *"In order to grasp the specificity of the regional structures in a given mode of production (e.g., of the capitalist state in the capitalist mode of production) we must determine its place inside the matrix specifying this mode."*[7]

This rule spells out the major element of his method. Even though each particular form of the capitalist state will differ, the difference can be explained only if we conceptualize the state as a whole, "inside the matrix," as he puts it in this quotation, or "in its unity," as he phrases it elsewhere.[8]

This means we must be able to show the connection between forms of the state (resembling our lower-order or regime structure) and concurrent changes in the relations of production (the economy), the class struggles and the rest of the mode of production.[9] "Only *after* having established the relation of a form of State as a unity, *that is, as a specific form of the system of State apparatus as a whole*, with the 'exterior,' can the respective role of the mutual internal relation of the 'branches' [executive *vs.* legislative] of the State apparatus be established."[10]

This last quotation is the foundation on which Poulantzas's whole analysis of the state rests. To understand what happens to the internal structures of the political system we need to look at modifications in all other elements of the mode of production external to the state. Since the economic is "determinant in the last instance," changes in economic relations, as from competitive to imperialist or to state capitalism, will have a direct bearing on the types and forms of states.

This rule argues against the theory that the relations of production (the economy) or the forces of production (as G. A. Cohen would claim for Marx)[11] determine the nature of the state. The state is a creature of the whole "ensemble," the overall structure of a social mode of production, of the way the three major instances hang together, their practices and class struggles associated with them, and in a given society, the influence of the combination of modes of production that may be present historically.

In affirming the significance of the mode of production for state types and forms, by implication this transformation rule is also denying that these can be the deliberate product of the efforts of any group that may seek to control the state. For example, he counts Miliband as wrong when the latter attributes the growing dominance of the military in democratic systems to the subjective efforts of big business.[12] In short, the rule reaffirms Poulantzas's postulate that the state neither emerges nor takes its particular forms from the will or desire of human agents. What the state is derives from the particular way in which the whole set of social relationships is organized or, as he so frequently describes it, "articulates."[13] The function of each part of the whole, such as the state, is determined by its place in the whole, not by any single factor or set of factors smaller than the whole set of relationships which constitute the mode of production, and certainly not by the form that the human actors would like such a part to take.

It would appear, therefore, that initially at least, the state is indeed determined, in the sense of being uniquely caused by,[14] the mode or modes of production in a social formation. However, as we have already seen about other matters, consistency is not one of Poulantzas's virtues. The determinant role of the mode of production appears to have been only an early formulation in his thinking. Poulantzas never abandons it entirely but he does gradually ease it onto a back burner from which he feels free to retrieve it as necessary. As he tries to account for the various exceptional states, and particularly about how one type of exceptional state, military dictatorship, may reverse its type to parliamentary democracy,[15] his determinism seems to dissolve into a kind of probabilism in the vein of much of contemporary social science. But I shall return to this shortly. At the outset he seemed to promise us that there is a determinate relationship between the types and forms of state on the one side and variations in the overall modes of production on the other.

Rule 2. *"The state of [a historically determined social formation] results from a combination of several types of state, the product of the different modes of production which come into combination in [a] formation."*[16]

This rule is based on the idea that each historical social formation consists of a combination of modes of production some of which have carried over from previous periods. Thus, under capitalism we may have elements of political institutions carried over from feudalism.[17] However, even though these remnants are present, one mode will dominate. When it is capitalism, then the social formation can be designated as capitalist. The state will assume its overall character from the dominance of this one mode although it will be shaped by the particular combination of modes in a society.

Specifically, under capitalism, because of the relative autonomy that this mode of production allows to each of the instances (subsystems), the capitalist state need not always be dominant. The economy, which, as we have seen, is determinant in the last instance, may dictate the dominance of a feudal type of state. For Poulantzas this helps us to understand how, under Bismarck, despite the fact that the capitalist mode of production prevailed, the state was feudal in nature, presumably because of the special power of the landed classes.[18] The very fact that under capitalism the instances are autonomous enables this mode of production to "permit" the existence "of a state dominated by a type other than that which characterizes the state of this mode" or totality of a formation.[19]

Here Poulantzas refines his meaning of the whole mode of production. It can be decomposed into various types, especially under capitalism, and by relating the state to these different types we can fine tune the determinants of the state.

Borrowing from Charles Bettleheim,[20] Poulantzas sees each social formation as passing through two *phases* and any number of *stages*. Every social formation or society has a beginning phase in which it is in transition from one kind of formation to another, as from feudalism to capitalism. Once it has passed through this great moment, it enters into the phase of an "expanded reproduction" of its structure. Here the competition among different modes of production in the transition phase has been settled[21] and one of the pure forms (slavery, feudalism, capitalism, socialism) dominates, although, as we have seen, it may share the formation with remnants of other modes of production.

Poulantzas's analysis is largely confined to this settled phase and deals only with the capitalist mode of production in any detail. The capitalist mode of production (the generic social system) and its social formation (a specific society) are character-ized, for Poulantzas, by an economic "periodization" of its own. This he divides into five periods or stages: simple market production, private capitalist production or competitive capitalism, social capitalist production (for example, welfare capitalism under Roosevelt's New Deal),[22] monopoly capitalism (the advanced industrial period in which capitalist society now finds itself), and state monopoly capitalism.[23]

None of these stages exists empirically in its pure form, but whatever the mixture, one or another stage will dominate. Furthermore, these stages need not be historically consecutive. They are just different types and may appear in any order depending on the way the economy is organized, even though Poulantzas spends little time in explaining how these variations occur. They are his givens, in effect. Nevertheless, once they do occur, once the economic instance (subsystem) enters into one or another of these stages, the "articulation" of the whole system will alter and with it the form of the state.[24] That is to say, under each stage in the mode of production the state will continue to serve its postulated constant functions, but it does so by assuming different structural forms that are appropriate to or that "articulate" with the given stage. The state, therefore, will "depend on" or "reflect," to use Poulantzas's terms, the stage of economic periodization.

In this way Poulantzas sets the stage for his analysis of different types and forms of states. Initially he introduced two different types of states that need to be accounted for: the liberal and the interventionist. In Poulantzas's lexicon these terms retain their normal connotation. The economically liberal state interferes little in the economy and the rest of the social formation; the interventionist manifests considerable involvement in all areas of society. With this minimal typology we can now proceed to analyze the way "economic periodization" affects the state and its structure under capitalism.

B. Transformation Rules for All Capitalist States

Rule 3. *The liberal "form" or type of state "corresponds to" the pre-monopoly stage of production in a society; the interventionist stage "corresponds to" the monopoly capitalist state.*[25]

Why should there be this connection between a given mode of production and the structure of the state? The argument is even more complex than Poulantzas's normal complexity, although we need not make our way through all the labyrinths of his thought.

Poulantzas seems to pursue his point at two levels. At the first he argues, in a straightforward manner, that the periodization in the mode of production in a given society influences the way the instances interpenetrate. This seems to be an objective consequence of the way the capitalist system hangs together. During the period of private capitalism, the cohesion of the formation can be guaranteed with little state intervention at the economic or ideological level. This unifying function of the state, which prevents a society from "bursting apart," as we saw earlier, was posited as its major function. In other stages of capitalism, however, to achieve the same effect the state must intervene with increasing frequency at the economic and ideological levels.[26] This intervention takes the form of all kinds of government regulations such as social welfare regulation, financial support for industry, legislation in the area of trade and commerce, trade union rules, and the like. As the mode of production changes from one to another type, the same state function will be served by a different form (interventionist as against liberal) of state.[27]

At another level, however, Poulantzas seems to be saying that if we wish to understand the actual mechanisms at work which link the shift in economic stages to transformations in the state, we need to look below the surface facts of such intervention, beneath the mere assertion of objective consequences. These mechanisms are to be found not in the structure of the mode of production but in the specific political practices or class struggles of the various dominant classes.

In turning from the formal stages of the capitalist mode of production, however, to the class struggle, we find that in effect Poulantzas abandons his initial unmistakable claim that the type of state is determined by or directly "corresponds to" (a frequently used weaker formulation) economic stages through the effect of the latter on the whole social system. (We will recall that the economy is "determinant in the last instance.") In the end, this claim to direct determination unobtrusively disappears, as we shall see. To be sure, it is periodically resurrected in the formal assertion that the mode of production influences the nature of the class struggles. However, unless he can argue that the nature of these struggles and their outcomes are also uniquely determined by the given stage of a mode of production then the effects of the class struggles are essentially unpredictable. In that event the presumed determining effects of the mode of production are lost in the unpredictability of the effects of the class struggle. And this is precisely what happens. Poulantzas hoists himself on his own petard once he takes into consideration the variability of the class struggles.

We need, then, to turn to the class conflicts. Although the struggle between the dominant and dominated classes (Poulantzas's terms) is not ignored, it does not receive anything like the attention that he gives to the struggles within the dominant classes. As it turns out, he sees these as being very responsive to shifts in the stages of the mode of production.

In short, then, Poulantzas's train of thought is as follows: the state is determined by the mode of production (the social system as an overarching or higher-order entity); the economic periodization within the mode enables it to influence the state in different ways; the mode of production manages this by influencing the nature of the class struggles; the struggles within the dominant classes are most relevant for an understanding of what happens to the structure and policies of the state. The grand conclusion to this sequence is, therefore, that if we wish to account for variations in state forms, we must first understand how the internal conflicts in the dominant classes are themselves influenced by changing stages in the mode of production.

The reader has been forewarned of the complexity of Poulantzas's analysis, and we are about to see further evidence of it. To deal with the internal conflicts in the dominant classes as they contribute to transformations in the state, Poulantzas now introduces the notion of the *power bloc,* an idea that he claims is already implicit in Marx. This bloc is central to struggles within the dominant classes. It is through changes in the character and composition of this bloc that the mode of production ultimately makes itself felt. As an aside, we may observe that the power bloc looks very much like a competitor for the bourgeois concept of the politico-economic elite. Although it goes beyond our interest or need to pursue the matter, there are many parallels between the two concepts despite the gulf that separates the theoretical perspectives out of which each has emerged.

In any event, the power bloc consists of a number of the dominant classes or "fractions" (parts of classes) which share power in the social system.[28] Any society (social formation), as we have noted, may consist of a number of different and overlapping modes of production—feudal and capitalist modes being typical. These deposit a number of different classes in a given society. For example, capitalism in Europe for some time contained remnants of feudalism, such as a landed aristocracy or squirearchy, which have not all died out even now. All these classes normally subdivide into a number of fractions. The capitalist class, to take one illustration, can be decomposed into financial, industrial, commercial, export-import fractions, and the like. These are all part of the dominant classes under capitalism even though they may not all share equally in political power at a given historical moment. For Poulantzas the continued dominance of these classes requires that only some, not all these classes or their fractions, hold and share power. Those that do, at any time, constitute the *power bloc*,[29] a politically dominant minority.

This bloc itself arises out of the internal conflicts over power among the dominant classes and fractions. For Poulantzas, its existence depends on objective circumstances, on the presence of a plurality of classes and their fractions under capitalism with each competing for special political influence so as to be able to twist the system to its own purposes. Given their resources of various sorts, one or another combination of classes and fractions may be able to join together to form a power bloc.

In Poulantzas's view, like the dominant classes themselves the power bloc is not an undifferentiated whole or composed of egalitarian elements. There is always one class or fraction that assumes the dominant role among the various fractions or classes that form the power bloc. Poulantzas calls this the hegemonic class/fraction, borrowing and adapting Gramsci's term.[30] On the hegemonic class/fraction rests the ultimate burden of providing for the "contradictory unity"[31] out of the conflicts among the dominant classes/fractions themselves. That is to say, the policies of the bloc and its hegemonic class/fraction always promote a postulated common interest of the dominant classes as a whole, despite the internal differences among the latter which may at times arise as to how this is to be done. Why the hegemonic class/fraction should provide unity for the dominant classes, despite their internal contradictions, is never explained. It seems to be taken as a given, as part of the objective consequences of the way the capitalist system works.

In any event, we now have some inkling of the mechanism that serves to bring about state type transformations under capitalism. It is to be found in the power bloc. This enables us now to state the transformation rule in finer detail.

Rule 4. *Variations in the capitalist mode of production and its social formations influence the composition and interrelations of the classes/fractions within the power bloc. As the competition and relationships within this bloc change, the state will be transformed into either a liberal or interventionist type.*

It would appear, then, that the form of the state that emerges, whether liberal or interventionist (and whether, within these limits, as we shall see, the executive or legislative is ascendant), will depend upon the concrete way in which all these elements—the dominant classes and their fractions as well as supporting classes outside the bloc, which we need not note further—combine in a historical moment or "conjuncture."[32]

This new rule now enables us to restate the issue raised in general by Rule 3. Why should the state shift from a liberal to an interventionist type as the social formation moves from one dominated by private capitalism to monopoly capitalism? The linkage here lies in the way the class struggles threaten the legitimacy of the dominant or ruling classes.

Poulantzas argues that in the advanced stages of capitalism, reached in the last half of this century, as represented in imperialism and monopoly capitalism, these conflicts within the power bloc, between it and the rest of the dominant classes, and between it and the dominated classes, threaten the legitimacy of the state and the very position of the dominant classes as a whole. To hold the formation together and to reassert the legitimacy of the dominant classes, the hegemonic class/fraction in the power bloc must turn to the economy for leverage.[33] It must use the power of economic intervention particularly, to disorganize and buy off the dominated classes, and even parts of the dominant classes, through allocating rewards and benefits.

Since the state is the point of "condensation" for the various class struggles in society, as we have already noted,[34] we would expect the state to change its own behavior to meet the new requirement for maintaining the unity of the social formation under the domination of the power bloc. Regardless of the intention or preferences of the dominant classes, therefore, the impact of the class struggles on legitimacy forces the state to intervene in the economy, through government regulation and the like, to revive the flagging legitimacy of the dominant classes and with them, of the capitalist state it self, if the capitalist mode of production is to be maintained.

Clearly the argument here is no longer that the form of state is determined by the "stage of economic periodization," as seemed to be implied in Poulantzas's initial formulation. Intervention is a mechanism always available regardless of the stage of capitalist economic relations. It would make life easier if we could find in Poulantzas a rule which said that there is a unique relationship between each economic stage and each type of state. But this is not the story. Interventionism, surprisingly, may occur in any economic stage, even under private or competitive capitalism! Correspondingly, monopoly capitalism may at times be relatively free of intervention.[35] This means that both economic liberalism or interventionism are only *possible*, not necessary strategies. They depend on how the class conflicts within the power bloc, within the dominated classes as a whole and between them and the dominant classes, work themselves out. In any economic period, if legitimacy is endangered, the state may alter its policies in the direction of regulation of the economy so as to rebuild the legitimacy of the state and the dominant classes.

In the end, then, the form of state is tied to the class struggles and the way they affect the legitimacy of the ruling classes. The effect of the class struggles on legitimacy are not uniquely related to any one or another stage in the mode of production. Since the conditions of the class struggles, under which legitimacy waxes or wanes, are not spelled out, we have no way of discovering whether one or another form of state will appear.

In effect, what we end up with under transformation Rule 4 is a theory of possibilities, not a theory of determination. The two forms of states are not uniquely determined by a given stage in the mode of production after all. They are contingent on the response of the state to variations in the class struggles and represent only mechanisms for coping with a decline in legitimacy. In this way Poulantzas manages to free the forms of states from inescapable dependence on economic periodization, despite his initial claims to the contrary. The interventionist state may spring up, almost as a voluntaristic strategy, at any of the many stages of the mode of production.

Although Poulantzas does not choose this methodological vocabulary to deal with the matter, he does seem to be dealing with what looks like interaction effects. In his later writings, for example, he states his position somewhat more clearly although still without any real awareness of its methodological implications. He acknowledges that the mode of production at a particular stage does not "by itself"[36] determine variations in forms of the state. The mode of production is "relevant"[37] only through the fact that it

> determines the conjunctures of class struggles, the transformations of classes and the internal balances of socio-political forces which alone can explain these [state forms] . . . and their evolution. . . . it is none the less clear that the concrete forms that [the] state assumes—fascism, military dictatorship, 'democratic' republic, etc.—depend on the internal factors within these [authoritarian] societies.[38]

The internal factors (class struggles in particular) mediate between the mode of production and the types as well as the forms of states,[39] so that the former (mode of production) no longer uniquely determines the latter (types and forms of states). Presumably the mode of production will make possible certain kinds of class struggles and allow certain power blocs to develop. The specific configuration of these, a nonpredictable pattern of class struggles, will then lead to one or another kind of regime.

The most that Poulantzas could be saying here is that changes in the mode of production, that is, in the higher-order social system, must now be considered a necessary condition for one or another type or "form" of state or lower-order structure. The social system generates certain kinds of classes, various kinds of conflicts within and among them, and the resources available to them. But the outcome of their conflicts, in terms of liberalism or interventionism, appears not to be determined.

In brief, then, this basic transformation rule is less than helpful. It takes two forms. Initially it posits that the forms of states are determined by the historical modes of production. In the end, it reduces the modes of production to limiting conditions within which the chance outcomes of the class struggles seem to be more important in shaping the forms of state. In this way, however unwittingly, Poulantzas manages to distance himself from determinism and to move toward a probabilistic form of explanation.

C. Transformation Rules for *Normal Interventionist* Capitalist States

Rule 5. *As the composition and unity of the power bloc and hegemonic class/ fraction change and as the political struggles among these classes/fractions and between them and the dominated classes change, so too will the forms of the normal interventionist states.* (Poulantzas designates these changes as changes in regime, thereby coming close to my usage of the latter term.)

As we have seen, Poulantzas initially differentiates between liberal and interventionist types of capitalist states. He has relatively little to say about the former type. Most of his attention is devoted to the interventionist state, the more recent historical stage.

He further subdivides interventionist states into two major categories: normal as against exceptional (or crisis) types. Poulantzas wants to know why states are transformed into one or the other category and why various subtypes (what he calls forms of states or regimes) of both normal and exceptional states arise or collapse from time to time. I shall postpone discussion of the exceptional states until the next chapter. As the normal state is the starting point of his detailed analyses, here I shall begin by examining the different forms assumed by these normal interventionist states.

In the end I shall be making the point that just as with types of states so here, with forms (or subtypes) of states, what he calls regimes, the whole system or mode of production does not determine them. Rather, the whole system of relationships constituted by capitalist society makes itself felt only through the limits it imposes on the nature of the class struggles. But within these limits, the regimes may take different forms depending upon variations in class relations. These class relations, however, are not predictable from the mode of production itself except that the latter may impose broad limits within which class struggles occur, such as is found in the existence of dominant and dominated classes under the capitalist mode of production.

Accordingly, Poulantzas will not be able to argue here, with respect to the regime, any more than he was able to argue with regard to types of states (liberal as against interventionist), that the observed structures are in any sense derivative from the mode of production. They are only possibilities within the broad constraints of a given social formation.[40]

Let us now turn to an analysis of the way Poulantzas attempts to explain variations in regimes of normal, interventionist states. Such regimes represent one form of observed or lower-order structures.

To begin this analysis, however, we must clarify two points. First, what does Poulantzas mean by normal, interventionist regimes. In effect, it turns out that, despite the terminology, these regimes are nothing other than contemporary representative democracies, the "modern representative state,"[41] operating under conditions which Poulantzas describes as the monopolistic capitalist mode of production. He defines these normal types of regimes as those in which we find universal suffrage, plural political parties and other political organizations, specified relationships between executives and legislatures, and judicial regulation of the respective spheres of competence of the various organs of the state.[42]

It is clear then that Poulantzas is addressing himself to the very issue of conventional political science that is at the focus of my own inquiry in this book: How can we account for the variety of regimes that we find in modern democracies? As Poulantzas himself puts it, "The next question is the transformations of the State according to the stage and phase of capitalism, as well as *the different forms taken by the State and the regime*."[43] These regimes incorporate most of what I have been characterizing as observed, lower-order political structures.

The major interest his analysis has for us is the understanding it offers of the extent to which Poulantzas is able to bring his methodology to bear in explaining or describing why such structures vary in the way they do. Is he able to show that they are determined by the whole higher-order structure, that is, in his terminology, by the mode of production? As I have already indicated, he does not carry his argument as far in the case of the regime as he did with respect to types of states.

The second point requiring clarification is: What does Poulantzas mean when he speaks of regimes? Here we run into a little additional trouble. As we have repeatedly discovered, consistency in the use of terms is not one of Poulantzas's strong points, and this is especially true as he seeks to differentiate regimes from other forms of the state. In *Political Power and Social Classes*, for example, the regime explicitly covers what he calls "the political scene"[44] (a phrase that he borrows from Marx) in "combination" with one or another legislative or executive type of state. The "political scene" appears to be a synonym for what we would call the political party system ranging from one party to multiparty types. The reason for combining the party system and the type of separation of powers into a single category called the regime is to be found in Poulantzas's hypothesis, following Duverger in this respect,[45] that the way the parties and the separation of powers operate will depend in a significant way on whether the legislature or executive is predominant in a system.

At other times, however, the regime is used in a conventional sense to encompass the overall institutional arrangements or divisions of formal power, as when Poulantzas writes about constitutional, monarchical, parliamentary, presidential, two-party or multiparty regimes.[46] In the *Crisis of Dictatorships*, for example, he has forgotten his more restrictive definition of regime as the combination of party system with a particular form of the separation of power and in a matter-of-fact way uses the labels of parliamentary as compared to fascist or dictatorial regimes.

We shall have to do the best we can with Poulantzas's loose language and try to penetrate to the substance of his meaning rather than haggle with him over any linguistic infidelities. For the most part it is fair to assume that in the end, for Poulantzas, the regime represents all the institutional arrangements and political relationships that attain some degree of stability in a political system. It includes what we would normally think of as the formal structure of government and the stable relationships among nongovernmental organizations that are directly and explicitly involved in the political processes of modern mass industrialized society. What appear to be omitted are the rules of political action and the goals of the political system or its major components, elements that a comprehensive and more useful conceptualization of regime might wish to include.[47]

Although Poulantzas writes much about regimes, the part in which he is particularly interested and which he attempts to account for is variations in the separation of powers.[48] He does spend some time on political parties and bureaucracies. But the analysis of these hinge on the basic differences he finds between the executive and legislative dominated forms of states. This aspect of the separation of powers seems to be decisive, for Poulantzas, in establishing the character of a regime.[49]

In turning to the differences between the legislative and executive branches of government, Poulantzas descends to almost the lowest level of determination of observed structure. From the broadest level of determination, that of the influence of overlapping modes of production on the emergence of different kinds of capitalist states, we have moved with an unrelenting logic toward the level that deals with very particular kinds of lower-order structures of government. This is in accord with the intention he expresses at the outset of *Political Power and Social Classes*. In this progression Poulantzas fulfills his initial commitment to seek to account for variations in types and forms of states, the political superstructures, a necessary goal if Marxism is, for him, to measure up to its responsibilities as a social science. It must be able to show that it can do better than conventional political science, even if for different reasons and from a different problematic.

How can we account for the attention that Poulantzas almost lavishes on this particular lower-order structure, the separation of powers? His focus on it as the key aspect of regimes in normal states is rather surprising. On the surface, it would not seem to have profound implications for the transformation of capitalism to socialism, the ultimate and central concern of Marxism as a social theory. We may well ask why Poulantzas, as a Marxist, chooses so unlikely a structural candidate for particularly close scrutiny.

Outside the Marxist perspective the shift from parliamentary to executive democracy under industrialization has, of course, often commanded the attention of political scientists. It constitutes one among a number of central factors influencing the efficacy, representativeness, and responsiveness of democratic institutions and possible tendencies toward authoritarianism. Poulantzas's theoretical perspectives apparently compel him to take this part of the agenda of bourgeois social science with equal seriousness. He sees the separation of power as no minor structural detail, as might be the opinion of other Marxists. This lower-order structure is not just another incidental part of the "state apparatus" which can be glossed over. Nor is it for him just a "simple juridical" structure.[50] Rather, "it corresponds both to the precise relations of political forces and to real differences in the functioning of state institutions."[51]

For Poulantzas, the separation of power plays a central role in allowing the state to rise above the classes contending for power without, however, thereby diminishing the capacity of the state to fulfill its stipulated objective function of maintaining the unity or coherence of the system under the control of the dominant classes. The separation of powers has this effect since it provides alternative "power centres" where the hegemonic class/fraction can exercise its influence, as we shall see in a moment.

The mechanisms through which this function of the separation of power is fulfilled become clear when we take into account the functions that Poulantzas assigns to political parties. We will recall that these form the second major component of the regime in Poulantzas's terminology, the first being the separation of powers itself. Where the political parties directly represent the interests of the dominant classes the latter can depend on them to express their class needs in the legislative branch. The power of the dominant class/fraction is "concentrated" there. However, at a certain stage, under monopoly capitalism, the monopolist class/fraction may find itself no longer able to organize, through its own parties,[52] its hegemony vis-à-vis either the nation as a whole or other classes/fractions in the power bloc.[53] This encourages the hegemonic class/fraction to beat a partial retreat from the legislative branch as its main forum and to turn to the executive instead where its reliance on parties is reduced. Hence, the balance of political power in the state between these two branches of government will be explainable by the relationship of the dominant classes, and especially of those in the power bloc, to the political parties.

The rationale behind this kind of relationship rests on the notion that the legitimacy of the dominant classes and the state can be successfully maintained through the party system as long as the latter is representative of these classes, establishes working coalitions for these class/fractions, and mediates between them and the "people-nation." Poulantzas concludes that under monopoly capitalism political parties, in their search for political office, are compelled to cater to the wishes of the dominated classes. Once the class struggle results in the parties thereby falling under the direct influence of the dominated classes, however, their capacity to represent the dominant classes is undermined. This may ultimately threaten the ability of the state itself to maintain its legitimacy in the eyes of the "people-nation." When the hegemonic class/fraction loses control of its parliamentary parties, however, it finds itself better able to pursue the long-term interests of the power bloc and of the dominant classes as a whole by "concentrating its power" in the executive and bureaucracy. There it can hope to shape policy more effectively through its influence on government regulations or other kinds of intervention, and conceal its power more successfully than in the open arena of a legislature in which the parties are no longer sympathetic to its cause. At the same time this will help the monopolists assure the legitimacy of their own rule and that of the state itself since the latter, in principle, can only act on behalf of the dominant classes,[54] as I have noted.

In this way Poulantzas tries to account for the emergence of executive power and the decline of parliament in modern times. As he himself expresses it,

> This predominance [of the executive] corresponds to the hegemony of monopolies, and to their incapacity to organize this hegemony over the power bloc and over the people-nation by means of their own political parties in parliament. Hence there is a decline of the parties in the power bloc, a recrudescence of the political role of the state apparatus, and an organization of this hegemony by means of the state in the executive itself.[55]

Relationship between Regime and Higher-Order Structure

Now that we have a description of the way in which Poulantzas sees changes in regimes, a type of lower-order political structure, we can return to our main problem. To what extent does Poulantzas seek to explain such transformations in the regime by appeal to the way in which the political or social system as a whole operates? Does he demonstrate a plausible linkage between variations in the regime and changes in the mode of production, the "matrix" within which all previous transformations have occurred?

It might appear indeed that this is precisely the kind of argument he is presenting. After all, he is hypothesizing, or perhaps we might better say, declaring, that the monopolistic stage of the capitalist mode of production generates a certain type of class struggle between the dominant and dominated classes. This, in turn, leads to the transformation of the regime, as we have just seen, to one in which the power of the hegemonic class/fraction is centered in the executive rather than the legislature. This apparent relationship, however, demands closer scrutiny. We will find that he fails to push his argument so far as to find in the mode of production itself the original source of variations.

It is rather surprising, given the weight he puts on the mode of production or "ensemble" of instances as the determining "matrix," that he makes no claim for it as the determinant of the regime. His position about the regime, therefore, is substantially different from the one he consciously espouses for types of states (interventionist as against liberal). It is true, at the outset he stipulates that just as the mode of production as a whole undergoes changes in response to economic periodization, so the interventionist state will experience changes in the regime. These kinds of changes he describes as *political* periodization.[56] However, as we saw earlier, *economic* periodization was supposed to reflect variations in the whole mode of production, ultimately converting it from an economic liberal to a monopolistic type of capitalism. In the process, as part of the mode of production, the type of state was supposed to shift from liberal to interventionist. As we also saw earlier, however, in practice Poulantzas was not able to make as direct a connection between the two as he seems to have wished or intended. The type of state seemed to be more closely connected to unpredictable variations in the class struggles.

For regimes, however, Poulantzas spares himself a similar inconsistency, for reasons he does not advance, by avoiding the claim that variations in regimes are directly influenced by the mode of production. In his own words, "The factors differentiating the *forms of regime* are the concrete methods of the political class struggle in a determinate *conjuncture.*"[57] He had already generalized this position in *Political Power and Social Classes* by holding that the kinds of regimes will depend only on the "rhythm and scansion"[58] of the political level itself (the political class conflicts), within the limits, presumably, of the liberal or interventionist character of the state.

Poulantzas has little to say about this "rhythm and scansion," however; its nature is never fully defined. We are left to infer that it is found largely in the possible oscillations between the executive and legislative predominance in the policy processes. This grand phrase is, therefore, reduced from what seems like a promise of a description of some broad patterns of change over substantial periods of time to the humbler movement of policy-making power from the legislature to the executive. The rhythm looks more like a single beat, a one-time, definitive shift in one direction in part of the regime rather than a patterned change in the regime as a whole.

It is true that this shift is associated with the rise of monopoly capitalism. But as we have just seen in the quotation above, Poulantzas does not attribute the regime change directly to the emergence of a new stage in the mode of production, monopoly capitalism. The regime transformation occurs only as a result of the "concrete methods of the political class struggle in a determinate conjuncture." Translated, this simply means that the regime will depend upon the vagaries of the class conflict, and Poulantzas makes no suggestion that the particular outcome of the class conflicts can be predicted as part of any pattern, at least insofar as it concerns the regime. Indeed, as he does imply, what does happen will depend on the particular *conjuncture*, that is, set of historical circumstances. Whatever the "rhythm and scansion" may be, it is not foreseeable. The "political periodization" with respect to the regime has none of the identifiable stages of "economic periodization" and, indeed, looks more like a Paretan unpredictable flux than a set of stages.[59]

In effect, therefore, with respect to the regime, Poulantzas takes, at the outset, the same position into which his analysis of types of states finally and unwittingly led him. The types of regimes, like the types of states, are a product of (or as he would put it, in his ambiguous and uncertain vocabulary, "correspond to," "are related to," "mirror," "depend on") the vagaries of the class struggle within the limits set by changes in the mode of production.

At most, therefore, the stage of the mode of production with which executive dominance is associated, does not determine (cause) such dominance. It only creates the conditions of its possibility within certain limits. As with the relationship of economic periodization to types of states, so political periodization (whatever it may mean) is related to regimes only by virtue of the fact that it creates *possible*, not necessary outcomes. Once again we have here, not a theory of determination (or unique outcomes) but a theory of possibilities within limits.

At this point, it appears, when Poulantzas descends to the lowest level of political structures, as it were, he shifts gear. The observable structures are no longer directly determined by the mode of production, that is, by the whole social system or higher-order structure. The latter has effects, but only indirectly, through variations it may permit rather than bring about in the class struggles.

Conclusion

Poulantzas's analysis is complex to say the least. In part this is due to its formalistic character. As we have seen, Miliband has accused Poulantzas of structural superdeterminism and structural abstractionism.[60] This criticism owes much of its validity to Poulantzas's failure to specify a plausible deterministic linkage between the mode of production—the three instances and the way they combine under the hierarchical "determination" of the economy in the last instance—and the policies and observed political structures. In fact, Poulantzas usually tries to avoid the term *determination* but otherwise offers little by way of describing the relationship. As he encounters difficulty with the notion of determination, which I have already noted, he uses such flaccid phrases as "governs," "mirrors," "accounts for," and the like, terms that leave us uncertain about the exact nature of the relationship. But what does come through in his rhetoric is that he wishes to convince us that no single important structure can be understood except in terms of the way each of the three instances interrelates with or "interpenetrates" each of the others[61] as they serve their foreordained functions.

As we have pursued the analysis, however, we have seen that this strong statement about the connection between the observed structures and the social system as a whole becomes somewhat attentuated. When it comes to deriving from this relationship the various types of states and the various types of regimes, these seem to be more a product of chance concatenations of circumstances flowing from the way the various class struggles manifest themselves than of any direct linkage to the functioning of higher-order structures.

It is true, of course, that the kinds of classes and their interrelationships are circumscribed or constrained by the nature of the capitalist mode of production. The latter sets some outer limits, apparently. One of the most prominent of these is the built-in or objective necessity for the dominant classes to seek to guarantee the reproduction of the system, that is, its system-maintaining and /-reproducing tendencies. Another is the inevitability of the actions of the dominant classes, especially of its hegemonic class/fraction, operating so as to maintain the unity of the state under the power of these classes. But within these limits, the range of alternative types of states (liberal versus interventionist) and, as we shall shortly see, alternative forms of regimes (normal versus crisis) are the result of historical circumstances. They seem to be essentially unpredictable, depending, as they do, on the way the particular class struggles evolve, within the limits set by the mode of production at whatever stage it happens to be. We would seem to have here, then, an explanation of lower-order structures that fails to deliver on Poulantzas's apparent promise to show a strong connection between such structures and the overall structure of the social system.

16

The Transformation to Authoritarian Political Structures

In the last chapter we saw how Poulantzas seeks to explain changes that occur within the confines of representative democratic regimes, especially with respect to the shift of actual power from the legislative to the executive arena. We saw that he attempted to trace these changes back to the mode of production, that is, to the overall social system and the way it operates. But the direct linkage between the various forms of the political system and the social system as a whole, that is, between lower- and higher-order structures, tended to break down, at least insofar as the latter could be said to explain variations in the former. At the very most, the social system influences observed structures only by serving as a limit on the forms that the political system might assume, not as a determinant. We shall now discover that when Poulantzas applies the same analytic tools to the shift from democratic to authoritarian political systems, he gives us no greater explanatory leverage despite his initial aspirations to the contrary.

Crisis (Exceptional) Regimes

As we noted earlier, Poulantzas classifies interventionist states according to whether they are marked by normal or exceptional regimes.[1] The latter kind of regime takes its name from the exceptional or crisis conditions out of which it arises. Poulantzas then subdivides exceptional regimes into three types: fascism, military dictatorship, and Bonapartism. It leads him to propose that "the specific political phenomenon of fascism can therefore only be analyzed by positing at the same time a theory of the political crisis and the exceptional State [regime, strictly speaking] which also fits other types of exceptional capitalist regimes."[2]

The reason for Poulantzas's special interest in exceptional regimes is transparent. They represent the same kinds of regimes which conventional political science usually calls authoritarian, totalitarian, and dictatorial. Poulantzas seeks to formulate a special subtheory to cover their emergence—an achievement, Poulantzas might have warned us, that has eluded conventional political science. Poulantzas for his part proposes that there is something in the nature of political crises under the advanced stage of capitalism, in his language, that leads to the rise of the different kinds of exceptional regimes. The "specific forms" of the exceptional regime "correspond," Poulantzas maintains, to "the particular kinds of political crises."[3] His theory is in part a theory of the structural effects of political crises.

To what does he trace back these crises? Given his original project to derive types of states and their regimes from a theory about variations in the mode of production, we would have expected him to relate these crises and their outcomes to the capitalist mode of production. We shall see that in one sense he does exactly that—he seeks to demonstrate that the capitalist mode of production, in its stage of monopolism and imperialism, can be expected to generate such crises. The outcomes of these crises, however, will prove not to be objectively determined. These fluctuate with the uncertain fortunes of the class struggle.

We shall end up here, as we have with so much of Poulantzas's theorizing, not a little confused. After promising us an "account" (we know by this time that we are seldom offered anything Poulantzas himself calls an "explanation") based on the determining effects of the mode of production, we shall find that once again he is unable to escape serious ambiguity about whether he intends to identify objective determinants or just the limits of regime structures. When we are through we shall be left with no greater help in establishing the effect of the whole on the parts than we have already received, in the previous chapter, from his discussion of normal regimes.

Furthermore, we shall find him seriously wanting at the theoretical level. Despite the accusation frequently levelled against him for his formalism and abstractionism in *Political Power and Social Classes,* in his later works the pendulum frequently swings to the other extreme even though his critics have usually neglected to draw this to our attention. In these writings we shall discover, despite his lofty language and the broad net within which he casts his conclusions, that his implicit transformation rules are usually mere descriptions of the way in which historical "normal" systems, such as Germany, did convert to fascism. In effect, under the cloak of a generalizing historical social scientist, Poulantzas becomes a historian of the unique. We will need to penetrate this disguise.

Conditions for the Rise of Exceptional Regimes

I shall now briefly examine the elaborate arguments through which he intends to demonstrate theoretically the conditions under which exceptional regimes arise and the kinds of states that can be expected to experience transformations into exceptional regimes. Thereby we shall be in a position to assess the extent to which he can explain, through this theorizing, variations in these kinds of lower-order political structures.

Not all states are likely to see their regimes transform themselves into exceptional kinds. For example, liberal states either are able to escape such transformations or, if not, Poulantzas shows sufficiently little interest in the liberal state to take the trouble to explain why he overlooks them. Technically, as we observed earlier, the liberal state could flourish under monopoly capitalism. Since the exceptional regime is closely "related to" this monopolist stage in the capitalist mode of production, theoretically liberalism could also undergo an exceptionalist transformation. In practice, Poulantzas totally ignores this possibility.

For Poulantzas it turns out that crises which lead to exceptional regimes occur, in effect, only during interventionist periods in the lives of states. They are the "normal" regimes within which exceptional types can emerge. As we shall see, in the monopolist stage of the capitalist mode of production conditions arise that may lead the dominant classes to abandon representative institutions. But even within the interventionist state only the executive-dominated regime seems to be a victim of crises of this sort. Noticeably missing are the legislative-dominated states, for reasons that will become apparent.

In short, Poulantzas limits his writings to only two broad classes of regimes. These seem for him to be typical of the capitalist mode of production, at least in its monopolist stage: interventionist, normal, executive-dominated regimes as compared to the interventionist, exceptional (crisis-generated), executive-dominated regimes. Poulantzas claims to be able to "account for" the latter through a "theory of political crises."

To explore whether in this area Poulantzas is better able to instruct us about how to establish the effects of the whole social system on one of its parts—the state or political system—I shall analyze Poulantzas's treatment of exceptional regimes in much the same way that I did normal types. I shall try to extract the major transformation rules implicit in the description that Poulantzas gives us of the conditions "related to" the emergence of exceptional regimes. Furthermore, I shall confine my remarks largely to only one type of exceptional regime, fascism. Poulantzas's later works, dealing with other types of exceptional regimes such as military dictatorships and Bonapartism, add little to our understanding of how he derives lower-order structures from his structuralist base.

Since Poulantzas has promised us a "regional" or partial theory of the exceptional "state" (regime, strictly speaking), we might have thought that we would have been able to discover a number of at least implicit transformation rules (or dynamic laws) that cut across all exceptional states. The fact is that at most he offers us only two major rules of any significance. That we can infer only these rules for generalization to all exceptional regimes, exposes the limitations of the theory he has promised us.

We shall learn that this want of rules, at the most general level, is no accident. It reflects the fact that, upon inspection, most of Poulantzas's rules, as I have already indicated, are more likely to be descriptions of the unique historical circumstances surrounding the emergence of one type of exceptional regime, fascism, than statements of the relationships among all exceptional regimes and the conditions that generate them. He is prone to describe rather than to theorize, always, however, in the guise of theorizing. For translating his general social theory (of modes of production) into specific forms of regimes, these rules will, therefore, offer us less help than we might have expected.

The Role of Political Crises

Rule 6. *Political crises, not economic crises alone, transform normal, interventionist, executive-dominated regimes into exceptional ones.*[4]

Put more fully, this rule states that all exceptional regimes, whether fascist, military dictatorship, or Bonapartist, are responses to specific types of *political* crises.[5] For Poulantzas a political crisis is not just confined to the political sphere. It is an indicator of a *crisis* in the whole social system. This is his central point.

Hence, to understand why a normal regime breaks down we need to trace it back to the crises that give birth to exceptional regimes.

Poulantzas developed his position, expressed in this rule, in opposition to the theoretical interpretation of the Third International. The latter had designated fascism as primarily an offspring of an *economic* crisis.[6] Poulantzas argues that far from being so, the direct economic effects of severe unemployment, inflation, and the like were already on their way to being overcome when fascism came to power in Germany.[7] This suggests to Poulantzas that fascism, as an exceptional regime, owes its existence rather to political crises which occur in certain historical periods of the capitalist mode of production. Since, as we have seen, the state "condenses" or is the focal point of "contradictions" throughout society,[8] fascism as a political phenomenon indicates that something is amiss in the social system as a whole, not just in the economy alone.

Poulantzas explicitly and carefully wants to distinguish his theoretical position from that of the Third International before the Seventh Congress. At that time the Third International construed fascism "as that form of the capitalist state which corresponds to monopoly capitalism and imperialism."[9] Poulantzas maintained that there can be no automatic relationship between monopoly capitalism and imperialism, on the one hand, and fascism on the other. Otherwise every capitalist state, at the monopolistic-imperialistic stage, would be "fascist in varying degree."[10] He considered fascism to be a product of a variation in the way in which not only the economic but the political and ideological instances (subsystems) were interrelated. For him, fascism mirrors the whole social formation rather than a particular stage of the economy alone.

To prove his point he enters into an involved analysis of what he calls the "imperialist chain." Through it, he argues, monopoly capitalism leads to the internationalization of the class struggle at all levels (instances) of the social formation. Fascism arises, he agrees with the Comintern, because of a desperate economic crisis. But for Poulantzas this is only part of the story; the economic crisis is but one ingredient in a political crisis. The latter is, as always, the focal or condensation point of a crisis in the mode of production at large. For Poulantzas, the source of the crisis lies in the fact that the capitalist mode of production, during the twentieth century, is in the throes of change from its competitive to its monopolistic-imperialistic stage.

The final step of the argument is that each social formation responds to the ties created by imperialism—the imperialist chain, as he later labels it[11]—in ways that conform to the social formation's own stage of development. Characteristically, capitalism, in this transition stage, develops "unevenly" in different countries, that is, at different rates. It is this that leads to political crises in some social systems, as it did in Russia, with one outcome and as it did in Germany and Italy with a very different one. Even though the results were at different socioeconomic poles, the political crises of change in each of these countries revealed them as weak links in the "imperialist chain."

For Poulantzas, to attribute the political crises in such countries to economic forces alone, such as the rise of monopoly capitalism and imperialism, would be to descend to economism—economic monocausality. Fascism is due not just to the relative economic position of a country but to the "particular nature of the ensemble of the social formation [which] helps determine the allocation of [its] position [in the imperialist chain], and any changes in it, such changes being determinant for the conjuncture."[12] From Poulantzas's point of view, to understand the transformations into exceptional regimes it behooves the analyst to examine the way in which the political crises encapsulate the crises in the other instances of the mode of production, that is, in the economic and ideological subsystems, other parts of the "ensemble" of the social formation.

Nature of Political Crises

Since politics is symptomatic of the state of health of the whole social system, we may well ask: What makes up a political crisis? For Poulantzas, crises are composed of several distinctive elements.

First, the kinds of crises that yield exceptional regimes occur only in certain historical periods of capitalist social formations, during their monopolist-imperialist stage. Imperialism is one of the major conditions that stimulates a fascist solution to such crises. For example, for Poulantzas it is the fact that Germany and Italy were "weak links in the imperialist chain," having been late arrivals on the scene during the imperialist stage of the capitalist mode of production, that compelled the monopolists in these countries to seek to "consolidate [their] dominance" internally through an exceptional regime.[13] Once they achieve this the monopolists could then "retreat," as they did after World War II, and accept the reintroduction of a normal (parliamentary) state.[14]

Second, the historical period does not operate directly to produce exceptional regimes. It is true, the "'economic' factors actually determine a new articulation of the ensemble of the capitalist system thereby producing profound changes in politics and ideology."[15] We will recall, for Poulantzas, as for Althusser, the economy is always, in their unrelentingly opaque phrase, "determinant in the last instance." But it is not the mode of production in its imperialist stage, in some abstract sense, that objectively determines the crisis to which the exceptional state is an automatic response. What ultimately counts is the fact that the new economic stage "affects" the class struggle.[16] Or as he puts it even more positively, state forms or regimes "often undergo radical change, corresponding to a modification in the relation of forces [class struggles], and due among other things to the instability or lack of hegemony."[17]

This is a central point in Poulantzas's understanding of crises. They arise out of circumstances contingent on the fortunes of the class struggles. Again in his own words, the "essence of a political crisis which can lead to the emergence of an exceptional State lies in particular characteristics of the *field of the class struggle*."[18]

What is left dangling here is the relationship between the mode of production and the class struggle. Does the former determine not only the latter's existence but its course and outcome as well? Or is there some less influential connection?

Answers to these questions are critical for an understanding of the way the mode of production shapes the regime, and I shall return to them shortly.

Third, a crisis erupts not just because capitalism is in its monopolistic-imperialistic stage but because in the course of the class struggles during this period the various dominant classes and fractions within the power bloc are unable to resolve their internal conflict. *"No dominant class or fraction seems able to impose its 'leadership' on the other classes and fractions of the power bloc, whether by its own method of political organization or through the 'parliamentary democratic' State."*[19] In other words, no one class or fraction can manage to assert its hegemony. At the same time the dominant classes are in collision with the dominated classes who are seen to be making excessive social and economic demands.[20] When such conflicts in class relationships—within the power bloc and between it and dominated classes— cannot be resolved, a crisis is at hand; fascism, as one type of exceptional regime, for example, becomes an acceptable solution for the dominant classes (preeminent among which, at this economic stage, are the monopolist-imperialists).

To repeat, the trigger for the political crises is not an economic crisis alone with its obvious dislocations, as the Third International had proclaimed. It is the "contradictions" brought about by the class struggles over hegemony, within the power bloc itself especially, which the bloc, as then constituted, is unable to resolve. The crisis appears to be determined by the stage of production. Once again, whether or not the outcome, in the form of an exceptional regime, is similarly determined, is a different question.

Fourth and finally, the political crisis is not confined within the bloc alone. It infects the ideological instance (subsystem) as well. As a result of internal political instability, the ideological state apparatus (parties, schools, mass media, trade unions, churches, and the like, in Gramsci's sense) is no longer able to hold the bloc together or to bind the dominated classes to the bloc as under normal conditions. Furthermore, the crisis reveals itself through "profound fissures in the institutional system,"[21] that is, in the repressive state apparatus (police, army, administrative services, and governmental agencies) and in other governing institutions. This institutional component, revealed in such things as the breakdown of parliamentary and administrative processes, flows from the irreconcilable differences in the various class conflicts. The crisis in these areas, however, is, for Poulantzas, not an independent cause of the general crisis as it appears to have been for the Third International. The institutional breakdown is only a symptom, not a cause, which, once it appears, can only aggravate the general crisis.

The total effect of these crisis conditions throughout the social system, "condensed" as they are in the state, is to create a need for the state to assert a greater degree of autonomy from the social classes than we find under normal conditions. This enhancement of the autonomy of the state, and the reorganization of the repressive and ideological state apparatuses that are part of it, permit the exceptional regime to impose a settlement on the power bloc and thereby to do two things.[22] First, by reasserting the hegemony of the power bloc over the popular masses, as Poulantzas puts it,[23] the state staves off any threat from the dominated classes; otherwise the latter might have been able to take advantage of the cleavages in the ruling classes. Second, the state saves the system for the dominant classes even if the latter may not all see the swelling of state intervention and control in this light and may even actively resist it.

What, however, is the nature of these changes that come about as a result of this transformation from a normal to an exceptional state? We might have expected the transformation rule we are considering to offer us some surprises or at least some capacity to move from the general statement to the particular. Poulantzas had clearly intended us to interpret him as making a theoretical statement of the sort I summarized in transformation Rule 6. After all, in the extension of this rule it declares that the change occurs under the impetus of a political crisis, broadly defined to mean a crisis in the whole mode of production at a time when competitive capitalism is passing over into the monopolistic mode of production. However, when Poulantzas actually applies this rule, he presents us with little more than a historical description, in his own special language, of what happened in Germany and Italy. In effect, he does no more than formulate empirical rather than theoretical generalizations, drawing them from the specific historical experiences of these two systems.

We can see this from the list of transformations that Poulantzas offers us as derivative, in effect, from his implicit major transformation rule (Rule 6). They are as follows:

(1)   There is a reorganization of the relative autonomy of the ideological apparatuses from the state repressive apparatus (in Poulantzas's special language), typical of a pluralist-type capitalist society. In its place there emerges a political system in which all institutions or organizations are brought under the control of the state. They therefore lose their autonomy.[24]

(2)   The dominant position in the repressive state apparatus may go to one or another branch, as, for example, to the political police or to the party.[25]

(3)   The judicial system is typically displaced by the police system.

(4)   A single-party system replaces the pluralistic electoral system.

(5)   Cooptation, appointment, and corporatist representation replace the electoral principles of recruitment.[26]

The general nature of these changes—including those in observed structures—accompanying the reorganization of the power bloc through the agency of the state itself is clear. The new regime form destroys the pluralism of the normal regime and brings all structures under the domination of one or another branch of the state apparatuses. In addition, the exceptional regime will find it necessary to transform its juridical system from a legal (normal regime) into a police state[27] and, depending upon whether it is fascist, a military dictatorship, or Bonapartist, displaces any existing plural electoral principles with a one-party system.[28]

In arguing that the transformation of capitalist states to exceptional forms, as here defined, is a consequence of political crises, Poulantzas seems to be using this formulation to present his case for the determination of exceptionalism by the mode of production (the social system conceived as an entity). The determination appears to be at least a two-stage process. The monopolist period of capitalism generates class conflicts under certain conditions of transition from competitive capitalism, as in Germany and Italy. These conflicts, in turn, spark political crises in the form of irreconcilable differences within and among the classes; the state manages to cope with these through the reorganization of hegemony in the power bloc. The crises are not confined to the state alone. They take root in all three instances or subsystems of the social system and are just "condensed" in the overall political crises. On the surface at least, it would appear that, when faced with crises composed of the elements just noted, the capitalist state, in its stage of monopolism, must turn to exceptionalism if it is to continue to function as the guardian of the long-term interests of the dominant classes.

This interpretation of the necessary relationship between the mode of production and the crises that give birth to exceptional regimes must be recognized if later we are to understand the tension that pervades Poulantzas's overall analysis. This tension flows from the fact that what here appears as virtually inescapable will once again turn out, after all, to be only a mere possibility.

Necessity versus Possibility

To demonstrate this vacillation in Poulantzas's analysis, we need to examine the basis upon which Poulantzas sees an apparently necessary connection between the mode of production and exceptionalism. This necessity seems to flow logically from Rule 6 about the transformation of the normal into the exceptional regime. This rule takes the form of a theoretical statement; hence the plausibility of a necessary connection.

When, however, it comes down to developing the reasons why this shift should occur—under the impetus of instability within the power bloc and irreconcilable conflicts between the latter and the dominated classes—this theoretical approach in effect dissolves, as I have pointed out. It becomes little more than a historical description of what Poulantzas sees as having taken place in Germany and Italy during the 1920s and 1930s. His theoretical propositions are really not much more than descriptive ones.

I would not argue that Poulantzas is necessarily wrong in his description of the conflicts that had prepared the ground for fascism in Germany, for example. It is plausible to argue that inter-faction conflict among the various dominant classes and "fractions" (heavy industry, the export trades, commerce, etc.) contributed to the readiness by their leaders to accept fascism, even if reluctantly at times, as a resolution of the various political impasses.[29] Business also certainly felt that it could make no further concessions to labor, and indeed that those already made had gone too far. Various business groups had also lost their influence in parliament because of the ineffectual parties to which they normally looked for representation of their interests.

It is one thing to describe what did indeed happen, in Germany and Italy as prototypes, as Poulantzas does, and quite another to generalize this description of the actual historical situation to the rules that must always govern the transformations from representative democracies to totalitarian fascist or other "exceptional"

228 The Structuralism of Nicos Poulantzas

regimes. Even if these observations were valid for both these cases of fascism, they represent only a recounting of history, not a theoretical explanation of why even paralyzing conflicts should lead to the particular kinds of regimes that they did. They do not tell us why, when the state, in Poulantzas's terms, asserts greater autonomy and steps in to manage conflicts over hegemony, it must erase preexisting observed political structures or regimes to the degree it did in these political systems. Or why it selects a fascist alternative rather than a military dictatorship, or why it might even retain a modified form of democracy. The changes could easily have been a product of the particular local conditions in these two countries, without being extendable to all situations of this sort, at least under capitalism. Poulantzas presents no evidence that would lead us to a different conclusion. Once again, at best, Poulantzas's science of politics, as he calls his work, offers us presumed generalizations that he would find difficult to distinguish from mere descriptions of unique historical events.

The other side of the coin is that, in committing himself to the historical model of fascism as the only class of outcomes, Poulantzas does not take into account the possibility that the state, even as he defines it, might have been able to cope with the situation through very different structural arrangements. In other words, even though I shall later try to show that he builds his whole edifice—about the transformation from a normal to an exceptional regime—around the indeterminacy of the outcome (within the limits set by monopoly capitalism at its imperialistic stage), at this point he seems to be declaring a unique and inescapable connection between an exceptional regime, such as fascism, and the historical structures through which it happened to manifest itself.

No logical reasons or empirical necessities are advanced for this tie between hegemonic instability and the particular form (regime) of the German and Italian response, as I have already argued. All Poulantzas is able to show in reality is that the given response serves the function which he postulates the state needs to serve, namely, to assure the power of the dominant classes by imposing a settlement of their internal conflicts on them and by reducing the threat of the popular masses. He does not go even so far as other functionalists and recognize that this necessary function of the state—to preserve the power of the ruling classes, in his view— could perhaps have been served by a variety of alternative structural arrangements. His declaration of a necessary connection between the class struggles and the structures delineated in the transformation rule above is no more than that, an unsupported assertion seeking plausibility through what is essentially a description of the historical experiences that we call German and Italian fascism.

At the very best the transformation rule we are discussing here describes sufficient, perhaps, but certainly not necessary conditions and must be considered theoretically deficient. Historically, it is true, irreconcilable conflicts among the various social classes and "fractions" in Germany did precede fascism. But the theoretical question is whether there was any necessity in this transformation into a new kind of regime, as Poulantzas wishes to maintain, and this he fails to demonstrate. We do not know the nature of the connection—necessary, possible, or accidental—between the mode of production (the whole system), its crises, and exceptional regimes.

Even if we disregard the theoretical shortcomings of Poulantzas's formulation about the relationship between the form of the regime and the mode of production as mediated by class struggles, the basic issue remains. Does Poulantzas intend to leave the matter as one of necessity, however unconvincing in fact his case may be? Does he really stick by his initial convictions that there is this kind of inescapable connection between the regime (the observed lower-order structures) and the mode of production, what I have been calling the higher-order structure?

As I have suggested, we shall see that, in *Fascism and Dictatorship* particularly, he has second thoughts, and these lead him to vacillate between determinism and mere possibility. This indecision will mean that, after all, we may have no explanation of the observed regime structures that is anything more than a historical possibility within the broad constraints laid down by the mode of production at its particular stage.

So much, then, for the exceptional state or regime as a type of structure that diverges from the normal one. For Poulantzas, the change manifests itself in three different forms or regime types, as we have seen: fascist, military dictatorship, and Bonapartist. These types of regimes bring us down to the most visible kinds of structures that usually command the attention of conventional political science and that parallel the same level of detail that Poulantzas had discussed for normal regimes.

Let us now look at the rules governing transformations into specific kinds of exceptional regimes. Poulantzas has spelled these out most explicitly for the fascist regime, so I shall confine myself to this type.[30] What he has to say boils down to a single rule.

Fascism: An Inevitable or Only a Possible Regime?

Rule 7. *Fascism, as one kind of exceptional regime, is a particular response to class-struggle related political crises in the period of transition from competitive (liberal) capitalism to the stage (in Poulantzas's technical sense) of monopoly capitalism in its imperialist phase.*

I have deliberately constructed this rule from Poulantzas's writings to leave open the issue as to whether fascism is a necessary or only a possible conclusion to the kind of political crises that Poulantzas sees as underlying all exceptional regimes. In fact, Poulantzas's treatment of the exceptional regime designated as fascism marks a predictable transition from, if not a marked break with his earlier work. In *Political Power and Social Classes*, we will recall, he delineated a philosophy of social causation in which the mode of production, the overall social system, was to account for variations in lower-order structures. He was never fully at ease with this formulation, however. He could bring himself to use the idea of determination in only selected cases, when speaking, for example, of the economy as "determinant in the last instance." And he constantly undermined his own deterministic objectives by opening the door to alternative historical or "conjunctural" possibilities depending on the circumstances rather than on given structuralist arrangements. In his analysis of fascism he finally peels off most of his restraint and calls upon the consequences of the class struggles, with less predictable outcomes, rather than on obscure objective social forces of the mode of production.

It is true, in his early writings on fascism, no less than in Rule 7, as we have already observed, he pays lip service, even if ambiguously so, to structuralist determinism. Fascism was interpreted by him as a different form of articulation of the instances of the capitalist mode of production, as a state that "corresponds" to this difference.[31] There was, then, a real and important distinction between his position on fascism and that of the Third International. For economic determinism he was opting in favor of determination by the whole social formation (the higher-order structure), or mode of production, to put the matter theoretically. For economism he would substitute total system causation.

Where he continued to be vague about differentiating himself from the position of the Third International, however, was in his own acceptance, albeit ambiguously, of some degree of automaticity, if we may use the word, between this new articulation among the instances (brought about by the change to monopoly capitalism and imperialism) and the appearance of the fascist regime. Even though class struggles mediate between the mode of production associated with monopoly capitalism and imperialism, on the one side, and fascism, on the other, in *Political Power and Social Classes*, at least, the class struggles and their outcomes in fascism seem to be as automatically determined, for Poulantzas, as fascism was for the Comintern. It would appear that the monopolistic mode of production, and not the economy alone, determines the nature of the class struggles, these lead to political crises, and these in turn account for fascism. The regime is thus explainable, ultimately, by reference back to the inescapable consequences of shifts in the mode of production.

Even when Poulantzas came to write his book on fascism he retained his early bent toward structuralist determinism. As he typically phrased the matter there, "The contradictions between the dominant classes and class fractions often take on sufficient importance to determine the forms of State and of regime."[32] This declaration, made in the context of a discussion on fascism, would seem to be definitive enough, despite the protective cover of the word "often," when the weight of his discussion characteristically leans in the direction of "always."

Nevertheless, despite this apparent continuing commitment to at least a half-hearted determinist interpretation of fascism, in *Fascism and Dictatorship* it is really atavistic in light of the thrust of the discussion in the book as a whole. Indeed, the book foreshadows an uneasy tension in Poulantzas's later writings between determinism and what we might call possibilism. A fascist regime is no longer determined, whether unreservedly or cautiously. It becomes only a possibility. In this book Poulantzas now sees the stage of the mode of production (monopoly capitalism combined with imperialism), in his technical sense of the meaning of stage, as providing, not the driving force behind the transformation to fascism, but only necessary conditions for regime changes. Fascism is no longer unequivocally determined even by the whole social formation. It becomes only a historical possibility[33] explainable by the "concrete situation" of the class struggles.[34]

In this light, once the social formation makes it possible for any exceptional state to arise, fascism as a particular kind of exceptional regime *could* appear. It arose, in Germany and Italy, not for any inescapable conjuncture in the class struggles, to use Poulantzas's terminology, but simply because as "weak links in the imperialist chain," these countries provided a more hospitable environment for the kind of crisis out of which fascism, now as one among a number of options, might emerge as a solution. In the international linkages forged by monopoly capitalism, these countries arrived late on the scene of industrialization and monopolism. They were in process of "transition"[35] from competitive (liberal) to monopolistic and imperialistic capitalism, somewhat later than other Western industrialized countries. The problems created by the resulting internal and international conflicts in which these countries found themselves made it possible, but by no means necessary, for a fascist type of regime to ease the burden of transition for the dominant classes.

We would be wrong, of course, to say that in *Fascism and Dictatorship* Poulantzas now denies to the capitalist mode of production, as an objective structure, some salient place in the transformation of the normal regime into an exceptional one. The capacity of the normal regime to respond to political crises through conversion to exceptionalism is itself made possible by the structure of this mode of production. The reason the budding exceptional regime is able to flower is that it is still a capitalist state, Poulantzas argues. As such it has both major characteristics of all such states: the economic, political (the state), and ideological instances, the ensemble of which make up the mode of production, are each relatively autonomous from the dominant classes and fraction.[36] These are important features of the emerging exceptional regime since they enable it to take two kinds of actions critical to their birth and survival: to reorganize the hegemony within the power bloc as a means of escaping the political crisis, as we have seen;[37] and to reorganize the whole state apparatus including the relationship between the repressive and ideological apparatuses. That is to say, what we find in all exceptional regimes is that as a response to political crises created by the class struggles, the state uses its relative autonomy or freedom from all social classes to attempt to impose a resolution.

In addition, the relationship between the repressive (public) and ideological (private) apparatuses—relatively independent of each other in the normal state— is now subject to a reorganization in which the repressive dominates the ideological.[38] In this way, Poulantzas argues, the general theory of the capitalist state provides a basis for understanding how normal regimes are transformed into exceptional ones. It is another matter, however, to infer from this that these properties of the state provide anything more than a necessary (but not a sufficient) basis, a point I have already made and to which I shall again return.

The tension, however, between this continued structuralist element in his thought and his new discovery of the crucial significance of the human agency in the form of class struggle—which I noted in an earlier context—as well as of its unpredictability, leads Poulantzas to relax if not to abandon his objectivism. He begins to hedge on his claim that exceptional regimes are determined regardless of the wishes, intent, or motivations of human actors, who take the form of social classes in this case.

For example, in the process of making a case for fascism arising in the weakest links in the "imperialist chain" in Europe, he cautions that "in no sense do I mean that fascism was fated to happen there. . . . I simply mean that in the particular *conjunctures* of class struggles in these countries [Germany and Italy], which for a whole series of reasons led to such different results, their position in the imperialist chain was of crucial importance."[39] The capitalist mode of production, therefore, at its imperialist-monopolist stage, provides only the background limit which makes fascism possible. It takes a particular "conjuncture" or unique combination of circumstances to bring it about.

Fascism and Dictatorship is larded with caveats of this sort "Fascism can only be explained by reference to the *concrete situation* of the class struggle as it cannot be reduced to any inevitable need of the 'economic' development of capitalism."[40] "The non-correspondence between base and superstructure does not automatically spell out some future catastrophe for a social formation: the explosion of this contradiction [between the production process, combining productive forces and relations of production on one side and the superstructure on the other] and also the possibility of its eventual readjustment within the same mode of production, depends on this [class] struggle."[41] The driving force for change here is not the mode of production but the class struggle; and this has certain elements of unpredictability. If the base (mode of production) and superstructure (state) are in contradiction, there is no longer anything inevitable about the base winning out. It all depends now on how this conflict is worked out through the class struggle. Nowhere does Poulantzas offer any guarantees that in the conflict among the various classes and fractions any outcome is certain except that, whatever the result, it must serve the long-range interests of the dominant classes in the aggregate.

If the class struggle, unpredictable in its resolution, now takes over as the mechanism through which the fascist transformation occurs, what is the function of the objective underlying structure, the mode of production? It appears to become the necessary but not sufficient condition. It provides the limits within which the class struggle itself must operate. Within those limits the class struggle *may* take a turn toward fascism, but the latter may also be avoided depending on the strategy of the class actors, a surprising human or subjective element in Poulantzas's thinking. There are means, Poulantzas insists, "of successfully struggling against the resistible rise of fascism."[42]

In this vein Poulantzas now points out that fascism is not even restricted to the period in which it did in fact occur. For Poulantzas, as we have seen, this was the period of transition in the imperialist phase of capitalism toward dominance of monopoly capitalism. But, he writes, *"the fascist phenomenon is by no means restricted to this 'period'*. The 'period' is important only insofar as it circumscribes the conjunctures of the class struggle, and contributes to the emergence of the *political crises* to which fascism corresponds, political crises which are not determined solely by the character of the period, and which may well occur in other periods too."[43] Clearly, what is necessary and sufficient for fascism, according to Poulantzas, is the confluence of the imperialist-monopolist period of the capitalist mode of production with its political crises in weak links of the imperialist chain and certain actions, the occurrence of which is unforeseeable, resulting from the class struggles within the social formation.

In effect, Poulantzas has presented us with several conditions for the rise of fascism. First, there must be an appropriate mode of production in a stage that gives rise to "contradictions" in the form of class conflicts. Second, the conflicts must lead to political crises—in the power bloc and between the dominant and dominated classes. The important conclusion, however, is, finally, that even under these circumstances the emergence of fascism is not inevitable. It is "resistible," and although how it is to be resisted is not clear, presumably it would depend upon a subjective factor, the strategy followed by the classes and fractions in conflict, including the working class and other dominated classes.

The outcome of this line of analysis is clear. The fascist regime is, after all, not derivable from the objective higher-order structure, the mode of production, as, we have seen earlier, Marxist structuralism would normally have it. Fascism as an exceptional regime is only a possibility subject to the strategy of class actors, not a necessity under the appropriate conditions provided by this mode. Nor is it a necessary outcome of the class struggles generated by capitalism at its monopolist stage. Its occurrence seems to depend not upon objective factors, even though they are necessary components, but upon the actual, and unpredictable, practices followed by the participants in the various class struggles.

Once again, the fascist regime does not just "correspond" to a stage in the development of capitalism viewed, not as an economic system, but as a total mode of production. At an earlier period in his thinking, as I have noted, Poulantzas might have been inclined to have said this. In *Fascism and Dictatorship*, however, despite the continuing tension between his early determinism and his growing possibilism, the fascist regime is finally interpreted as a specific response of the monopolist state to cope with particular historical circumstances created by the class struggles of the period which threaten the dominance of the monopolists. These struggles, of course, relate back to the nature of the mode of production which gives birth to monopoly capitalism. However, as we have seen, this now provides only the necessary conditions or backdrop, not the sufficient conditions, of the political crisis which yields fascism as its outcome.

As Poulantzas himself writes, "The non-correspondence between base and super-structure does not automatically spell out some future catastrophe for a social formation: the explosion of this contradiction, and also the *possibility* of its eventual readjustment within the same mode of production depends on this struggle."[44] The automatic operation and single-minded direction of the mode of production are in process, here, of being displaced by the less predictable and even reversible consequences of the class struggles. He had already made this point in *Political Power and Social Classes*, where he had written that "the fascist state . . . can be studied only by examining the relation between the social forces in the concrete conjuncture."[45] But as we have just seen, the outcome seemed at that time predetermined, if only obscurely so. In *Fascism and Dictatorship* his thinking had clarified to the point where he was prepared to declare that fascism is, after all, not inevitable but can be explained only "by reference to the *concrete situation* of the class struggle, as it cannot be reduced to any inevitable need of the 'economic' development of capitalism."[46]

Structuralism versus History

Poulantzas begins, therefore, as an explicit structuralistic determinist. The human agent is a mere "Träger" of history, as Marx expressed it, an agent or bearer. Poulantzas ends, if not an unrestrained voluntarist, at least as what we might call a possibilist. In moving in this direction he gives up all hope of being able to derive observed lower-order structure from knowledge of how the whole system is organized and operates, a necessary inference in structuralist thinking as, we have seen, Piaget had pointed out. If fascism as an exceptional regime is itself unpredictable for Poulantzas, then its particular form or structure has a broad latitude for variation.

Whether Poulantzas really recognizes that, in his own later formulations, the human actor has a historical and potentially effective role to play, is difficult to say. He studiously avoids formulations such as fortuitousness or accident of history or chance. Conjuncture is as close as he comes to this. The unpredictable nature of the outcome of the class struggles is never explained or even recognized as posing a problem for his general theory of determination or "inevitabilism." If the instances have some relative autonomy under capitalism, it would have been both interesting and important to know what the mechanisms are through which this autonomy is exercised. Does it consist of random policy choices by the state? Or do the relatively autonomous actions permitted to the state really represent a disguised way of bringing human actors, with their historical experiences and fateful choices, back into the scheme of things? If the class struggles may or may not end in an exceptional regime, what is the source of the indeterminancy?

Poulantzas could have argued the case for objective determination by demonstrating that the mode of production, in his broadest sense, throws differential resources into the various social classes depending upon such circumstances as rates of economic development, means of access by rulers to the masses, skills as political entrepreneurs, and the like. He might then have turned to the obvious complexity of such circumstances to demonstrate the futility of trying to predict any specific outcome, such as the utilization of an exceptional regime.

He does not push his argument in this direction, however. Instead he only leaves us with the bald assertion that the class struggle may end up in exceptionalism. If it does not, even the probable or possible alternatives are not indicated. All we know is that, contrary to his initial indications, exceptional regimes, such as fascism, are no longer inevitabilities; they are only possibilities, all within the limits of the overall higher-order structure of the capitalist mode of production at its imperialist-monopolist stage. This mode is a limit, presumably, because no regime could survive that did not place the monopolist class/fraction in a hegemonic position within the power bloc, unless, of course, the capitalist state itself was destroyed entirely and with it the capitalist mode of production.

All sense of real determination becomes lost. Human intervention, in the form of actors in the class struggles, overrides objective necessity. We are presented only with conditions that make certain structural outcomes, such as fascist regimes, possible; and the effects are even reversible.

As his writings progress Poulantzas thus seeks to distance himself from the very accusation of inevitabilism that Miliband and Laclau, among others, had leveled against his use, in *Political Power and Social Classes*, of the mode of production and its influence on the state. Objective structure or the system of relationships constituted by a mode of production, is no longer the driving force, in some abstract and formalistic way, in shaping the observable or lower-order structures. Poulantzas increasingly liberates the class struggles, as an intervening mechanism, from structural compulsions to reach a determinable, let alone a predetermined, outcome. Forms of regimes become less automatic and ineluctable. In this way, in *Fascism and Dictatorship*, Poulantzas would seem to be responding, wittingly or otherwise, to the very kind of criticism directed toward him, not for his economism, of which he could not be accused, but for his "formal abstractionism" and "abstract superdeterminism."[47]

Necessity evaporates.[48] Structuralism seems to be yielding to the events of history as made by actors. Not only is Poulantzas not successful in deriving lower-order from the higher-order structures, but he no longer even tries. The fascist regime looks increasingly like a product of the historical course of political crises created by the inability of the parliamentary democratic type of bourgeois state to alleviate the stresses of the class struggle. This in turn invites institutional collapse of the democratic regime. Circumstances could have been such that fascism might have been avoided.

In the end, as others have also pointed out,[49] his analysis does not offer us much more than the literature of such writers as Daniel Guerin or Franz Neumann had already discovered about fascism. Implicitly but unfortunately *only* implicitly, it shares with them the suggestion that to understand the emergence of fascist structures we must know first, the conditions which make it possible, and second, the confluence of circumstances which trigger the actual transformation. This is not a negligible thought, but it certainly is not a new one.

Salvage from Poulantzas's Work

Structuralist Marxism, at least as represented in Poulantzas, is, then, deficient in its capacity to demonstrate a compelling relationship between the mode of production, his higher order-structure, and variable forms of political regimes, the observed structures. Part of the difficulty lies, of course, in the ambiguity in the notion of mode of production itself, to the extent that it is defined as elements in which the economy is dominant in the last instance. But if for the moment we ignore this carryover from the privileged position that Marxism traditionally gives to the economy, a major value to us of Poulantzas's analysis lies in the way in which he broadened Marxism. Although he was not alone and just applied, to political phenomena, new tendencies already initiated in the work of Gramsci and Althusser, nonetheless in bringing these changes to bear on politics he was moving in a direction already prevalent in conventional social science as a whole and not in Marxism alone.

As I noted at the outset, structuralism, as a general point of view reaching beyond Marxism, can be fully understood only if we recognize in it a way of coming to terms with the systems transformation taking place, in thought, during the twentieth century. Poulantzas took his place in that transformation by spelling out its implications, in effect, for the study of politics from a Marxist perspective. He no longer sees political phenomena as only society-determined. They can have a life of their own, virtually. We need the reservation of "virtually" only because of his reluctance to give up the special place of the economy. But with Gramsci and Althusser he recognizes what the latter called "the relative autonomy of the state" and with both of them the independent effect of ideology (the cultural subsystem) as well.

In going this far Poulantzas was only a hair's breadth away from recognizing that the state of society at any historical juncture is a product of the interaction of all social subsystems—economic, cultural, psychological, political—without providing in advance any special position for the economy. And specific concatenations of these subsystems yield a particular product called feudalism, capitalism, socialism. In short, they stand as a higher-order set of relationships that in some way influences all lower-order phenomena. We cannot understand capitalist democracy, totalitarianism, dictatorship, or even socialist democracy, Poulantzas was saying, in effect, without a complex analysis in which we need to trace out how each subsystem, in combination with all others, affects the particular regime and is, in turn, affected by the latter. Any element in the social system is a product not of some special and isolated other element or combination of a limited number of such elements, but is, in some unexpressed way, the resultant of all elements combined.

Even though the language available to Poulantzas would not have permitted him to formulate it in this way, he was clearly searching for a way of demonstrating the impact of the whole social order on each of its parts. Despite the opacity of much of his analysis, through his failure or unwillingness to understand the new direction in which his own reformulation of Marxism was carrying him and the circumlocutions into which his commitment to the privileged position of the economy drove him, he was in fact groping for a way of identifying the influence of the whole social system, as such, on its parts. He was searching for a way of doing this without fracturing the analysis by decomposing the whole into its parts and sorting out the independent effects of each part on the other. And, of course, in contradistinction to the whole we have in mind, that of the *political* system alone, Poulantzas was concerned about the effects of the whole *social* system.

Can we carry away with us anything of use from Poulantzas as we seek to resolve the vexatious problem of the impact of the whole on each of the parts of a political system? Poulantzas is at least very suggestive with regard to where we ought to look for these effects.

First, by implication he addresses political life as a system of some sort, however imprecise or downright confusing his conception of the state and politics may be. Second, despite the "relative autonomy" he attributes to the state in its capacity to make policies and contribute independently to the state of the whole social system, he sees this subsystem as being affected in central ways by the environment in which it exists. For Poulantzas the total environment consists of two other instances or subsystems: the economic and the ideological (cultural, as we have noted), in combination with the state itself. Third, he instructs us that in trying to trace out effects of the social system as a whole on any one of the subsystems, we need to be sensitive to the way they "interpenetrate." The term is suggestive, at least in the sense that it foresees an intimate connection that is perhaps obscured by the conventional notion of interaction. System relationships in these terms are much more like an interwoven mass of spaghetti than a set of sequentially interacting billiard balls.

This latter idea is in itself highly suggestive even if it does not carry us very far methodologically. At the very least it alerts us to the existence of relationships the enormous complexity of which may escape us if we restrict ourselves to purely interactionist vocabulary. And yet to trace out the enormously involved interconnections among the various social subsystems, especially as they relate to the political system, was Poulantzas's primary objective. The fact that he was less than successful certainly points not only to the deficiencies of his method but undoubtedly to those of his "theory," as well, or if that is too strong a term for what he offers, of his conceptualization.

Yet the harshness of any judgment on this score needs to be tempered by the realization of the inherent difficulty of the enterprise. Contemporary research has still to devise a set of methods appropriate for the resolution of the task posed by Poulantzas. One way of handling the matter is simply to deny its validity or utility as an issue. Another is to assert in advance that even if it were a sensible one, the difficulties are insuperable and our time would be better spent in identifying and addressing more readily researchable tasks. Once we are prepared to acknowledge the validity of the question itself, however, the more responsible procedure must be to accept the challenge of the need to trace out the precise linkages between the higher-order broader political structures and the lower-order ones and to devote the attention and resources necessary for inventing the appropriate methodological tools. Bringing us to an awareness of this need has of course been one of my overarching purposes.

What is this whole—the higher-order structure—at least as it refers to political structures? How does it contrast with lower-order structures which, I have been proposing, cannot be understood except by reference to the broader structures? How may we to hope to penetrate the relationships between the two? Now that we have looked at the way political science in general and structuralism in various guises have faced up to these issues, it is time for us to address them directly.

Part 3

Higher-Order
Structures

17

Higher-Order Structures: As Explanation

Can we hope to be able to explain or predict the character of observed structures by calling upon higher-order ones? If this is too strong a way of putting the matter, can we at least expect to be able to derive these lower-order structures in some way? Or are lower-order structures only a product of a particular society and its history? Do they take their character from a unique conjuncture of events or, at most, from particular relationships at a given moment? We are now at a point where we can directly address this issue as to whether higher-order structures can enter into an explanation of lower-order ones and, if so, how this might occur. These questions have been our central concern.

The Higher-Order Structure and Explanation

From our analysis of the way in which the structuralists[1] and political scientists in general have dealt with structures one central conclusion has emerged. If we are to begin to appreciate the conditions that help to explain the obvious variations in political structures, it may prove useful to classify them into two types: higher- and lower-order ones. The latter structures are those we are so familiar with that I have called them observable; the former are less likely to be immediately obvious, so we may say they are not directly observed but have to be inferred.

In truth, of course, as noted in chapter 8, both observed and non-observed structures are abstractions and, as such, are inferences from observation or can be confirmed through observation. The lower-order ones are thought of as observable, we will recall, only because we are accustomed to the inferences involved. Thus, it takes little effort to think of legislative, judicial, administrative, or party structures and hold some image of them in our mind's eye, as it were.

The higher-order structures, however, come from a different level of abstraction. Even though, as ethnomethodologists contend, we do acquire competence to cope with such structures as these, their nature is such that we need to conceptualize them deliberately and in some new way. They need not be given to us by common sense or out of day-to-day experience. That is why in attempting to get at them the structuralists invoked a geological imagery to depict them as nonobvious underlying structures, and the Marxists have typically thought of them as the base or infrastructure. Regardless of the terminology describing the relationship, what we learn from these efforts of the structuralists is that there is a level of structure, which I have been describing as a lower-order one, that is not readily explained or understood at its own level. We need to call upon some more general forms that order those

241

forms that are more directly accessible to customary observation. As I observed earlier, in Piaget's phrase, we need to explore the form of forms.[2]

When we turn to this higher-order structure as an explanatory factor, however, we encounter its own set of intractable problems. In the first place, the debate has long been joined as to whether structure can ever be a force with an objective status, an ontological reality that compels or limits behavior, or whether the individual has overriding degrees of freedom to create and recreate the surrounding world. This has been a question that has lurked in the background of our analysis and one that I have yet to address. Do lower-order structures merely reflect individual choices for action, a kind of residue from past rational selection of options? Does the human subject play a more important role than a focus on the relationship between different levels of structure would suggest or even seem to allow?

I have avoided a frontal confrontation of this persistent issue not because I think it unimportant; rather, in the literature the changes have been rung on all sides of the matter so extensively that there is truly little more that can be, or, for that matters, needs to be said. It is transparent that neither polar extreme could be correct. The individual is not totally free to create society out of whole cloth, as Marx had long ago declared. But then neither is society able to determine ineluctably the fate of its constituent actors under all circumstances. The truth undoubtedly lies somewhere in between, even if the critical question is exactly where.

As we have seen, Poulantzas, in his early years, had argued against any central contribution from the individual, as had Lévi-Strauss. Observed social relations for the latter and superstructure for the former are derivable, not from knowledge of individual choices but from certain underlying forces, the determining structures of a society. But as we have also seen, Poulantzas's arguments did not make the sense he thought. He was unable to point to the specific mechanisms through which these underlying forces do in fact shape observed structures; they operate in some formal and abstract way. At most, as we have noted, he could claim to have discovered factors that might limit the range of variation among lower-order structures, not those that would uniquely determine their form.

Of necessity, at any moment the social system does serve as a given set of relationships which impose certain kinds of constraints, a subject to which I shall return, more systematically, in the next chapter. There will be limits to what individuals may do without destroying society entirely or within which they may plausibly act to bring about change. Yet it is transparent that as individuals make their way in a social system, through their actions they help to construct and reconstruct it. Ethnomethodology had sought to detail the process. Although individuals may at times be helplessly buffeted about by some impersonal structure, this need not always be the case. Actors do have the capacity to change social relationships fundamentally. Lenin was scarcely a cipher in bringing about a change in Russia's mode of production. Few counterfactual scenarios would give the October revolution half a chance without him. Similarly for Gorbachev in the perestroika movement in the USSR that began in the late 1980s. And even if these two leaders played roles exceptional for individuals, actors in the aggregate may bring about substantial transformations in social relationships, as happened, for example, during the Russian Revolution itself, in Hungary, East Germany, and Czechoslovakia, in 1989, in bringing down the existing authoritarian regimes in those countries and in the United States through the countercultural revolution of the 1960s and 1970s.

After the vast debates, over the ages, about the relative role of the subject as against objective conditions, it should be transparent by this time that both may play significant but varying parts depending upon the given circumstances. This fact is coming to be recognized and may indeed flow from what has been described as "the new spirit [that] is manifest in a growing willingness to engage in dialogue by opposed naturalist-humanist wings in the philosophy of social science."[3] Once the principle has been established that actor and objective conditions may share an outcome and that the actor is not totally imprisoned by social forces but helps to reshape the prison walls themselves, the relative contribution of each can only be empirically, not theoretically, resolved despite the torrents of ink that continue to be loosed on the subject in favor of one or the other extreme.

Aside from this perennial division about the relative importance of subject and object in social action, when we turn specific attention to higher-order structures there is a second difficulty, a methodological one, that regularly arises. It is far easier to describe the need to call upon the explanatory power of higher levels of structural elements than to provide a readily defined and communicable method for relating them to the lower-order structures. This, we saw, was a great shortcoming of Poulantzas as a structuralist, even if he failed to realize it, let alone to acknowledge it openly.

As I shall argue again, later, acknowledgment of the difficulty of handling the matter ought not to reduce its significance, however, or the need to specify its nature as carefully as possible. Insufficiency of method for dealing with a problem is seldom justification for sweeping it under the rug. Yet this practice had become only too common during the height of the behavioral movement in political science, fed by the prevailing misconception that scientific method requires immediate operationality or a metrical solution.

Political Structure as the Overarching Context

The place of the individual in social action as against the objective effects of social structure and the tools for unearthing structural effects are two hurdles that historically have confronted structural analysis. To locate higher-order structure in its appropriate explanatory space, however, let us go back to the beginning of our argument. Can it be assumed and maintained, as it all too frequently is, that the lower-order structures can be understood by reference to phenomena at the same level? Can we calmly assume that in trying to understand these structures it does little if any harm to overlook, ignore or just take as a given the way in which the whole political system is organized and operates?

Normally we look for explanations of lower-order phenomena within themselves, without serious reference to the broadest context within which they operate, as we saw in chapter 10. With the development of the argument beyond that chapter, we are now able to consider this way of handling such structures a little further. Observed structures are often interpreted as a product of such factors as the conflicting interests of social and political groups and classes at the given time. For example, details about the struggles over the adoption of the formal structures provided for in the American, French, and Weimar constitutions are intended to reveal how each clause was constructed and supported or opposed by the interests involved, how costs and benefits were estimated, what the intentions of the various participants were, what each major social force and its representatives hoped to achieve, what resources they brought to bear on pressing their ambitions, and the like. Inquiries such as these attempt to explain a given set of compromises incorporated into the constitutional arrangements as finally adopted. In effect, it appears that each formal part of the regime, so created by the given constitution, is to be understood and explained by the nature of the struggles that went into it, the forces that were engaged, the negotiations involved, and the final compromises achieved.

In one sense no one could deny that such historical descriptions of the actions of the contenders for power do constitute an important part of an explanation. Each proponent of a structural arrangement embodied in the final constitution hopes to be able to provide a set of incentives for members of society to conform to the behavior prescribed therein. Whether or not these incentives are sufficiently strong or cleverly enough designed to bring about actual conformity in the future is another question entirely. Even if they are effective at the moment a constitution is adopted, times may change, the constitutional prescriptions may lose much of their force and political actors may look for ways to avoid structures contrary to their perceived interests.[4]

Of course, formal constitutions are not the only source of structures, and certainly not by any means necessarily the most important. As we have seen in chapter 5, when we speak of political structures we have in mind far broader categories of political phenomena—the patterns of relationships among interest groups, parties, elites, publics, and so on, none of which need even be mentioned in the fundamental law of the land. However, even if, for the moment, we were to confine ourselves just to constitutionally specified structures, we would be remiss if we failed to take into account what I have been calling the higher-order structure.

In the construction of constitutional arrangements, for example, higher-order structures are implicated in at least two different ways. In the first place, all the negotiations and compromises for the specific clauses of constitutions take place within a social context. In the case of the French Revolution, that context reflected a fundamental shift in power among the various social classes. The historical conflicts over the details of the document reveal the processes through which this shift in power was working itself out. In their detailed forms, the particular lower-order structures that arose out of the constitutional debates could vary enormously depending upon the interaction of the personalities involved, the particular judgments of individuals, the accidental resources available to one person or group as against another, and so on. But fundamental limits had been set by the success of the revolution in displacing the monarchy and the landed aristocracy at the moment.

That was the accepted social context. It established a certain framework of relationship among classes that would have been difficult to overcome without a reversal of the major events of the French Revolution. It provided the historic shift in a part of the higher-order social structure within which the details of the realignment of political power had to be worked out.

A higher-order structure is involved in a second sense, one that calls upon the strictly political rather than the societal context. Constitutional debate concerns the establishment of a formal political framework for making authoritative decisions for a society. In agreeing to compromise with regard to disputes about various constitutional provisions in one area, different contenders will normally wish to take into account what has been won in other areas in dispute. If you lose out on the nature of the franchise and it is broader than you would wish, you may seek to win part of the control over policy, lost to the electors, by trying to strengthen the hand of the chief executive or the courts. In any negotiation about a series of interlocked issues, the compromises and agreements about one clause can be appropriately understood only in light of the whole document and of the way in which participants balance their gains and losses in one disputed area by strategies in another.

This is why, in debate about large documents or even resolutions with a number of parts, votes may be taken item by item; and even if all clauses are approved, at the end, normally the document or resolution as a whole will still need to be voted upon. Each part may look satisfactory to one or another coalition of persons or groups and may win their approval. Yet there still needs to be some expression of opinion about the document as a whole. The tradeoffs made on individual items may in the end not seem to be worth it if the document as a whole does not create a set of arrangements with which any given contending force feels it can or must live. It is a process such as this that reveals the underlying rationale of the whole assent process in groups composed of complex competitive factions. They need always to return to the acceptability of the package as a whole.

Analogously, for example, the structures of British parliamentary democracy may in part be understood through the history of the struggle of various social classes to obtain a share in effective political power. The residual power of the Crown, the party structure in and out of parliament, the weakness of the interest group structure in relationship to parliament and even to the civil service, the dominance of the House of Commons in the legislative structure, and so forth, all have their historically specific explanations. If we were to adopt a rational-actor perspective,[5] the stability of the political regime at any moment might be traced perhaps to the tradeoff that occurs on the basis of a rational calculation of benefits that the dominant political actors may feel they obtain from a given arrangement. And, on rationalistic assumptions, the broad masses, excluded interest groups, or excluded social classes may have no choice—even if they had specific mechanisms for informing themselves of a range of options—but to accept a regime as it has evolved. The costs of change might be too great even if they had the organizational skills and other resources to pursue a course intent on bringing about basic changes in the political structure. Regardless of the precise nature of rationality-based explanation, its essential character is to sort out the probable choices of the political and social groups that have participated in shaping the political relationships and that have seemed to benefit or lose from them.

However, if we stopped at that point, as much research does, we would be overlooking other important influences that are at work. The blindness that develops toward such other influences is one of the central hazards of the decompositional method we have inherited from the seventeenth century. To understand an entity we break it down into its components, explain the latter by breaking them down into their own components, and so on in a never-ending descending order of fragmentation of the object of inquiry. Physics is the model *par excellence*. Matter is decomposed into molecules, the latter into atoms, and so on down to the smallest bit of matter (at one time the quark, which itself appears to be subject to further fragmentation of sorts). Physicists do this in the hope and expectation that some day they will be able to bring all knowledge about the increasing number of decomposed parts back together into some kind of understanding of how the whole functions.

Somehow, however, in political analysis, it does not work quite that way, as we have seen in chapter 10. Unless we have already taken into account that the whole is itself worth investigating, as such, and not just in terms of its parts, we are not very likely to be able either to return to the whole or to try to bring our knowledge about the parts back together again. We push the Humpty Dumpty of knowledge off the wall and seldom even try to put it back together again. We are even less likely to explore ways in which this might be done or to entertain the question as to whether reassembly of the parts is even possible and whether or not we ought to have pushed the egg of knowledge off the wall in the first place.

Yet, it has been the contention of my analysis, unless we are prepared to take the strictly political whole into account, at the very outset, we will have excluded the very element that has a significant part in shaping the varying forms of regimes in political systems. If we want to complete our understanding of such lower-order structures—the components of regimes in political systems, for example—we need to appreciate their relationship to the structure of the political system as a whole, the higher-order structure in the context of which each of the interrelated parts can be more appropriately understood. It is this very kind of understanding that Lévi-Strauss and Poulantzas were striving for, however unsuccessful they have been. And it is this very insight of structuralism that we threaten to discard in rejecting, very appropriately, many of the other elements of their approach to the analysis of structure.

Thus, to return to our British example, whatever the validity of any particular explanation for the form of any structural parts—party relationships, parliament-Crown-administrative ties, mass-representative connections, political cleavages, and the like—no one of these parts of the system stands in splendid isolation. Each may have a degree of autonomy, if we wish to put it in this way. Or to use a somewhat less ambiguous language, we can decompose a political system into subsystems whose independence from or influence on each other may vary.[6] Changes in one subsystem, such as political parties, may bring about considerable changes in another, such as parliament. Changes in another, such as the civil service, may be relatively insulated from the rest of the system, by historical evolution or by design. Hence, it may take great changes in the civil service to influence, say, the power of the Crown or the structure of political parties. In the end, however, the position of interest groups, their relative weakness as compared to other subsystems, cannot be adequately explained in historical terms exclusively or by reference to the structure of parliament or of the party subsystem and the like, either alone or in some limited combination.

As the Weberian interpretivists, if we may so call the intuitive practitioners of Weber's method of empathic understanding, or as the configurative analysts in comparative politics—the single-system case-study advocates—insist, we need to have some sense of the way the whole system is put together and, where a particular substructure fits into that whole, to be able to comprehend a part adequately. This is what I have been trying to suggest by the notion of higher-order political structure.

As we saw much earlier, in chapter 10, the Teune and Ostrowski study had already pointed in that direction, even if the authors were not quite prepared to recognize the signpost as they passed it. And even in the 1980s the return of some political scientists, specifically the neostatists, to an effort to redefine the domain[7] of political science as the study of the state represents a groping toward a more comprehensive context in which to place political phenomena. In this neostatist view, the state provides a broad setting for lower-level structures that privileges some members of a political system by giving them control over resources and public policies and a certain autonomy from other social forces. Whatever kinds of structures may be intended by the notion of the state—and, as I have already noted, the term is filled with ambiguity and fraught with analytic danger[8]—at the very least a strong message is being sent by this tendency in political inquiry. Only at our peril, it is warning us, can we lose sight of the significance of the overall way in which a "state" (the political system?) is organized, a level of structures higher than those usually attended to by traditional political research into political power and policies.

Relationship between System Structure and Subsystems

Several further points need to be made about my way of looking at the explanatory relationship between a component of the political system and the latter's overarching structure. First, this point of view needs to be clearly distinguished both from a holistic and from a decompositional mode of analysis. Holism has typically argued that the whole is logically, if not, in some ineffable way, empirically prior to its parts. Decompositionalism, if I may coin a term, might profess that the whole is merely the sum of the parts, whatever that may mean,[9] or at least can be reconstituted from knowledge of the parts. I am arguing, rather, that the parts are inextricably interlocked with the way they are organized into a given whole, in this case, the political system. We can fully understand why the parts are related to each other in a particular way, why they operate as they do, and how they have come to have the consequences they do, only if we take into account their particular relationship to the whole complex of which they themselves are part. This means that if we are to be able to understand and explain the observable structures of a political system, we need to identify their relationship to other relevant and significant parts of the political system, the rules that describe their relationships, and the power relationships in this complex, as we shall see in the next chapter.[10]

Second, as I have already intimated, I am not suggesting that the higher-order structure need constrain all parts of a political system equally. The relationship between subsystems and the overall structure of a political system may vary enormously, ranging from one in which any given subsystem may be virtually independent, and hence almost free of any influence from the higher system, to one in which the slightest change in the overall organization of the system will be felt in some nontrivial way by a given part. Where a subsystem, as a component of the higher-order structure, stands on this continuum of effects will hinge on the degree of connectedness among the parts.[11] In other words, the overall structure of systems will show variations in a property that we may call the connectedness of the parts.

Political systems, for example, would represent very hazardous structures if every change in one part, such as in the organization of a legislature, were necessarily to have serious ramifications for all other parts of the system. Some degree of independence or relative isolation of the parts of a system is normal if the system is not to be sent reeling from one state to another with each fluctuation in the structure of a subsystem, or if, out of fear of such consequences, change is not to be entirely stifled. There are indeed political systems where, for this very reason, change is brought to a virtual standstill. In many dictatorial systems even what may appear as a trivial change proposed for a significant substructure in the system may at times be seen as a major threat to those in power. In such cases the parts of the structure are tightly coupled. In short, the property of looseness or tightness in the connections among lower-order structures of a political system has a critical bearing on the capacity of a system to promote or tolerate change.

The obverse of this recognition of varying degrees of independence among the parts of a system is the fact that not all parts of a system need be affected, in equal measure, by the overall structure of the system. Some may be more isolated than others from the effects of the structure; they may have varying degrees of independence (autonomy). This was indeed the very point that Poulantzas, in less general terms, sought to make about the "state" and its capacity to make policy. In arguing that the state was "relatively autonomous" from the rest of society, he joined Althusser in liberating this part of the superstructure from the base so that the political subsystem is no longer to be considered uniquely determined by the mode of production. It is subject to other kinds of influence in varying degrees to be established through historical inquiry. In effect, Poulantzas was declaring that the state is loosely coupled to other parts of the social structure (mode of production, in his terms) and, therefore, has a relative degree of independence from their influence. Other structural Marxists, as well as newly emerging neostatists, have followed him in this course—often without giving him his due—and have sought to document the degree to which the "state" (and its policies), because of its position in the capitalist mode of production (the higher-order *social* structure), is shaped less by societal factors than by its own composition and interests. Hence the claim that our research on the "state" should be less society-centered and more state-centered.[12]

The fact that parts of the political system may stand in varying relationships to the higher-order structure is an important theoretical as well as empirical consideration. For our purposes, however, it simply serves to reinforce our main point: Parts of the political system cannot be fully understood as such. Their relationship to the overall way in which a political system is organized needs to be taken into consideration systematically if we are to be able to explain how they, the parts, come to take the form they do and have the consequences associated with them.

Higher-Order Structure as the Overall System

How can we take into account the influence of the whole complex of structural elements that make up a political system if this is necessary for an understanding of any of its structural parts? It is certainly not new to suggest that this question represents a fundamental challenge facing all political analysis. A French critic of structuralism itself has pointed to the need to be able to cope analytically with the system viewed as a whole entity in itself. "In fact, structuralist revolutions are initiated," Boudon has written, "not when it is understood that languages, personalities, markets and societies are systems, but when the conceptual tools are devised that permit the analysis of these systems as systems."[13] The system, by implication, constitutes the higher-order structure.

Implicitly at least, the literature offers us a number of answers to our question as to how to distinguish the system, as an overall structure, from its parts. Let us look at some of them.

System State versus System Structure

There are those who would distinguish between the structure of a system and its varying states within that structure, borrowing this notion from the natural sciences. In effect, this would offer us a method for grappling with the effects of a whole system on lower-order structures.[14] This method suggests that we identify the basic relationships among those elements in a system which constitute its significant structural components. We would then need to figure out the different states that the system would assume as the values of the variables that enter into the stable relationships change. In an ideal sense, the relationships could be described by a set of differential equations that provides a formal expression of system properties.[15]

Some time ago Brunner and Brewer, in a computer simulation experiment, attempted this very method, on a limited scale, in relation to a developing country, using Lerner's *Passing of Traditional Society* as their test case. In their own words,

The *structure* of a class of systems . . . is the set of components X_t and the set of relationships G. . . . A *model* of any one of the systems is the general structure with the magnitudes of the variables and parameters specified to represent the particular context. The *behavior* of a model is the set of time series of the $x_{i,t}$ that are produced as the relationships generate successive state descriptions.[16]

The authors explicitly see themselves as trying to sort out the impact of a whole system on its operation. As they phrase it,

> There will always be a need for specialization and for simplifying assumptions and procedures, but these simplifications are costly. The task of studying complex political systems has a quality of 'wholeness' just as the systems themselves do. . . . The promise, in short, is to extend our present capacity to deal with complex political systems as wholes. . . .
>
> To the extent that our intellectual tasks as well as the systems themselves have the quality of 'wholeness' which frustrates partial analysis, this use of computer simulation is significant."[17]

Aside from the failure of others to pick up on this approach, its limit, for our purposes, is that differentiating between structure and states may indeed clarify the possible effects of the structure of a system on its policies and practices, or system behavior, as the authors characterize it. It offers us no clue, however—nor was it designed to do so, it should, of course, be said—as to how the approach might be applied to show the way the basic structure, that is, the overall system structure, shapes other structures, such as those of the regime. This is the issue at stake here of course.

Furthermore, it is one thing to isolate those variables which influence the socio-economic development of a social system. It is quite another to attempt to identify the basic structural elements that constitute the higher-order *political* structure of a system, to find a way of describing variations in the values they assume and then to demonstrate their consequences for lower-order structures. To talk, at our present level of understanding, of representing the structure of a political system in a set of simultaneous equations simply boggles the mind, to put it bluntly. Intuitively, at least, even the less ambitious approach of Brunner and Brewer does not seem to lend itself readily to the analysis of observed structures, however interesting its potential for ascertaining effects on rate and direction of social development or on other aspects of system behavior.

System Structure as Context

Others, in their efforts to resolve difficult issues with regard to what has come to be called contextual effects, have also been forced to grapple with the problem of whole-system effects. The reason for this is not difficult to appreciate. The political system as a whole is clearly the most comprehensive political context in which action can take place.

Since I have borrowed the concept of higher and lower levels from Scheuch but diverted and reformulated it to make it more useful for the analysis of structures, it is appropriate to turn to his original article on the importance of recognizing levels as an aid in coping with the impact of the context. We will then be able to determine the extent to which this attempt to guide contextualism in the right direction might also assist us in finding a method to take the whole into account in explanation.

Scheuch broadly defines contextual analysis, which I touched on in chapter 10, as a "description of a member of a collectivity by using properties of the collectivity."[18] Its explicit concern, therefore, is with individual behavior and not, of course, with observable structure. As I pointed out in chapter 10, beginning with Robinson we have been cautioned to avoid the reductionist individualistic fallacy in which we may mistakenly seek to derive higher-level properties from the properties of constituent individuals. Similarly, we have been warned about the opposite extreme, the ecological fallacy, of assuming that properties of aggregates of individuals necessarily enable us to predict characteristics of single individuals. To penetrate the relationship between the individual and the social context in which he or she operates, Scheuch proposed considering this context as a higher-level environment to which the individual reacts.

His specific interest lay in the mechanisms through which this reaction might occur. He proposed that we would find it in the fact that the individual does not respond to the whole environment (context) in some vague and generic way but, rather, very selectively. In other words, the context or environment is not an undifferentiated whole. The individual only reacts to one or another part of this whole. It is this fact that enables us, in the end, to account for different individual responses to what appears to be the same context. For each individual, because of this selectivity of response, the context is indeed different.[19]

Thus, if we view the whole social context as the individual's environment, then the individual is influenced by this whole through this selective process and not in some undefined global way. Scheuch labels these selective aspects of what we are calling the whole, to which individuals react, their subjective environments.

The proposal for disaggregating, in this way, the context to which individuals respond is highly suggestive. It enables us to understand why individuals may seem to be responding differently to what appears to be the same social context; they may just be reacting to different parts of that environment.

For purposes of survey research this may well be a helpful way of approaching the effects of the overall context. Whether or not it points in a useful direction for detecting the influence of the whole political system on parts of its observed structures may be a somewhat different matter, however, but one that bears some further consideration.

We might plausibly argue, for example, that the relationships among political parties may represent selective reactions to their higher-level structural environment. In Britain, for example, parties are clearly shaped by the cabinet form of parliamentary democracy and, indeed, are an integral part of it. In the United States, party relationships certainly represent a reaction to the separation and balance of powers and to state powers. The arrangements help to explain a kind of party structure different from that found in Britain, a commonplace interpretation in the literature. We might advance similar arguments for the structure of interest group relationships, legislative forms, and the like, showing how each has its own subjective environment to which it may selectively react.

Unfortunately, however, as helpful as this procedure might be in bringing out some of the aspects of the influence of the overall structural context on an observed structure, what it would clearly fail to do is to direct attention to the overall way in which the political system is organized and the effect of this very organization of relationships on the subsystems or parts. We can certainly appreciate the value of paying attention to the specific effects, of a given part of the totality, on the lower-order structures. What is still missing, however, is the constraint that the very organization of the system as a whole imposes such that if that organization is fundamentally transformed, as happens in the extreme during social revolutions, for example, the lower-level structures themselves will normally undergo radical change. The lower-level structures are not free to assume any character that their participants might wish.

Comparative Historical Analysis

We can recognize the nagging nature of this unresolved issue in the continued attention that the overarching context has drawn during the 1970s and 80s. It would appear to be one of the major goals behind the turn to historical interpretive analysis in the field of comparative historical sociology, arising in this period, not only in political research but in social research in general. This revived historical approach to the study of politics clearly represents an attempt to compensate for the inability of rigorous decompositional analysis to take many essential factors of the whole into account simultaneously.[20] It takes much of its direction from hermeneutics, as initially developed by the Frankfurt School and as it has evolved since then.[21] And as I have pointed out, this is what the configurative analysts, proponents of case-study approaches, Weberian ideal-type methodologists, and recent neostatists have all been seeking. It is this direction of their attention to the whole context that is undoubtedly a major basis of their appeal.

Their success in this endeavor has, however, been limited. For the most part, with minor exceptions, they remain at a semi-impressionistic and historical-interpretive level, an outcome that had been found wanting in the immediate post–World War II period and which is no less so in the 1980s. Indeed, comparative historical inquiry, as usually practiced, represents a *methodological* regression, despite its frequent substantive insights. In expressing dissatisfaction with the decompositional approach of conventional science, its practitioners have mistakenly rejected the messenger with the message. In appropriately seeking to compensate for the failings of decompositionalism and in looking for a way out by founding explanation on the influence of the higher-order structure or whole, historical sociologists may unnecessarily slight or even abandon the rigor and intersubjective verification required by normal science. They offer instead what we may call qualitative (as against possible analytic) holism, case-history accounts filled with rich cross-sectional description and detailed chronology.[22] For recognized canons of empirical validity they seem to be relying heavily on intuitive intelligibility, coherence, consistency, and articulation of relationships rather than on time-dependent (causal) or relational (reciprocal associations) connections. It remains perhaps for the next generation to take their insights, formalize them, and devise ways to test them rigorously.[23]

The most that can be said about these alternative explanatory methods or approaches—state of a system as against its enduring structure, contextualism, and revived comparative historical interpretation—is that they intuitively recognize the central issue. Indeed, the history of recurrent return to the matter in the face of the overwhelming explanatory strength of decompositionalism is perhaps the strongest evidence we need of the fact that neglect or indifference to the issue and to methods for dealing with it within the logic of science are not likely to lead to its disappearance.

Alternative Views of Overarching Structures

To be sure, there are approaches to the explanation of lower-order social structures—seldom applied to political structures, however, even if there is no reason why they could not be—that take a tack very different from a holistic one. It is worth glancing briefly at their implications for the study of higher-order structures as a set of explanatory variables. They are arguing for one of two alternatives: that such broad structures have no effects at all and, therefore, can be virtually ignored—all understanding must be confined to the level of purely individual interactions; or if they do have effects, we can discover them only by looking at the individual level, the so-called micro level.

Network Analysis

Network analysis, in sociology at least, would seem to offer an example of the second category. As noted in chapter 6, this kind of analysis sees large structures as having important consequences, but to detect them it argues for the need to reduce these structures to individual relationships. It has faith in the capacity to identify and describe the vast variety of stable patterns of connections among individuals that are called networks. This might seem to suggest that we do have within our grasp a means for specifying the detailed relationships among individuals so that we might thereby overcome any difficulty in reducing group properties to the micro level.

We need not pause long over this approach, however. As I have already observed in chapter 6, network analysis tends to be atheoretical and largely descriptive in character. It emerged out of small-group research and digraph theory, misleadingly called theory when it was, and in fact remains, largely descriptive. We did note in that earlier chapter, however, that efforts are currently under way to extend it to larger structures, although it is still too early to be able to say whether the application will be successful there. In any event, to this point there is as yet no substantial indication about the relevance of this mode of inquiry to the broad range of political phenomena, although there is no reason in principle why it should not be.

Ethnomethodolgy

An example of another and more radical approach to the analysis of structure is to be found in ethnomethodology, an approach I have already touched on in chapter 6 as well, at least as to its conceptions about the effects of structure. As our earlier discussion has already shown, unlike those who advocate a network approach, some ethnomethodolgists reject the notion that causal consequences can be attributed to structure under any interpretation of the concept. They deny any objective ontological status to macrostructures and would, therefore, reject any suggestion that such structures do influence behavior. This is the extreme position, at least as compared to the structuralists. If we can make no reasonable claim to the existence or reality of macrostructures there can be no issue about the way they influence behavior. And if they have no influence there would be little point in being concerned about the sources of variation in their forms. This point of view among ethnomethodologists can contribute little to our understanding of these matters except insofar as they imply that they are nonissues.

Not all ethnomethodologists go so far, however. Others are prepared to attribute some reality to larger social structures; they see them as composites of relationships among individuals in much the same spirit as network analysts, even if their methodology is substantially different. They insist that only through building from the ground up can we make sense of any macrostructural influences, whether as determinants or limits, imposed on behavior. Hence they start at the microlevel, with individuals in discrete relationships with each other, and they painstakingly describe the precise activities involved. In this view we would need to postpone the day for attempting to understand macrostructures until we had built up a sufficient body of knowledge about microrelationships out of which to weave our understanding of the whole.

To this position, the ultimate in reductionism, still other enthnomethodologists have replied that this may be so. But in that case macrostructures are in the end impossible to describe since this would require "an explication of every cognitive moment in the lives of every individual"[24] referred to in the structure, a complaint not inconsistent with my own[25] but from which these ethnomethodologists draw somewhat different inferences. They conclude that since we can never expect to be able to "explicate every cognitive moment" we can never get at any possible influence of higher structures. I, on the other hand, would argue that this merely offers us a challenge to discover possible technical means, of a *nonreductionist* sort, for discovering this influence.

Even among those who are willing to entertain the notion that macrostructures may exert some effect on individual or collective behavior, however, there are some who would restrict the operation of these effects very narrowly. These ethnomethodologists do not find it necessary to attribute an existential quality to structure or any direct consequences from them. To the extent that structures do shape behavior in any way, they do so only indirectly, as representations that persons carry in their minds. The effects are mediated through the perceptions of the actors. In this way such structures do not become an objective force out thère compelling or limiting individual behavior in some mysterious manner, a position they attribute to most past structural analysts. Rather, to the extent these structures have any influence they do so only through the way they are filtered through the minds of individuals, a position that bears strong phenomenological overtones. Persons are not influenced directly by some macrostructure but only by the idea that they hold of that structure.

This interpretation preserves the basic position, namely, that even if macrostructures are not mythic creations the source of their influence lies not in some special constraint they impose on behavior but in our images of them to which alone we react. We are impelled not by some uncertain objective structure out there, behind the backs of the individual, as Poulantzas might have put it, but simply by our perceptions of some structure. In this view the influence of structures derives not from their status as real forces; rather the idea of structures is merely a rhetorical device to deceive people into thinking that they, the structures, are indeed real influences, beyond us, that have to be taken into account.

To say, for example, that the working class is part of the social structure and represents the destiny of mankind or requires certain social policies is, in this view, not a statement about the actual or potential existence and influence of such a class as part of a class structure. It is, rather, a mythical device to mobilize individuals on behalf of certain policies by persuading them that there is such a class and that it does indeed represent what it is said to represent. In other words, the working class, as part of the relationships included in the social structure, does not function "as a term with an empirical referent but as a device for making points, taking up a stance and so on; in short. . . . It forms part of the apparatus of the expressive order."[26]

Other ethnomethodologists, who operate from this perspective, may even at times go further and accept the ultimate reality of structures such as class, society, system, authorities, or government. They would also trace their influence, however, not to these structures as objective forces existing independently of constitutive individual relationships and operating "behind their back" but only to the representations of these objects that people carry in their minds and that thereby help to influence their behavior as they respond to these images.[27]

The limits of these kinds of ethnomethodological explanations are apparent. If basic structure could influence behavior only by virtue of its representation in the minds of the actors, out of mind, out of sight might well describe the situation. But the fact is that actors typically find themselves constrained, at the very least, by "forces" about which they may have little knowledge and over which they may have little or no control. We all want to get to work on time but may find ourselves caught in a traffic jam that we did not anticipate and that is not of our own making, *whatever the image we may carry in our minds about the likelihood of traffic jams*. When we withdraw money from a bank, even if we know little about the way banks are organized, the structure dictates our behavior. We fill out withdrawal slips, append our usual signature, present identification, and so on in the expectation of getting access to our funds.[28] We are acting in roles predefined for us and from which there is little chance of any single individual escaping if we wish to have access to what we legally own. This influence of the banking structure is independent of our image of it.

Similarly, in politics we may hope for a responsive legislature, but the structure of power in a political system may be such that the legislature is responsive to a network of invisible groups who dominate the economic resources of key legislative players. We may wish to influence the political authorities, but the disposition of economic and organizational resources in a political system may be such that we lack the capacity to implement our desires. In short, there are arrangements in the political system which impose severe constraints on individual or even group choices and actions, independently either of whether we are aware of them or if we are, whether we prefer them. There are "absent totalities," the linguists say, that not only structure the meaning of the "presences" or speech acts of the moment but that do so whether or not we are conscious of these totalities.[29] In much the same manner, the effect of the way a political system is organized through its basic structure need not await its recognition by or awareness of members of that system.

This small sampling of alternative conceptions of structure—as networks or microrelationships—either denies the existence of the issue of higher-level structural influence or seeks to cope with it through radical reduction of all meaningful structures to the individual level. To the extent that these approaches do so, of course, within their framework the independent effect of a higher-order structure becomes a nonissue. The result of such a denial of what, to others, appears only too obvious, is predictable. It leaves the field to a continued intuitive grasping for explanation based on impressionistic holistic assumptions about the nature of reality. Even contextualism, which, of all approaches to structure, we might have expected to venture into what might well appear to be the treacherous shoals of higher-order, overall structures, has shown little appetite for taking such a risk. Perhaps contextualists have felt too beleaguered by their own difficulties in resolving the lesser problems of the effects of lower-order structures to have wished to complicate their life further. Whatever the source of this neglect of systematic and rigorous attention to higher-order structure, the fact of its continued neglect cannot be denied.

"Pragmatic Holism" as Explanatory Base

Lest any reader think that the call for attention to the higher-order structure, as a major explanatory factor, is just a concealed way of reviving the tired, venerable issue of methodological individualism, I would put any anxiety on that score to rest.[30] The kind of holism, as the basis for explanation, that I am talking about here, if we cannot escape using that aged pigeonhole, does not require commitment either to an individualist or to a presumed holist methodology as such. In fact, *if I had to confine myself to this dichotomy*, I would prefer to describe myself as a *pragmatic* holist, joining Herbert Simon in this designation,[31] and, at one and the same time, a *theoretical* methodological individualist. In this way it would be possible to bridge the gulf separating the two positions.

To my way of thinking, there can be no question but that empirical explanation ultimately requires that all phenomena, in principle, be reducible to individual behavior or interactions. How could the objects of our analysis be otherwise? We are not dealing with ghosts or abstracted entities which have presences or influences devoid of human beings; we saw the difficulties into which this got Poulantzas. Political science, like all social science, deals with human beings in those relationships with each other that we designate as political. Of necessity all social scientists ought to be reductionists; the explanation of social behavior must be reducible to the activities of persons and their empirically traceable connections with each other.

This conclusion does not mean, however, that our methods will at any historical moment be refined enough to permit us to pursue inquiry built upon such reductionism, as I have already observed. In practice the shortcomings of our technical means of inquiry forces us to be methodologically holistic. We may need to recognize that many of the properties of political relationships—often called emergent ones— may be accessible only if dealt with at the collective level. We have little other choice. This is equally true of the natural sciences. Individual cells, for example, do not have the capacity to think even though the particular organization of the cells in the human mind do give rise to thought processes.

Thus, we scarcely need to point out that the properties possessed by political parties—authority structures, legislatures, and other such macrostructures or large-scale subsystems, as well as systems as a whole—are products, not of individuals in isolation, but of individuals in multiple and complex relationships with each other. As such, we need to be able to recognize the limits of available ways of obtaining understanding of them, given our present research technology. It is not a matter of whether we are methodological individualists or holists but rather of whether our present research tools permit us to understand macrostructural properties by reducing them to the individual or micro level. If they do not, as I have been assuming, we cannot escape macrostructural analysis.[32]

When I have suggested elsewhere that the structures of systems have properties which cannot be inferred from the properties of their constituent individuals, it should now be clear that all that I meant is that the behavior of individuals in relationship to each other generate such properties.[33] Hence we need to look to these relationships to discover them. From what I have been saying above about the difficulty of using individual reductionism to understand complex political relationships, it is clear that inability to infer structural properties from our knowledge of individual relationships is a practical one only. In principle such inferences are possible, from this point of view, even if, in practice, we are unable to do so. To hold otherwise would be to attribute to macrostructural concepts, such as system, authority, political outputs, or feedback, mysterious qualities the search for the source of which would take us beyond the limits of empirical inquiry.

In principle we should be able to reduce party structures, authority structures, elite patterns, and other observable political structures to their constitutive individual behaviors and thereby explain those properties as products of the relationships among individuals. In practice the enormous research detail that would be required to track all persons engaged in those patterns of relationships or structures simply surpasses our technical capacity, a deficiency which looms large in ethnomethodology, as I have already pointed out. Nor is it foreseeable that we will ever achieve such technical skill or, for that matter, that we will ever need it. We are left, therefore, with the *practical* irreducibility of structures, or at least of macrostructures, to the level of described individual interactions. Since individuals interact with each other, proximately or at a distance, in numerous and complex relationships, we are compelled through the sheer enormity of the task of unraveling these ties to turn, instead, to the collective results of their actions, as group properties, so called.

Feedback in a political system, for example, represents an enormously complex set of relationships. It is a product of the way such a system is organized.[34] In that sense it is a group property, not the property of specific individuals. *In principle* we should be able to trace out each stable pattern of individual actions and reactions that goes into creating a feedback structure. Feedback can occur only if individuals behave in appropriate ways in responding to output stimuli and in communicating information to others. *In practice*, however, such a detailed empirical description of individual actions defies any sensible conception of research that we have today. Even if it were considered to be desirable, the cost of the required technical skills and resources would be prohibitive. Accordingly, we must assess feedback at the level at which it appears, namely, as a structure (and set of processes) associated with the way political systems operate. It has to be understood as an abstracted product of the myriads of interwoven transactions among individuals that cannot be directly traced in all their complexities but can only be seen in their collective outcome.

It could be that Bourdieu was groping for a position such as this when he stated that

> it is not possible to understand the functioning of bureaucractic institutions unless one moves beyond the fictitious opposition between, on the one hand, a structuralist view which tends to see structural and morphological characteristics as the basis of the "iron laws" of bureaucracies, which it regards as mechanisms capable of defining their own teleology and imposing it on their agents; and, on the other hand, an "interactionist" or psycho-sociological view which tends to see bureaucratic practices as the product of the agents' interactions and strategies, ignoring both the social conditions of production of the agents (both inside and outside the institution) and the institutional conditions in which they perform their functions."[35]

Bourdieu is clearly searching for some middle ground, one that takes into account properties of the whole without losing sight of the actors who make up social relationships.

We have to bear in mind a point that is easily overlooked by critics of holism in general. Whether or not higher-order structures are reducible to individual interactions has little to do with the objective consequences of such structures, that is, with their ontological status as real relationships which influence the activities of individuals or institutions. The mere existence of a democratic or an authoritarian regime, for example, may constrain or shape the behavior of its parts and may have certain autonomous or independent properties associated with that higher order. Thus, a democratic regime is expected to offer feedback systems that are more responsive than those in authoritarian systems and that have a higher degree of fidelity in communicated information. We may well suspect such effects without, however, having the technical skills or resources to trace precisely the means through which they are realized. Reducibility refers to the research process, to levels, such as that of individual interactions, underlying a phenomenon that may need to be explored in attempts to understand the phenomenon. The consequences of a structure will be present, however, whether or not we have the tools to understand them by reducing them to their components.

This difference between plausibly suspecting the effects of a structure as a whole and having the tools to determine how they occur is not always understood or taken into account in the criticisms of structural or of structuralist analysis.[36] The hint of so-called holistic effects needs to be seen as an inducement to seek to develop adequate analytic and research tools to uncover them, not as an argument against looking for such an explanation of effects or for neglecting their existence because of the difficulty presented by our current incapacity to trace them empirically.

Conclusion

The continued insufficiency of the alternative approaches to analyzing broader structuralist effects may derive, in part, from overconcentration on the methods of decomposition, as I have suggested. In some cases, however, as in that of comparative historical interpretation, this lack of recognized success in confirming the effects of the whole on its parts may be attributable to the largely intuitive way in which scholars have been forced, by the very lack of attention to the necessary methodology, to deal with the epistemological issue. This issue, of course, addresses the relationship of an understanding of a part of a system to its place in the relationship, organization, or articulation of all the parts viewed as a system. Acceptably reliable methods have yet to be devised for demonstrating the effect of higher-order structures on their constituent parts.

Bearing in mind the little assistance we can get from the empirical literature on methods of analysis for this area, nonetheless by this time we can have little doubt that a macrostructure, in the form of a higher-order type, exists "out there," that it is independent of individual will and that it has major effects on the political system, especially on the way in which its components, such as the regime, are themselves organized.

Just what the nature of this kind of overall structure is, what its influence may be, and how we might go about exploring it are issues to which the whole of my analysis has, of course, been explicitly directed. For that reason we are now at a point where we are ready, finally, to probe more deeply into the nature of this structure and its possible influence.

18

Higher-Order Structures:
Their Composition and Influence

Now that we have explored the way in which higher-order structures enter into an explanation of lower ones, it is time to ask: What does it mean to speak of a higher-order structure of the political system and of its influence on lower-level structures? These issues have been implicit in my analysis to this point, or I have touched on them lightly in passing. As I concluded in the last chapter, we have now come to the point where we can face up to the tasks, first, of clarifying this idea directly, and second, of exploring the kinds of influence such a structure might have on other structures in a political system.

Lower-Order Structures

I have invoked the notion of higher-order structures as a way of helping to explain why it is that political systems may take the forms they do. The latter forms constitute the lower-order or observable structures that we are seeking to explain and understand, as discussed in chapter 5. In the language of empirical research, they are the dependent variables at issue. It is appropriate, therefore, before we turn to a specification of the nature of higher-order structures or search for the nature of their relationships to lower-order structures, to begin by reminding ourselves, in general terms, about what the idea of lower-order structures refers to.

In the most comprehensive sense, lower-order structures represent the way in which members of a political system relate to each other for performing their characteristic activities, namely, the production and implementation of binding decisions for a society. To understand the way political systems produce such outputs, I proposed, some time ago, that we may usefully view political systems as composed of certain invariant elements—inputs, outputs, conversion processes, and feedback. The activities implied in these elements are performed through the relationships of such variable units as political roles, legislatures, courts, interest groups, parties, publics, and so on. To ensure that we all had in mind the same structural realities of a political system, I illustrated various recurring types of such political structures in some detail in chapter 5.

These structures are not randomly related. They tend to be connected with each other in relatively stable ways, at least if systems are not undergoing rapid change. In that sense these units and other patterns of interaction constitute an order or set of relationships or structures.[1] I have called this order or form of organization of a political system, its regime structure.[2] The structures of which it is composed represent major means through which a society is able to make and implement

260

decisions that most of the members consider binding most of the time. At least in structurally differentiated systems, such as modern societies, regimes and their associated structures visibly and concretely help to distinguish the political from the economic, cultural, or religious aspects of society, for example. And we have also noted, in chapter 6, that it is this set of structures that has a potentially vital influence on the behavior of political actors as well as on systems and their policies. Through these structures, demands and support are converted into public policies. Insofar as the "state" has any autonomy, as Poulantzas argued and as neostatists today join him in insisting, its influence must reveal itself through the operation of these regime structures.

As I have proposed from the very beginning, it is, therefore, of more than passing interest to seek to understand variations in these structures. Why do they take the form they do, as a merely constitutional order, or as a democratic, dictatorial, or totalitarian one, for example? Why does one democracy assume a parliamentary structure, whereas others adopt a presidential or collegial pattern? Why does one regime support multiple parties, whereas in another they may be only dual? Why do interest groups coalesce into peak organizations in some European systems, especially smaller ones, but not in others, such as the American? In short, how can we account for a given type of regime structure and for its transformation into some variant within the type?

Structure as Relationships among Parts

Let us look at this regime structure a little more closely than we were able to in chapter 5. There are different ways of describing its structure. The one we choose to use will depend upon the conceptual and methodological tools at our disposal and the purposes we have in mind.

One way of analyzing a regime structure, as a subsystem of the political system, is through the identification of the patterns of relationships among the basic components of the system.[3] How a regime functions, within the context of a higher-order structure, will be reflected in the specific relationships among its parts.

If the relationships among constituent structural parts (whether constant or changing) were to undergo some fundamental alteration, we could expect that a political system, by definition, would have experienced what I would describe as a regime change. We see this most vividly in transformations from democratic to totalitarian or authoritarian systems, and *vice versa*, as under the reformist communist transformations, beginning in the late 1980s, in the communist bloc countries, inspired by perestroika in the USSR. In the latter instance, for example, whether or not the structural components of the system change, the rules governing the relationship among these components seem likely to become basically different. Thus, without radically changing its own internal structure, it would appear that in the late 1980s the Supreme Soviet of the USSR had moved in the direction of changing its external relationships, as, for example, with respect to the Communist party and to the governmental executive apparatuses. If these changes were to continue, they would represent a distinct regime transformation offering far greater opportunity for popular intervention for control of administration and of public policy. They could therefore be expected to have important implications for the overall operation of the Soviet political system.

Structure as Transformation Rules

As we saw in our analysis of Poulantzas, another way of describing the fundamental character of a regime is by describing the relationships among structural parts of a political system as so-called transformation rules or "laws."[4] The latter are designated as such rules since they are presumed to depict the way in which changes in the value of one or more variables that enter into these relationships in the regime will change (transform) the present state of the regime. "Were it not for the idea of transformation[,] structures would lose all explanatory import," suggests Piaget, "since they would collapse into static forms."[5]

Let us now look more closely at what the idea of transformation rule might mean. For one thing, it may simply describe relationships, not explain them. For example, marriage rules are transformational; they describe the process through which the relationship between two people is transformed, in a given culture, into that of a married couple. They are not the cause or explanation of marriage; persons marry for reasons other than the procedures that couple them.

Transformation rules may, however, be normative, specifying how things should be related. As such, we have already seen,[6] the rule is better thought of as part of the structure of culture and therefore may or may not help to structure behavior. As we know, there will often be a divergence between the transformation rule that describes a connection and the normative (cultural) rule that prescribes it. In a democracy, for example, the norm says that a loser in one election should be free to become a winner in a later one. Whether in fact that rule does prevail depends, of course, on the actual practice. Similarly for other normative rules of the democratic game.

Transformation rules, viewed as part of the behavioral structure of a democratic regime, are just that: they describe the operations through which a political relationship changes. They are not cultural rules depicting the way the democratic game of politics *should* be played; they are descriptive of the way the relationships are actually organized, that is, of the rules used in practice. They will coincide with the norms expressed in constitutions, statutes, judicial decisions, or administrative regulations only to the extent that these documents reflect reality.

As indicated earlier,[7] it is useful to adopt the notion of the regime as a way of referring to three elements of a political system: its goals, its norms and, in addition, its structure or form. Here we have been considering only the latter element. In earlier publications I have already developed the idea that this element—the structure of the regime—encompasses the relationships through which a political system transforms (converts) inputs of support and demands into public policies.[8] Accordingly, one way of identifying this structure would be through specification of the rules through which this important type of transformation (conversion) actually occurs. We would thereby be able to distinguish changes in the structure of a regime, that is, changes in the relationship between inputs and outputs, from mere changes in its state (condition).

In the work of Brunner and Brewer, we have already looked at an illustration of this method, applied to the political system as a whole.[9] To pursue the matter further, let us take an oversimplified and unrealistic example and assume that policies stand in a linear relationship to demands. For every specified number of demands put into a system, a certain number of policies will be produced. If that were true, then changes in the number of demands that are formulated and presented for action would lead to changes in the state of the regime without necessarily altering its structure, that is, the relationship among its constituent parts—in this case, demand inputs and policy outputs. In this scenario, the structural elements of the regime would be demands and support; the relationship between them, their structure, would be described by their ratio, a descriptive transformation rule.

If, for example, a regime were of a character such that every three demand inputs (DI) produced one policy output (PO), we could say that the structure of the regime is such that 3DI = 1PO. The state of the regime at any moment of time depends on this transformation rule or ratio—a three-to-one relationship between demands and outputs. Hence, if there were twelve demand inputs we could predict four policy outputs. The present state of the regime would have changed as there are now more inputs as well outputs in the system. However, the basic structure would have remained the same as the relationship between demand inputs and outputs, the transformation rule, has not been altered; every three demands still result in a single output.

If, however, as a result of changes in the regime, for whatever reasons, the ratio, as a description of the relationship, should now change and require six demand inputs to produce one policy output (6DI = 1PO), clearly the very structure of the regime itself would have changed. It is not just a matter of the state of the regime having been altered; the relationship between inputs and outputs is now no longer the same. The units of the system which produce demands—such as interest groups or parties or individuals—may remain the same, as may the producers of the outputs—such as a legislature—yet the relationship between them would have been altered. It now takes many more demand inputs to bring about a single policy decision. The regime structure could accordingly be said to have changed.

Although the structure of a regime in terms of its transformation rules has not been worked out, not even in a purely formal model, other rules of operation of, for example, democratic regimes, are well known even if they are not usually characterized as transformation rules. In fact, they are often presented as a mixture of descriptive and prescriptive rules. Typically, we speak of the rules of the game in a democracy: the winner takes all; minorities may become majorities; members of the system are free, within variable limits, to express their opinions, associate for political purposes, criticize, and oppose; leadership is subject to periodic renewal; those who win are accessible and responsive to the losers as well; rules for resolving conflict are impartial and known (rule of law); and so on.[10] At times these rules are used as norms constituting a theory about what democracy should be like. In effect they are cultural exhortations and inducements for members of a regime to relate to each other in the specified ways. At other times they are presumed to describe actual relationships among the actors in a democratic regime and, therefore, would operate to convert inputs of demands and support to policies. In this latter sense they would stand as transformation rules describing the actual structure of the regime.

Within the limits of these rules the regime may assume a large number of states. Winners may be many or few in number; minorities may have greater or lesser degrees of freedom; leadership may remain in power for longer or shorter periods of time; and the like. Nonetheless, despite the different outcomes of these variations, the structure of the regime remains constant, insofar as the system can continue to be considered democratic as defined by normative rules.

It is, of course, commonplace to recognize this difference between change in the *state* of a regime and change in its *structure*, even if we may not use it as a self-conscious tool of analysis. In any event, this view of structure leaves open the possibility that when we talk of a change in the regime structure of a political system we may have in mind just this aspect of the structure, namely, its transformation rules—the rules describing the presumed invariant relationship among the parts.

Structure as Political Resources

When we speak, even impressionistically, about changes in a regime or lower-order structure, however, we might have in mind more than changes in the transformation rules of a given type of political system or in some of the parts as they relate to each other. We might wish to refer to a third aspect of structure, one that would take into account differential effects in the operation of the rules even where the actors, as parts of the structure, and the basic relationships among them do not themselves change. I refer here to effects that depend upon the distribution of political resources available to participants in political processes.

Not all participants in the structure are likely to have equal access to centers of decision making and equal resources to execute their will. The distribution of resources will have their own structure such that certain participants will be in a position to exercise greater influence than others over the input of demands and support and over their conversion to policies. In this sense there will normally be a nonobvious structure of power relationships, whatever the factors may be that determine it, that provides the driving force behind the operation of the elements in the structure of the regime and the transformation rules that govern their relationships.

We can now see that the idea of a lower-order regime structure is somewhat more complex than might have appeared initially. It comprises several major interlocking components: patterns of relationships among the basic components of a political system (elites, legislatures, courts, parties, roles, etc.); the relationships among such units that enable any system to conduct its normal activities (converting inputs of demands and support into outputs), describable as transformation rules; and a power structure that interweaves and influences the nature and operation of the other two aspects of this structural level.

To explain these differences in patterns of relationships, rules, and power relationships in a regime, as I have already argued, we must certainly look to the specific interests, pressures, distribution of power resources among groups and classes, and the like which have favored one or another way of organizing political processes. But by this stage in our discussion it is no secret that to complete an explanation we would be passing over a central desideratum if we did not recognize the significance of what I have been calling the higher-order structure, the overall political system itself, of which the regime is but a part.

Meaning of Higher-Order Political Structure

Just what does this term *higher-order political structure* refer to? In the first place, we need to bear in mind that I have been speaking about *political* structures only. Other kinds of social structures are, without the slightest doubt, of vital importance for helping to shape political life, a point I have made a number of times throughout this book, so that there can be no mistake about the importance I attach to them. For the moment, however, they are outside our range of interest, even though shortly I shall want to say a word about them.[11]

In the second place, as we concluded early on,[12] structure is just a property of things in space and time, and not a concrete entity in itself. And in the third place, our interest has been in structural properties as they are found in political behavior or activity, not in culture, attitudes and beliefs, personalities, or in society in general (social structure, so-called).[13]

External Higher-Order Constraints

The reason for reminding ourself of these limits of our inquiry is that there has been much discussion in the 1980s, as noted earlier,[14] about social constraints and our recent rediscovery of their presence and importance. When writers began to signalize such constraints on politics, however, all too frequently they had in mind not the overarching limits imposed on political activities by the structure of the political system itself but rather the way in which other kinds of constraints, nonpolitical ones, operated on the political system as a whole. This was the thrust of the work of both Lévi-Strauss and Poulantzas. In the one case, what looked like a cognitive structure, the intellect, was the operative constraint and in the other, a social structure, in the form of a broadened conception of the Marxist notion of mode of production.

Even when we look at other latter-day discoveries of such constraints, we find scholars preoccupied with constraints external to the political system—nonpolitical social forces—that operate in some way on the system as a whole. For example, Lindblom interprets the economic market as a prison restricting the range of policies open to government. In his words, "Policy is imprisoned in market oriented systems. . . . The feature of market systems that is at the core of the recoil mechanism is the inducement system that we use to motivate one great category of organizers and coordinators to do their work."[15] Implied in this quotation is the idea that the most significant constraints external to the political system are not necessarily behavioral in nature. In speaking of inducements and punishments as the mechanisms to coordinate behavior, the structure external to the political system but influential for it seems to be more psychological (an "inducement system") than behavioral.

In short, it is transparent that the political system does not operate in splendid isolation. Axiomatic as this statement may be, the popularity, in recent years, of trying to establish the independent effect of the actions or policies of the political authorities (the "state") may easily divert attention away from the context in which these actors operate. It is strangely necessary to reaffirm that the political system is subject to critical influences from its social environment. The general culture, economy, psychological subsystem, and social structure all help to determine (or limit?) where political power lies, and they do this through shaping the inputs of demands and support and the nature of the conversion of these to outputs. I have elaborated on these influences in my earlier publications, so there is no need to do more than mention them here.[16] Others have gone further to argue that we cannot understand contemporary political events (and structures?) without seeing them as products of the great historical movements of the last two centuries: (1) the development of capitalism as a process of production with its attendant industrialization, territorial expansion, urbanism, migration, etc.; and (2) the accompanying growth of the power of the "state" itself with its monopoly, in Weberian terms, of legitimate control and violence.[17]

It should be clear by his time that I do not seek to deny in any way the significance of these external factors for the functioning and structure of the political system and any of its parts, such as the regime. In this work, however, I have turned to a different and separable issue, one that rests on a *politically centered* explanation. To what extent does the political system itself, as a specific and identifiable set of relationships (the overall political structure), also help to generate, shape, or limit the ways in which individual members of and organized units in a political system use their power to make and implement policies? Specifically, how might the overarching political structure affect the regime structure, that is, that substructure of the political system through which policies are shaped and implemented?

To be clear about what I mean by higher-order political structure, therefore, we must bear two points in mind. As I have just indicated, I am speaking first and foremost about a property of the behavior or interactions of members of a political system, not about a property of their motives or culture, for example. And since I am seeking to identify structure as a property of these interactions, what I have in mind is the structure of the political system itself, rather than constraints working on the system from the outside, of which there are many.

Internal Higher-Order Constraints

To return, then, to my main point. I wish to clarify what I mean by higher-order structure, as a property of political interactions themselves, that is, as a property that is internal to and an aspect of the whole political system.

As I have already indicated, put most simply the structure of a political system consists of the invariant elements of that system and their interdependencies. As such, we can know and understand this structure only by identifying the important constituent elements of a political system together with their significant relationships. An effort such as this clearly involves exactly what we would do if we sought to formulate a general theory about the operation of political systems. Such a theory would require the identification of the major elements of a system and their relationships, in their totality. My previously published analyses of the political system were designed to present at least the major conceptual outlines of such a theory. As such, it should, therefore, already contain the major components of the overarching political structure.

Implicitly, this way of defining the overall political structure denies the utility or necessity for considering that this structure somehow underlies (as an infrastructure) observable political relationships, as both Lévi-Strauss and Poulantzas imply, or that, in structural linguistic terms, it represents a "deep" structure, something that lies below "surface" phenomena. The overarching political structure is nothing more than the nonobvious relationships among observed phenomena. This higher-order structure is, therefore, inherent in the way in which observed or lower-order ones, in their totality, are interrelated. It is not necessary to invoke an imagery that sees it as a separate entity that somehow underlies them like some overwhelming geological formation or that "stands behind their back" as an *éminence grise*.

In effect, this is perhaps what Piaget had in mind when he interpreted structures as a theory about systems and their transformation laws. It is also what both Boudon and Runciman probably meant when they argued, as I observed earlier, that structuralism, as a school of interpretation, is no less than a general theory built out of the observed elements in society and not a special theory about structure, as such, at all.[18] From this perspective, the higher-order structure to which I have been referring ought not to be thought of as *above* lower-order ones any more than we ought to think of them as *underlying* the latter. As we shall shortly see, they are higher only in the sense that they incorporate, in a hierarchically nesting sense, the lower-order structures and describe the way the latter articulate as a set. They are not superimposed on the lower structures any more than they might act as an infrastructure on which the lower ones rest. In place of this layering or geological imagery I am substituting one of system interrelatedness.[19]

From my earlier writings, it is clear that major elements of the structure of political systems would consist of patterns of activities involved in generating demand and support inputs, their conversion to policies, and feedback processes. The relationships through which these activities are performed can be classified into empirically specifiable units abstracted from the total political activity of society: the political authorities, regime, and political community. Each of these gross structural elements, decomposable into its own constituent parts, plays some significant role in determining the input, output, conversion, and feedback processes, the basic activities characteristic of any and all political systems. These structural elements, in their many and complex relationships, internal as well as external, together form what I have been calling the higher-order structure of political systems.

To speak of this structure, then, is to identify the totality of basic political relationships. These, it is true, need to be specified in and derivable from some theory of politics, in this case a systems-analytic one. We must be careful to note, however, that structural analysis by itself is not coterminous with such a theory. Systems analysis is more comprehensive. It deals with processes as well, that is, with the significant activities of any and all political systems that we must understand, such as inputs, conversions, and feedback. But the way the processes work can themselves be understood only through the structural means that shape, limit, determine or facilitate them, kinds of relationships to which I shall return in a moment. Hence, a theory about political structures is only part of systems analysis, not identical with it.

Structure as an Integral Aspect of the Whole System

What is clear from this way of describing the higher-order or system structure is that we do not see it as something separate from and independent of its theoretically defined parts. The overall structure of a political system is, of course, different from any single part or limited combination of structural elements. But as a property of all of them as found in their relationships to each other, the structure is inherent in them. On the other hand, each part by itself takes its particular quality from its participation in the complex organization constituting the political system in its totality.[20] It is this relationship (between any part and the whole complex), I have been arguing throughout this work, to which we need to be alerted in seeking to understand variations in any part of the political system, and hence of the one we call its regime.

This total structure of the system needs to be clearly distinguished, of course, from the regime. The latter is the particular form that a given system takes at a given time and place—democratic, authoritarian, dictatorial forms, and their variants, about which I have already spoken. Why such forms arise will be contingent in a significant way, I have been proposing, on the relationships among *all* elements of the system—demands, support, and conversion and feedback relationships as well as the political authorities, regime, and political community. Different kinds of these relationships—that is, variations in the higher-order structure thus conceived in its totality—will influence variations in types of regimes.

For example, as I have sought to show,[21] political systems will differ in the way in which demands are generated and processed, in the nature of the gatekeepers that restrict or facilitate the input of demands, in the kind and level of support available for the political authorities, in the regime itself, or in the political community. I am suggesting here that to understand variations in such lower-level structures as are found in the regime and its associated structures requires more than historically informed inquiry into the social forces that gave them birth, the interests and power resources that have sought to shape them,[22] or the extent to which they are based, for example, on imitation of other systems.[23] We would also need to go beyond knowledge about the forces behind the current regime structure at any given moment, whether they be the conflict among classes as proposed by Poulantzas, the "people" in some undifferentiated Rousseauean sense of conventional democratic theory, a fixed power elite in Paretan terms, varying decision elites in power pluralist theory, or even presumed rational choices. Variations in the regime structure need to be traced back to the broader relationships, found in all political systems, among demands, support, and the like, which, in different ways to be addressed in a moment, may circumscribe the range of variations possible for such lower-order structures.

What do we mean by variations in the overall structure of a political system, in specific terms, as contrasted to variations in regime structures? It should be evident by this time that to describe such variations we would need to be able to identify differences in the inflow patterns of demands, in the typical patterns of support for the three basic political objects of a system (political authorities, regime, and political community), in conversion and feedback structures, and in the regime structures themselves. We would also need to bear in mind the patterns of power distribution as well as the various cleavage patterns among ethnic, linguistic, regional, cultural, ideological, etc., groups in the political community."[24]

The structure of a regime and the way it operates, whether it can tolerate one or another kind of relationship within the authority structure (among the executive, legislature, bureaucracy, and judiciary, for example), party system, interest group structure, and the like, could be understood in significant part as a function of the relationship of the regime to the way the overarching political system itself is organized. The regime does not stand separate and apart; it functions in a broader context. As we have noted, this point has been the inherent message among configurative analysts, Weberian interpretivists, and, most recently, the historical neostatists. The specific properties of a given regime structure (as well as its capacities) need to be understood in the broader context of the structure of the total political system.

Hierarchical Ordering of Political Structures

As already noted, I do not propose to direct our attention to reasons why the structure of the whole political system should itself take the form it does. To engage in the pursuit of such explanations would raise us to a still higher level of analysis, to the social system itself (the society level in Diagram 18.1), certainly an important task but one that would take us too far afield and would be redundant of my earlier work.[25]

Although the focus of my interest in this book has been on the neglect of one aspect of the explanation for regime variations, in fact the same kind of analysis can be applied to the relationships between any two levels of a political system. It is illuminating to explore this thought further.

If part of a political system, such as a party structure, interest group formation, or judicial subsystem, can be adequately understood only by considering it in relation to its position in a higher-level structure, is it correct to imply that the latter is singular in character, that there is only one higher-level structure? To this point I have been speaking at times as though this were indeed the case. This has been somewhat misleading. The fact is that we can expect to encounter more than one level of higher structure and, accordingly, a multiplicity of levels for lower-order structures as well, points that have already been implied in our earlier discussions.[26]

Diagram 18.1 displays the conceptualization suggested by these remarks. It can be described as a hierarchy in which we begin with the highest level of structure, the total social order, and descend to the lowest level, the more numerous patterns of individual behavior (political roles). In effect, this way of describing the relationships among various levels of structures returns us, not surprisingly, to a systems analytic view of political behavior and institutions.

The diagram indicates that each class of subsystem, beginning with individuals as occupants of subsystems called political roles, can be usefully interpreted as being contained within a higher-level subsystem, moving to the highest order of all, the total social system. For this purpose, then, it is useful to conceive of the overall political system as a set of structures at different levels each of which may have variable effects on the levels above and below it.

Diagram 18.1 presents pictorially a conceptualization appropriate to such an analysis. This diagram depicts an ascending order of structures in hierarchical form. Each lower level can be understood only by taking into account its position in the next higher level of which it serves as a constituent element. Each higher level helps to organize the next lower level of the system and thereby creates new properties in the system.

This hierarchical structure need not exert its influence through the fact that it represents a "boss" or command structure in which the higher level has authority over a lower one or, for that matter, need determine that lower level in the sense of having a compelling influence. It can be viewed rather as what we may call a containment or *nesting* hierarchy.[27] Lower levels are included in higher ones and take part of their character from this fact. The former are conditions under which the latter must operate. Illustrative of this kind of hierarchy, not usually thought of

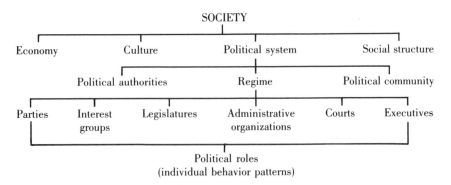

Diagram 18.1   Hierarchy of Structures

as such, are Chinese boxes or Russian dolls in which each box or doll contains a smaller one, which, in turn, contains a still smaller one to some limit. The nature of the influence of one level on another is deliberately left moot, for reasons that will appear shortly.

Even without the power to command, upper hierarchical levels, by virtue of their nesting character, set limits or, in appropriate instances, physical boundaries on the range of variation available to lower ones and, in that sense, help to organize the lower levels. In short, the hierarchical ordering is a way of declaring that properties of a next-lower level cannot be fully understood without reference to the totality in which it is included as represented by the higher levels.[28]

The diagram is, of course, limited to depicting the relationships in the political system and between political systems and the broader social systems within which they are contained. In effect, it asserts that a political system is included within the broader society and that the latter, in one way or another, influences the forms that a political system may take (the importance of which I have already stressed at several points in our discussion). But it also says that within a political system there are subsystems, such as the authorities, regime, and political community. And, of course, the regime itself has its own subsystems, such as those described in chapter 5—parties, interest groups, electorates, and the like. The structures constituted by the latter can be fully understood only if we take into account their nesting relationship to their higher-order subsystem, the regime. Understanding of the latter, in turn, requires us to look to its relationship to the encompassing higher-order structure of the political system as a whole. In effect, this nesting relationship is probably what is meant when linguists, following Saussure, talk about the "absent totality" represented by the taken-for-granted language system that shapes the meaning of any string of words in a culture—a phrase that is occasionally used, as well, by social scientists to describe taken-for-granted broad, structural factors.

Such a conceptualization alerts us to what we intuitively know, namely, that if we transfer one type of regime, such as responsible parliamentary democracy (as in Britain), to another society (as in Canada), the operation of this type and its consequences are likely to be vastly different from what they were in the original society. Each society with its own overall political system is likely to set some limits, at the very least, on the imported regime.

The identification of a hierarchical ordering of this sort is not the only thing that can be said of the relationship between a political system and the society of which it is part, of course. It omits reference to important *interactions* of the political system with the economic, psychological (personality), and cultural systems, interactions which may be different from any asymmetrical relationships found in a hierarchical ordering. I have had much to say about this in earlier publications, demonstrating there the way in which other social systems help to shape the nature of the inputs and outputs of a political system (and, I might add, the way in which the political system, through its outputs, shapes other social systems as well). In other words, the nesting hierarchy may do more than just set limits. Under some circumstances it may contain processes that determine, in the strict sense of the term, the kinds of demands that become part of the political agenda, the way in which support is mobilized, the distribution of power resources, and the like. To include a discussion of these kinds of consequences here would take us too far afield, and in any event I have dealt with them at length in my earlier writings.[29]

The important thing is first, that the political system itself constitutes a higher-order structure; initially, we do not need to go outside the system to find such a constraint. And second, this structure, when unpackaged, reveals various theoretically specified components: demands, support, conversion structures, feedback, political authorities, regime, and political community. All these, with their own internal structured components, form a complex of relationships. It is this complex that we need to bear in mind when we speak of the highest-order political structure, the whole political system itself.

My contention has been that if we seek to understand why and how a regime structure assumes the form that it does, we cannot do so ultimately without reference to the hierarchy in which it nests. I have focused on that part of this hierarchy that involves the relationship of the regime to the higher-order structure of the overarching *political system* itself. But *pari passu* we could have focused on other individual structures, such as the relationships among political roles. In that case a complete explanation would have depended on showing their connection to the next higher-order structures in the hierarchy, as shown in Diagram 18.1. This could appropriately have led us to the next higher level and, finally, to the overall political system as the highest level. From there we could seek to show the effect of the highest hierarchical level, the societal system. Indeed, we can now see that Poulantzas was engaged in precisely the latter task, and much of the analysis by neostatists today is of the same character. They seek to show the way in which society (or certain aspects of it, such as social classes, conflict, property relations, profit, and capital accumulation) has influenced the structure of the "state," its policies, and practices.

From this point of view, it is now clear that contemporary neostatists have jumped a level in the hierarchy, from society directly to the state structure. Neglected here is the way in which society shapes or limits the organization of the political system as a whole and through the latter, the structure of the state (assuming the state refers to something less than the whole political system). However important societal influences may be, they are refracted through the way in which the overall political system is organized. Accordingly, the task would be to distinguish carefully among the levels being analyzed. Society influences the state through the way it affects the overall political system; in this sense, the state would be subject to the effects of society derivatively, in addition, of course, to whatever direct relationship there might be. Here I am assuming that neostatists are using the concept *state* to identify something close to what I am calling the *regime*.[30]

This complex order of the overall political system, in the totality of its constitutive relationships, I have been arguing, forms the context, a macrostructure with respect to any single part of a political system.[31] It is this overall or system level structure the impact of which needs to be taken into account and understood if we are to be able to help explain why the parts, or any combination of them, such as a regime, assume the form they do. The relationships among the components of a system do not order themselves, as it were; their order is influenced in various ways by the overarching structure of the system itself. In these ways, to be examined in a moment for their variety, the higher-order system helps to structure the relationships among its component subsystems.

This is undoubtedly what the structuralists were striving to express, when, as we saw earlier,[32] they converted structure from a noun to a verb, arguing the need to conceptualize the total context as a system. This very neglect of the effects of this "structuring" systemic whole has hitherto handicapped us in attempts to compare the differences in forms of political systems and the differences in consequences of similar organizations or political units across systems.[33]

Relationships between Lower- and Higher-Order Structures

When we speak in this way of the higher-order system structuring lower-order subsystems and their operations, and use the imagery of a nesting hierarchy, what kinds of influence between these two orders might we envisage? The fact is that the relationships between the hierarchical levels will themselves vary. Let us look at these differences for a moment.

In the first place, the extent of the influence itself may vary depending upon the tightness of the coupling or connectedness between subsystems and the political system as a whole. We need only mention this condition here as I have already drawn our attention to it in the preceding chapter. There we saw that subsystems may be loosely coupled to other components of the political system so that even large changes in the latter may have little influence on the subsystem (as well as the reverse, of course). Indeed, I had suggested that this is precisely the kind of relationship to which those who speak of the autonomy of the "state" were directing our attention. In this interpretation, the state, at least with respect to its policy-making activities, is relatively sheltered from societal influences, that is, from variations in other political and social subsystems. Otherwise we could scarcely describe it as being autonomous.[34]

In the second place, even in those cases where there is a tight connection between the higher- and lower-level structures, we ought not to assume that this relationship is always the same. We will recall that Lévi-Strauss and Poulantzas had seemed to insist on the empirical relationships being determined (asymmetrically caused by) an underlying structure, even though, in the end, Poulantzas, at least, softened his position, as we have seen. This suggests that the relationships between the two orders of structure may be of more than one kind. At times the one may indeed be uniquely *determined* by the other. In addition, however, we would be neglecting very important aspects of their relationships if we failed to recognize that higher-order structures may also *facilitate* the emergence and operation of lower-order ones. Finally, the former may at times only *limit*, rather than determine, the latter. Let us examine these three types of possible relationships: determination, facilitation and limitation.

Relationship as Determining

As I have just indicated, Lévi-Strauss and Poulantzas had little doubt about what structuring meant for them. They saw the so-called underlying structure as determining the social relations or superstructure. And by determination, which figures so prominently, especially in Poulantzas's work, they presumably meant that there was an *obligative* or compulsory relationship;[35] the one was inescapably shaped by the other. For them, to say that A determines B means that A virtually reduces the variety of B's choices to one. No narrower constraint could be imposed.[36]

This is essentially what was involved in Poulantzas's use of the term. He seemed to wish to say that the mode of production, the highest-order macrostructure in his conceptualization, legislates, as it were, for the lower-level ones.[37] For him, initially at least, the mode of production seemed to do more than just set broad limits on the range of opportunities among political regimes. Given the internal contradictions in the capitalist mode of production, they would necessarily bring about the collapse of capitalism through the inability even of democratic forms to deal with the crises so generated. Actors, as mere *Träger* of history, would be able to do little to stem the tide. We saw the great lengths to which Poulantzas went[38] to demonstrate the determining power of the mode of production, in its various phases and stages, over the structure of the state.

Similarly, although not so obviously, for Lévi-Strauss kinship ties must directly reflect the intellective tendency to think in terms of binary and complementary opposites. On the surface, kinship groups may seem different but underneath these appearances they reveal the balanced oppositional form of all basic human relationships. It is in the very nature of the human "mind" that it cannot escape establishing empirical relationships of this sort.

Setting aside questions about the validity of the claims made by either Lévi-Strauss or Poulantzas, determination in this obligative sense undoubtedly does represent one kind of possible relationship between the two levels. How frequently it occurs empirically would, however, be an entirely different question.

Relationship as Facultative

Relationships between higher- and lower-order structures, other than of an obligative kind, are, however, possible and appear empirically. Higher-order structures may be only *facultative* in nature.[39] They may serve only as a potential that facilitates and guides behavior in certain directions. Some scholars, such as proponents of rational political models, would argue indeed that that is the main consequence of structures. For example, structures such as constitutions are presumed to provide incentives to coordinate behavior, as I noted earlier. To the extent that a higher-order structure contains relationships that are introduced for specific purposes—such as the creation of a new regime through a constitution—the facultative consequences would be pronounced.

Thus, a democratic structure offers opportunities for popular electoral participation, but only infrequently does it compel such involvement. It normally also provides incentives for members of the system to organize parties or interest groups of various sorts, but it need not make such action obligatory. Nor need it dictate the form of interest group structures, such as whether they coalesce in peak organizations or remain more fragmented, an issue at the heart of contemporary corporatist analysis. But the rules and relationships may make one or another form of organization easier or more difficult to achieve.

Relationship as Limiting

Most structures, however, whether deliberately generated or crescive,[40] that is, emerging as part of informal or natural processes, have a third aspect that is well understood in practice although not always explicitly noted. As I have tried to demonstrate, in my analysis of Poulantzas in particular, higher-order structures are likely to create kinds of effects that need not compel or facilitate but may only *limit* the range of variation of lower-level structures.

Determination is often used in this way. It suggests that certain parameters may set limits on the range of variation of some phenomena subject to them, in the sense that many choices may be possible but that certain ones are excluded. In this meaning a fence determines the area on which cattle may graze; it limits the range of choices without reducing variety to one choice alone. It does not compel them to feed in one spot or to follow a particular path within the bounded area. Their freedom to select their activities may be very wide. Yet they must conduct those activities within the fenced area, however appealing the greener pastures in an adjacent field. Or, to change the analogy, gravity does not compel us to jump, nor does it facilitate our doing so.[41] We are free to jump or not, as we see fit. But if we choose to do so, whatever the form and direction of the leap, gravity imposes recognizable limits on our capacity.

Similarly, the regime of a political system may take many different forms. But its range of variation is not infinite or unrestricted. The form of regime is limited by the fact that it is part of a political system which includes more than the regime itself. The organization of the political system as a whole provides a higher-level environment within which the observed or lower-level structures function and which normally impose limits on the variety of subordinate political relationships that can be formed.

Concretely, for example, the ordering of relationships in a democracy under capitalism does not compel the creation of a congressional legislative subsystem or a parliamentary or a French presidential form. Historically, each of these lower-level regime structures is possible, as are numerous other as yet untried and undreamed of types. But in each of the respective systems the form of legislature that can arise is limited by the need to conform to the higher level of relationships. An appointed unicameral legislature, for example, or one able to select its own successor would fall outside the limits of most overall political structures that presume to operate by democratic rules. Similarly, a capitalist-based democracy, the members of which seemed to wish to transfer effective power to a working class ideologically unsympathetic to the prevailing social and economic order, might run up against a resistance that is built into the very structure of that order, as Allende discovered in Chile. These represent the so-called structural constraints on a system about which we hear so much, and appropriately so, in neostatist analysis. But as we can see, this is only one among a number of kinds of constraints, albeit an important one, on the actions of the members of a political system.

Illustrations of claims about higher-order structures and their presumed determinate relationship to lower-order ones, which really describe limits, are not hard to come by. General theoretical approaches to political systems are particularly prone to make such apparently obligative assumptions. Thus, elitist theory suggests a particular overarching set of relationships between leaders and the masses such that a predominance of power must always rest in the hands of the former. This was the essential message of the elitist theories of Mosca and Pareto, as well as of Michels with his iron law of oligarchy. Whatever observed form the actual political institutions might take, whether democratic or autocratic, they must assume an elitist structure. As such, an elite ultimately has the last say in determining the course of political events. The elements of the higher-order structure are the elites and masses, the basic transformation rule allocates dominant power to the elite so that the overlying power structure, although not necessarily observable, effectively disfranchises the masses even in a democracy.

Despite the appearance of the claim to an obligative relationship, however, the reality is one of limitation only. What the elitists are saying, in effect, is that the observable, lower-order, or regime structures—relationships among political authorities in legislatures, administrative organizations and courts, together with parties, interest groups, and the like—may take any number of forms. But regardless of this, in the end the higher-order relationships, which define the power of the elite as against the masses, will always limit the range of variation possible. No form can arise that will effectively dispossess the elite; their power position in the overall complex of relationships, which constitutes the political system as a whole, at the very least sets outer limits on the structures through which the system may operate. That is why democracy is free to assume so many different forms without, however, being able to deprive an elite of its power.

Power pluralism as a theory is no less suggestive of a higher-order structure which conditions the particular democratic forms of a political system. Although there are elites, these are competitive, rather than a coherent bloc in the Paretan sense, and are built on the shifting sands of particular issues. The imagery here is interestingly kaleidoscopic. As policy issues change, existing coalitions of leaders recede and new ones, with alternative resources, emerge around the new issues. There is a continuous flux and flow of changing—if, at times, overlapping—elites. Through competition among them for popular support, popular demands are more likely to be met.

The overall structural imagery suggested here is one in which competitive elites are governed by democratic transformation rules and the resulting fragmentation in the distribution of power redounds to the benefit of the masses. Within the limits of an overarching structural arrangement such as this, the lower-level institutions take their form. Conditioned as they may be by historical circumstances associated with their evolution, they ultimately take an important part of their character from the fact that they must facilitate the competition among elites or, at the very least, not erect insuperable barriers to their emergence and periodic withdrawal as dictated by the nature of the decisions to be made. The forms of the government itself and its associated party structure, interest group arrangements, and electoral organization may not be *determined* by this higher structural order composed of competitive elites. They are, however, at least *limited* by it, if the basic form of the regime as a liberal democracy is to be retained.

Of course, there is a still higher-order structure, it is now commonplace to point out, that power pluralism had sadly neglected. It used to be spoken about as the various faces of power that were concealed through the power-pluralist imagery. The power resources available to various groups and leaderships are themselves limited by basic power relationships within a political system, a key constraint or limit on the free play of plural groups. Furthermore, since the existence of issues as a precipitant in the political process was central to the power pluralist conceptualization, it inherently neglected various issues that failed to get on the agenda and around which elites, therefore, could not have the opportunity to cohere, even if they had the resources to do so. This inability to get consideration could only too easily lead to the neglect of the interests and demands of various segments of a democratic society.

In our terms this is just a way of saying that however democratic the structure of a regime may be, the overall structure of the political system, including its basic power relationships, may impose certain limits not only on the way that structure operates but on the very structure of the regime itself. As with elite theory, so with power pluralism, we need not assume that the way in which the overall system is structured need compel the generation of any particular kind of democratic regime; there would be ample room for variety. Many types of regime structures would presumably be consistent with the emergence of plural power elites for control over policy.

Regardless of the type of democratic structure that was introduced, however, if the varied-faces-of-power theory is correct, such elites would run up against certain limits or boundaries, inherent in the power relationships of the system as a whole. These would represent the outer limits of constraints on the regime. They would impose implicit barriers against the construction of a regime which would permit the other faces of power to be ignored or flaunted. Hence, even if the power pluralist conception of democratic structure, however inarticulate it is in the theory itself, were an accurate representation of how some democracies operate, it would still leave unexplained the way in which these higher-order kinds of structures can seriously limit the organization and functioning of the democratic regimes themselves.

In brief, then, to say that the political system as such serves as a determinant of its subsystems is in itself insufficient. The notion of determination is ambiguous; it conceals a number of possible relationships. We need to clarify the nature of the constraints the higher-order structures impose: whether and to what extent they reduce the variety of options open to lower-level structures to a single type (determination in the narrowest and strictest sense), facilitate the emergence of various structural alternatives, or just set broad limits within which alternative forms are possible, depending upon historical circumstances. In short, we need to know whether what is meant is that the lower order is determined in an obligative or facultative sense by the higher order, or whether the lower-order structures are only limited in their range of variation, as part of a nesting hierarchy.

It is, of course, hazardous to speculate as to whether in any particular historical situation one or another of these three possible relationships—obligative, facultative, or limiting—between higher-order and lower-order (observable) structures need dominate. This would be a matter for empirical discovery. Yet our discussion of Poulantzas has already suggested that it is difficult, theoretically and consistently, to demonstrate the obligative relationship, one in which observable structures are necessarily the exclusive resultant of higher-level forces. Despite Poulantzas's apparent intention to the contrary, all that he could reasonably show was that such higher-level structures were inescapable constraints that limited the range of lower-level structural alternatives. And his borrowing from Althusser of the notion of relative autonomy of the state revealed his intuitive recognition of this limit in his own deterministic scheme of things. Of course, the great counterfactual debates among historians hinge on being able to give plausible answers as to whether a particular outcome was necessary, just possible or even fortuitous.

It should be clear that this classification of possible relationships between hierarchical structural levels also offers a useful way of handling systematically the role of the subject in the structure of social action. Where constraints are such as to eliminate all options but one, the subject disappears as a factor in social action. Objective social forces take over. But in the other instances, where the higher structural levels only facilitate a choice or limit the range of choices, there remains ample room for the human agent, as the role of Gorbachev in the USSR from the late 1980s on would seem to indicate.

We can now appreciate the full significance of theories about the relative autonomy of the state. In effect, they signal the implicit abandonment of any pretence of strict determinism. We can now see that this has been the whole point about the turn toward state autonomy; it represented a way of coping with structuralist determinism, both of the Marxist and other varieties. In putting the emphasis on the state rather than on the human subject, Poulantzas, as well as contemporary neostatists, have converted the state into a surrogate for the human actor. As such, its actions and structure are no longer seen as uniquely determined by society; at most, they can only be limited by social forces. To hold otherwise would be to deny the state its autonomy. Thereby Althusser and subsequent neo-statists could make room for the human actor. Agents are once again given a significant role in social change, even though they are now cloaked in the state, itself a concept laden with heavy ambiguity, as we have seen,[42] or imbedded in social classes as aggregate actors.

Without making an issue of it or even avowing it, in this indirect way Althusser and Poulantzas, together with contemporary neostatists, have been able to escape from the voluntarist-determinist dilemma. The state, with its social class actors, becomes the vehicle for the expression and implementation of human choices and for asserting human autonomy from surrounding social forces.

In effect, our way of classifying relationships between levels in the structural hierarchy offers a somewhat different escape from the vise of the artificial, if not arbitrary voluntarist-determinist dichotomy. We no longer need to see them as polar alternatives between which we must choose. We need not claim in advance that the "state," assuming it refers to the regime structure and its occupants, is autonomous or not. Instead, our classification offers us a continuum between strictly obligative connections in which objective social conditions determine behavior in the strict sense and limiting circumstances in which human choices can be implemented within specifiable constraints. Human choice, as embodied in "state" action, may be limited in varying degrees depending upon the situation, ranging from virtual total freedom (unlimited options) to virtual determinism (only one option). In other words, the degree to which the state is autonomous may vary from zero to some indeterminate magnitude short of total freedom of action.[43]

The imagery of a nesting hierarchy of strictly political structures, as depicted here, suggests just such a continuum for every structure. Each lower-level structure is constrained in varying degrees by the higher-order ones, as we saw, ranging from zero to some upper limit. The "state," as such a lower-level structure in the nesting hierarch, may indeed, therefore, have a high degree of autonomy on occasion; but under other circumstances it may also be very severely constrained. Just where any "state" stands on such a continuum would have to be discovered empirically or preferably, through some special subtheory about state autonomy.

Our responsibility at this moment is not to try to resolve the issue, at least theoretically, as to which relationship dominates a particular historical situation. The important point to note is that in concluding that the forms of observed structures are shaped by the overarching structure of which they are part, we need to bear in mind that this influence may derive from the different kinds of relationships as depicted in the three alternatives we have been discussing in this chapter.

19

Substance versus Methods

The constraints engendered by the overarching structure are very real, even though they are invisible and are seldom identified and recognized for what they do. They go to the heart of the degree to which any political system can be reformed or transformed and the barriers that may need to be surmounted or reduced. Only by discerning their vital impact can we hope to account for the often frustrating discrepancy between the vast hope for political reforms, for example, and their failure to materialize despite the support and fervor they may inspire. As we saw at the outset, it was this apparent contradiction in the United States between the high expectations of the counterculture movement of the 1960s and 1970s and the subsequent conservative reaction that helped to drive the search for an explanation. We discovered an important and neglected part of this explanation in the higher-order political structure.

We sought to penetrate an understanding of the influence of this kind of political structure by approaching it from one direction, central to the formulation of any theory about politics: How do higher-order structures become translated into observed or lower-order kinds? An answer to that question showed promise of enabling us to understand and explain the emergence of different regime structures, or, for that matter, of any other political structures. Beyond that, however, this very understanding could provide the basis upon which we might be able to overcome critical, unsuspected limitations on action, represented in such higher-order structures, and thereby to try to attain otherwise elusive goals.

The Quest

It should now be clear where research about lower-level structures stands in the whole enterprise of political science. In the past the idea of structure has been taken for granted in the discipline. It has scarcely even been considered, let alone been considered problematic. At the outset of this book I had indicated the almost total absence of specific attention to the idea of political structure in the literature of political science. I hope that the importance of structure has now been established, as a critical beginning.

Once we recognized the neglect of structure in political science, we had a number of options. We could have chosen to inquire into the effects of structures, especially on the distribution of political power and on shaping and limiting political outputs, or the compatibility of various types of structures within a political system and their change over time, to mention only two. Instead, to narrow our focus within a

280

manageable range, I chose to concentrate on one of the central and classical issues of political inquiry: How can we explain the variety of regime structures and their changes that we observe in political systems across space and time.

The bread-and-butter activity of empirically oriented political inquiry, from time immemorial—meaning, in Western civilization, from Plato and Aristotle onwards—has been to classify political systems according to their structural arrangements: democratic, oligarchic, dictatorial, with numerous variants of these categories and varied names for similar kinds of regime structures. Regardless of the labels we have put on these different structural types, a dominant set of concerns has persisted across the ages, motivated as often by normative intent as by a desire for understanding: What is the best form of government and what criteria should be used to determine this? How can we assure its stability and survival? How can we explain any particular ordering of political relationships at a given time and place and its possible change? It is this last question that became the focus of my present inquiry.

To address this question systematically we found it necessary to clarify what we might mean by structure. This led us to explore its place in explanation and to conclude that it was not a physical entity out there in space and time but a property of things. As such we were led to differentiate behavioral from psychological, cultural and organismic structures. To give content to our meaning of political structure we looked at the variety of structures typically appearing in political inquiry, including formal as well as informal kinds. And, to persuade ourselves that it was worth pursuing an understanding of such structures, we had to develop evidence—not uncontested for some structures, however—that they do have important effects on political life.

To aid us further in defining the meaning of structure and revealing its possible significance, we turned to structuralism, a description of an approach that by its very name showed the privileged place it gave structures. Despite the transparent shortcomings of a structuralist view and the turn, in recent years, toward its virtual antithesis, deconstruction, we found that structuralism did have some unmistakable salvage value. It had seized upon a neglected aspect of social research—the place of the whole context in an understanding of any of the parts. An analysis of what appeared to be a persistent concern for this issue in comparative politics led us to conclude that, in fact, even in this subfield of political science where we might have expected the matter to have been addressed forthrightly, it had been dealt with either intuitively—which at least had the effect of keeping the matter alive—or not at all.

Strangely, as it turned out, one of the few place in which *political* as contrasted with *social* structure in general became a live issue, subject to serious and indeed vigorous if not acrimonious debate, was in Marxist thinking. And since Poulantzas was the first and only Marxist to seek self-consciously to develop a strict theory of politics with particular attention to structure, it seemed appropriate to analyze in detail his interpretation of Marxism, especially from the point of view of the assistance it might give us in understanding variations in regime structures.

As we pursued this long and not uninvolved analytic path we found it useful to distinguish between lower- and higher-order structures, to recognize their hierarchic relationship, and to conclude that this very relationship was really part of a much broader issue—the connection between a political system as a whole and its parts or subsystems. By this point our quest brought into question what almost seemed like a basic operational tenet of empirical science, namely, that parts could be adequately understood without taking into account their position in the whole.

If, however, there is no necessary validity to this assumption, it left us with the further question as to how the whole might be introduced into scientific research without prejudicing the rigorous empirical foundations on which all confirmable inquiry must ultimately rest. Although I was not prepared to offer any solution to the methods that might be appropriate for unpackaging the connections between the overall system structure and its substructures, such as political regimes, our identification, justification, and substantiation of the problem provide the necessary if not inescapable first step.

The Substance

Most political research about political structures, such as those involving parties, interest groups, governmental organizations, and the like, seeks to show their determinants in the sense of necessary and sufficient conditions. The latter are sought in formal prescriptions such as constitutions, in social forces external to the political system itself, such as the economy (command of economic resources, state of industrialization, class conflicts), in culture (attitudes, conventions, historical traditions, values), in society (ethnic, religious, regional and other cleavages, socio-economic status), in the kinds of decisions that are dealt with, in the distribution of political and social power, and so on. These constitute the day-to-day research concerns of political science as a whole. They represent the conventional approach to the search for an understanding of why the forms we see in political life take the shape they do. It is the limitation of this kind of inquiry that I have been calling into question throughout this book.

My argument has been not that such research lacks merit or that it is unnecessary. Far from it. As I have repeatedly affirmed, there can be little question that it does indeed reveal part of the reason why observed structures take the form they do under given spatiotemporal conditions. Thus, we could not hope to be able to understand why the American regime has the shape it has if we did not begin with the intentions of the founding fathers as central actors in the making of a nation and with how, through the Constitution, they sought to provide incentives for behavior that would prevent the domination of government by a single major organ or by the populace itself. Neither would the structure of the British parliamentary system be understandable without attention to the historical conflicts over the Corn Laws and mercantilism and the desire of the emerging middle classes, using the muscle power of the working classes, to displace the landed aristocracy from the seats of political power. Nor could we hope to help explain modern liberal as against social corporatist structures[1] if we did not see their relationship to differential industrial policies followed by various small states. And we could not adequately explore the structures of administrative agencies without relating them to the needs of the clientele, interest group pressures, the professional aspirations of the administrators, and the place of the particular agency in the formal governmental apparatus.

In short, nothing that has been said in this book should be interpreted as denying the appropriateness of conventional substantive studies of observable political structures. Within the limits imposed by the higher-order relationships, a wide range of observed types of lower-level structures is possible. Insofar as political research has been concerned with accounting for variations in these structures, most of it has been invested in seeking out their presumed specific determinants. Research of this kind clearly helps us understand why, among all possible observable structures, certain ones have arisen, changed, or survived.

The only question that I have raised is why, with all the variance in such structures that has been explained, we still find that somehow we have not got an adequate explanation.[2] I have proposed, first, that a major source of this shortcoming lies in the failure to take into account the overall structural context, the higher-order nesting hierarchical structures, within which observable structures operate; and second, that this overall context may at times determine, in an obligative sense, the nature of these observable structures, even though in practice it is more likely just to facilitate or limit them.

In the literature there are, of course, some important exceptions to this neglect of the limits imposed by the very structure of the political system itself. McFarland, for example, distinguishes between critical and routine decisions, clearly groping for a theoretically acceptable way of understanding these limits.[3] Similarly Bachrach and Baratz and Lukes, in talking of the various faces of power, were moving in the same direction, as I have noted.[4] And neo-Marxism, together with contemporary neostatism, are directed toward such basic constraints, as I have observed more than once, even though their historical interpretive methods still leave much to be desired in terms of evidential rigor for purposes of empirical confirmation. From my point of view, to be sure, another of their major shortcomings derives from the fact that they focus only on the broad societal limits rather than on the strictly political ones. Both in neostatism and in the general literature there is little awareness of the need to turn to the effects of the whole political system through which societal structures are themselves refracted.

The reasons for the preeminence of the overall structural context in fleshing out an explanation should now be transparent. To return to the analogy between higher-order structure and gravity, in effect we have hitherto confined our research largely to trying to understand when we leap, how we leap, and why we leap. What we have consistently omitted as a major focal point of research are the immediate forces of gravity that impose ultimate limits on our leaping options and habits.

We seem to know a great deal about why political life takes the various forms it does and how these forms operate to shape political interactions and public policies. But what we still lack is a way of grappling with our forces of gravity, as it were: that is, with the boundaries that may limit the range of possible variation in our lower-order structures and may even serve to determine those structures in an obligative sense or to facilitate behavior. Not only that, but, with some few exceptions already noted, we have not been sufficiently aware of or persuaded about the importance of these boundaries to have sought, on the one hand, to identify and describe them and, on the other, to theorize about them. If we had done so, we would now be better prepared for developing a method for rigorously analyzing them as well as for exploring their relationship to lower-order structures, in a way consistent with our empirical traditions in science.

To change the analogy, if we were to strip a person of all warm clothing and set him "free" in the Arctic wastelands, he would have the sovereign choice to move about as he chooses. He would be free to make rational choices based on his preference schedules. The subject reigns supreme. The basic interest in survival would provide him with a good incentive to behave rationally and to repeat those movements that seem to reward him most, such as running to keep warm, building cold-resistant igloos, preferring sun to shade, hunting animals for food and clothing, and so on.

We might perhaps be able to explain his behavior through a rational-choice model, at least at this one level of explanation. But there would still be an unanswered question: Who stripped him of his warm clothing in the first place and let him loose in the hostile environment? Who fixed the overall structure, composed of the ecological and social conditions, under which this person was "free" to operate as he chose? If, indeed, the range of options is already limited by a prior structuring of his context of operations, neglect of this context would clearly lead to the omission of a significant explanatory factor. The rational model of inquiry, or any other model that limits itself to the observed elements in the situation in which actors find themselves, is adequate only as long as we accept as givens the outer limits of the constraints under which the actor operates. Hence the need to inquire, systematically and not just episodically, into these outer limits, especially the important one that we have established as the overall structure of the political system. In the illustration, because of its simplicity, the importance of the givens is transparent. For the political system at large, because of its complexity, the givens are more likely to be comfortably set aside, assumed, or even forgotten.

Furthermore, what has seldom been recognized explicitly is that a higher-order structure such as this, despite our hierarchic imagery, is really "neither above, nor in addition to, its part, but *is* its parts in systematic interconnection."[5] This hierarchic image, it will be recalled, referred to a nesting relationship, not a command ranking. The higher order so conceived is the whole system that is no more than its parts viewed in their "systematic interconnection."

The whole so created has properties that cannot be inferred from knowledge about the parts and does not represent some kind of summation of such parts. Stability, ease of change, levels of performance, feedback, character of conversion processes, and the like are properties of the political system as a complex set of interdependent relationships and not of any of its parts alone. And just as all parts in their interconnect-edness generate properties arising from these interconnections, so they have consequences for the structural parts of the system that cannot be understood by reference to those very parts alone and their immediate determinants. These consequences need to be traced back to the system viewed as a complex entity.

The Methods

It is one thing to recognize the possible existence of higher-order structures and their likely influence on lower-order ones and, thereby, on the disposition of political power in a political system and on control over outputs (public policies). It is quite another thing, we have seen, to be able to identify a research technology that will permit us not only to describe this higher-order structure but to trace out the ways in which it facilitates, determines, or limits lower-order ones.

A specific set of methods needs yet to be devised. Their purpose, however, ought not to be to continue decomposing the interconnection among the parts of the complex political structure for separate and detailed study; that we already have and will continue to have and to benefit from, as already discussed. Rather, we need instruction on how to detect specifically the way in which the structure of the political system, taken as a complex whole, facilitates, determines, or limits the range of alternative patterns of relationships open to a constituent element, whether that element itself be a structural unit, a set of specific relationships among such units, or a pattern of action in which such units engage, all of which are embraced in the concept *regime structure*. In failing to produce reliable procedures for such analyses, we will abandon the field to those who, lacking more rigorous alternative, are forced to rely on the impressionism of Weberian interpretive analysis,[6] a stage in the shift away from nineteenth-century *Kulturwissenschaft* out of which we have only recently escaped.

At the outset I had indicated that although I hoped to be able to establish the undeniable presence and importance of the overall system structures, I would not be able to provide a rigorous set of methods for determining their influence. This is not incomprehensible, nor ought it to be discouraging. Since Descartes, at least, decompositional analysis has been the name of the game in the pursuit of knowledge. We have had at least three hundred years of effort devoted to solving the problems attending the use of decompositional methods. Relatively few years have been spent in exploring methodologically rigorous means for looking at wholes, discovering the properties they give rise to which cannot be inferred from their parts, and isolating the specific influence on their parts. In the last quarter-century or more there has been considerable debate over the so-called holistic as against individualistic methods. But most of this debate has been just that: statements of philosophical positions, intellectual posturing, rather than efforts to work out a set of methods for taking the whole systematically and rigorously into account, according to accepted canons of scientific inquiry. Little wonder at the complaint that "the rhetoric of totality . . . is the object of a kind of instinctive or automatic denunciation by just about everybody."[7]

It is apparent that this book adds another rhetorical element to that debate, and that is not unintended. But I have sought to go further. I have attempted to clear away some of the conceptual underbrush, with regard to overarching structures, which has seemed to be concealing the nature of the problem in political science. Without improved conceptual clarity, the problem remains that much less open to solution through the necessary methodological innovations.

The part-whole puzzle has been with us for centuries, during which time its resolution, through decomposition, has been repeatedly attempted. The critical point is that we tend to ignore the higher-order structure if only because of the difficulty of discovering a way of coping with it, one that is compatible with the decompositional and reductionist research technology that our civilization has refined (and appropriately so, given the undeniable success it has had in both the natural and social sciences). The time has surely come, I have been proposing, not only to recognize its limitations but to concentrate our theoretical and technical resources on a search for alternative methods, and not only *not* to shy away from the issue because of the inadequacies of our current methods, but for this very reason to deal with it head-on. To do otherwise is to leave the field to those who see the significance of the issue but who would slip away from the demanding canons of scientific inquiry. Only when we have devised the means for reliably explaining and understanding the ways in which such structures limit our capacities for action will we be in a position to control or overcome them for the better attainment of our social and political goals.

The Present against the Future

Many years ago, when I first began to sketch out a theoretical framework for the analysis of political life, the intellectual context was very hospitable for such an enterprise. Within scholarship the pursuit of reliable understanding through the methods of science was beginning to establish itself as a fundamental assumption of research. Outside academia the social issues were troubling—the cold war among nations and the cold war, as evidenced by McCarthyism, within. But there seemed many sensible ways out. At least enough people were still optimistic that we could reconstruct our future and that indeed the world had a future.

As the 1990s begin, all these assumptions have been brought into question. The methods of science for the study of human behavior have on more than one occasion been declared dead, although strangely they have refused to accept this fate. Instead, their assumptions and justifications have undergone a number of needed modifications and transformations. The future of the world at large has itself been called into question. Even if we were to learn how to cope with the end of the cold war and the outbreak of a possible enduring international peace among nations, globally we confront equally threatening issues of environmental pollution, the greenhouse effect, and the perilous conditions of global maldistribution of wealth and resources.

To surmount these new crises may require extraordinary efforts of global purpose and cooperation which neither our nationally oriented will nor our nationally centered and overspecialized social science knowledge have had to cope with before. In short, the world faces crises the proportions of which it has never had to confront, with an international political structure fundamentally at odds with the global nature of the issues and their solutions.

One may well ask: What room is left for the continuation of the search for basic knowledge of the sort I have been pursuing in this book? Ought we not to be concentrating all our intellectual energies and resources on the immediate solution of these crises? Ought we not to devote ourselves to spending whatever intellectual capital we have hitherto accumulated in the form of fundamental knowledge and understanding? Ought we not to leave to future generations the task of restoring this capital accumulation, when our global future is more secure?

In face of a compelling argument such as is implied in the very way these questions are posed, in the present book I have in effect still held out, as I have in the past, for the need to discount the future somewhat less heavily. Despite the perils that we clearly face as we move toward the twenty-first century, there is good reason to devote at least a small part of our intellectual resources as a hedge for the future. If the world does manage to cope successfully with its present lumbering toward environmental self-destruction, there will be greater need than ever before, in the even more complex global society that is clearly emerging, for a deeper and richer understanding of the nature of political life, what makes it work in the way it does, and the nature of constraints on its transformation. In particular, we will require new kinds of political structures, domestically and internationally (if that division continues to make future sense), to address the new needs for cooperation and participation in global decision-making. In other words, there is not only room for but a continuing need for an understanding of how we are to go about generating the kind of basic knowledge about politics that will be even more important than ever before.

It may seem appalling that the times call upon us to explain the necessity for a continuing interest in fundamentals. It only serves to reveal the crisis state of mind of contemporary society and within it, the unfortunate state-of-siege mentality forced upon long-range scholarship. The saving factor, however, is, as I have noted elsewhere, that apparently fundamental understanding may frequently and unexpectedly turn out to have a direct bearing on important short-run social issues.[9]

In this vein, then, I have not dealt here with immediate policy issues—how we are to surmount our present critical problems to achieve a more certain future. Much less have I sought to advance such issues as criteria by which to determine the selection of research foci. I have assumed, rather, that there is still room for at least some few scholars to continue the pursuit of basic knowledge. There the problems for inquiry are set by the logic of the state of our understanding, that is, by the problems that theory dictates as requiring attention, not necessarily by the pressing and urgent issues of the day. In the disposition of time and effort in the social sciences, it would seem to be the height of wisdom for at least a small proportion of our human and material resources to be devoted to the continued accumulation of such basic knowledge. This book, as an attempt to cut a new path for a basic understanding of the nature and determinants of political structure, has been offered in that spirit.

Notes

Chapter 1

1. See D. Easton, *A Framework for Political Analysis* (Englewood Cliffs: Prentice Hall, 1965); reissued, University of Chicago Press, 1979 and *A Systems Analysis of Political Life* (New York: Wiley, 1965); reissued, University of Chicago Press, 1979.

2. "Contemporary political theory [rational actor theory?] is probably overly sanguine about the possibilities for a theory of politics that ignores political institutions." In J. G. March and J. P. Olsen, "The New Institutionalism: Organizational Factors in Political Life," 78 *American Political Science Review* (1985) 734–48 at p. 742.

3. See P. Bachrach and M. S. Baratz, *Power and Poverty: Theory and Practice* (New York: Oxford University Press, 1970); P. Bachrach, *The Theory of Democratic Elitism* (Boston: Little, Brown, 1967); and S. Lukes, *Power: A Radical View* (London: Macmillan, 1974).

4. See my article "Political Science in the United States: Past and Present," 6 *International Political Science Review* (1985) 133–52.

5. My cautious way of putting this, saying that the subject matter is put in terms of the state, reflects my own reservations about the state as a broad orienting concept for research. I shall return to this later.

6. For this term see G. Almond, "The Return to the State" (Stanford University, 1987, in manuscript). Compare it with my earlier paper, "The Political System Besieged by the State," 9 *Political Theory* (1981) 303–26. I use the term in this present context to refer to all those in the 1980s who have revived the state as a central orienting concept with regard to the internal analysis of political systems. As my paper points out, they range from Marxists and neo-Marxists to archconservatives who would drive out any and all state interference with society.

7. See S. G. McNall, "On Contemporary Social Theory," 13 *The American Sociologist* (1978) 2–5.

8. This has led to the emergence of a new discipline, the cognitive sciences.

9. See the very important book by S. Rosenberg, *Ideology, Reason and Politics* (Princeton, N.J.: Princeton University Press, 1988), as well as D. Graber, *Processing the News* (New York: Longman 1984) and R. Lau and D. Sears (eds.), *Political Cognition* (1986). Rosenberg makes the point that actors are not rational in a uniform way. They use different modes for reasoning about things, which Rosenberg identifies as sequential, linear, and systematic. Regardless of the acceptability of this classification, the point is that the means-end form of reasoning built into the economic model of the rational actor is probably only one of the types found in the real world. Of course, this is no answer to those positive economists who see the rational actor only as a useful model for understanding the real word, not as a representation of it. See my next note.

10. Not all proponents of rational modeling formally accept the conformity of behavior to the model. For some, particularly those in economics from whom the model was, of course, borrowed, the rational choice model is only a norm, the way people would behave if they were indeed rational. Behavior may in fact deviate from this norm and if so, in this so-called positive theory of economics, the deviance needs to be explained. See the classical statement of this position in M. Friedman, *Essays in Positive Economics* (Chicago: University of Chicago Press, 1953).

11. See P. B. Evans, D. Rueschemeyer, and T. Skocpol (eds.). *Bringing the State Back In* (Cambridge: Cambridge University Press, 1985).

12. See especially the work of Otto v. Gierke and F. W. Maitland, who made the case for the

consideration of groups as "real personalities" with wills and minds as concrete as those of individuals and separate from their constituent individuals. When this was transformed into legal doctrine it meant that groups and associations could have the same rights and obligations as individuals, could enter into contracts, sue and be sued, etc. This thinking about the prior existence of groups formed the basis for twentieth-century pluralism. Compare this approach with J. Coleman, *Power and the Structure of Society* (New York: W. W. Norton, 1974), who discusses the emergence of the "juristic person" or corporate actor as a major locus of power in modern society, displacing the concrete agent as occupant of corporate roles.

13.   See, for example, J. E. Toews, "Intellectual History after the Linguistic Turn: The Autonomy of Meaning and the Irreducibility of Experience," 92 *American Historical Review* (1987) 897–907.

14.   We find a very early and virtually ignored warning along these lines in M. Fainsod, "Some Reflections on the Nature of the Regulatory Process," in C. J. Friedrich and E. S. Mason (eds.), *Public Policy* (Cambridge, Mass.: Harvard University Press, 1940). For later references to the institutional and other constraints within which plural groups must operate and must therefore be constrained, see the notion of critical decisions in A. S. McFarland, *Power and Leadership in Pluralist Systems* (Stanford: Stanford University Press, 1969).

15.   See J. G. March and J. P. Olsen, *op. cit.*; and K. A. Shepsle, "Studying Institutions: Some Lessons from the Rational Choice Approach," 1 *Journal of Theoretical Politics* (1989) 131–47.

16.   See C. H. Achen, "Toward Theories of Data: The State of Political Methodology," in A. Finifter (ed.), *Political Science: The State of the Discipline* (Washington, D.C.: American Political Science Association, 1982) 68–93; and a doctoral dissertation at the University of California, Irvine, by D. M. Eagles, "An Ecological Perspective on Working-Class Politics: Neighborhoods and Class Formation in Sheffield, England" (1986). See particularly the extensive bibliography on contextual analysis in that thesis.

17.   Compare: "The problem of agency is the problem of finding a way of accounting for human experience which recognizes simultaneously and in equal measure that history and society are made by constant and more or less purposeful individual action *and* that individual action, however purposeful, is made by history and society. How do we, as active subjects make a world of objects which then, as it were, become subjects making us their objects? It is the problem of individual and society, consciousness and being, action and structure; a problem to which the voices of everyday life speak as loudly as those of scholars." P. Abrams, *Historical Sociology* (Somerset, England: Open Books, 1982) pp. xiii–xiv. See also contemporary neo-Marxism and those influenced by it who have turned to the history of capitalism and the development of the modern state for a theoretical approach to an understanding of the present. Representative of this turn to history is of course the seminal work of Ferdinand Braudel and the *Annales* school in France and the research of the many who have been inspired by him.

18.   See my book *The Political System: An Inquiry into the State of Political Science* (New York: Knopf, 1953; 2d ed., 1971; reissued, Chicago: University of Chicago Press, 1981) and "The Political System Besieged by the State."

19.   *Ibid.*, and *A Framework for Political Analysis.*

20.   See E. A. Nordlinger, *On the Autonomy of the Democratic State* (Cambridge: Harvard University Press, 1981). This revision of state theory has arisen largely as a response to the general policy analysis movement in social research; see the suggestive article by D. A. Gold, C. G. H. Lo, and E. O. Wright, "Recent Development in Marxist Theories of the Capitalist State," 27 *Monthly Review* (1975) part 1, pp. 29–43; part 2, pp. 44–51.

21.   See V. O. Key, Jr., *Politics, Parties and Pressure Groups* (New York: Crowell, 1958) 4th ed. Chapter 25 is entitled "Administration as Politics," with one of the subheads reading "Administrative Agencies: Actors in the Political Process." See also J. D. Kingsley, *Representative Bureaucracy* (Yellow Springs, Ohio: Antioch Press, 1944).

22.   As we shall see in later chapters on Nicos Poulantzas, he elaborates fully on this point.

23.   In chapter 5 I shall raise some questions about the validity of this assertion, at least if it stands without qualification.

24.   See *A Systems Analysis of Political Life*, chapter 12. For further discussion of regime structure, see chapters 5 and 18 below.

25.   See *A Systems Analysis of Political Life*, p. 193.

26. *Ibid.*, p. 210.

27. See chapter 8.

28. Relationships that will be explicitly examined in chapter 18.

Chapter 2

1. *Institutions, organizations,* and *structure* are competitive terms (see my later discussion of them) in the sense that they are at times used synonymously and at others with substantially different meanings. Outside of political science there is a sizeable literature which seeks to show the relationship among these terms. For the moment I shall avoid engaging in the debate over the appropriate terminology, especially as the literature is replete with such discussions. Rather, I shall simply define my usage of structure as we move along and come back to this terminological problem in a later chapter.

2. With one of which I shall deal at length, namely, the neo-Marxist, Nicos Poulantzas. As I suggested in the preceding chapter, he is a major, if unrecognized, intellectual source of what limited theoretical interest political science has shown in structure.

3. See B. Barry and R. Hardin, *Rational Man and Irrational Society* (Beverly Hills: Sage, 1982); K. Monroe, *et al., op. cit.*; J. G. March and J. P. Oleson, *op. cit.*, and their bibliography.

4. See for example, D. E. Apter, *The Politics of Modernization* (Chicago: University of Chicago Press, 1965); F. W. Riggs, "The Comparison of Whole Political Systems," in R. T. Holt and J. Turner (eds.), *The Methodology of Comparative Research* (Glencoe, Ill.: The Free Press, 1970) pp. 73–121.

5. As one essay puts the matter, "That a society's institutions usually have a critical role in structuring the actions of its citizens would appear so obvious a point as to require no elucidation. In fact, in some respects, institutions can be said to occupy the kind of position of centrality in the research of social scientists as natural and physical phenomena occupy in the investigations of physical and biological scientists. Nonetheless . . . one casualty in the study of newer societies has been institutional analysis." A. Kornberg and S. M. Hines, Jr., "Legislatures and Modernization of Societies," 5 *Comparative Political Studies* (1973) 471–91 at p. 476. There is some basic discussion, of course, as in H. Eckstein and D. E. Apter, *Comparative Politics: A Reader* (Glencoe, Ill.: The Free Press, 1963) and D. E. Apter, *op. cit.*, but these are notable exceptions. And of course there is, most recently, the "new institutionalism" mentioned in the preceding chapter, about the relevance of which to structure, however, much more will be said later.

6. The same holds true for the later multivolume *Handbook of Political Science* by F. I. Greenstein and N. W. Polsby (eds.), (Reading, Mass.: Addison-Wesley, 1975) and for the more recent *Blackwell Encyclopaedia of Political Institutions* (Oxford: Blackwell, 1987) by V. Bogdnor (ed.).

7. See E. R. Leach, "Social Structure: The History of the Concept," in D. L. Sills (ed.), *The International Encyclopedia of the Social Sciences*, 2nd ed., (New York: The Free Press, 1968) vol. 14, pp. 482–89.

8. R. Boudon, *The Uses of Structuralism* (London: Heinemann, 1971) p. 1.

9. See the writings of T. Woolsey, J. W. Burgess, and W. W. Willoughby.

10. This was clear in the very title of E. R. Bentley's book *The Process of Government*. This continued to be true even as the behavioral movement got under way, as in the title of D. B. Truman's widely read book *The Governmental Process*. See also the emphasis on process in B. M. Gross, "Political Process," in the *International Encyclopedia of the Social Sciences*, vol. 12, pp. 265–73.

11. During the 1950s I recall Bernard Berelson, then head of the newly established Division of the Behavioral Sciences of the Ford Foundation, questioning me, with a puzzled note in his voice, as to why political scientists typically spoke about *the* political process, a question I continue to find difficult to answer to my own satisfaction, except on grounds of received usage.

12. T. S. Kuhn, *The Structure of Scientific Revolutions* (Chicago: University of Chicago Press, 1963).

13. See M. Lane, "Introduction," in M. Lane (ed.), *Structuralism: A Reader* (London: Jonathan Cape, 1970) pp. 11–42.

14. See R. T. de George and F. M. de George (eds.), *The Structuralists: From Marx to Levi-Strauss* (New York: Doubleday, 1972).

15. See M. Lane, *op. cit.*

16. Even in Europe, where there was a heightened awareness of the need to examine the conditions that structure politics, as I have noted, inexplicably there was only the occasional student of politics, aside from the structural Marxists, who even sought to apply structuralism to political phenomena. Note the marked absence of political scientists in the extensive bibliography prepared by J. Viet, *Les sciences de l'homme en France* (The Hague: Mouton, 1966).

17. J. Piaget, *Structuralism* (London: Routledge and Kegan Paul, 1971) p. 136.

18. See D. Easton and J. Dennis, *Children in the Political System* (New York: McGraw-Hill, 1969), esp. chapter 14.

19. See C. Reich, *The Greening of America* (New York: Random House, 1970).

20. J. S. Coleman, *Power and the Structure of Society*.

21. See T. Gitlin, *The Sixties: Years of Hope, Days of Rage* (New York: Bantam Books, 1987).

22. See R. A. Dahl, *A Preface to Economic Democracy* (Berkeley: University of California Press, 1985) and C. E. Lindblom, *Politics and Markets* (New York: Basic Books, 1977).

23. See P. L. Bergner and T. Luckman, *The Social Construction of Reality* (New York: Anchor, 1967). A similar point, of course, had been made by T. S. Kuhn, *op. cit.*, just as the vitalist philosopher Henri Bergson had much earlier proclaimed the distortion of reality to be found in every effort at conceptualization. Even earlier, Nietzsche had already inveighed against attempts at achieving "immaculate perception". The roots of phenomenology and their application to social phenomena descend deep into our intellectual heritage.

24. As I indicated earlier, the other two comings refer to the very limited reception of Marx's writings during his own lifetime and the far greater utilization of Marxism during the Great Depression of the 1930s.

25. See P. Bachrach, *The Theory of Democratic Elitism: A Technique* (Boston: Little, Brown, 1967) and K. Prewitt and A. Stone, *The Ruling Elites: Elite Theory, Power and American Democracy* (New York: Harper, 1973).

26. As we will recall from the preceding chapter, however, the structural tendency did not have the field to itself; it was quickly modified by efforts to discover a subjective element in political processes, as in the plea to return the "state," to a central position of analysis, with the state as an actor having a direct effect on political policy independent of the society by which it was shaped. Later, when we have occasion to look at ethnomethodological conceptions of structure, we will confront a different kind of return to the individual subject.

27. For the use of these terms in a similar sense, see M. Glucksmann, *Structuralist Analysis in Contemporary Social Thought: A Comparison of the Theories of Claude Lévi-Strauss and Louis Althusser* (London: Routledge and Kegan Paul, 1974) p. 45. See also chapter 4 below.

Chapter 3

1. In chapters 6 and 7 I shall return to this question, as to whether political structures do indeed have effects. There is greater questioning of this assumption than might be apparent at first glance.

2. For a similar point of view see A. Giddens, "Agency, Institutions and Time-Space Analysis," in K. Knorr-Cetina and A. V. Circourel (eds.), *Advance in Social Theory and Methodology* (London: Routledge and Kegan Paul, 1981) pp. 161–74.

3. See P. C. Schwartz and S. K. Schwartz (eds.), *New Directions in Political Socialization* (Glencoe, Ill.: Free Press, 1975) p. 10. See also J. N. Knutson (ed.), *Handbook of Political Psychology* (San Francisco: Jossey-Bass, 1973) and extensive bibliographies there; F. I. Greenstein, "Personality and Politics," in F. I. Greenstein and N. Polsby, *op. cit.*, vol. 2, pp. 1–92; and of course the classic work of Graham Wallas and Harold D. Lasswell in this area.

4. G. H. Mead, *Mind, Self and Society* (Chicago: University of Chicago Press, 1962) p. 223, n.25.

5. T. Parsons, *Societies: Evolutionary and Comparative* (Englewood Cliffs, N.J.: Prentice-Hall, 1966) p. 7; italics in original.

6. See R. C. Tucker, "The Georges' Wilson Reconsidered: An Essay on Autobiography," 61 *American Political Science Review* (1967) 606–18.

7. But see the attempt to give systematic meaning to it by L. W. Pye, "Political Culture," in

International Encyclopedia of the Social Sciences, 2d ed., vol. 12, pp. 218–24 at p. 218; and H. Eckstein, "A Culturalist Theory of Political Change," 82 *American Political Science Review* (1988) 789–804.

8. L. Pye, "Political Culture," *International Encyclopedia of the Social Sciences*, 2d ed., vol. 12, pp. 218–24 at p. 224. Similarly, Verba seeks to distinguish between beliefs on the one side and structure on the other when he points out that "our interest in this volume was to look beyond the structures of politics to the beliefs that affect the ways in which people act within these political institutions." S. Verba, "Comparative Political Culture," in L. Pye and S. Verba, *Political Culture and Political Development* (Princeton, N.J.: Princeton University Press, 1965). In the same vein, Almond and Powell see the patterned activities which constitute political roles as structure with the legal rules and ideal norms as their determinants. See G. A. Almond and G. B. Powell, *System, Process and Policy, Comparative Politics* (Boston: Little, Brown, 1978), 2d ed.

9. For the most recent literature, see E. O. Wilson, *Sociobiology: The New Synthesis* (Cambridge: Harvard University Press, 1975); T. C. Wiegele, *Biopolitics: The Search for a More Human Political Science* (Boulder, Colo.: Westview, 1979); T. C. Wiegele (ed.), *Biology and the Social Sciences* (Boulder, Colorado: Westview, 1982); A. Somit, S. A. Peterson, W. O. Richardson, and D. S. Goldfischer, *The Literature of Biopolitics* (Northern Illinois University, Center for Biopolitical Research, 1980); A. Rosenberg, *Sociobiology and the Preemption of Social Science* (Baltimore: Johns Hopkins University Press, 1980); A. Somit (ed.), *Biology and Politics: Recent Explorations* (Paris: Maison des sciences de l'homme et Maison Mouton, 1976); and the journal of *Politics and the Life Sciences*.

10. See, for example, an early statement of this in B. Tursky, M. Lodge, and D. Cross, "A Bio-Behavioral Framework for the Analysis of Political Behavior," in A. Somit (ed.), *op. cit.*, pp. 59–96, which argues for "a bio-behavioral approach to the evaluation of the cognitive and evaluative components of political attitudes" (p. 59). In the same book see also D. C. Schwartz, "Somatic States and Political Behavior: An Interpretation and Empirical Extension of Biopolitics" (pp. 15–44).

11. See E. O. Wilson, *op. cit.*; R. Masters, *The Nature of Politics* (New Haven: Yale University Press, 1989). It should be noted that the field of biopolitics has broadened out from its initial base as described here and now includes the study of policy in the area of biotechnology, biomedicine, and health, and includes as well the study of evolution as it impinges on our conception of the biological nature of human beings.

12. For a discussion of the ontological status of structure, see R. Grafstein, "The Legitimacy of Political Institutions," 14 *Polity* (1981) 5–20; "Structure and Structuralism," 63 *Social Science Quarterly* (1982) 617–33. See also B. H. Mayhew, "Structuralism and Ontology," 63 *Social Science Quarterly* (1982) 634–39.

13. In *A Framework for Political Analysis* I sought to show the influence of social structure, general culture, general personality, etc., on the political system. It is clear that there I was directing my attention to systems in the environment of the political system. Here I am looking at comparable kinds of (sub)systems which are usefully viewed as being internal to the political system, that is, within it, not outside of it, in its environment. An understanding of the relationship between environmental and internal systems—that is, between the general culture and the political culture, for example—is vital, of course, but not central to our concerns at the moment.

14. Compare with M. J. Levy, Jr., *The Structure of Society* (Princeton, N.J.: Princeton University Press, 1952), p. 88.

15. See my reference in chapter 6, note 27, to this early work by A. Bavelas, who experimented on the effect of different forms of relationships on various aspects of communications.

16. See my discussion of the empirical nature of analytic properties in *A Framework for Political Analysis* (Chicago: University of Chicago Press, 1979), first published in 1965.

17. J. G. Miller, *Living Systems* (New York: McGraw-Hill, 1978) p. 22; italics in original. See also Miller's statement that "structure is the static arrangement of a system's parts at a moment in three-dimensional space." J. G. Miller, "Living System's Basic Parts," in 10 *Behavioral Science* (1965) 193–237 at p. 211. Perhaps a theoretically more appropriate way of putting this might be that structure is indeed a "static arrangement" but that it is only a property of "a system's parts at a moment in three-dimensional space."

18. The term institutions is used here loosely. For problems with its usage, see chapter 4 below.

19. See D. E. Apter, *op. cit.* and his article "Government" in *International Encyclopedia of the Social Sciences*, 2d ed., vol. 6, pp. 214–29.

20. For an effort to make a similar distinction, see A. Giddens , "Agency, Institution and Time-Space Analysis," in K. Knorr-Cetina and A. V. Cicourel, *Advances in Social Theory and Methodology*.

21. See M. Glucksmann, *Structuralist Analysis in Contemporary Social Thought*, p. 15.

22. *Ibid.* and E. R. Leach, "The History of the Concept," *International Encyclopedia of the Social Sciences*" 2d ed., vol. 14, pp. 482–89.

23. See A. Leighton, *My Name Is Legion: Foundations for a Theory of Man in Relation to Culture* (New York: Basic Books, 1959), pp. 221–22; cited in J. G. Miller, *op. cit.*, p. 23.

24. A. Leighton, *op. cit.*

25. *Ibid.*

26. *Ibid.*

27. We must recognize, however, that behavior has structure in another sense, one that is recognized by both natural and social scientists. This structure is an aspect of the behavior of objects over time. History may have patterns—cycles, stages, fluctuations, trajectories, such as progress or decline, and so forth. In this respect, however, it is equally impossible to separate structure from behavior over time or historical process. The one is but a property of the other.

Chapter 4

1. See my book *A Systems Analysis of Political Life*, *passim*.

2. Radcliffe-Brown, *Natural Science of Society*, quoted in T. Bottomore and R. Nisbet (eds.), *A History of Sociological Analysis* (New York: Basic Books, 1978) p. 576; italics in original.

3. See J. Viet, *Les méthodes structuralistes dans les sciences sociales*.

4. A. L. Kroeber, *Anthropology* (New York: Harcourt, Brace, 1948), revised edition, quoted in C. Lévi-Strauss, *Structural Anthropology* (Garden City, N.Y.: Doubleday, 1967) p. 270, and in R. Boudon, *The Uses of Structuralism* (London: Heinemann, 1971), first English edition, p. 11–12.

5. R. Boudon, *op. cit.*, p. 3.

6. See *ibid.*, p. 7ff.

7. See F. E. Emery, *Systems Thinking* (Middlesex, England: Penguin, 1969) and D. Easton, *A Framework for Political Analysis*.

8. R. Boudon, *op. cit.*, p. 16; italics added.

9. *Ibid.*, p. 133. Compare with J. Piaget, *Structuralism* (New York: Basic Books, 1970) and W. G. Runciman, *Sociology in Its Place* (Cambridge: Cambridge University Press, 1970), chapter 2, who seem to share his view. As elsewhere in this book, I am here using the term *structuralist analysis* in a special sense to be distinguished from *structural* analysis, as indicated at the end of chapter 2 above.

10. "Therefore, social structure cannot claim a field of its own among others in the social studies. It is rather a method to be applied to any kind of social studies, similar to the structural analysis current in other disciplines." C. Lévi-Strauss, *Structural Anthropology* (Garden City, N.Y.: Doubleday, 1967) p. 271.

11. I shall return to structuralism in chapter 8.

12. See P. Bachrach and M. Baratz, *op. cit.*; S. Lukes, *op. cit.*; and A. S. McFarland, *op. cit.*

13. S. F. Nadel, *The Theory of Social Structure* (Glencoe, Ill.: Free Press, 1958) p. 8. He also points out that "in describing structure we abstract relational features from the totality of perceived data, ignoring all that is not 'order' or 'arrangement'; in brief, we define the positions relative to one another of the component parts." P. 7.

14. P. M. Blau (ed.), *Approaches to the Study of Social Structure* (New York: Free Press, 1975) p. 3. But compare this with another view of social structure that he presents: "a multidimensional space of social positions among which a population is distributed; its complexity has been defined as the great number of different positions and the wide distributions of people among them." *Inequality and Heterogeneity: A Positive Theory of Social Structure* (New York: Free Press, 1977) p. 247.

15. C. Lévi-Strauss, *op. cit.*, p. 271. It should be noted that at the same time that Lévi-Strauss speaks of structure as a model, he claims it is "a method to be applied to any kind of social studies" (p. 271). Clearly, he seems to think that a model is a method rather than a theory!

16. *Ibid.*

17. See chapter 2 for the source of these terms.

18. In chapter 18 I shall look at the facilitative aspect of structure.

19. Quoted from R. W. Ashby in R. Lilienfeld, *The Rise of Systems Theory* (New York: Wiley, 1978) p. 48; italics in original. Compare with A. S. McFarland, *op. cit.*, chapter 7, esp. p. 128.

20. Although Walter Bagehot thought that France just about reached that point during the period of the Paris Commune; and Lebanon seemed to be there during the 1980s.

21. See P. M. Blau, *Equality and Heterogeneity: A Primitive Theory of Social Structure* (New York: Free Press, 1977). There he argues that showing the effects of the parts of a structure on behavior should not be counted as the study of structural effects. Structural effects should be reserved for the consequences of the patterns made by the part. Also see chapter 6 below for the further development of this thought.

22. K. P. Langton and R. Rapoport, "Social Structure, Social Context and Partisan Mobilization: Urban Workers in Chile," 8 *Comparative Political Studies* (1975) 318–44 at p. 318; italics added.

23. See P. M. Blau, "Parameters of Social Structure," in P. M. Blau (ed.), *Approaches to the Study of Social Structure* (New York: Free Press, 1975) pp. 220–54; and P. M. Blau, *Inequality and Heterogeneity: A Primitive Theory of Social Structure* esp. p. 1.

24. Compare: "Patterns of belief . . . may be termed latent cultural structures, e.g., the belief in luck, rather than 'hard work', as the vehicle for upward mobility." A. W. Gouldner, "Some Observations on Systematic Theory: 1945–55," in *Sociology in the U.S.A.* (Paris: United Nations Educational, Scientific and Cultural Organization, 1956) 34–42 at p. 40.

25. For a contrary point of view, one that interprets what I am calling the structure of culture as the core of social structure, see O. and J. M. Collins, *Interaction and Social Structure* (The Hague: Mouton, 1973). In that book they argue that structure, meaning social structure, "does not apply to actual interaction. It applies, rather, to the governance of the interaction. Echoing Piaget, Von Neumann says 'the game is the rules.' . . . All cultures must 'guide' or 'map' the interactions of persons. We are not here talking about a separate 'part' of culture. We are, rather, talking about the manner in which a culture relates actors one to another. . . . It is this special functioning of culture which anthropologists and sociologists have increasingly in mind when they have talked about 'social structure'"(p. 140) "By way of summary, over the last century the use of the term 'social structure' has emerged as denoting the ordering of interpersonal relations in a culture"(p. 147). In short, the structure of culture as represented through rules appears to be social structure; social interactions are social phenomena reflecting those rules, that is, reflecting the social structure. See the next note for a different interpretation of rules which sees them as determinants of social structure rather than as constitutive of the latter.

26. It may not be self-evident that, in a strict construction of the term, rules are not behavior but rather norms which behavior may or may not follow. They are different from those regularities of behavior which may at times be described as rule-governed behavior. Thus: "Does 'rule' ever refer to bodily behavior? Behavior can exhibit rules by being in accordance with them, behavior can show rules in actions, and so forth. But does the word refer directly to any bodily actions? I think not. . . . Behavior expresses, exhibits, is directed by rules, among other things, and the fact that such relations are necessarily introduced to describe connection between rules and behavior points to a relation between two distinct things." J. F Ganz, *Rules: A Systematic Study* (The Hague: Mouton, 1971) p. 14. Also: "Scholars agree that rules are followable. . . . Not only are rules followable, but those who are knowledgeable of a rule also know that they can be held accountable if they break it. Like followability, prescriptiveness is a characteristic of rules. . . . Prescriptiveness is another means of distinguishing rules from scientific laws. Prescriptiveness implies that something should happen and that a deviation from this behavior is subject to evaluation." S. B. Shimanoff, *Communication Rules: Theory and Research* (Beverly Hills, California: Sage, 1980) pp. 40–41. See below, in chapter 16, for further discussion of rules and structure.

27. See J. L. Wahlke, H. Eulau, W. Buchanan and L. C. Ferguson, *The Legislative System* (New York: Wiley, 1962).

28.   *Cf.*: "Microsociological theory seeks to explain human relations in terms of the psychological and social processes underlying them, such as processes of symbolic communication, of competition and cooperation, of social exchange. Its focus is on the social processes that shape the interpersonal relations of individuals in a social structure, which is conceptualized as a configuration or network of social relations among individuals." P. M. Blau, *Inequality and Heterogeneity*, p. 2.

29.   G. C. Homans, *Social Behavior: Its Elementary Forms* (New York: Harcourt Brace, 1961) and S.R. Waldman, *Foundations of Political Action* (Boston: Little, Brown, 1972).

30.   *Cf.* P. M. Blau and R. W. Scott, *Formal Organizations* (San Francisco: Chandler, 1962) p. 14.

31.   See R. Firth, *Elements of Social Organization* (London: Watts, 1951).

32.   J. G. March and J. P. Olsen, "The New Institutionalism: Organizational Factors in Political Life," 78 *American Political Science Review* (1984) 734–49; and by the same authors, "Popular Sovereignty and the Search for Appropriate Institutions," Manuscript, September 1986; E. Ostrom, "An Agenda for the Study of Institutions," 48 *Public Choice* (1986) 3–23; E. Ostrom, "A Method of Institutional Analysis," in F. X. Kaufmann, G. Majone, and V. Ostrom (eds.), *Guidance, Control and Performance Evaluation in the Public Sector* (New York: de Gruyter, 1985) pp. 459–78; V. Ostrom, "A Forgotten Tradition: The Constitutional Level of Analysis," in J. A. Gillespie and D. A. Zinnes (eds.), *Missing Elements in Political Inquiry: Logic and Levels of Analysis* (Beverly Hills: Sage, 1982) pp. 237–52; K. A. Shepsle, "The Role of Institutional Structure in the Creation of Policy Equilibrium," in D. W. Rae and T. J. Eismeier (eds.), *Public Policy and Public Choice* (Beverly Hills: Sage, 1979) pp. 249–83; K. A. Shepsle, "The Positive Theory of Legislative Institutions: An Enrichment of Social Choice and Spatial Models," 50 *Public Choice* (1986) 135–79; K. A. Shepsle, "Studying Institutions: Some Lessons from the Rational Choice Approach," 1 *Journal of Theoretical Politics* (1989) 131–47; K. A. Shepsle and B. R. Weingast, "The Institutional Foundations of Committee Power," 81 *American Political Science Review* (1987) 85–104; W. H. Riker, "Implications from the Disequilibrium of Majority Rule for the Study of Institutions," 74 *American Political Science Review* (1980) 432–47.

33.   See E. M. Sait, *Political Institutions: A Preface* (New York: Appleton-Century, 1938).

Chapter 5

1.   See the quotation from his work in chapter 2 above.

2.   In *Structural Anthropology* on p. 271, Lévi-Strauss, of course, spoke of them as *social relationships*.

3.   See my discussion of the concept political regime in chapter 1 above and the references noted there, as well as chapter 18 below.

4.   See D. E. Apter, *Choice and the Politics of Allocation* (New Haven: Yale University Press, 1971) pp. 21ff.

5.   *Some Conceptual Approaches to the Politics of Modernization* (Englewood Cliffs, N.J.: Prentice-Hall, 1968) p. 10, my italics.

6.   *Ibid.*, pp. 10–11.

7.   "Government," *International Encyclopedia of the Social Sciences*, vol. 14, pp. 214–30.

8.   *Some Conceptual Approaches to the Study of Modernization*, chapter 5. See also *Choice and the Politics of Allocation*, pp. 71 and 132–38, and especially p. 15, where he distinguishes between government and the elite, which he interprets as more general than government and which also has an effect on society.

9.   Conclusive evidence for this drifting between a narrower and broader conception of government lies in the fact that with such a central function for "government" in the modernization process, a large part of Apter's thinking is devoted to examining alternative forms of structural arrangements, clearly regimes by this time, through which government, in its narrow and formal conception, is organized. It leads him to distinguish among regimes ("governments") organized hierarchically, pyramidally, and segmentally, and to construct broad, complex structural types in order to determine their different effects on development as defined by his two test criteria, choice and equity. Clearly, in this focus of his analysis, government returns to its original implication, formal regime structure.

10.   For A. R. Radcliffe-Brown, for example, structure consists of prevalent articulated rules establishing rights and obligations among members of a system. Formal structure so defined was

understood in terms of certain postulated functions. See *A Natural Science of Society* (Glencoe, Ill.: Free Press, 1957) and *Structure and Function in Primitive Society* (Glencoe, Ill.: Free Press, 1952). R. Firth (*Elements of Social Organization* [London: Watts, 1951]) and others preferred the notion of "social organization" to direct attention to the way people actually related to each other as against Radcliffe-Brown's emphasis on formal rules (statements of how persons should interact). This distinction in research on nonliterate societies finds an analogue in political inquiry in the distinction I have been suggesting between formal and informal structures.

11. See chapter 4 for discussion of rules as related to the structure of culture.

12. See P. M. Blau and W. R. Scott, *Formal Organization: A Comparative Approach* (New York: Chandler, 1962) for the introduction of this term.

13. The concept level is being used here in the ordinary sense of the term, that is to say, a ranking based on inclusiveness. At the moment I am assuming what I shall later call a "nesting" hierarchy (discussed in chapter 18 below) in which one set of relationships may include other relationships as a subset. In such cases, the first set is considered to represent a higher level, the second, a lower level. Thus, the concepts *higher* and *lower order* simply divide the structures of a political system into two levels. The higher-order structure represents the highest (most inclusive) level structure in a political system. I define it explicitly (see especially chapters 17 and 18) as well as implicitly through the way I use it throughout this book. As we shall see in chapter 18, it embraces, through a nesting hierarchical arrangement, all other structures. Lower-order structures, on the other hand, refer to all levels of relationships below that of the highest (the higher-order structure). Hence these lower-order structures may have many different levels of relationships within themselves depending on how finely we need to decompose a political system for research purposes. (For example, see diagram 18.1 for a number of different levels.)

14. See H. Eckstein, *Division and Cohesion in Democracy: A Study of Norway* (Princeton, N.J.: Princeton University Press, 1966) chapter 8 and especially p. 136.

15. See D. Easton, "Political Anthropology," in B. J. Siegel (ed.), *Biennial Review of Anthropology* (Stanford: Stanford University Press, 1959) pp. 210–62; and I. Schapera, *Government and Politics in Tribal Societies* (London: Watts, 1956).

16. G. B. Adams, *Constitutional History of England* (London: Jonathan Cape, 1963) rev. ed., and W. S. Holdsworth, *A History of English Law* (London: Methuen, 1956) 7th rev. ed.

17. For the difference between groups and groupings, see an early explicit statement in D. Easton, *The Political System* (Chicago: University of Chicago Press, 1971) 2d ed., pp. 186–87.

18. P. M. Blau, "Parameters of Social Structure," in P. M. Blau (ed.), *Approaches to the Study of Social Structure* (New York: Free Press, 1975) pp. 221–22.

19. See V. Pareto, *Mind and Society* (New York: Harcourt, Brace, 1935) and C. W. Mills, *The Power Elite* (New York: Oxford University Press, 1956).

20. For additions to such interest groups, in the 1980s, of the so-called new social movements, such as those organized around environmental, feminist, peace, and similar issues, see R. J. Dalton and M. Kuchler (eds.), *Challenging the Political Order: New Social and Political Movements in Western Democracies* (manuscript, 1988).

21. See H. G. Skilling and F. Griffiths (eds.), *Interest Groups in Soviet Politics* (Princeton, N.J.: Princeton University Press, 1971).

22. See the well-known writings of T. Parsons and the too little known work of S. F. Nadel, *The Theory of Social Structure* (Glencoe, Ill.: Free Press, 1957). Also, N. Gross, W. Mason, and A. McEachern, *Explorations in Role Analysis* (New York: Wiley, 1958) and M. Banton, *Roles: Introduction to the Study of Social Roles* (London: Tavistock, 1965).

23. See G. A. Almond and G. B. Powell, *Comparative Politics: A Developmental Approach* (Boston: Little, Brown, 1966) chapter 3; D. E. Apter, *Choice and the Politics of Allocation*, esp. chapter 1; H. Eulau and K. Prewitt, *Labyrinths of Democracy* (New York: Bobbs and Merrill, 1973); and J. C. Wahlke, *et al.*, *The Legislative System, passim*. See as well B. J. Biddle, *Role Theory: Expectations, Identities, and Behaviors* (New York: Academic Press, 1979); J. L. Foster and J. H. Jones, "Role Orientation and Bureaucratic Reform," 22 *American Political Science Review* (1978) 348–63; D. W. Ink, "The President as Manager," 36 *Public Administration Review* (1978) 508–15; C. Johnson, *Revolutionary Change* (Boston: Little, Brown, 1966); M. Lee, *"Why Few Women Hold Public Office"* 91 *Political Science*

Quarterly (1976) 297–314; D. R. Matthews, "Senate Folkways and Legislative Effectiveness," 53 *American Political Science Review* (1959) 1064–74; J. C. Moses, "Indoctrination as a Female Political Role in the Soviet Union" 8 *Comparative Politics* (1976) 525–47; D. L. Yarwood amd D. D. Nimmo, "Subjective Environments of Bureaucracy: Accuracies and Inaccuracies in Role-Taking among Administrators, Legislators and Citizens," 29 *Western Political Science Quarterly* (1976) 337–52.

24.   T. Parsons is, of course, a major exponent of of this normative position, which has been widely adopted in sociology and anthropology.

25.   See G. P. Murdock, *Social Structure* (New York: Macmillan, 1960).

26.   See, for example, G. A. Almond and S. Verba, *Civic Culture* (Boston: Little, Brown, 1965), where participant, subject and parochial role patterns define an important part of the structure; D. E. Apter, *The Politics of Modernization*, p. 123; H. Eulau and K. Prewitt, *op. cit.*, pp. 43, 49–51; G. A. Almond and G. B. Powell, *System, Process and Policy: Comparative Politics* (Boston: Little, Brown, 1978) 2d. ed., p. 12.

27.   See J. C. Wahlke *et. al.*, *Legislative Behavior*; D. E. Apter, *op. cit.*, where he classifies various kinds of roles and seeks to show the way they both reflect and influence modernization and help to cope with the strains of social and political change; and an early study that draws on role analysis, D. R. Matthews, *U.S. Senators and Their World* (Chapel Hill: University of North Carolina Press, 1960).

28.   See chapter 4 above.

29.   See chapter 2, above, and the beginning of the present chapter.

30.   See chapter 2, above, and chapter 4.

31.   I continue to refer here only to *political* structures, of course. In much the same way, however, we might seek to show the importance of *social* structures for the political system, except that the parts are, of course, located in the social system, and, therefore, are not the same as those found in the political system itself. In my conceptualization the social structure lies in the environment of the political and is, accordingly, external to it. As we know, such external factors are often vital to the state of the political system so that locating a phenomenon there in no way belittles or underestimates its possible influence. See my book *A Framework for Political Analysis*.

32.   O.W. Anderson, *Health Care: Can There Be Equity?* (New York: Wiley, 1972) p. 24.

33.   See C. Tilly, *Big Structures, Large Processes, Huge Comparisons* (New York: Russell Sage, 1985).

Chapter 6

1.   See J. G. March and J. P. Olsen, "The New Institutionalism: Organizational Factors in Political Life" and the literature cited there; and, by the same authors, "Popular Sovereignty and the Search for Appropriate Institutions" (manuscript dated September 1986).

2.   This doubt is not confined to political science of course. "While most social scientists would probably endorse programmatic declarations about the importance of social structure, the issue becomes more difficult as soon as one presses for a specific definition of what, exactly, is meant by 'social structure.' Is it the *effects of social interaction* on individuals' beliefs, expectations, and behaviors as in the study of conformity, contagion, diffusion, or influence processes? Is it the particular *pattern of social relationships* that in turn constrains, channels, or otherwise determines the distribution of opportunities for such interactions? Is it the specific *content of transactions* which take place among interacting individuals that determines the effects of social structure? Must the operational concept of social structure itself be made contingent on the particular *types of social interaction* that are assumed to affect individual outcomes? *Unfortunately even those who advocate the theoretical importance of social context tend to leave the meaning of this message somewhat ambiguous.*" L. Erbring and A. A. Young, "Individual and Social Structure: Contextual Effects as Endogenous Feedback," 7 *Sociological Methods and Research* (1979) 396–416, at p. 397. All italics, except the last sentence, in original.

3.   The case for this phrase was made initially by Louis Althusser in the 1960s and then elaborated by Nicos Poulantzas in the same decade.

4.   I place this term in quotes because of its ambiguity. It can refer to a wide range of phenomena, from the governing authorities at the one extreme, to the "condensation of class relationships," as we shall see Poulantzas puts it, at the other. As readers familiar with my writings know, I have carefully

avoided this concept, for reasons thoroughly discussed in *The Political System*; in "The Political System Besieged by the State," 9 *Political Theory* (1981) 303–26; and in chapter 12 below. As described in these publications, I prefer to speak instead about the political system and its authorities. I am pleased to see that my reservations in these publication have been followed, a few years later, by a number of other discussions along the same lines about the appropriateness of the state as a central orienting concept for theoretical and empirical research. See the symposium around G. A. Almond, "The Return to the State," 82 *American Political Science Review* (1988) 853–904.

5. See T. Skocpol, *States and Revolutions: A Comparative Analysis of France, Russia and China* (Cambridge: Cambridge University Press, 1979); P. B. Evans, D. Rueschemeyer, and T. Skocpol, *Bringing the State Back: State and Social Structure Newsletter*, publication of the State and Social Structure Committee, Social Science Research Council, New York; A. C. Stephan, *The State and Society* (Princeton: Princeton University Press, 1978); S. D. Krasner, *Defending the National Interest* (Princeton: Princeton University Press, 1978); E. Nordlinger, *On the Autonomy of the Democratic State*.

6. For evidence that, despite claims to the contrary by both sociologists and political scientists, students of politics have not really neglected the influence of government (the state?) on politics and society, see J. D. Kingsley, *Representative Bureaucracy*; V. O. Key, Jr., *Politics, Parties and Pressure Groups*; the quotations from A. Kornberg and S. M. Hines, "Legislatures and Modernization of Society," in chapter 2, note 5; and D. Rae, *The Political Consequences of Electoral Laws* (New Haven: Yale University Press, 1967), among others, and the references in the symposium cited in note 4 above.

7. See W. Bagehot, *The English Constitution* (New York: Oxford University Press, 1928).

8. W. Wilson, *Congressional Government* (Boston: Houghton Mifflin, 1885).

9. For reference to the extensive literature on the relationship between outputs (public policy) and structures, see M. S. Beck, "The Relative Importance of Socioeconomic and Political Variables for Public Policy," 71 *American Political Science Review* (1977) 559–66.

10. T. R. Dye, *Policy Analysis* (University, Alabama: University of Alabama Press, 1976) 25–26. Dye's research in this area had been preceded by the innovative efforts of R. E. Dawson and J. A. Robinson in "Inter-Party Competition, Economic Variables and Welfare Policies in the American States," 25 *Journal of Politics* (1963) 265–89. The latter had concluded that structural variables do have some influence on the way in which budget allocations are distributed in a population. However, the per capita GNP was a better predictor than structure on the level of expenditures for social welfare.

11. T. R. Dye, *op. cit.* p. 29, italics in original.

12. There has been some suggestion that if we disaggregate effects it will turn out that party structure and participation do make a difference, if not on the quality of the outputs at least on their distribution among various social groups and social classes. Also, as V. O. Key, Jr. and others before him suggested, the degree of party competition may influence voter turnout and political interest. In addition, see the challenge to studies (such as Dye's) that insist on the "primacy of economic influence upon government policies" in I. Sharkansky, "Economic and Political Correlates of State Government Expenditures: General Tendencies and Deviant Cases," 11 *Midwest Journal of Political Science* (1967) 173–92. Finally, these studies were done at a time when ideological conviction may have played a less obvious or less central role in government policy than has been the case since the beginning of the 1980s.

13. D. E. Apter, *The Politics of Modernization*.

14. P. Cutright, "Political Structure, Economic Development and National Security Programs," 70 *American Journal of Sociology* (1965) 537–48.

15. In his own words, "The specific activities that engage the attention of national governments are not independent of the general level of development. Quite the contrary is true. In spite of very great differences among nations in ideological orientation as well as in type of political organization, we found that . . . nations with high level of economic development but with less that 'perfect' [that is, democratic] political systems had government activities highly similar to those undertaken by democratic governments." *Ibid.*, p. 548. As I cautioned in an earlier note, whether, during the 1980s, the rise of strong and explicit convictions opposing safety-net social welfare legislation has changed the significance of the effects of ideology on public policy would need to be taken into account in assessing the conclusions of these earlier studies.

16. C. A. Reich, *The Greening of America*.

17. *New York Times*, Op-Ed page, March 8, 1971.

18. See P. M. Blau, *Inequality and Heterogeneity*.

19. The method that he recommends to discover the effects of such structures are instructive. In his own words, they involve the following steps: "*First*, empirical measures are obtained that pertain to those characteristics of the individual members of the groups that have direct or indirect bearing on their relations to each other, such as group identification, sociometric choices, initiation of interaction, or promotions. *Second*, the measures that describe individuals in one respect are combined into one index for each group, and this index no longer refers to any characteristic of individuals but to a characteristic of the group. Examples of such group attributes are the proportion of members identified with the group, the average number of in-group sociometric choices, the degree of variation in rates of interaction, and the homogeneity of interests. *Third*, to isolate a structural effect, the relationship between a group attribute and some effect is determined while the corresponding characteristic of individuals is held constant." P. M. Blau, "Formal Organization: Dimensions of Analysis," 63 *American Journal of Sociology* (1957) 58–69, at p. 63.

20. *Union Democracy* (Glencoe, Ill., Free Press, 1956) p. 165–67.

21. The phrase used in P. M. Blau, *op. cit.*

22. *Ibid.*, p. 65.

23. "a network [or pattern] of social relationships" *ibid.*, p. 63.

24. *Suicide: A Study in Sociology*.

25. S. A. Stouffer *et al.*, *The American Soldier* (Princeton, N.J.: Princeton University Press, 1949), vol. 1, pp. 250–54.

26. J. A. Davis, J. L. Spaeth, and C. Huson, "A Technique for Analyzing the Effects of Group Composition," 26 *American Sociological Review* (1961) 215–25.

27. A. Bavelas, "Communication Patterns in Task-Oriented Groups," 22 *Journal of the Acoustical Society of America* (1950) 725–30.

28. F. Harary, R. Z. Norman, and D. Cartwright, *Models: An Introduction to the Theory of Directed Graphs* (New York: Wiley, 1965). Also see A. P. Hare, E. F. Borgatta, R. F. Bales, *Small Groups: Studies in Social Interaction* (New York: Knopf, 1962).

29. See T. Newcombe, *The Acquaintance Process* (New York: Holt, Rinehart and Winston, 1961).

30. F. Harary, R. Z. Norman, and D. Cartwright, *op. cit.*, p. 3.

31. For example, H. C. White, *Chains of Opportunity: System Models of Mobility in Organizations* (Cambridge: Harvard University Press, 1970). For references to the literature in this area, see especially the journal *Social Networks*.

32. B. Anderson and M. L. Carlos, "What Is Social Network Theory?" in B. Anderson (ed.), *Essays on Social Action and Social Structure* (Stockholm: Almqvist and Wiksell, 1988) pp. 70–89 at p. 73.

33. For the difficulties and complexities encountered and for ingenious ways of trying to overcome them, see, for example, B. L. Foster, "An Exchange Network Approach to Thai Social Organization" (manuscript n.d.) and "Domestic Units and Larger Social Structures" (manuscript, 1982). For a useful introduction to this whole area of social network analysis, see L. C. Freeman, *Social Networks: A Beginner's Bookshelf* (Irvine: University of California, Irvine, and University of California, Santa Barbara Preprints in Social Network Analysis, no. 1, Aug. 15, 1980). See also the work of world-systems analysts.

34. See K. Knorr-Cetina, "Introduction: The Micro-sociological Challenge of Macro-sociology: Towards a Reconstruction of Social Theory and Methodology," in K. Knorr-Cetina and A. V. Cicourel (eds.), *Advances in Social Theory and Methodology* (Boston: Routledge and Kegan Paul, 1981) pp. 1–48 at p. 4.

35. See A. Giddens, "Agency, Institutions and Time-Space Analysis," in K. Knorr-Cetina and A. V. Cicourel (eds.), *op. cit.*, chapter 5.

36. K. Knorr-Cetina and A. V. Cicourel (eds.), *op. cit.*, p. 4.

37. T. Skocpol, *States and Social Revolutions*, p. 284, my italics. See also J. A. Goldstone, "Theories of Revolution: The Third Generation," 32 *World Politics* (1980) 423–53.

38. The views of the neostatists are reinforced by the so-called new institutionalists. They, too, build, wittingly or otherwise, on Poulantzas's claims about state autonomy, having discovered (or just

rediscovered?) the possible significance of state action for influencing all aspects of social life, including the political. See J. G. March and J. P. Olsen, "The New Institutionalism: Organizational Factors in Political Life," p. 738.

39. *Ibid.*

40. The literature is now fairly large in this area, but early on some of the basic issues were addressed in the writings of T. Skocpol and in E. A. Nordlinger, *op. cit..*

41. For example, until the end of the 1980s the Supreme Soviet in the USSR was a purely administrative organization with little if any legislative consequences. In the late 1980s it appeared that that situation changed substantially.

Chapter 7

1. F. F. Ridley, "Political Institutions: The Script not the Play," in 23 *Political Studies* (1975) 365–80 at p. 375.

2. For this term, see D. Easton, *A Systems Analysis of Political Life*, pp. 86 and 222.

3. See W. Bagehot, *English Constitution*; M. Ostrogorski, *Democracy and the Organization of Political Parties* (New York: Macmillan, 1922); and W. Wilson, *Congressional Government: A Study in American Politics* (New York: Meridian Books, 1956).

4. (New York: Oxford University Press, 1942)

5. See J. G. March and H. A. Simon, *Organizations* (New York: Wiley, 1958).

6. H. A. Simon, D. W. Smithburg, and V. A. Thompson, *Public Administration* (New York: Knopf, 1965), p. 5, and J. G. March and H. A. Simon, *op. cit.*

7. P. M. Blau and R. W. Scott, *Formal Organizations*, p. 14.

8. I. D. Duchacek, *Power Maps: Comparative Politics of Constitutions* (Santa Barbara, Calif.: ABC Clio, 1973), chapter 1.

9. See H. Eckstein, *Division and Cohesion in Democracy*, p. 25, and H. J. Spiro, *Government by Constitution: The Political Systems of Democracy* (New York: Random House, 1959) on various legalistic cultures. See also R. Hardin, "Why a Constitution?" (draft manuscript), and other papers prepared for a "Conference on the *Federalist Papers* in Public Choice Perspective: The New Federalism and the Old," University of California, Irvine, 1987, Bernard Grofman and Donald Wittman, cochairmen.

10. C. E. Merriam, *Political Power* (New York: McGraw-Hill, 1934).

11. For the possibility of nonlegitimate authority, see D. Easton, "The Perception of Authority and Political Change," in C. J. Friedrich (ed.), *Authority* (Cambridge: Harvard University Press, 1958) pp. 170–96.

12. The argument can and has been made that all public-choice theory assumes the inescapable presence of broad institutional influences of the sort that would be included in what I have been calling higher-order structures. (See T. Schwartz, *"The Federalist Papers*, Public Choice, and Bureaucratic Usurpation of Legislative Power" and B. E. Cain and W. T. Jones, "Madison's Theory of Institutional Design and His Application of It to the Question of Representation," prepared for the conference on the *Federalist Papers* referred to above.) These provide the context within which rational choices may be made and therefore limit or determine such choices. This raises central issues about the limitations of choice theory. It is still too early in our analysis, however, to address these matters. Hence we must set them aside for the moment.

13. See our earlier discussion of the difficulties with institutions as a concept. Here I shall use the term in the loose and relatively undefined way in which it appears in rational-choice literature to avoid getting mired in the morass surrounding the possible meaning of the term. Where necessary in my discussion, I shall specify the meaning I wish to attribute to it in the given context.

14. This interpretation of public choice theory would seem to follow Parsons's conception of motivation—that it is not part of psychology but is a social phenomenon generated by the institutional context. As Schwartz puts it, "Producers, for example, are assumed to maximize profits. But that assumption is institutional rather than psychological: people may or may not be avaricious by nature, but those who do not act avariciously do not long survive in the role of producer: the role selects for avarice" (*op. cit.*, p. 7; this statement is classically Parsonian). Formal rule structures select out of the

range of human motivations those that serve the functions of the wider social processes. In the case of the neoclassical conceptions of the market place and of what we may call a neoclassical view of political structures, assuming the strong propensity of persons to follow a course based on self-interest rather than altruistic motives, political structures will be able to achieve the objectives of their designers to the extent to which they are able to appeal to and evoke these self-directed motivations. In this sense we must view public-choice theory, Schwartz correctly argues (*ibid.*), as resting on certain presuppositions about the presence of appropriate institutional arrangements to enhance the probability of outcomes predicted by rational theory. Not only do institutions (read, formal rule structures) have effects; they are central to the effects envisioned in public choice analysis.

15. See the papers to the conference on the *Federalist Papers* referred to above.

16. "Once we have settled on a constitutional arrangement, it is not likely to be in the interest of some of us then to try to renege on the arrangement. Our interests will be better served by living with the arrangement. And this is generally true not because we will be coerced to abide if we choose not to (although we may be, as the southern states were at the end of the Civil War) but because we generally cannot do better than to abide. To do better we would have to carry enough others with us to set up an alternative, and that will typically be too costly to be worth the effort. For [contracts which are different from constitutions] the ultimate source is sanctions from an external body; for the constitutional case, the ultimate source is the internal costs of collective action for recoordination [realignment of the coalition of forces behind a constitution?]." R. Hardin, "Why a Constitution?" draft of a paper prepared for the conference on the *Federalist Papers*.

17. See H. Eckstein, *op. cit.*, p. 154

18. H. J. Spiro, *Government by Constitution: The Political Systems of Democracy.*

19. L. Pye, *Politics, Personality and Nation Building* (New Haven: Yale University Press, 1962), cited by H. Eckstein, *op. cit.*

20. As against the newly named "new institutionalism" as proclaimed by J. G. March and J. P. Oleson, "The New Institutionalism: Organizational Factors in Political Life."

21. See Lord Balfour's amendment to Walter Bagehot's interpretation of the British constitution, noted above.

22. F. Hunter, *Community Power Structure* (Chapel Hill: University of North Carolina Press, 1953).

23. Perhaps this revealed his disciplinary origins and commitments in sociology. One would like to think that someone trained to look for political phenomena might not have overlooked such an obvious source of power in the hands of the political authorities, however little use for this last resort power there may have been in the community Hunter studied.

24. D. Cartwright and A. Zander, *Group Dynamics Research and Theory* (Evanston, Ill.: Row, Peterson, 1953) pp. 436ff.

25. See D. Easton, "The Political System Besieged by the State."

26. E. A. Norlinger, *On the Autonomy of the Democratic State.*

27. The state "refers to all those individuals who occupy offices that authorize them, and them alone, to make and apply decisions that are binding upon any and all segments of society. Quite simply, the state is made of and limited to those individuals who are endowed with society-wide decision-making authority" (*ibid.*, p. 11). This definition is almost identical with my earlier description of the political authorities: "If we use the concept 'authorities' to identify these [role] occupants, generically it can be said to include members of a system who conform to the following criteria. They must be recognized by most members of the system as having the responsibility for these matters; and their actions must be accepted as binding most of the time by most of the members [of society] as long as they act within the limits of their roles" (*A Systems Analysis of Political Life*, p. 212). The state here also looks very much like the state described by R. Miliband in *The State and Capitalist Society* (London: Quarter Books, 1973) and like Poulantzas's state apparatus, as we shall later see.

28. "The state is autonomous to the extent that it translates *its* preferences into authoritative actions . . . " (*op. cit.*, p. 19, my italics). Presumably, by this measure, to the extent to which official U.S. governmental policy, during the 1980s, supported the Contras in the civil strife in Nicaragua while public opinion opposed such support, the "state" was demonstrating its autonomy.

Chapter 8

1. See, for example, T. Bottomore and R. Nisbet, "Structuralism," in T. Bottomore and R. Nisbet (eds.), *A History of Sociological Analysis* (New York: Basic Books, 1978) pp. 557–98, at p. 557.

2. *Ibid.* Italics in the original.

3. See M. Glucksmann, *Structuralist Analysis in Contemporary Social Thought: A Comparison of the Theories of Claude Lévi-Strauss and Louis Althusser* (London: Routledge and Kegan Paul, 1974), p. 52.

4. This interpretation goes beyond structuralism, of course, to the heart of inquiry in the social sciences. The goal of nomothetic science is to discover an inferrable body of relationships, not directly or intuitively obvious, which determines or sets limits on the behavior and structures in political systems, as on those who exercise power. Such limits are often referred to globally as structural constraints. Presumably it is about the nature of these constraints that structuralism is offering various interpretations. See A. Megill, " 'Recounting' the Past," 94 *American Historical Review* (1989) 621–43, p. 631.

5. See M. Lane (ed.), *Structuralism: A Reader*, Introduction, pp. 69–72.

6. As M. Godelier, a prominent Marxist structuralist put it, in his article "Structure and Contradictions in Capital," "They constitute a *level of reality* invisible but present behind the visible social relations." R. Blackburn, *Ideology in the Social Sciences* (New York: Vintage, 1973) pp. 334–68 at p. 336, italics in original.

7. Even R. K. Merton seems to wish to associate his distinction between manifest and latent structures with this geological imagery. ". . . It is analytically useful to distinguish between manifest and latent levels of social structure as of social function (with the aside that structuralism as expressed in other disciplines—for example, by Jakobson, Lévi-Strauss, and Chomsky—finds it essential to distinguish 'surface' from 'deep' structures)." "Structural Analysis in Sociology," in P. M. Blau (ed.), *Approaches to the Study of Social Structure* (New York: Free Press, 1975) pp. 21–52 at p. 36.

8. See chapter 11, note 9.

9. See C. Lévi-Strauss, *Structural Anthropology*, pp. 37ff.

10. For this idea, see M. Glucksmann, *Structuralist Analysis in Contemporary Social Thought*, esp. chapter 1.

11. *Ibid.*

12. There are some who see little if any difference between these two approaches. See, for example, W. G. Runciman, "What Is Structuralism?" in A. Ryan, *The Philosophy of Social Explanation* (London: Oxford University Press, 1973), pp. 189–202, and R. Boudon, *Uses of Structuralism*.

13. Quoted in E. Lazlo, "Systems and Structures—Toward Bio-social Anthropology," 2 *Theory and Decision* (1971) 174–92, at p. 186.

14. See *Structural Anthropology*, p. 271.

15. See *Structuralism*, p. 142. See also R. Boudon's interpretation of structuralism in his *Uses of Structuralism*. There he argues that "to be able to speak of structure in this type of context [as an operative definition, in Boudon's sense of the term], it is first necessary to conceive the object to be analyzed as a *system*. In other words, it must be conceived of as a whole made up of interdependent elements." (p. 56, italics in original). Or, as he states even more forcefully on his own behalf, "The purpose of this study will be to demonstrate that in all cases in which the concept [of structures] appears in this type of context [again, as an operative definition in Boudon's usage], it is related to a theory concerning an object considered as a system" (p. 57).

16. See also, in the area of literature, L. Goldmann, "Structure: Human Reality and Methodological Concept," in R. Macksey and E. Donato (eds.), *The Languages of Criticism and the Sciences of Man* (Baltimore: Johns Hopkins University Press, 1970), pp. 98–124. Others, such as Bottomore and Nisbett draw too sharp a distinction between holistic (totality) and structural or structuralist analysis. See their article "Structuralism" in T. Bottomore and R. Nisbet (eds.), *A History of Sociological Analysis*, pp. 557–98 at pp. 586ff.

17. See Lévi-Strauss, *Structural Anthropology* pp. 37ff.

18. See S. M. Lipset, "Some Social Requisites of Democracy: Economic Development and Political Legitimacy," 53 *American Political Science Review* (1959) 69–105.

19.   For which, see the following chapter.

20.   See the discussion of Piaget in the following chapter. Lévi-Strauss also refers to his structuralism as a model but he interprets models to be methods rather than special kinds of theories, a view that cloaks his approach in a certain scientific cloudiness since his models look very much like theories to any ordinary practitioner of scientific inquiry. See his *Structural Anthropology*, pp. 127 and 271–72.

21.   M. Glucksmann, *op. cit.*, p. 31.

22.   For a discussion of structuring as a "problematic," that is, as a fundamental theoretical position guiding inquiry, see P. Abrams, *Historical Sociology*. Structuring is here (see especially pp. ix and xv) seen as a way of overcoming the artificial dichotomy between agent and society, individual and system, action and structure and, in addition, as a means of introducing time into social analysis. Piaget, too, saw this clearly. As he said, "If the character of structured wholes depends on their laws of composition, these laws must of their very nature be *structuring*; it is the constant duality, or bipolarity, of always being simultaneously *structuring and structured* that accounts for the success of the notion of law or rule employed by the structuralists" (quoted in T. Bottomore and R. Nisbet, *Structuralism*, pp. 585–86, footnote 69, italics in original). See also A. Giddens, *Central Problems in Social Theory* (Berkeley: University of California Press, 1979), whose term *structuration* clearly implies structuring; and A. Dawe, "Theories of Social Action," in T. Bottomore and R. Nisbet (eds.), *History of Sociological Analysis*, pp. 362–417.

Chapter 9

1.   See D. Easton, "Limits of the Equilibrium Model in Social Research," 1 *Behavioral Science* (1956) 96–104.

2.   See D. Easton, *A Systems Analysis of Political Life*, pp. 363–468.

3.   See D. Easton, *A Systems Analysis of Political Life* and *A Framework for Political Analysis*, *passim*.

4.   *Ibid.*, and see as well L. von Bertalanffy, *General Systems Theory* (New York: Braziller, 1969).

5.   Of course, for some students of contemporary philosophy of science, this statement about the possible existence of universal regularities in human behavior simply begs the question. Yet despite all the questioning that has gone on during the 1970s and 1980s about the validity of searching for general social regularities, little has really been said that had not already been thoroughly debated in the past century. To the extent that no better answers have been given now than in the past, the positivist search for universal regularities of human behavior still remains a valid objective, in my mind, however deficient we can now understand various other aspects of the positivist conception of science to be. The fact is that positivism had misconstrued much about the procedures and canons of science. These are now in process of being corrected. But the fact that we may need to revise our understanding of the nature of scientific method and its products does not mean that we must throw out the wheat with the chaff. The ultimate objective of positivist science—the search for generalizations about human behavior—remains intact.

6.   *Structuralism*, p. 13.

7.   J. Piaget, *op. cit.*, p. 5. Elsewhere Piaget includes equilibrium as one of the necessary conditions of structure. There is no reason, however, for thinking that all systems and, therefore, all structures in this structuralist sense must tend toward a state of equilibrium. Long ago I argued against the utility of this term in political research. We simply lack adequate measures to determine when a system is in a state of equilibrium, has left it or is returning to it. See note 1 above.

8.   J. Piaget, *op. cit.*, p. 98.

9.   *Structural Anthropology*, esp. pp. 271ff.

10.   *Ibid.*, chapter 15.

11.   See chapter 5 above.

12.   L. Althusser, *For Marx* (Middlesex, England: Penguin, 1969), first published in France, 1966.

13.   For the definition of these terms, see the preceding chapter as well as chapters 2 and 4.

14.   "The peculiarity of authentic (analytic) structuralism is that it seeks to explain such empirical

systems by postulating 'deep' structures from which the former are in some manner derivable." J. Piaget, *op. cit.*, p. 98, italics added.

15. Having said this, however, we must also remember that there has been considerable variety among structuralists themselves. It would take us too far afield to pursue their internecine conflicts. Suffice it to say that some structuralists, such as the Marxist variety, do go beyond a special concern for observed patterns of relationships. They seek to offer an overarching social theory. Yet it is also fair to say that what leads others to call certain Marxists, such as Althusser and Poulantzas, structuralists, is the special effort they devote to accounting for the particular form of society at a given time and place. This is especially true of Poulantzas, as we shall see. He chooses to stress the truly structuralist aspect of his Marxist general theory of the mode of production. With that in mind he seeks to plumb the depths of the presumed connection between the changing structures of a system (variable types of states) and the forms (modes of production) in which the system manifests itself.

16. C. Lévi-Strauss, *op. cit.*, p. 275. As we noted in the preceding chapter, I am not alone in assimilating structuralism to model or theory building. See W. G. Runciman, "What is Structuralism?" and J. Piaget, *op. cit.*, p. 5 ("A structure is a system of transformations" and exhibits "transformation laws," all elements of a theory). In assessing structuralism, Boudon defends the view that "the structural description of an object is defined as the whole set of *theorems* based on the application of axioms to this object. Both the axioms and the theorems constitute a theory of the object viewed as a *system*." "Thus no 'structural method' exists" (*op. cit.*, pp. 137 and 140). He insists that what distinguishes such theories is not their structural(ist) or nonstructural(ist) "method"—structuralism is virtually synonymous with theorizing—but only their variations in validity, clarity, precision, testability and scope (*ibid.*, chapter 3).

17. "The unconscious activity of the mind consists in imposing forms upon content, and . . . these forms are fundamentally the same for all minds—ancient and modern, primitive and civilized." *Op. cit.*, p. 21.

18. For further comments on this ambiguity, see chapter 11 below, especially note 9.

19. See esp. L. Althusser, *For Marx*, part 3.

20. See, for example, the range of essays in M. Lane (ed.), *Structuralism: A Reader* (London: Jonathan Cape, 1970).

21. "Loose talk", as one social scientist has deprecatingly called it. See B. H. Mayhew, "Structuralism versus Individualism," part 1, in 59 *Social Forces* (1980) 335–75 and part 2, in 59 *Social Forces* (1981) 627–48.

22. See chapter 8, note 15.

23. *Op. cit.*, chapter 1.

24. See chapter 4, note 4 above.

25. See J. Viet, *Les méthodes structuralistes dans les sciences sociales* (Paris: Mouton, 1965) and R. Bastide, *Sens et usage du terme structure* (Paris: Haugue, 1972).

26. For evidence of this influence, for example, see J. A. Goldstone, "Theories of Revolution," 32 *World Politics* (1980) 423–53 and T. Skocpol, "Explaining Revolutions," in L. A. Coser (ed.), *Use of Controversy in Sociology* (New York: Free Press, 1976) pp. 155–75. As we shall see in chapter 10 and later, despite the limited diffusion of Poulantzas's ideas, at least one of them, "relative autonomy of the state," continues to have a significant impact.

27. See D. Ross, "The Development of the Social Sciences," in A. Oleson and J. Voss (eds.), *Organization of Knowledge in Modern America, 1860–1920* (Baltimore: Johns Hopkins University Press, 1976), pp. 107–38, for evidence of Germany's commitment to empiricism from the beginning of the nineteenth century.

28. C. Lévi-Strauss, *op. cit.*, p. 127.

29. See D. Easton, *The Political System* for reasons for the emergence of empirically oriented theory since the 1950s.

30. See, for example, P. L. Berger and T. Luckman, *The Social Construction of Reality* (New York: Auchor, 1967).

31. See chapter 12 below.

32. L. von Bertalanffy, *General System Theory*; L. J. Henderson, *The Order of Nature* (Cambridge: Harvard University Press, 1917); and W. B. Cannon, *Wisdom of the Human Body* (New York: Norton, 1932).

33. See P. Feyerabend, *Against Method* (London: Lowe and Brydone, 1976).

34. "A sudden upsurge of interest in 'the state' has occurred in comparative social science in the past decade. Whether as an object of investigation or as something invoked to explain outcomes of interest, the state as an actor or an institution has been highlighted in an extraordinary outpouring of studies by scholars of diverse theoretical proclivities from all of the major disciplines." T. Skocpol, "Bringing the State Back In: Strategies of Analysis in Current Research," in P. B. Evans, D. Rueschemeyer, and T. Skocpol, *Bringing the State Back In*, p. 1.

35. This law states that if for the first time a child is given a hammer, it will suddenly discover all kinds of things it wants to strike that had never even occurred to it before!

Chapter 10

1. Cf. R. Boudon, *Uses of Structuralism*, chapter 4, and A. Lijphart, "II The Comparable Cases Strategy in Comparative Research" 8 *Comparative Political Studies* (1975) 158–77.

2. See a recent statement in defence of case studies in S. Goldsmith and K. Boo, "The Case for the Case Study," in *The Washington Monthly* (June 1989) 18–25.

3. See T. Skocpol and M. Somers, "The Uses of Comparative History in Macrosocial Inquiry," 22 *Comparative Studies in History* (1980) 174–97.

4. For the concepts higher order and lower order, see E. K. Scheuch, "Social Context and Individual Behavior," in M. Dogan and S. Rokkan (eds.), *Quantitative Ecological Analysis in the Social Sciences* (Cambridge: MIT Press, 1969).

5. J. S. Mill, *A System of Logic* (London: Longman, Green, 1949) book 4.

6. Thus, it has been said that "in short, we use the term comparative method to refer to social scientific analyses involving observations in more than one social system, or in the same social system at more than one point in time." (D. P. Warwick and S. Osherson, "Comparative Analysis in the Social Sciences," in D. P. Warwick and S. Osherson, *Comparative Research Methods* [Englewood Cliffs, N.J.: Prentice-Hall, 1973]). For an alternative point of view about the importance of giving a distinctive connotation to the term *comparative method* which leaves it as a description of a method to be contrasted with statistical analysis as a different kind of method, see A. Lijphart, "Comparative Politics and the Comparative Method," 65 *American Political Science Review* (1971) 682–93 and "The Comparable-Cases Strategy in Comparative Research," 8 *Comparative Political Studies* (1975) 158–71. See also T. W. Meckstroth, " 'Most Different Systems' and 'Most Similar Systems': A Study in the Logic of Comparative Inquiry," 8 *Comparative Political Studies* (1975) 132–57.

7. See, for example, F. W. Riggs, "Comparison of Whole Political Systems," in R. T. Holt and J. E. Turner (eds.), *The Methodology of Comparative Research* (New York: Free Press, 1970) pp. 86–87.

8. See A. Lipjhart, "Comparative Politics and the Comparative Method," p. 686.

9. See A. Lijphart, "The Comparable-Cases Strategy in Comparative Research," p. 163. And, as he goes on to say, "In general, the problems of reliability and validity are smaller for the researcher who uses the comparative [rather than the statistical] method. He can analyze his smaller number of cases more thoroughly, and he is less dependent on data that he cannot properly evaluate. He can also use the availability of reliable data as a subsidiary criterion in the selection of his cases" (p. 171).

10. D. Easton and J. Dennis, *Children in the Political System: Origins of Political Legitimacy* (New York: McGraw-Hill, 1969); reissued, University of Chicago Press, 1979.

11. S. M. Lipset, "Some Social Requisites of Democracy," in C. F. Cnudde and D. E. Neubauer (eds.), *Empirical Democratic Theory*, p. 156. The editors of the work, however, find that this correlation does not hold (p. 146). See also G. A. Almond and S. Verba, *The Civic Culture* (Princeton: Princeton University Press, 1963) p. 317. The fact that the political systems are not the same did not, in their analysis, play a significant role in accounting for differences in political attitudes. Cf. S. Verba, N. H. Nie, and J. Kim, *The Modes of Democratic Participation: A Cross-National Comparison* (Beverly Hills, Calif.: Sage, 1971).

12. See M. Czudnowski, *Comparing Political Behavior* (Beverly Hills, Calif.: Sage, 1976).

13. See H. Teune and K. Ostrowski, "Political Systems as Residual Variables," 6 *Comparative Political Studies* (1973) 3–21.

14. D. P. Warwick and S. Osheron, *op. cit.*, p. 3.

15. See A. Lijphart, *op. cit.*; R. T. Holt and J. Turner (eds.), *The Methodology of Comparative Research* (Glencoe, Ill.: Free Press, 1970); and M. Czudnowski, *op. cit.*

16. For the issue of multiplication of variables, see N. Smelser, "Notes on the Methodology of Comparative Analysis of Economic Activity," 2 *Transactions of Sixth World Congress of Sociology* (1966) 101–17, esp. p. 109.

17. For the ambiguity inherent in this sentence, see F. Nagel, "Whole, Sums and Organic Unities," in D. Lerner (ed.), *Parts and Wholes* (Glencoe, Ill.: Free Press, 1963), pp. 135–55.

18. H. Teune and K. Ostrowski, "Political Systems as Residual Variables."

19. *Ibid.*, p. 6.

20. *Ibid.*

21. *Ibid.*

22. *Ibid.*, p. 8.

23. *Ibid.*, p. 9.

24. See T. Skocpol and M. Somers, "Uses of Comparative History in Macrosocial Inquiry," 22 *Comparative Studies in Society and History* (1980) 174–97. Among three types of historical comparative methods that the authors mention (parallel comparative history, contrast-oriented comparative history, and macro-analytic comparative history), the second type, "contrast-oriented comparative history," comes close to taking whole structures into account. (See an alternative classification of comparative historical methods in C. Tilly, *Big Structures, Large Processes, Huge Comparisons* (New York: Russell Sage, 1985.) As they describe it, it does seek to show how the particular historical evolution in contrasting systems brings about different outcomes and, therefore, must be assumed to have some overall effect on the constituent parts of the social system (pp. 178–81). However, the authors virtually end up attributing differences to unique historical developments, which is the equivalent of using proper names as causal variables, a violation of a cardinal rule of nomothetic inquiry.

25. "The relation between ecological and individual correlations which is discussed in this paper provides a definite answer as to whether ecological correlations can validly be used as substitutes for individual correlations. They cannot." W. S. Robinson, "Ecological Correlations and the Behavior of Individuals," 15 *American Sociological Review* (1950) 351–57 at p. 357.

26. See M. Eagles, "*An Ecological Perspective on Working-Class Politics: Neighborhood and Class Formation in Sheffield, England*" (Ph.D. diss.), University of California, Irvine, 1988). For an interesting study of the impact of regional social class base and partisan political support, see K. P. Langton and R. Rapoport, "Social Structure, Social Context, and Partisan Mobilization," in 8 *Comparative Political Studies* (1975).

27. We could assume, of course, with the ethnomethodologists, that what we might call the total system context is simply built up out of all microcontexts. (See my further discussion of ethnomethodology in chapter 17.) However, such an approach would raise numerous problems about the ethnomethodological approach for which no solution appears in sight, not the least of which is the difficulty of undertaking the number of microstudies that would be necessary and of spanning the chasm that would still separate those microstudies from a macro-level analysis. If we are to continue our belief in empirically-based knowledge, in principle the ethnomethodologists are undoubtedly correct. There can be no phenomenon, whether macro or otherwise, that lies beyond the realm of specifically observable behavior and relationships or inferences therefrom. In practice, however, we can have no reasonable expectation of being able to provide explicit and detailed empirical data for the behavior of complex whole entities. In principle it may be necessary to retain one's faith as a reductionist even though in practice we cannot escape behaving as holists.

28. Some contemporary historians have taken up this same theme, although they look to history, as we might expect, to provide the tools for bringing all elements together and revealing their effects. See, for example, C. Tilly, *op. cit.* Of course, this is not a new perspective for history. In the past many historians have construed their discipline as the master discipline capable of linking together all knowledge. See an early statement of this in F. J. Teggart, *Prolegomena to History: The Relation of*

History to Literature, Philosophy and Science (Berkeley: University of California Press, 1916) and *The Process of History* (New Haven, Conn.: Yale University Press, 1918).

29. Compare with Wilhelm Windelband, *Geschichte und Naturwissenschaft* (1904), who, at the end of the nineteenth century, sought to preserve for history its authority as a science (*Wissenschaft*) by distinguishing nomothetic (*Naturwissenschaften*—natural sciences) from idiographic (or historical) type of sciences (*Geisteswissenschaften*—sciences of the mind). Nomothetic science deals with general laws; idiographic "science" seeks laws pertaining to individual or particular instances. See W. Windelband, "Rectorial Address, Strasbourg, 1984" in 19 *History and Theory* (1980) 169–85, esp. pp. 174–75, cited in A. Megill, "Recounting the Past: 'Description,' Explanation and Narrative in Historiography," 94 *American Historical Review* (1989) 627–53 at p. 633.

In seeking to justify the scientific study of individual personality, Allport joins Windelband in separating the nomothetic from the idiographic "sciences" such as history, biography, and literature (sciences of the mind, in Windelband's terms). As Allport puts it, these disciplines seek to understand "some *particular* event in nature or in society." In this view, a "psychology of individuality would be essentially idiographic." However, for Allport the division between these two approaches, the nomothetic and idiographic, is

> too sharp: it requires a psychology divided against itself . . . It is more helpful to regard the two methods as overlapping and as contributing to one another. In the field of medicine, diagnosis and therapy are idiographic procedures, but both rest intimately upon a knowledge of the common factors in disease, determined by the nomothetic sciences of bacteriology and biochemistry. Likewise, biography is clearly idiographic, and yet in the best biographies one finds an artful blend of generalization with individual portraiture. A complete study of the individual will embrace both approaches. . . .
>
> If there are psychologists who . . . still declare that the study of the individual is not and never can be a part of science, they must now be left alone with their views. The psychological study of individuality is being undertaken with profound seriousness; no blind loyalty to an anachronistic ideal can prevent it. One may call it science or not science, as one chooses. Long before the method of natural science attained its commanding position with psychology paddling in its wake, there was an ancient meaning of *Scientia*. It prescribed no method; it set no limits; it signified simply knowledge.

G. W. Allport, *Personality: A Psychological Interpretation* (New York: Henry Holt, 1937) pp. 22–23, italics in original.

30. See C. Geertz, *The Interpretation of Culture* (New York: Basic Books, 1973), chapter 1, "Thick Description: Toward an Interpretive Theory of Culture."

31. See D. Shapere, "Discovery, Rationality and Progress in Science," in K. Schaffner and P. Cohen (eds.), PSA 1972 *Proceedings of 1972 Biennial Meetings of Philosophy of Science Association* (Dordrecht, Holland: Reidel, 1974); F. Suppe, *The Structure of Scientific Theories* (Urbana, Ill.: University of Illinois Press, 1977); S. Tulmin, *Human Understanding* (Princeton: Princeton University Press, 1972); and N. R. Hanson, *Perception and Discovery* (San Francisco: Freeman, Cooper, 1969).

Chapter 11

1. In *Structuralist Analysis in Contemporary Social Thought* (p. 43), M. Glucksmann seeks to show the relationship that Lévi-Strauss sees between Marx and himself. Glucksmann points out that in *The Critique of Political Economy* and *Eighteenth Brumaire of Louis Bonaparte*, Marx revealed that he was not an economic determinist but that he believed in a certain relative autonomy for the superstructures, an idea that he never did explicitly or systematically develop further. Lévi-Strauss, however, sees himself as exploring this relationship, the one left unelaborated by Marx even if, in his own writings, Lévi-Strauss never does actually find use for this notion of relative autonomy. In any event, in this sense, Glucksmann maintains, Lévi-Strauss sees himself indebted to Marx.

2. *Structural Anthropology*, pp. 31–32 and 308–09; or as Glucksmann put it, some "principles of operation underlying observed data" (*op. cit.*, p. 31)."

3. "Structure is not immediately visible in the 'concrete reality.' . . . When we describe structure . . . we are, as it were, in the realm of grammar and syntax, not of the spoken word." *Structural Anthropology*, p. 297.

4.   *Structural Anthropology*, p. 272.

5.   *Ibid.*

6.   As, for example, in the work of G. P. Murdock, *Social Structure and Outline of World Cultures* (New Haven: Human Relation Area Files, 1983) 6th rev. ed.

7.   We may note that his mode of analysis is identical formally with that of the functionalists stemming from Malinowski, passing through Talcott Parsons and still with us, in many concealed ways, today. Both Lévi-Strauss and the functionalists search for certain constants which various visible relations somehow fulfill. Thus, the functionalists discover one or another number of constant functions which are met through variable structures in different systems. Lévi-Strauss finds a constant structure which is met by variable social relations or surface structures.

8.   It appears that even though he shares with Marx the idea that the economy is part of the infrastructure, this together with other aspects are "not principally the ethnologists concern, for ethnology is first of all psychology." C. Lévi-Strauss, *Savage Mind* (Chicago: University of Chicago Press, 1962) pp. 130–31. It appears, therefore, that Lévi-Strauss reserves to social anthropologists the task of exploring only one part of the infrastructure, that of the activities of the mind and the way it is translated into various parts of the superstructure such as kinship, myths, totems, and even cuisine or gustatory practices.

9.   "The unconscious activity of the mind consists of imposing forms upon content." *Structural Anthropology*, pp. 21, 41, and 64; *Savage Mind*, pp. 8–9 and 13; and *Totemism* (Boston: Beacon, 1962), pp. 96–97. For the inherent ambiguity in Lévi-Strauss's use of mind as a central concept, see E. Leach, "The Legitimacy of Solomon: Some Structural Aspects of the Old Testament," in M. Lane (ed.), *Structuralism: A Reader* (London: Jonathan Cape, 1970) pp. 248–92, esp. pp. 248–49; and S. Clarke, *Foundations of Structuralism* (New York: Barnes and Noble, 1981) pp. 40ff.

10.   At one point he even went so far as to disclaim that he might be a spokesman for an authentic Marxism. "For there can be no such things as orthodox Marxism. No-one can presume to behave as the keeper of holy dogmas and texts; nor have I sought to clothe myself in them. It is not that I claim to speak in the name of some genuine Marxism, but rather the opposite. I assume responsibility for what I write and speak only in my own name." N. Poulantzas, *State, Power, Socialism* (London: NLB, 1978) p. 8.

11.   See *For Marx, Lenin and Philosophy and Other Essays* (London: NLB, 1971); *Essays in Self-Criticism* (London: NLB, 1976), and L. Althusser and E. Balibar, *Reading Capital* (New York: Random House, 1970).

12.   See *Framework for Political Analysis*, chapter 5.

13.   For example, as I have mentioned earlier, we may note the central role played by the notion of relative autonomy of the state in the thinking of the Social Science Research Committee on *States and Social Structures* (established in 1986) as well as of many other neostatists, and yet we may wonder at the infrequent references to Poulantzas or Althusser. For a possible explanation, although not an adequate excuse, surely, see the quotation from S. Clarke *et al.* in my next note.

14.   E. Laclau, "The Specificity of the Political: The Poulantzas- Miliband Debate," 4 *Economy and Society* (1975) 88–110 at p. 88. In the same vein, Laclau elsewhere writes that Poulantzas's work "has an importance [for the development of Marxist political sociology that] can hardly be exaggerated." *Politics and Ideology in Marxist Theory*, (London: NLB, 1977) p. 79; see also E. P. Thompson, *Poverty of Theory and Other Essays* (New York: Monthly Review Press, 1978), in which Poulantzas is described as a "formidable opponent" (p. 4). Compare with the following remarks about Althusser, on whose ideas Poulantzas leaned so heavily: "The Althusserian movement is a very recent phenomenon, and yet it has come to dominate the interpretation of marxism, at least in the French and English-speaking worlds. Althusserian concepts have been assimilated into the discourse of many Marxists who have never heard of Althusser and are used with such an easy familiarity that many believe they come from Marx himself." S. Clarke, V. J. Seidler, K. McDonnell, K. Robins, and T. Lovell, *One-Dimensional Marxism* (London: Allison and Busby, 1980) p. 6.

15.   *Political Power and Social Classes* (London: NLB and Sheed and Ward, 1973) pp. 9ff.

16.   In *State, Power, Socialism* (London: NLB, 1978) pp. 22–25, Poulantzas talks about the impossibility of a general theory of the state as contrasted with a theory of the capitalist state which he seeks to construct.

Chapter 12

1. Poulantzas had, of course, adapted his conceptions from the original statement by Althusser. As I indicated in chapter 10, it would, however, take us too far afield to pursue the important and interesting Althusserian connection. For example, there are those who would argue that in separating economy, ideology, and politics and postulating their relative autonomy, Althusser puts parts ahead of the totality and he has thereby destroyed the fulcrum on which all of Marx's original thought was balanced. (K. McDonnell and K. Robins "Marxist Cultural Theory: The Althusserian Smokescreen," in S. Clarke *et al.*, *One-Dimensional Marxism*, pp. 158–59.) Whatever the case may be for Althusser, Poulantzas goes to considerable pains to argue for the retention of what he interprets as a holistic view of society, one that he sees as consistent with Marx's intentions, as I shall explain later in this chapter.

2. See B. Ollman, *Alienation: Marx's Conception of Man in Capitalist Society* (Cambridge: Cambridge University Press, 1971).

3. See my essays "The Current Meaning of 'Behavioralism' in Political Science," in J. C. Charlesworth (ed.), *Contemporary Political Analysis* (Glencoe, Ill.: Free Press, 1967) and "The New Revolution in Political Science," 63 *American Political Science Review* (1969) 1051–61.

4. See, for example, the work of Talcott Parsons.

5. In chapter 9.

6. *Ibid*.

7. See my discussion in chapter 9.

8. Perhaps it was some kind of intuitive awareness of this that led his critics to accuse Poulantzas of succumbing to bourgeois social science. For systems thinking as a twentieth-century intellectual movement, see my writings.

9. For example, a work in which one of the authors is a Marxist, has argued that "a reconstruction of [Marx's argument in *Capital*] would demonstrate clearly that Marx's reasoning proceeded along lines of systems analysis" (F. Cortes, A. Przeworski, and J. Sprague, *Systems Analysis for the Social Scientist* [New York: Wiley, 1974] p. 291, note 12). See as well S. M. Lipset, "Social Structure and Social Change," in P. Blau (ed.), *Approaches to the Study of Social Structure* (New York: Free Press, 1975) pp. 172–209 at p. 174, who, quoting from Robert Friedrichs makes the point that "contrary to the impression of most sociologists, Marx's stance . . . is at a number of points startlingly congruent with system theory as we have come to know it in Western sociology." For the reception of systems thinking by modern official Soviet Marxism, see I. V. Blauberg, V. N. Sadovsky, and E. G. Yudin, *Systems Theory* (U.S.S.R.: Progress Pubs., 1977).

10. From another point of view we might wonder whether Marxism, without abandoning any of its substantive theories, might not today be conceptually better off if it gave up the fuzzy notion of the state. See chapter 14 below and my essay "The Political System Besieged by the State."

11. *State, Power, Socialism* and *Political Power and Social Classes*, pp. 9ff.

12. *Political Power and Social Classes*, p. 99.

13. As M. Godelier phrases the issue, a specific structure is to be explained "by seeking the reasons for it in the specific determination of different modes of production." "The Problems of the 'Reproduction of Socioeconomic Systems', " in I. Rossi (ed.), *Structural Sociology* (New York: Columbia University Press, 1982) pp. 259–91 at p. 272.

14. L. Althusser and E. Balibar, *Reading Capital* (New York: Random House, 1970) pp. 182–83.

15. *Political Power and Social Classes*, p. 37.

16. *Ibid*, p. 13.

17. See D. Rosenberg's review of *Fascism and Dictatorship* in 24 *Sociological Review* (1976) 658–75 at p. 671.

18. *Political Power and Social Classes*, p. 13; and see p. 41, where Poulantzas speaks of political practice as bearing on all four levels.

19. See L. Althusser, *For Marx*.

20. It may be that since Althusser considers Marxism as the only truly scientific knowledge and all

else as ideology disguised as knowledge, this might have created problems of analysis for Poulantzas that he was not quite ready to face up to.

21. E. Laclau, *Politics and Ideology in Marxist Theory*, p. 73.

22. *Political Power and Social Classes*, pp. 13–14, italics in original. G. A. Cohen, *Karl Marx's Theory of History: A Defence* (Princeton: Princeton University Press, 1978) p. 280, finds that "in the last instance" is an "unexplained" (he might have said, murky) phrase that was clearly borrowed from Engels, who once wrote about "determination in the last resort."

23. *Political Power and Social Classes*, p. 14, italics in original. See also *Fascism and Dictatorship*, p. 325.

24. *Political Power and Social Classes*, p. 209.

25. The fact that it has been frequently borrowed, either in name or in substance, by both Marxists and conventional social scientists has unfortunately not contributed very much to its clarity.

26. *Ibid.*, p. 37

27. For the affinity of this idea to Marx's own theories, see the interpretation of the latter in holistic terms by B. Ollman, *Alienation: Marx's Conception of Man in Capitalist Society*.

28. *Political Power and Social Classes*, p. 14, italics in original. Note the confusing and inconsistent use of the notion of dominance. Sometimes it means "determined by" and at other times something of a less powerful influencing factor.

29. *Ibid.*, pp. 29 and 32.

30. See K. McDonnell and K. Robins, "Marxist Cultural Theory: The Althusserian Smokescreen," in S. Clarke *et al.*, *One-Dimensional Marxism*, pp. 157–231 for the claim that Althusser, at least, has failed to make the case for an interpretation along these lines.

31. *Political Power and Social Classes*, p. 26.

32. *Ibid.*, p. 27.

33. Poulantzas virtually abandons the older concept of superstructure, however, so that the term finds little place in his analysis.

34. A similarity already noted by an unsympathetic Marxist critic, S. Clarke, "Althusserian Marxism," in S. Clarke *et. al.*, *One-Dimensional Marxism*, pp. 7–102 at p. 22.

35. Poulantzas's interpretation of ideology is influenced by Gramsci, hence it comes close to what we would have to consider culture.

36. See S. Giner and J. Salcedo, "The Ideology and Practice of Nicos Poulantzas," 17 *Archive of European Sociology* (1976) 334–65, esp. pp. 349 ff.; S. Clarke, *op. cit.*, who accuses Poulantzas of being a bourgeois social scientist; and the review by D. Rosenberg of N. Poulantzas, *Classes in Contemporary Capitalism*, in 26 *Sociological Review* (1978) 679–94 at p. 685. With appropriate changes in terminology, the following sentence might have been taken from a description by Parsons of the interaction among the major social subsystems. "With regard to the relations among the instances [subsystems], their so-called 'interaction' . . . consists of the *limits* within which one level [subsystem] can modify another." N. Poulantzas, *Political Power and Social Classes*, p. 94. In fact, S. Clarke, *op. cit.* at p. 37, remarks on "the uncanny resemblance of the complex whole structured in dominance [as phrased by Althusser] to *The Social System* [of Talcott Parsons]."

37. For example, p. 316, line 10.

38. See *Fascism and Dictatorship*, pp. 305, 307–08, 314, 319–20, 324–22.

39. "The relation between the bourgeois class and the State is an *objective relation*. This means that if the *function* of the State in a determinate social formation and the *interests* of the dominant class in this formation *coincide*, it is by reason of the system itself." 58 *New Left Review* (1969), italics in original; reprinted in R. Blackburn (ed.), *Ideology in Social Science* (London: Fontana, 1972) pp. 239–53 at p. 245.

40. See R. Miliband, *The State in Capitalist Society* (London: Weidenfeld and Nicolson, 1969). This position is virtually implied in one of Poulantzas's last pieces where he writes that "a theory of the new type of state that has developed in the countries of dependent capitalism is called for, all the more urgently in that, whereas a great deal of research has been done into the economies of dependent countries . . . no 'general theory' on the political system peculiar to these countries has so far been

evolved." "Research Note on the State and Society," in 32 *International Social Science Journal* (1980) 600–608, at p. 603.

41. This is not true for all Marxists however. See chapter 1.

42. See my *Framework for Political Analysis*.

43. For the importance of decomposability in all analysis of social systems, see H. A. Simon, "The Architecture of Complexity," in *The Sciences of the Artificial* (Cambridge: MIT Press, 1969), and A. Ando, F. Fisher, and H. A. Simon, *Essays on the Structure of Social Science Models* (Cambridge: MIT Press, 1963). I shall turn to this theme in a later chapter.

44. From this interpretation we can appreciate the extent to which neostatists, in their newly discovered contribution of the "state" to social policy and social change, must be deeply in debt to Althusser and Poulantzas for their development of the notion of "the relative autonomy of the state." Yet it is very strange to find that they are only infrequently referenced or in other ways given their due in the discussions during the 1980s.

45. S. Giner and J. Salcedo, "The Ideology and Practice of Nicos Poulantzas," 17 *Archives of European Sociology* (1976) 344–65, at p. 352.

46. There are several ways of approaching the work of Poulantzas. One is to interpret him as a partisan member of the Communist party of France, follow his fortunes in that area and seek to account for his analyses in the light of these changing relationships. The other is to assess his works on their merits from the point of view of our particular purposes. I shall select this second alternative. Whether the limitations we shall find in his writings stem from his lack of insight, inadequate background in the social sciences, necessities of partisan loyalty, class position, and the like are interesting questions but ones that need not detain us here.

Chapter 13

1. See *State, Power, Socialism*, pp. 127–36, esp. p. 136.

2. See N. Poulantzas, "The Capitalist State: A Reply to Miliband and Laclau," 95 *New Left Review* (1976) 63–83.

3. For Poulantzas's views on the state, see chapter 14 below.

4. See S. Giner and J. Salcedo, "The Ideology and Practice of Nicos Poulantzas."

5. For example, intuitively he explains ideology in functionalist terms: "It is apparent that the juridico-political ideology is the dominant region in bourgeois ideology in the CMP [capitalist mode of production] and in a capitalist formation. This is also closely linked to the specific role [function] played by the real juridico-political level, i. e. the state and law. The 'cement' of ideology permeates every layer of the social structure, *including economic and political practice*." *Political Power and Social Classes*, p. 213, italics in original.

6. See E. Laclau, *Politics and Ideology*, pp. 69ff. Also R. Miliband, "Poulantzas and the Capitalist State," 82 *New Left Review* (1973) 83–92.

7. See *Political Power and Social Classes*, p. 5.

8. *Ibid.*, p. 50.

9. *Ibid.*, p. 17.

10. *State, Power, Socialism*, p. 17

11. *Ibid.*, pp. 16–17.

12. Poulantzas clearly anticipates and, in advance, rejects the contrary claims of S. Clarke in "Althusserian Marxism," in S. Clarke *et al.*, *One-Dimensional Marxism*, pp. 7–102. There Clarke sees Althusser as returning Marxism to the very disciplinary approaches the shortcomings of which holistic Marxism was able to overcome.

13. See *Political Power and Social Classes*, p. 16–17.

14. *State, Power, Socialism*, pp. 18–19, italics in original.

15. See Glucksmann, *Structuralist Analysis in Contemporary Social Thought*, pp. 147–49.

16. *State, Power, Socialism*, pp. 26–27

17. *State, Power, Socialism*, p. 26.

18. See *Political Power and Social Classes*, p. 89. Undoubtedly he is here arguing against a hidden opponent, systems analysis, which does use as its point of departure the interaction of subsystems. See my *Systems Analysis of Political Life*.

19. "What distinguishes one mode of production from another and consequently specifies a mode of production is the particular form of the articulation maintained by its levels." P. 15.

20. *Political Power and Social Classes*, p. 17.

21. *Ibid.*, pp. 76–77 and p. 94.

22. *Ibid.*, p. 297.

23. *State, Power, Socialism*, pp. 26–27.

24. *Fascism and Dictatorship*, p. 334.

25. See another effort to cope with this problem in *State, Power, Socialism*, p. 15.

26. M. Glucksmann, *op. cit.*, pp. 147ff.

27. *Political Power and Social Classes*, p. 90, italics in original.

28. K. Marx and F. Engels, *On Britain* (Moscow: Foreign Languages Pubs., 1962).

29. *Political Power and Social Classes*, pp. 90ff.

30. *Ibid.*

31. *Ibid.*, p. 90.

32. *Ibid.*

33. B. Ollman, *Alienation: Marx's Conception of Man in Capitalist Society*, p. 33.

34. *Ibid.*, p. 253.

35. N. Poulantzas, "The Problem of the Capitalist State," in R. Blackburn, *op. cit.*, p. 246.

36. *Political Power and Social Classes*, pp. 13–14, italics in original.

37. *State, Power, Socialism*, pp. 18–19.

38. *State, Power, Socialism*, p. 128, italics added. Compare also: "The State maintains its relative autonomy of particular fractions of the power bloc . . . so that it may *ensure* the organization of the general interest of the bourgeoisie under the hegemony of one of its fractions" (*ibid.*, italics added.). The italicized verbs in these two quotations indicate that the state has no choice; its functions are almost preordained. It is not a matter of probability but of necessity.

39. *Ibid.*, pp. 18–19.

40. *Political Power and Social Classes*, pp. 13–14.

41. For a discussion of the presumed ways through which this is achieved, see *ibid.*, pp. 50–54, 130ff and 191ff.

42. For alternative meanings of the concept determine, see R. Williams, *Keywords: A Vocabulary of Culture and Society* (New York: Oxford University Press, 1985).

43. See chapter 11 above.

44. *Political Power and Social Classes*, p. 297.

45. For Poulantzas the state and social classes represent "objective structures, and their relations . . . an objective system of regular connections, a structure and a system whose agents, 'men', are in the words of Marx, 'bearers' of it, *Träger*." N. Poulantzas, "The Problem of the Capitalist State," in R. Blackburn (ed.), *Ideology in Social Science: Readings in Critical Social Theory* (Bungay, Suffolk: Fontana/Collins, 1972) p. 242. It should be noted that toward the end of his life, and before he had an opportunity to develop his position fully, his views began to change radically. Actors, not objective social contradictions, were becoming the driving social force. See his "Research Note on the State and Society," in 32 *International Social Science Journal* (1980) pp. 600–608.

46. *Fascism and Dictatorship*, p. 41.

47. *Political Power and Social Classes*, p. 115, footnote 24, italics in original.

48. R. Miliband, *The State and Capitalist Society*, p. 57. Miliband sees the political elite as involved

in a far more complex relationship with the rest of the political system and society than Poulantzas's structuralist determinism would seem to allow, at least as it is presented in *Political Power and Social Classes*.

49. Miliband agrees. See *ibid.*, p. 69.

50. S. Lukes, "Outclassed: A Review of *Classes in Contemporary Capitalism* by Nicos Poulantzas," 90 *The New Statesman* (Sept. 12, 1975).

51. Poulantzas was not alone in Marxism, or even original, in seeking to resolve the whole-part dilemma. Here he was clearly influenced by Althusser in whose footsteps he was following, even if not slavishly. Althusser saw this dilemma as a primary epistemological issue before him. See L. Althusser and E. Balibar, *Reading Capital* (New York: Random House, 1970) esp. pp. 182ff.

52. For a defense of Marx's own functionalism as a form of explanation, see G. A. Cohen, *Karl Marx's Theory of History: A Defence* (Princeton, N.J.: Princeton University Press, 1978) esp. chapters 9 and 10.

Chapter 14

1. N. Poulantzas, "The Problem of the Capitalist State," in R. Blackburn (ed.), *Ideology in the Social Sciences*, p. 238.

2. *Political Power and Social Classes*, pp. 46ff.

3. See *ibid.*, pp. 41 and 93.

4. *Ibid.*, chapter 1.

5. N. Poulantzas, "The Problem of the Capitalist State," 58 *New Left Review* (1969) 67–78; R. Miliband, "The Capitalist State: Reply to Nicos Poulantzas," 59 *New Left Review* (1969) 53–60; N. Poulantzas, "The Capitalist State: A Reply to Miliband and Laclau," 95 *New Left Review* (1976) 63–83.

6. Poulantzas shares Gramsci's view that the nominally "private" institutions of church, parties, unions, mass media, and so on which "embody" the dominant ideologies represent "the ideological state apparatuses," whereas those institutions such as police, army, courts, and government are the "repressive state apparatus." See N. Poulantzas, *Fascism and Dictatorship*, esp. p. 301.

7. N. Poulantzas, *Political Power and Social Classes*, p. 256.

8. *Ibid.*, p. 117; see footnote 5 as well.

9. N. Poulantzas, *State, Power, Socialism*, p. 131.

10. *Ibid.*, p. 129.

11. N. Poulantzas, *Political Power and Social Classes*, pp. 258ff.

12. See N. Poulantzas, *State, Power, Socialism*, pp. 128ff.

13. *Ibid.*, p. 191.

14. *Ibid.*, p. 17, italics in original.

15. N. Poulantzas, *Political Power and Social Classes*, pp. 48–49.

16. *Ibid.*, p. 50.

17. N. Poulantzas, *State, Power, Socialism*, although in his concluding chapter he seems to modify his view on this matter substantially. See also *Political Power and Social Classes*, p. 44.

18. For this term, see M. J. Levy, Jr., *The Structure of Society* (Princeton: Princeton University Press, 1952) p. 77.

19. N. Poulantzas, *Political Power and Social Classes*, p. 42.

20. *Ibid.*, p. 93.

21. *Ibid.*, p. 104.

22. *Ibid.*, p. 43, my italics.

23. *Ibid.*, p. 8.

24. *Ibid.*, p. 115, footnote 24.

25. *Ibid.*, p. 116.

26. *Ibid.*, p. 115, footnote 24, italics in original.

27. *Ibid.*

28. N. Poulantzas, *Fascism and Dictatorship*, p. 301, footnote 3.

29. *Ibid.*

30. *Ibid.*, pp. 301ff.

31. Poulantzas, *Political Power and Social Classes*, p. 115, footnote 24.

32. See note 5 above.

33. N. Poulantzas, *State, Power, Socialism*, p. 128, italics in original.

34. *Ibid.*

35. *Ibid.*, pp. 128–29, italics in original.

36. *Ibid.*, p. 133.

37. N. Poulantzas, *Political Power and Social Classes*, pp. 130–31.

38. N. Poulantzas, *State, Power, Socialism*, p. 132.

39. *Ibid.*

40. A. Koestler, *The Ghost in the Machine* (London: Hutchinson, 1967).

Chapter 15

1. N. Poulantzas, "The Problem of the Capitalist State," p. 248, italics in original; See also *Political Power and Social Classes*, p. 142.

2. *Political Power and Social Classes*, pp. 12ff.

3. *Ibid.*, p. 142, italics in original.

4. The material for the classification is drawn from *Political Power and Social Classes*, supplemented by Poulantzas's other publications.

5. Somewhere, I believe, in E. Laclau, *Politics and Ideology in Marxist Theory*.

6. *Political Power and Social Classes*, pp. 157 and 187ff.

7. *Ibid.*, p. 142, my italics.

8. N. Poulantzas, "The Problem of the Capitalist State," p. 248.

9. This contains a higher-order structure. But whereas I have been concerned with higher-order *political* structures, Poulantzas is clearly referring to the broader *social* structure and pays little specific attention to the overall political structure.

10. *Ibid.*, p. 248.

11. G. A. Cohen, *Karl Marx's Theory of History: A Defence*.

12. See N. Poulantzas, "The Problem of the Capitalist State."

13. *Ibid.*, pp. 249ff, and *Fascism and Dictatorship*, pp. 311ff.

14. For the variety of meanings associated with the word determination see R. Williams, *Keywords: A Vocabulary of Culture and Society*, 2d ed. (New York: Oxford University Press, 1983).

15. *The Crisis of the Dictatorships*, p. 90.

16. *Political Power and Social Classes*, p. 144, my italics.

17. *Ibid.*, p. 47.

18. *Ibid.*, p. 144.

19. *Ibid.*, p. 149.

20. *Ibid.*

21. See Table 15.1.

22. *Political Power and Social Classes*, p. 272.

23. *Ibid.*, pp. 271–72.

24. *Ibid.*, p. 150.

25. *Ibid.* "Type" of state refers to states reflecting different modes of production—for example, capitalist or feudal states. "Form" of state seems to be reserved by Poulantzas for interventionist as against liberal and, as we shall see, for what he calls normal as compared to exceptional states. But at times he also designates these as "types of states." As we have already found and will continue to find, Poulantzas's terminology is notoriously unstable. I shall use type and form indiscriminately as they both seem to refer to categories or classes of states. To distinguish between them is to try to make a difference without a difference.

26. *Ibid.*, p. 55.

27. *Ibid.*

28. *Ibid.*, p. 141.

29. *Ibid.*, p. 230.

30. *Ibid.*, pp. 140–41.

31. *Ibid.*, pp. 229, 237, and 296.

32. *Ibid.*, pp. 242–43. Poulantzas adopts Lenin's definition of conjuncture as "equivalent to that of the 'present moment' which is the specific *object* of political practice." (*Ibid.*, p. 93, italics in original.)

33. *Ibid.*, p. 151.

34. Chapter 14 above.

35. *Political Power and Social Classes*, p. 155.

36. *The Crisis of the Dictatorships*, p. 21.

37. *Ibid.*

38. *Ibid.*, p. 21.

39. For the difference between types and forms of state, see above.

40. Compare: "It would be necessary to trace historically how each crisis imposes on capital a new relation between its economic and political form of domination, a new relation shaped in practice by concrete class struggle. . . . It is . . . a shift in the form of capital's rule imposed upon capital by the pressure of class struggle expressing the contradiction of its own domination, a shift in the [political] form of capital's crisis-ridden struggle to accumulate." J. Holloway and S. Picciotto, "Capital, Crisis and the State," in 2 *Capital and Class* (1977) 76–101 at pp. 94–95.

41. *State, Power, Socialism*, p. 12.

42. *The Crisis of the Dictatorships*, p. 91. Why states such as these should be designated as "normal," when they have been so few in number in modern times, may be cause for wonder. In the twentieth century, democracies have been really no less exceptional than other kinds of regimes. Unobtrusively, Poulantzas seems to have introduced an evaluative criterion. Since such democracies are clearly not statistical norms, they must represent norms in the evaluative sense. Representative democracies are normal for him, perhaps, because something like this is the form that he feels the preferred state should take? It fits in with "normal" human needs in some manner?

43. *State, Power, Socialism*, p. 159, my italics.

44. *Political Power and Social Classes*, p. 317.

45. *Ibid.*

46. *Ibid.*, pp. 153–54.

47. See my discussion of regime as a concept in chapter 5 above and chapter 18 below.

48. For what he calls his political rather than a conventional juridical definition of the separation of powers, see *Political Power and Social Classes*, pp. 308ff, esp. footnote 1.

49. *Ibid.*, pp. 317ff.

50. *Ibid.*, p. 303.

51. *Ibid.*

52. The identification of parties with specific classes or fractions thereof is typically a European

phenomenon found elsewhere, of course, but less often in the United States. Here a distinguishing and not fully understood feature of both major parties is their capacity to embrace most major classes/ fractions, to use Poulantzas's terms, even though one or the other party may tilt toward big business or labor.

53. *Ibid.*, p. 315.

54. *Ibid.*, p. 151.

55. *Ibid.*, p. 316.

56. *Ibid.*, p. 245.

57. *Fascism and Dictatorship*, p. 311, italics in original.

58. *Political Power and Social Classes*, p. 246.

59. For V. Pareto's theory of change, see his *Mind and Society* (New York: Harcourt, Brace, 1935).

60. Chapter 13 above.

61. See my earlier discussion of his "method" of interpenetration.

Chapter 16

1. See Table 15.1.

2. *Fascism and Dictatorship*, p. 11. In his usual loose way with language, Poulantzas in this single sentence manages to characterize the exceptional regime as a type of state as well as a type of regime. See my Table 15.1 and the discussion about it for the problem of terminology in Poulantzas's work. Henceforth, except for occasional deliberate lapses for special reasons of understanding Poulantzas's meaning, I shall reserve the attributes normal as compared to exceptional, for regimes only.

3. *Fascism and Dictatorship*, pp. 12 and 16.

4. *Fascism and Dictatorship*, pp. 17–47. Note that I am here numbering the transformation rules so that they are continuous with those in the preceding chapter.

5. *Fascism and Dictatorship*, p. 59. It should be noted that a number of years later, in *States and Social Revolutions*, T. Skocpol joins Poulantzas in attributing special importance to political crises in bringing about changes such as social revolutions and makes this idea one of the centerpieces of her analysis.

6. *Fascism and Dictatorship*, p. 18.

7. *Ibid.*, p. 54.

8. See above, chapter 14, on the State.

9. *Fascism and Dictatorship*, p. 18.

10. *Ibid.*

11. *The Crisis of the Dictatorships*, p. 19.

12. *Fascism and Dictatorship*, p. 24.

13. *Fascism and Dictatorship*, p. 21.

14. *Ibid.*

15. *Ibid.*, p. 20.

16. *Ibid.*, p. 17.

17. *Ibid.*, p. 334.

18. *Ibid.*, p. 63, italics in original.

19. *Ibid.*, p. 72, italics in original.

20. *Ibid.*, pp. 58 and 334.

21. *Ibid.*, p. 63.

22. "The exceptional State needs this relative autonomy to reorganize hegemony and the power bloc." *Fascism and Dictatorship*, p. 313.

23. *Ibid.*, p. 112.

24.   *Ibid.*, p. 314.

25.   *Ibid.*, p. 319.

26.   *Ibid.*, p. 326.

27.   *Ibid.*, pp. 320–24.

28.   In this analysis of the origins of the authoritarian and totalitarian types of regimes it is interesting to note that no more light than we had before (see chapter 14) is shed on the nature of the object called the *state* despite the latter's very central and active role in the transformation process. Hopefully, by this time we have learned to live with the ambiguity, if not opacity, of the meaning of the state as a term. Whatever the state is, through changes in the observed structures (its apparatuses, in Poulantzas's terms) it does increase its control over policy and the social classes. Furthermore, we now have a better understanding of why Poulantzas considers the exceptional regime to be a variant of the executive-dominant interventionist state. To resolve the economic-political-ideological crisis, the state finds it necessary to intervene in all areas of the social formation and not only in the economy. The instrument of the intervention on behalf of the state and of the dominant classes which, of necessity, as we have seen, it serves, is the executive branch of government. The exceptional regime can, therefore, be said to originate in the same stage, in Poulantzas's technical sense, as the executive interventionist state under capitalism. (*Fascism and Dictatorship*, p. 327). We have here the major reason for the considerable if not excessive attention that Poulantzas has seemed to pay to the function of the executive as against the legislative arms of government under capitalism.

29.   See D. Abraham, *The Collapse of the Weimar Republic: Political Economy and Crisis* (Princeton, N. J.: Princeton University Press, 1981), even though his critics have not at all been convinced by his analysis. See also an assessment of Poulantzas's history in D. Rosenberg's review of *Fascism and Dictatorship* in 24 *Sociological Review* (1976) 658–75 and in J. Caplan, "Theories of Fascism: Nicos Poulantzas as Historian," 3 *History Workshop* (1977) 83–100.

30.   In *The Crisis of the Dictatorships* he does deal with military dictatorships. There, however, he does not consider the rules that generate this kind of regime, nor does he explain this omission. Rather he accepts the existence of such dictatorships and reverses the question he asks in *Fascism and Dictatorship*. In effect, although he is not as self-conscious of his own approach as we might have wished, he there poses the question of how these regimes are transformed back to normal ones, that is, to representative democracies, as in Greece and Portugal, and later in Spain, especially where the reversal has not been brought about by revolutionary means. This is the problem of redemocratization. Two points may be made about his treatment of transformation rules for the reverse direction. His rules continue to be an unsurprising account of the historical way in which these political systems have moved back into the democratic fold. As a result, whatever we can glean from his analysis of the way military dictatorships are transformed into democracies would not radically modify the transformation rules as we understand them from his interpretation of fascism.

31.   *Political Power and Social Classes*, p. 294, footnote 29.

32.   *Fascism and Dictatorship*, p. 71.

33.   *Ibid.*, p. 40.

34.   *Ibid.*, p. 39.

35.   *Ibid.*, p. 20.

36.   *Ibid.*, p. 312.

37.   *Ibid.*

38.   *Ibid.*, pp. 294–309.

39.   *Ibid.*, p. 23.

40.   *Ibid.*, p. 39, italics in original.

41.   *Ibid.*, pp. 41–42.

42.   *Ibid.*, p. 52.

43.   *Ibid.*, p. 53, italics in original.

44.   *Ibid.*, pp. 41–42, italics in original.

45.   P. 293.

46. *Ibid.*, p. 39, italics in original.

47. See chapter 14 above.

48. For further evidence of this we need only turn to the last chapter of *State, Power, Socialism* where he changes his mind about the objective necessity for "smashing the State apparatus." He sees this as leading to a nondemocratic socialist system. Instead he now favors infiltrating and taking over the capitalist State apparatuses through a gradualist program of workers' management and control, rank-and-file democracy. This new policy clearly moves in the direction of a "subjective problematic."

49. S. Giner and J. Salcedo, "The Ideology and Practice of Nicos Poulantzas" and D. Rosenberg's review of *Fascism and Dictatorship, op. cit.*

Chapter 17

1. As I have observed earlier, few structuralists, of course, found their way into political science, at least until the emergence of the neostatists in the 1980s.

2. For this phrase, see chapter 8 above and J. Piaget, *Structuralism*, p. 13.

3. W. T. Bluhm, "Synthesizing Rational and Cultural Models: An Empirical Survey and a Theoretical Suggestion," in W. T. Bluhm (ed.), *The Paradigm Problem in Political Science* (Durham, N.C.: Carolina Academic Press, 1982) p. 136.

4. See chapter 7 above.

5. *Ibid.*

6. See the discussion of this point below in this chapter, in reference to decomposability of systems.

7. I am using this term in the technical sense as represented in the post-positivist philosophy of science of D. Shapere, "Scientific Theories and Their Domains," in F. Suppe, *The Structure of Scientific Theories*, pp. 518–70.

8. See chapter 14 above and references there.

9. See E. Nagel, "On the Statement 'The Whole Is More Than the Sum of Its Parts'," in P. F. Lazarsfeld and M. Rosenberg (eds.), *The Language of Social Research: A Reader in the Methodology of Social Research* (Glencoe, Ill.: Free Press, 1955) pp. 519–27.

10. It is, of course, to the credit of Marxism that it has insisted on not losing sight of this relationship to the totality. "The Marxist principle, in contrast, is that one must first grasp the totality and then the way it appears as fragmented." K. McDonnel and K. Robins, "Marxist Cultural Theory: the Althusserian Smokescreen," p. 159. We need to bear in mind that the totality to which this quotation refers is the society, which Poulantzas, of course, calls the mode of production. For reasons already elaborated, without in the least denying the importance of the social totality, my focus has been on the neglected political totality and its influence.

11. For an elaboration of the possible relationships between parts of a system and consequences for the functioning of the whole, see A. Ando, F. M. Fisher, and H. A. Simon, *Essays on the Structure of Social Science Models* and H. A. Simon, *The Sciences of the Artificial*. They develop a vocabulary for dealing with the varying relationships among subsystem. Starting with a whole system they see the constituent subsystems as decomposable, nearly decomposable, and nondecomposable. This approach represents a possible systematic and theoretically more powerful way of dealing with the notion of relative autonomy of parts, such as the state, as proposed by Althusser, adopted by Poulantzas, and overutilized by a great many recent studies centering on the creative function of the state. Neostatists might well find that the literature on system decomposability illuminates a way whereby the notion of the autonomy of the state might be dealt with more rigorously.

12. For the academic interest group formed around this position, see the *States and Social Structures Newsletter*, Social Science Research Council.

13. R. Boudon, *The Uses of Structuralism*, p. 102.

14. In chapter 18 I shall exemplify this conception of structure as applied to the analysis of regimes.

15. See L. von Bertalanffy, "The History and Status of General Systems Theory," in G. J. Klir, *Trends in General Systems Theory* (New York: Wiley-Interscience, 1972) pp. 21–41 at pp. 32ff.

16. R. D. Brunner and G. D. Brewer, *Organized Complexity: Empirical Theories of Political Development* (New York: Free Press, 1971) p. 90, italics in original.

17.   *Ibid.*, pp. 86–87 and 170.

18.   I. Scheuch, "Social Context and Individual Behavior," in M. Dogan and S. Rokkan, *Quantitative Analysis in Social Sciences* (Cambridge, Mass.: MIT Press, 1969) pp. 133–55 at p. 142.

19.   In his own words, "Merely comparing the influence of large contexts such as the nation-states of Turkey or Greece would be too gross a description of environmental effects; for the individual returnee [returning emigrant], Turkey and Greece were, in part, abstractions that exert influences only through several mediating institutions" such as family, peer groups, or factories. "While the factory can be understood as one setting in which Turkey or Greece as economies become concrete for the individual returnee, the factory in turn is an individual unit influenced by the whole economic organization of the nation-state. In this way, the influence of the nation-state [the whole, in our terms] is filtered through many intermediate steps down to the individual." *Ibid.*, p. 158.

20.   See, for example, P. Katzenstein's justification for his dependence on historical analysis: "Although I use numbers in this book where relevant, I deliberately differ from statistically inclined investigations that seek to enhance our understanding by correlating small size with a broad range of economic, social, and political outcomes. In method of analysis I accord pride of place to historically informed comparisons rather than to statistical investigations. Granting the specifics of national settings, the historical evolution of these seven small European states justifies our particular attention." "The explanation this book proposes is, in a word, historical." *Small States in World Markets* (Ithaca, N.Y.: Cornell University Press, 1985) pp. 21 and 34. See also I. Wallerstein, "Should We Unthink Nineteenth-Century Social Science," in 118 *International Social Science Journal* (1988) 527–31 at p. 350. There he proposes that we "substitute for 'society' the concept of 'historical system'."

21.   Although hermeneuticists vary greatly among themselves, "yet most of them agree in attaching enormous importance to the idea of frameworks which give meaning and significance to individual phenomena. . . . Understanding [is] seen firstly as a holistic process mediated by a complex framework." "Hans-Georg Gadamer" by W. Outhwaite, in Q. Skinner (ed.), *The Return of Grand Theory in the Human Sciences* (Cambridge: Cambridge University Press, 1985) pp. 21–40 at p. 23. It would be interesting to analyze hermeneutic conceptions of the holistic context of understanding but, given the great variety of interpretations among them, it would distract us from our main concerns.

22.   See T. Skocpol and M. Somers, "Uses of Comparative History in Macrosocial Inquiry," 22 *Comparative Studies in Society and History* (1980) 174–97, esp. pp. 192–93.

23.   The long view in the evolution of social science would indicate that in the 1980s we may have been passing through a phase. It could be demonstrated that in the short history of social science there is a tendency for the pendulum of research to swing from commitment to empirical research—discovery of the "facts"—to theoretical attempts to make sense of them. Each new theoretical commitment raises the need for new kinds of "facts," given the problems that the theories raise, which in due course leads to the return to theory as a way of trying to understand the new facts, and so on in an endless cycle.

24.   R. Collins, "Micro-Translation as a Theory-Building Strategy," in K. Knorr-Cetina and A. V. Cicourel (eds.), *Advances in Social Theory and Methodology*, pp. 80–108 at p. 89.

25.   See my discussion of "pragmatic holism" later in the present chapter.

26.   R. Harré, "Philosophical Aspects of the Micro-Macro Problem," in K. Knorr-Cetina and A. V. Cicourel (eds.), *op. cit.*, pp. 139–60 at p. 150.

27.   See R. Collins, *op. cit.* and O. Collins and J. M. Collins, *Interaction and Social Structure* (The Hague: Mouton, 1973), as well as K. Knorr-Cetina and A. V. Cicourel (eds.), *op. cit.*, *passim*. Although it would take us too far afield to pursue the matter, it is interesting to see a similar point of view expressed by H. D. Lasswell in *Psychopathology and Politics* (Chicago: University of Chicago Press, 1930), chapter 13, "The State as a [Psychological] Manifold of Events"; and in his *World Politics and Personal Insecurity* (New York: McGraw-Hill, 1935). In the latter book, the whole of the structure of international relations seems to dissolve into the minds of individuals. See L. A. Coser's criticisms of the ethnomethodological point of view: "In general, it would seem to me, that we deal here with a massive cop-out, a determined refusal to undertake research that would indicate the extent to which our lives are affected by the socioeconomic context in which they are imbedded. It amounts to an orgy of subjectivism . . . [where the] private construction of reality serves to obscure the tangible qualities of the world 'out there'." "Two Methods in Search of Substance," 40 *American Sociological Review* (1975) 691–700 at p. 698.

28.   For this illustration see M. Mandelbaum, "Societal Facts," in A. Ryan, *The Philosophy of*

Social Explanation (London: Oxford University Press, 1973) pp. 105–18. There Mandelbaum identifies tellers, customers, banks, legal tender, contracts etc. as social facts, in a Durkheimian sense.

29. See A. Giddens, "Agency, Institutions and Time-Space Analysis" in K. Knorr-Cetina and A. V. Cicourel (eds.), *Advances in Social Theory and Methodology*, pp. 161–74.

30. See the extensive and well-known works of Karl Popper on methodological individualism and the considerable literature following from it.

31. H. A. Simon, *op. cit.*, chapter 4.

32. For a somewhat different view of the methodological issues involved here, see S. Lukes, "Methodological Individualism Reconsidered," in A. Ryan (ed.), *The Philosophy of Social Explanation* (London: Oxford University Press, 1973) pp. 119–29.

33. See my *Systems Analysis of Political Life*.

34. See *A Systems Analysis of Political Life*, part 5.

35. P. Bourdieu, "Men and Machines," in K. Knorr-Cetina and A. V. Cicourel, *op. cit.*, pp. 304–18 at p. 312. Compare also with the view of R. Collins, who suggests that "there are several advantages of attempting micro-reduction, and these advantages hold whether reduction proves to be fully possible or not. Reduction produces an empirically stronger theory, on any level of analysis, by displaying the real-life situations and behaviours that make up its phenomena. In particular, it introduces empirically real causal forces in the shape of human beings expending energy. It enables us to discover which macro-concepts and explanations are empirically groundable, and which are not." "Micro-translation as a Theory Building Strategy," in K. Knorr-Cetina and A. V. Cicourel, *op. cit.*, pp. 81–108 at p. 93. See also O. Collins and J. A. Collins, *op. cit.*

36. To recall the differences between structural and structuralist analysis, see chapter 2 above.

Chapter 18

1. This use of the concept order has little to do, of course, with the notion of orderliness in the sense of a low rate of change or of the absence of violence or disorganization.

2. See our earlier discussions about the regime and its structure in chapters 1 and 5.

3. See chapter 4 above.

4. For a discussion of a strict usage of rules as a concept, see chapter 4, especially note 25.

5. J. Piaget, *Structuralism*, p. 12.

6. Chapter 3 above.

7. Chapter 5 above.

8. See my *Systems Analysis of Political Life*.

9. Chapter 17 above.

10. See D. E. Neubauer, "Some Conditions of Democracy," in C. F. Knudde and D. E. Neubauer, *Empirical Democratic Theory*, pp. 224–35.

11. For a full discussion of the part played by the structures and processes in the social environment, see my extended discussions in *A Framework for Political Analysis*, chapter 5, and *A Systems Analysis of Political Life*, *passim*.

12. Chapter 3 above.

13. *Ibid.*

14. Chapter 7 above.

15. C. E. Lindblom, "The Market as Prison," 44 *Journal of Politics* (1982) 324–36 at p. 331.

16. See especially *A Framework for Political Analysis*, chapters 5 and 7.

17. See, for example, the writings of C. Tilly, I. Wallerstein, and M. Foucault.

18. See my discussion of this position in chapters 8 and 9 above.

19. Perhaps Poulantzas had something like this in mind when he spoke about "interpenetration." See chapter 13 above.

20. See S. Lukes, *Power: A Radical View*. The recognition of this was, of course, one of the merits

of structuralist Marxism. As Althusser put it, the "elements of a whole [are determined] by the structure of the whole" (quoted in S. Lukes, p. 52).

21. See *A Systems Analysis of Political Life.*

22. For a discussion of the way in which one pressure group in the United States, Common Cause, has sought to bring about reform of the regime structure there, see A. S. McFarland, *Public Interest Lobbies* (Washington, D. C: American Institute for Public Policy Research, 1976), esp. pp. 59ff. See also D. Abraham, *The Collapse of the Weimar Republic*, in which he writes about the influence of heavy industry in Weimar Germany which, by the 1930s, felt that social policy was bleeding off profits and capital accumulation and that a solution lay in reducing social gains (social welfare) of the working class and reducing the influence of the SPD. Heavy industry therefore aligned itself with the Nazi party—even if uncomfortable with its new bedmate—as a way of modifying the structure of the regime so as to reduce the power of labor.

23. For the role of imitation in the diffusion of parliamentary or presidential democratic regimes, among others, see R. Bendix, *Kings and People: Power and the Mandate to Rule* (Berkeley: University of California Press, 1978).

24. For the precise way in which I am using the notion of political community, see *A Systems Analysis of Political Life*, pp. 171ff.

25. In *A Systems Analysis of Political Life* I tried to show what we would have to look at to understand the various kinds of external social environments that shape and limit the range of variations of political systems.

26. See especially chapter 5 above.

27. For this term and a discussion of hierarchy in this sense, see H. A. Simon, *The Sciences of the Artificial*, chapter 4. See T. Parsons, *The System of Modern Societies* (Englewood Cliffs, N.J.: Prentice-Hall, 1971) p. 28, Table 1 for a different kind of hierarchical ordering. He seeks to establish a boss hierarchy in which culture seems to dominate. The hierarchy in my diagram makes no claim to the control exercised by any level; it simply shows a nesting relationship. The influence of one level on another is as varied as that among the various levels of a political system.

28. For hierarchical theory, see C. H. Waddington (ed.), *Towards a Theoretical Biology* (Chicago: Aldine, 1968–72) vols., 1–4, esp. 2 and 3; J. H. Milsum, "The Hierarchical Basis for General Living Systems," in G. J. Klir (ed.), *Trends in General Systems Theory* (New York: Wiley, 1972); H. H. Pattee (ed.), *Hierarchy Theory: The Challenge of Complex Systems* (New York: Braziller, 1973); L. L. Whyte, A. G. Wilson, and D. Wilson (eds.), *Hierarchical Structures* (New York: American Elsevier, 1969); P. A. Weiss (ed.), *Hierarchically Organized Systems in Theory and Practice* (New York: Hafner, 1971).

29. See *A Framework for Political Analysis* and *A Systems Analysis of Political Life.*

30. The English Marxist R. Miliband (*The State and Capitalist Society*) talks of the state as a component of the broader political system, for example. If, however, it is used as a synonym for the political system as a whole, then of course it would be appropriate to seek to establish the influence of the society on it directly, since state (whole political system) and society would occupy adjacent levels in Diagram 18.1.

31. See especially chapter 10 above.

32. Chapter 8 above.

33. As I sought to demonstrate in chapter 10 above.

34. Presumably the reverse cannot be true, that is, society cannot be isolated from the actions of the state. Thus, even though state policies will reflect the self-defined interests of the state, they should normally have important effects on other parts of the political system or of society. This much is clear in the state-autonomy literature. But what neostatists are not always so clear about is the influence of the higher-order political structure on the structure of the state. Some, however, do hold that despite the capacity of the state to pursue its interests or policies as it sees them, its structure continues to be shaped at least by society. We can infer as much from the laborious efforts of Poulantzas, as we have seen in chapters 15 and 16, to show the close connection between various forms of capitalist democracies and dictatorships, on the one hand, with various stages and phases of the capitalist mode of production on the other. It is difficult to reconcile the autonomy of the state from societal influences with respect to policy and yet hold that the structure of the state is subject to societal influences. One would think that these very forces that are powerful enough to shape the structure of the state would thereby gain

some important influence over policies as well. This possible contradiction reflects the analytic ambiguity that hangs over this whole notion of state autonomy despite the considerable attention it has received. At the minimum it seems to slight very seriously the mutual limits that base and structure, to use Marxist terminology, may impose on each other—a point of view which would at least seem to be implicit in the idea of "interpenetration" of the instances (subsystems) as developed by Poulantzas.

35. See as well R. Williams, *Key Words*, pp. 98ff. The terms *obligate* and *facultative* are borrowed from Grobstein, but I use them in a somewhat different sense from that suggested by their biological origins. See C. Grobstein, "Hierarchical Order and Neogenesis," in H. H. Pattee (ed.), *Hierarchy Theory: The Challenge of Complex Systems*, pp. 29–48.

36. See chapter 4 above for a discussion of this way of thinking about determination as a constraint.

37. For the concept "legislates," see my earlier effort to conceptualize relationships such as those we are talking about here, which appeared in "The Relevance of Biopolitics to Political Theory," in A. Somit (ed.), *Biology and Politics: Recent Explorations* (Paris: Maison des Sciences de l'Homme et Maison Mouton, 1976) pp. 237–47.

38. Chapters 15 and 16 above.

39. See C. Grobstein, *op. cit.*

40. See chapter 5 above for this term.

41. See M. Sahlins, *The Use and Abuse of Biology* (Ann Arbor, Mich.: University of Michigan Press, 1976) pp. 64–65.

42. See especially chapter 14 above.

43. Of course, totally free and unconstrained choices never exist in social reality. Every social relationship, by its nature as a relationship between two or more persons, must define some minimal constraint on choice.

Chapter 19

1. See P. J. Katzenstien, *Small States in World Markets* (Ithaca, N.Y.: Cornell University Press, 1985).

2. Chapter 10.

3. A. S. McFarland, *Power and Leadership in Pluralist Systems*.

4. See P. Bachrach and M. Baratz, *Power and Poverty* and S. Lukes, *Power: A Radical View*. We find later tendencies to take these limits seriously into account in C. E. Lindblom, *Politics and Markets* and R. A. Dahl, *A Preface to Economic Democracy*.

5. A description used for nonpolitical structures but which applies equally well to the latter. See E. Lazlo, "Systems and Structure—Toward Bio-social Anthropology," 2 *Theory and Decision* (1971) 174–92 at p. 180; italics in original.

6. Witness the recent revival of the notion of "thick description" (noted earlier in chapter 10) as a method for the analysis of culture despite the fact that the "thicker" the description, the greater and richer the number of facts, the more urgent the issue of the theoretical context within which the description can yield meaning. The piling of detail on detail represents a flight to hyper-empiricism as a way of coping with the genuine issue of seeking to grasp the broader context within which action takes place. In addition to the initial statement of "thick description" as a procedure, in C. Geertz, *The Interpretation of Culture*, see the abandonment of causality in favor of an interpretive approach to the part-whole relationship in H. D. Gadamer, *Truth and Method* (New York: Crossroad, 1986), despite the reservations Gadamer continues to express about interpretation as such.

7. Foreword by F. Jameson, in J-F. Lyotard, *The Post-Modern Condition: A Report on Knowledge* (Minneapolis: University of Minnesota Press, 1984, trans. from 1979 ed.) p. xix.

8. See my comments along these lines in "The New Revolution in Political Science," 63 *American Political Science Review* (1969) 1051–61 and in the new preface to the Phoenix edition of *A Systems Analysis of Political Life* (Chicago: University of Chicago Press, 1979).

9. See especially *The Political System: An Inquiry into the State of Political Science* (New York: Knopf, 1953; 2d ed., 1971; reissued Chicago: University of Chicago Press, 1981) p. 368; and "The New Revolution in Political Science," 63 *American Political Science Review* (1969) 1051–61.

Index of Names

Index of Subjects